The Indian Yearbook of Comparative Law

Series Editor

Mahendra Pal Singh, Centre for Comparative Law, National Law University, Delhi, New Delhi, India

The Indian Yearbook of Comparative Law (IYCL) is a Springer series in the field of Comparative Law, a field which has evolved from being seen as methodology only, to a full-fledged substantive discipline of study. It comprises both public and private law. With the yearbook, editors and publisher make a significant contribution to the development of this highly significant branch of study. Although much work has been done in the discipline worldwide, references to Global South in the discourse is still on the margins. The series attempts to bring narratives from Global South to the forefront. It also simultaneously engages with scholars from Global North too with a view to generate interactive comparative discourse.

IYCL covers all areas of comparative law. The series engages with contemporary issues and also with issues of perennial importance. This series primes inter-disciplinary approach to the study of comparative law. The view of comparative law taken by IYCL encompasses both jurisprudential and functionality approaches of the discipline.

Mathew John · Vishwas H. Devaiah ·
Pritam Baruah · Moiz Tundawala · Niraj Kumar
Editors

The Indian Yearbook of Comparative Law 2020

Springer

Editors
Mathew John
Jindal Global Law School
O. P. Jindal Global University
Sonipat, Haryana, India

Vishwas H. Devaiah
Jindal Global Law School
O. P. Jindal Global University
Sonipat, Haryana, India

Pritam Baruah
School of Law
BML Munjal University
Gurugram, Haryana, India

Moiz Tundawala
Jindal Global Law School
O. P. Jindal Global University
Sonipat, Haryana, India

Niraj Kumar
Centre for Comparative Law
National Law University, Delhi
New Delhi, India

ISSN 2524-7042 ISSN 2524-7050 (electronic)
The Indian Yearbook of Comparative Law
ISBN 978-981-99-5466-7 ISBN 978-981-99-5467-4 (eBook)
https://doi.org/10.1007/978-981-99-5467-4

This Springer imprint is published by the registered company Springer Nature Singapore Pte Ltd.
The registered company address is: 152 Beach Road, #21-01/04 Gateway East, Singapore 189721, Singapore

Paper in this product is recyclable.

Preface

The Indian Yearbook of Comparative Law (IYCL) was started in 2016 at the Center for Comparative Law, National Law University, Delhi (NLUD) to deepen engagement with comparative law from an Indian vantage point. We have tried to do so by juxtaposing and bringing into conversation the works of both established and younger scholars. The present volume is our fourth issue, and we hope to become more regular to truly live up to our ambition of being a yearbook of original scholarship in comparative law.

As Professor M.P. Singh moved from NLUD to Jindal Global University (JGU) beginning 2020, the *Yearbook* was also moved from NLUD to JGU. The Vice-Chancellor Prof. Dr. Raj Kumar of JGU was very encouraging in continuing *IYCL* and assigned two young Assistant Professors Ms. Abhilasha Ramakrishnan and Vandana Gyanchandani who faithfully and efficiently performed the editorial responsibility in the preparation of the final manuscript to be sent to the press. But in the milieu of Covid-19 the *Yearbook* appeared without the required communication with the Series Editor or any of the editors leading to a number of difficulties in responding to the queries from the contributors.

The *IYCL2020* has been unreasonably delayed because Abhilasha and some members of her family became victims of Covid-19 and Vandana decided to go on leave and lost interest in the *Yearbook*. Abhilasha boldly carried on the work alone for some time until she realized that it was too much work to be done alone. On consultation with the Vice Dean Vishwas Devaiah, Abhilasha was given the liberty to associate with her any colleague of her choice. She decided to have with her Maneka Nair, who on Abhilasha's leaving the University at the end of May, decided to have with her Sherin Sarah Philip.

As Series Editor I thank all the Editor colleagues for their contribution in bringing out the *Yearbook2020*. Due to the world-wide difficulties faced by almost everyone throughout the globe, this issue of the *Yearbook* has been unduly delayed for which I and my editorial colleagues express sincere apologies to all the contributing colleagues who have patiently waited for seeing their contributions in print. I also express my sincere gratitude for the help rendered by my younger colleagues,

Abhilasha Ramakrishnan, Vandana Gyanchandani, Maneka Nair, and Sherin Sarah Philip.

I hope the papers included in this volume will be found of interest to all its readers and they will patronize it in future too. Some innovations in the next issue onward of the *Yearbook* are also expected to be introduced to make it more thematic. Let us hope in the process of making constant improvements in the *Yearbook* it will acquire a distinct place in the literature on comparative law. Let us hope with the support of colleagues at Jindal Global University as well as colleagues in the universities globally, we will be able to produce worthwhile literature on comparative law. I wish that goal is realized sooner than later.

Finally, let us express our sincere apologies to all contributors to this issue of the *Yearbook* for giving them undue pain in the wait for its going into their hands. We sincerely hope that it will never ever happen in the future. With this promise, we take your leave until we return to you with the request for contributing to the next edition of the *Yearbook.*

Sonipat, India

Dipika Jain
Mahendra Pal Singh
Mathew John
Moiz Tundawala
Niraj Kumar
Pritam Baruah
Vishwas H. Devaiah

Summary

This yearbook is a compilation of thematically arranged essays that critically analyse emerging developments, issues, and perspectives in the field of comparative law. It comprises three parts wherein the first part focuses on public law and its relates issues, the second part comprises of issues in the field of private laws, and the third part discusses on general themes of comparative law. The yearbook intends to seamlessly tie together discussions on both public and private law aspects of comparative law. It encourages readers to gain a nuanced understanding of the working of law, legal systems and legal cultures while aiding deliberations on the constituents of an ideal system of law.

Board of Advisors

Contents

Editors and Contributors

About the Editors

Dr. Mathew John Professor at the Jindal Global Law School (JGLS), serves as the Executive Director of the Centre for Public Law and Jurisprudence. His research spans public law, legal theory, and the marriage of constitutional and political theory. He has enjoyed research fellowships from renowned institutions, such as the London School of Economics (LSE), Centre for the Study of Culture and Society, Bangalore, Jawaharlal Nehru University, and the Kate Hamburger Kolleg, Bonn. His credentials feature a doctoral degree from LSE, a master's from the University of Warwick, and a bachelor's from the National Law School of India University.

Dr. Vishwas H. Devaiah Professor at JGLS, serves as the Director of the Centre for Postgraduate Law School and Executive Director of CIPTEL. Additionally, he is the Co-director of JIRICO, driving its research and development. He has been the Managing Editor of Jindal Global Law Review. His research interests lie in intellectual property law, the overlap between IP and competition, health law, and biotechnology law. A published author in the Journal of Intellectual Property Law and Policy, Journal of World Intellectual Property, Asian Bioethics Review etc., he also won the 2015 Microsoft IP Teaching Fellowship.

Dr. Pritam Baruah is the Professor & Dean of BML Munjal Law School. His research revolves around legal philosophy and constitutional theory. Formerly a faculty at the National University of Juridical Sciences, Kolkata (WBNUJS), he has guest lectured at several universities globally. He co-founded UCL Legal Philosophy Forum and has published in international and Indian journals such as the Canadian Journal of Law and Jurisprudence, and the NUJS Law Review and edited volumes such as the Indian Yearbook of Comparative Law (IYCL). Besides academia, he practised law at the Supreme Court of India. Dr. Baruah holds a law and humanities degree from NALSAR University of Law, Hyderabad, and is a Commonwealth Doctoral Scholar at University College London.

Dr. Moiz Tundawala Associate Professor at JGLS, pursued his doctoral studies at LSE, Master's at SOAS and BALLB (Hons) at WBNUJS Kolkata on prestigious academic scholarships. Dr. Tundawala has taught and researched at various institutions including JGLS, LSE, WBNUJS and NLU Delhi, specializing in Indian constitutional thought, legal and political theory, modern intellectual history, and comparative public law. His works have been published or are forthcoming in renowned journals such as Global Intellectual History, Journal of Political Theology, Asian Journal of Comparative Law, IYCL, NUJS Law Review, and other edited volumes.

Dr. Niraj Kumar works as an Associate Professor at NLUD, where he co-directs a project exploring the nature of the Indian Legal System at the Centre for Comparative Law. Earlier, he taught at the Faculty of Law, University of Delhi. He coordinated a Ministry of Home Affairs project and was part of an Expert Committee constituted by the Ministry of Labor & Employment. He has published widely, including two books, and co-edited IYCL 2018. His research areas include comparative law, administrative law, constitutional law, environmental law, interpretation of statutes, and jurisprudence.

Contributors

Moslem Aghaeitogh University of Judicial Sciences and Administrative Services, Tehran, Iran

Punsara Amarasinghe Institute of Law, Politics and Development, Scuola Superiore Sant Anna, Pisa, Italy

Lalantika Arvind Centre for International Legal Studies, Jindals Global Law School, O.P. Jindal Global University, Sonipat, Haryana, India

Noriyuki Asano Kansai University, Osaka, Japan

Salmoli Choudhuri National Law School of India University, Bengaluru, India

Pratyush Gupta Centre for International Legal Studies, Jindals Global Law School, O.P. Jindal Global University, Sonipat, Haryana, India

Raunaq Jaiswal Jindal Global Law School, O.P. Jindal Global University, Sonipat, Haryana, India

George Katrougalos Democritus University, Komotini, Greece

prithviraj Khanna Centre for International Legal Studies, Jindals Global Law School, O.P. Jindal Global University, Sonipat, Haryana, India

Tonny R. Kirabira Faculty of Humanities and Social Sciences, University of Portsmouth, Portsmouth, UK

Niraj Kumar National Law University, Delhi, India

Neha Mishra Jindal Global Law School, O.P. Jindal Global University, Sonipat, Haryana, India

Judith N. Onwubiko School of Law and Social Sciences, London South Bank University, London, UK

Prabhash Ranjan Faculty of Legal Studies, South Asian University, New Delhi, India

Rashmi Raman Centre for International Legal Studies, Jindals Global Law School, O.P. Jindal Global University, Sonipat, Haryana, India

Rajnish Saryal Political Science, University Institute of Law, Panjab University Regional Centre, Ludhiana, India

Dinesh Singh National Law University, Delhi, India

Kevin Y. L. Tan National University of Singapore, Singapore, Singapore;
S. Rajaratnam School of International Studies, Nanyang Technological University, Singapore, Singapore

Moiz Tundawala Jindal Global Law School, Sonipat, India

Part I
Public Law: Constitutional Law

Chapter 1
Reclaiming *Rechtsstaat* from the Stuntmen of the State

Niraj Kumar

Abstract This review article is inspired by Gunter Frankenberg's work, "*Authoritarianism: Constitutional Perspectives*" (2020). The attempt is to understand the authoritarianism forays into constitutions. Specifically, whether this is a structural or episodic phenomenon. In doing so, the review article also tries to investigate the possibilities of constitutional bulwarks against such tendencies. To meet its end, the first part of the article culls out the basic idea of Frankenberg's work. In the second part, the author explores several key aspects of a liberal democratic state which has been discussed by the work under review in support of its fundamental argument. The third part investigates the possibilities of reclaiming *Rechtsstaat*. Finally, the last part talks about conclusions and suggestions.

1.1 Autocrats and Constitutions

1.1.1 Introduction

Frankenberg commences the work-at-hand by recording the presence of authoritarian regimes as rising global phenomena. It explores the enigma of the relevance of constitutions for autocrats. In the process, it challenges the intuitive argument of constitution and autocrat as antithesis to each other. Frankenberg begins by suggesting that, "more often, rights are adapted to autocratic purposes by doctrinal schemes, 'concretized' by laws or merely set aside in state practice."[1] He argues that autocracies are not opposed to the ideas of values and duties "because, by definition, values and duties must be enforced from above."[2] Besides, he views "constitution of politics," yet another facet of constitutional polities, "of [being] special interest

[1] Gunter Frankenberg, *Authoritarianism: Constitutional Perspectives* (Edward Elgar, 2020), 25.
[2] Ibid.

N. Kumar (✉)
National Law University, Delhi, India
e-mail: niraj.kumar@nludelhi.ac.in

M. John et al. (eds.), *The Indian Yearbook of Comparative Law 2020*, The Indian Yearbook of Comparative Law, https://doi.org/10.1007/978-981-99-5467-4_1

to autocracies, as long as it meets their increased demand for order."[3] In short, the utilitarian argument in favor of autocrats needing constitutions has to be different from the utilitarian argument in favor of liberal requirements is one of the fascinating themes of the book.

Certainly, the theme which Frankenberg has chosen to explore in this work: "Why Constitutions Matter?" is a common one and has been dealt with by several other legal minds. Nonetheless, his frame of reference to explore the question is different, which makes the work different from other such works exploring the same theme. As opposed to the liberal dispensation which views the constitution as providing a framework to achieve the political goals of the society at its foundational moments, Frankenberg argues that constitutions are viewed as instruments of legitimizing private aspirations by autocrats. In this context, the question that arises is whether constitutional defiance is also an oft-used *modus operandi* of revolutionaries too, so should all revolutionaries be thought of as autocrats. For instance, one can very well argue, factually, that Lincoln violated many of the tenets of the US Constitution during the Civil war. Rather, Noah Feldman argues that Lincoln violated the US Constitution in at least three ways. Firstly, by waging war against confederacy. Secondly, by suspending *habeas corpus* unilaterally, and thirdly, by believing that he also possessed the power to proclaim an end to slavery in the Southern states.[4] So should Lincoln be also clubbed with autocrats? Responding to it, Feldman argues that defiance of the US Constitution of 1787 by Lincoln helped in making it a "moral constitution." In contradistinction to above the defiance of the constitutions which aid infusion of morality in the documents, autocrats are motivated by personal benefits. In essence, therefore, they generally make "immoral constitutions."

The immoral constitution, neither in its origin nor in its objective, intends to trace any "Genealogy of Morals" (The phrase here is not intended to mean the construct as described by Nietzsche in his work of same title). The immoral constitutions are reflective of the tendencies of autocrats to use constitutions as instrumentalities of personal aggrandizement. This in opinion of Frankenberg requires the deployment of various "political technologies." Frankenberg defines political technology as "encompassing the totality of practices, norms and principles, forms of knowledge and skills, calculations, strategies and tactics that state (or international) actors and institutions bring to bear in their operations of social control, threat aversion, risk management and so on."[5] He argues that these defiance and different readings of the constitutions by autocrats are akin to the treatment of public power as private property.

He goes on to enumerate the techniques which are required to convert constitutions into some sort of special purpose vehicle to achieve private aims. To do so, he engages with the vexed problem of popular democracy and authoritarian regimes.

---

[3] Ibid.

[4] https://www.nytimes.com/2021/11/02/opinion/constitution-slavery-lincoln.html, visited on 02 May, 2022.

[5] See, Gunter Frankenberg, *Political Economy and the Erosion of the Rule of Law: Normalizing the state of exception* (Edward Elgar Publishing 2014).

The choice of a dictator to appeal to people or "public" is always a tricky issue. They defy the common logic of why, when, where, what, and how. But Frankenberg is almost successful in finding method in madness. The qualifier "almost" accounts for instances like Pinochet's failure in getting desired support. Frankenberg very convincingly enunciates such forays with the help of thesis of "the cult of immediacy." It serves the twin purpose, if not more, of need of legitimacy and dismantling the institutional check and balances. Frankenberg identifies the relevancy of it by asserting

> Immediacy prepares the stage for leaders to seduce their audiences to succumb to the authoritarian temptation and renounce their right to determine their own political existence. This script works if the totality of direct communications can disperse and condense into the cult of immediacy, which spreads-in word, writing and image-like a toxic fog over organizations, institutions, and procedures of representative democracy.[6]

Thereafter, Frankenberg unravels this complex web by suggesting that all these provide tools to an autocrat to create a miasma of the constitution in their own image. Lastly, he situates all of the above in the contemporary Covid crisis. He contrasts the approaches of autocrats and liberals. He argues, "Co-determination and voluntariness must be introduced as (new) principles, without which even the prohibition-supported and compulsively enforced imperatives against infection ultimately cannot work."[7]

1.2 Autocrats View About Some Tenets of a Liberal Democracy

1.2.1 Liberalism

Jacques Derrida suggested that meaning is often defined in terms of binary oppositions.[8] A deconstruction of autocracy will require an engagement with liberalism since autocracy is often posited as antithesis of liberalism (although it may not be always true). Therefore, it is quite pertinent to understand the foundational values of liberalism. Only then can one run a litmus test on autocratic regimes for their failures. John Gray describes liberalism in the following way:

> It is *individualistic*, in that it asserts the moral primacy of the person against the claims of any social collectivity; *egalitarian*, inasmuch as it confers on all men the same moral status and denies the relevance to legal or political order of differences in moral worth among human beings; *universalist*, affirming the moral unity of the human species and according a secondary importance to specific historic associations and cultural forms; and *meliorist* in its affirmation of the corrigibility and improvability of all social institutions and political arrangements.[9] (*Emphasis added*)

---

[6] Frankenberg (n 1), p. 200.

[7] Id at p. 279.

[8] Jacques Derrida, *Positions* (1992), p. 41.

[9] John Gray, *Liberalism* (Open University Press 1986), at x.

Frankenberg's autocrat is individualistic in a perverse sense of the personhood of the dictator. Whereas, when it comes to the according of individual status to their citizens, they always find ways and means for creation of the "others." Whether its *Fidesz* party in Hungary or *Junta* of Myanmar the "political technology" remains same. Egalitarianism in the sense of moral worth for an autocrat is chillingly analogous to "Homo Sacer" of Agamben, where a segment of populace deserves a lesser legal status. Universalism has never been of any appeal to the dictator. They always claim to confer privileges on their own people who have been denied their rightful place under the sun or in these cases in their motherland and fatherland. Meliorism is none of their concern. They always make an appeal to the past glory. Therefore, by natural logic, past must be better than future. So it is always an attempt toward restoration rather than any improvement. It appears John Gray's evaluation of an autocrat would be a polar opposite of a liberal.

The idea of liberalism has various connotations in legal sense. Fukuyama argues:

> Liberal societies embed rights in *formal law*, and as a result tend to be highly procedural. Law is simply a system of explicit rules that define how conflicts are to be resolved and collective decisions made, embodied in a set of legal institutions that *function semi-autonomously* from the rest of the of the political system so that it cannot be abused by politicians for short-term advantage.[10]

One may have qualms about a very simplistic role assigned to Law. But given the context of engagement with classical liberalism, it may not be of immediate concern for us. An autocrat sees law as conduit. He may not brook any parchment barrier either. In the same vein, autonomy of any kind is a matter of convenience. It can never be a matter of convenience. Till the time legislature isn't conducive, Hitler's game plan of third Reich, i.e., rule by executive fiats, serves the purpose. Frankenberg has established through many examples like Trump's infamous travel embargos, etc. that the executive fiat takes place of the legislative laws. Autocrats aren't even wary of unfavorable court's verdicts either. It is part of their theatrics. In any case, independent institutions are to be seen as untrustworthy. Therefore, either way executive fiat in its operation and demise serves the purpose. However, in present times there is also a tendency to justify illiberal shifts in state policies on the basis of liberalism.[11]

1.2.2 Constitutions

Bruce Ackerman wrote in 1997, "Turn back the clock sixty years, and glimpse into the future: What were the prospects for constitutionalism as they might have appeared in the late 1930s?. Grim."[12] He further writes, "Sixty years later, and how the world

[10] Francis Fukuyama, *Liberalism and its discontents* (Profile Books 2022), 2.

[11] See King, 1999.

[12] Bruce Ackerman, 'The Rise of World Constitutionalism', 83:4 Virginia Law Review 771.

has turned. Even the British are debating the need for a new-fangled written constitution".[13] The idea of Constitution, and largely written, became a widely accepted idea across the world.

David Singh Grewal and Jedediah Purdy, in review of Richard Tuck's book, "The Sleeping Sovereign: The Invention of Modern Democracy," write:

> To understand the original theory of modern constitutionalism, it is necessary to understand the original problem that constitutionalism was meant to solve: not whether but how "the people" were understood to participate in government, and specifically whether they could ever make their own laws-that is, rule themselves.[14]

Robert Tollison wrote in foreword to classic work of James M. Buchanan, "The Calculus of Consent: Logical Foundations of Constitutional Democracy," "Constitutional choice differs from ordinary political decision making in that it is devoid of self-interest."[15] This basic premise of Tollison is conspicuous by its absence in constitutional choices to be made by an autocrat. All the decisions of an autocrat are moved by an interest, which may not be a classic self-interest, but perpetuates the self of the autocrat. To use Freudian metaphors, the "self" of the autocrat is governed by *id*, and not *ego*, and never by *superego.* All these create an enigma about the relationship between an autocrat and the constitution.

Frankenberg writes, "The dispositive of authoritarian constitutionalism, regardless of its variations, encompasses an ensemble of discourses, forms of knowledge and institutions, regulatory decisions, political strategies and normative positions. This dispositive informs a technique of governing that combines constitutional opportunism with a special security agenda and imperative, and often informal action that consistently privilege the executive."[16] It is quite obvious that in case of an autocrat executive signifies the physical personhood of the autocrat and not the legal personality.

1.2.3 Democracy

Democracies work best and survive longer where constitutions are reinforced by unwritten democratic norms.[17] Levitsky and Ziblatt further argue (although in historical context of United States of America, it can be extended to most of other liberal democracies too) that two basic norms preserve democracy, viz., mutual tolerance and forbearance. They won't find even a mention in rule-book of an autocrat. The

---

[13] Id at 772.

[14] Grewal and Purdy, 'The Original Theory of Constituionalism', (2018) 127. The Yale Law Journal 669.

[15] The Collected Works of James M. Buchanan, Volume 3 (Liberty Fund 1999), p. ix.

[16] Gunter Frankenberg, *Authoritarianism: Constitutional Perspectives* (Edward Elgar 2020), 103.

[17] Steven Levitsky and Daniel Ziblatt, *How Democracies Die: What History Reveals About Our Future* (Penguin 2019), p. 8.

whole edifice of an autocrat is based on demagoguery. It strives to delegitimize the opposing political parties. Observing on similar lines, Runciman writes:

> Our political imaginations are stuck with out-dated images of what democratic failure looks like. We are trapped in the landscape of the twentieth century. We reach back to the 1930s and 1970s for pictures of what happens when democracy falls apart: tanks in the streets; tin-pot dictators barking out messages of national unity, violence and repression in tow.[18]

He rightly points out that new autocrats are not, at least in their appearances and *modus operandi*, like their predecessors.

Frankenberg's engagements also establish the same proposition. Therefore, it would be quite a tricky affair to sift through a regime for the purposes of lifting the veil. Most of them come through an electoral process. However, it does not stop them from questioning the process, if they fail to secure the electoral majority.[19] Electoral processes may not be sufficient safeguard to keep these autocrats at bay. More is required of independent democratic institutions to act as check and balances. Therefore, it is not surprising that after getting elected the immediate target of these strongmen is the credibility of these institutions. Tweets like, "What is our country if a judge can stop a Homeland Security travel ban?"[20] questions the credibility of the institutions. By relying on works of Forsythe and Henriksen, Frankenberg also argues, "Word has long since got around that even elections as a proof of democracy are not very reliable."[21]

1.2.4 Authoritarianism

Frankenberg argues the following in the context of identifiable markers of an authoritarian power:

> First, authoritarian constitutionalism (*although the term constitutionalism is a debatable construct here*) is characterized by an intimate dualism of power and property. Second, as far as circumstances permit, autocrats derive from this notion of power their right to decide high-handedly on the duration of their term of office and to determine who will be their successor. Third, not content with the psychological revenue they derive from commanding or oppressing others, or with mere perks, some autocrats seek to appropriate all form of state capital-all public good available within their grasp-for their own private benefit.[22]

Francis Fukuyama in book tracing the origins of political order asserted that, "Accountable government means that the rulers believe that they are responsible to the people they govern and put the people's interests above their own."[23] He further

---

[18] David Runciman, *How Democracy Ends* (Profile Books 2018), 2.

[19] One does not have to go far beyond January 6 event on Capitol Hill to appreciate it.

[20] Frankenberg, 129.

[21] Frankenberg, 172.

[22] Frankenberg, 134–35.

[23] Francis Fukuyama, *The Origins of Political Order: From Prehuman Times to the French Revolution* (Profile Books 2011), 321.

argues that, "Formal accountability is procedural: the government agrees to submit itself to certain mechanisms that limit its power to do as it pleases. Ultimately, these procedures (which are usually spelled out in constitutions) allow the citizens of the society to replace the government entirely for malfeasance, incompetence, or abuse of power."[24]

Frankerberg's authoritarian regime alters Fukuyama's Political order. The ruler doesn't see the people as plural as expounded by Jürgen Habermas. They refuse the identity to those who aren't on the same page. Therefore in authoritarian regime accountability appears to be of the people to the regime rather than other way around. Logical corollary to the above would be the ouster of inconvenient people from public life rather than ruler getting replaced. Further, since the public power and private property distinction is removed therefore the possibilities of abuse of power are not recognized. The distortions to classic liberal democratic models are generally traced to the idea of Populism.

1.2.5 Populism

It has to be said at the onset that as is the case with most of the other similar constructs like "democracy," "secularism," etc., the term populism can't be either confined to any specific doctrinaire limitations. But a few representative definitions may be a good starting point. Frankenberg describes populism as, "Populism designates a style that movements or parties use to mobilize potential followers (e.g., the population at large; the underclass; farmers) and to put issues on the political agenda that are widely negated".[25] Jan-Werner Muller argues that, "Populist governance exhibits three features: attempts to hijack the state apparatus, corruption and 'mass clientelism' (trading material benefits or bureaucratic favors for political support by citizens who become populist' 'clients'), and efforts systematically to suppress civil society".[26] There is a possibility of presence of traces of populism in all shades of political belief systems.[27] It appears that populism is the new "empirical mainstream." The possibilities of an alienated life in a world dominated by information warfare (although in classical sense the term is reserved for international relations) are ever looming large. It creates a very fertile ground for demagoguery.

Runciman catches the spirit of age of populism very aptly in following words:

> In an age of populism, while some anxious defenders of democracy are invoking the banality of evil, others are busy railing against the evil of banality. For many populists, mindless bureaucracy is not at risk of being invaded by a truly terrible idea it is powerless to resist. Instead, mindless bureaucracy is the truly terrible idea and the correct democratic response is to resist it. Both sides in populist politics-the populists and the anti-populists- believe they

---

[24] Id at 321–22.

[25] Frankenberg, 53.

[26] Jan- Werner Muller, *What is Populism?* (Penguin 2017), p. 5.

[27] See Muller (n 15).

> are fighting the good fight to save the democracy from itself. The central division of our time is not democracy v. conspiracy theory. It is conspiracy theory v. conspiracy theory in the name of democracy. It is not 1930s all over again. It is 1890s, without the prospect of resolution.[28]

Further, there is nothing to choose from left or right wing populism. Muller clearly establishes that, historically, it was a matter of which side of the Pacific is talking about it. Otherwise both sides deploy by and large same kind of toolbox for challenging the *status quo*. Schupmann's observations during Weimar republic are an indication in that direction," Weimar's anti-positivists were alarmed by the potential for the newly enfranchised German "masses" to become tyrannical-especially in the wake of right- and left-wing populists uprisings following the end of World War I (Schupmann, 2017).

1.3 Reclaiming the *Rechsstaat*

1.3.1 Rechtsstaat

The term "Rechtsstaat" is a German expression made up of the words "Recht" (law) and "Staat" (state). This term translates easily into some languages, for instance, "regstaat" (Afrikaans) or "Rechtsstaat" (Dutch); a similar combination of "law" and "state" is more difficult to achieve in others. However, the concept itself is expressed to a certain extent by the phrases "rule of law" in English, "regne de la loi" or "limitation des gouvernants" in French and "stato di diritto" in Italian.[29] The concepts of *Rechtsstaat* and of Rule of Law both express certain closely related values that have been advanced in respect of legal order. Some of the proponents of these values in the past and the present may have thought it possible to derive them from pure analyses of the concept of law and have thus been … in error.[30]

As is the case with several other important ideas, such as justice, liberty, democracy, etc., there is no universally agreed meaning, scope, conditions, and significance of rule of law. On the contrary, they are highly contested (Waldron, 2002). Nonetheless, in all versions, the rule of law is primarily concerned with the relationship between law and the exercise of power, particularly public power.[31]

Moreover, the local contexts and histories have also had lasting impacting on the idea of rule of law. That fact is apparent from the semantic difference between "rule of law," the term used in English, and its counterparts found in other European

---

[28] Runciman (n 18), 98–99.

[29] Loammi C Blauu, 'The Rechsstaat idea compared with the Rule of Law as a paradigm for protecting rights', (1990) 107 South African Law Journal [i].

[30] Neil MacCormick, *Questioning Sovereignty* (OUP 1999).

[31] Krygier, M., 2015. 'Rule of Law (and Rechtsstaat)' in James D. Wright (editor-in-chief), *International Encyclopedia of the Social & Behavioral Sciences* (Elsevier, Vol. 20, 2nd ed, 2015) 780–787.

languages. Put otherwise, the same idea of rule of law does not cover the same terrain in all contextual setting when studied historically. That said, however, in a host of European languages there is one thing commonly built into the concept, which is missing from the English phrase: the State. Whether it is *Rechtsstaat* (German: state of law; law-governed state), *état de droit* (French), *statto diritto* (Italian), *estado de derecho* (Spanish), *panstwo prawa* (Polish), or *pravovoe gosudarstvo* (Russian) law is inextricably connected to the state.[32]

The close connection between Law and State has not been the result of a linear development. But it has allowed a space for the autocrats to claim a conflation between Law and State and as a necessary corollary between themselves and the Law. Because for an autocrat, State is an entity in their own image not much distinct from their own personhood. Frankerberg's dictatorial centralism appears to come quite close to such a confluence. In the model of dictatorial centralism, the investiture-whether by dynastic succession, election or acclamation-leads to the joined ownership of supreme authority, whose holder is henceforth distinguished from the circle of constituted powers and acts as the constituent power.[33]

Rechsstaat or rule of law is dependent on the idea of a clear distinction between constituent power and constituted power. All subsequent exercise of power from the foundation moment has to be answerable to the constituent power. Of course, we are here assuming that the constituent power, in the first place, was a product of liberal democratic ideas. Frankenberg discusses various archetypes of the constitution.[34] All archetypes may not be amenable to a liberal outcome. Therefore, the idea of constitutionalism which is required to reclaim Rechsstaat must be weaned away from nation states. Martin Loughlin calls it as a process of constitutionalization.[35] Loughlin says it is born of the reconfiguration of the values of constitutionalism, an extension of their reach, and a loosening of the connection between constitutionalism and the nation state.[36]

1.3.2 Constitutionalization

Brazilian autocrat Getulio Dornelles Vargas is stated to have proclaimed: "For my friend, everything; for my enemies, the law."[37] In most of the cases, it is not the absence of laws, but it is about the selective application of laws. Ideally for an autocrat laws per se are to be drafted with selective appreciation and perception to

---

32 Ibid.

33 Frankenberg, 143.

34 Frankenberg (n 1), 21–24.

35 Martin Loughlin, 'what is constitutionalisation?' in Petra Dobner and Martin Loughlin (eds), *The Twilight of Constitutionalism* (OUP 2010).

36 Id at 68.

37 Guillermo A. O'Donnell, "Why the Rule of Law Matters", Journal of Democracy 15, no. 4 (2004): 32–46.

achieve a few of the goals of an autocrat. But till that is not achieved the existing state instrumentalities can be conveniently deployed for the purposes of signaling. In most of the circumstances, they are subtle like dog whistling.

It is a type of virtue signaling, where the proponent need not engage in moral reasoning. The virtue signaller is unduly concerned with herself rather than the issues she purports to discuss (Neil Levy, 2020). Levy further suggests, "...at least one of her primary motivations is recognition. She signals her supposed moral insight and her superior values, thereby turning moral discourse into a 'vanity project'." They essentially rely on the "halo effect (Thorndike, 1920)" phenomena rather than some argumentative justification. Autocrats indulge into virtue signaling in a manner which demolishes the idea of rule of law. The discourse is framed to elicit only a certain type of responses. In relation to political regimes, the authoritative/authoritarian distinction also presupposes that the rule can be characterized as legitimate or not.[38]

The problem faced in addressing the new archetypes of autocrats is somewhat captured by the following observation (albeit not exactly identical across the countries and continents) of Ginsburg and Huq, "Being old, and lacking an easy amendment mechanism, the US Constitution does not necessarily reflect the learning of subsequent years and decades. It instead calcifies the mistaken assumptions and prejudices of long-dead generation."[39]

1.4 Conclusions

Hayek lamented that liberty will not be preserved if the basic belief in the existence of abstract rules of law which binds all authority in action is shaken.[40] The stuntmen of the state intend to shake those belief systems. The conflation of state, government, and ruler can happen only if abstract rules of law are diluted, if not demolished. Any attempt to establish Rechsstaat has to begin with emphasizing the differences between state, government, and ruler. Loughlin proposed that the process of constitutionalization draws on some of the achievements of modern constitutions and constitutionalism in regulating government, but it jettisons those aspects of these modern processes which have rested on the particularities of history and culture.[41] Constitutions encapsulate the idiosyncrasies of a particular society. But it must also uniformly uphold universal human values to establish constitutionalism.

Frankenberg sounds hopeful, when he avers that, "Authoritarianism has no expiry date; but nor is its longevity guaranteed. There is no reason to view autocracies as inevitable and their constitutions as necessarily enduring."[42] But it is also important

[38] Frankenberg (n 1), 39.

[39] Ginsburg and HUQ, How to save a constitutional democracy (OUP 2019), 5.

[40] F. A. Hayek, The Constitution of Liberty (Routledge Indian Reprint 2012), 191.

[41] Loughlin (n 34), 68.

[42] Frankenberg (n 1), 284.

to realize that it can't be just wished away. We may be for a long haul. It will require an establishment of the following proposition of Kant:

> For since morality is a law for us only as rational beings, it must be equally valid for all rational beings; and since it must be derived solely from the property of freedom, we have got to prove that freedom too is a property of the will of all rational beings. It is not enough to demonstrate freedom from certain alleged experiences of human nature (though to do this is in any case absolutely impossible and freedom can be demonstrated only a priori): we must prove that it belongs universally to the activity of rational beings endowed with a will.[43]

Maybe sometimes one has to reinvent the wheels!

---

[43] Emanuel Kant, *The Moral Law: Groundwork of the metaphysics of morals* (Routledge, Indian reprint, 2012), 129.

Chapter 2
Selective Surname System and Its Constitutionality: Culture and Personal Dignity

Noriyuki Asano

Abstract One of the important issues of the constitutional/family law field in Japan is the selective surname system. In Japan, according to the provisions of the Civil Code, those who marry must use one surname. Among couples, most of brides change their surname to those of grooms. However, currently as more women enter the workforce, the unfairness of changing their surnames becomes a focus. In this article, first, I will give an overview of the family system and surname system in Japan, and then point out its legal problems. Then, two important judicial precedents, the Tokyo High Court judgment in 2014 and the Supreme Court decision in 2021, are reviewed, especially focused on matters relating to constitutional rights. At last, it is supposed that the nature of the family is in a state of constant flux in his dynamically changing society. So, I pointed out in the conclusion part that the appropriateness of basing constitutional judgments on a fixed image of the family needs to be further examined.

2.1 Introduction

The end of the so-called Edo period (1603–1868[1]) and the beginning of the Meiji period (1868–1912) marked the beginning of the modern era in Japan, with several changes in the legal system. This study discusses a matter relating to such a change, that is, the issue of personal names. In modern Japan, a person's name is a combination of the two words 'clan (shows surname)' and 'name (first name)', and one person is assumed to have one name. However, in pre-modern Japan in the Edo period, a woman's name was used to indicate her connection to the social group through the

[1] TherE are many theories about the end of the Edo period, but for the purposes of this paper, the end of the Edo period is 1868, when the name of era was changed to Meiji.

The author would like to thank Editage (www.editage.com) for English language editing.

N. Asano (✉)
Kansai University, Osaka, Japan
e-mail: asanon@kansai-u.ac.jp

M. John et al. (eds.), *The Indian Yearbook of Comparative Law 2020*, The Indian Yearbook of Comparative Law, https://doi.org/10.1007/978-981-99-5467-4_2

head of the family, for example 'XX's wife XX' or 'XX's daughter XX'. In the Meiji period, with the establishment of a system to control individual citizens, women were given names based on a combination of 'clan' and 'name' as same as men.

Nevertheless, as observed later, with the enactment of the Old Civil Code, it was ruled that women should take the surname of their husband upon marriage, that is, they should change their surname upon marriage. After the Second World War, the Civil Code was amended to require that the surname be changed to that of the husband or wife at the time of marriage, and this system of unified surname has remained unchanged.

In response to this situation, a system of selective separation of surnames has been proposed, whereby couples can choose to unify their surnames at the time of marriage or continue to use their original surname. This is because, although couples are allowed to choose either their own surname or their spouse's surname, in most cases the husband's surname is chosen, to the detriment of the woman. Therefore, lawsuits have been filed to argue that not introducing the proposed selective surname system violates the Constitution. However, as of 2021, no Supreme Court judgment has ruled that avoiding this system violates the Constitution. In addition, the name is a sign of social change, and judicial decisions on this issue may change in the future. In this article, the Supreme Court's decision on the system of selective surname change is reviewed as an opportunity to examine the relationship between social change and judicial decisions in Japan.

The first section describes the current situation and historical development of the surname system to understand the current system. The second section outlines the proposals for a system of selective surnames. In the third section, I discuss one high court judgment and the two Supreme Court judgments on the surname system for married couples. Finally, I conclude with a discussion of the prospects of the proposed system based on the judicial decisions.

2.2 Current Situation and Problems of the Surname System for Married Couples

2.2.1 Historical Background of the System of Married Couples with the Same Surname

The Japanese Civil Code is divided into five parts: 'General Provisions' (Part 1), which defines 'persons', 'things', and 'legal acts'; 'Property Rights' (Part 2), which defines 'ownership' and 'mortgages'; 'Claims' (Part 3), which defines 'contracts' and 'torts'; 'Relatives' (Part 4), which defines 'marriage', 'divorce', and 'parents and children'; and 'Inheritance' (Part 5), which defines inheritance. Of these, the surname of the husband and wife, which is the subject of this article, is provided for in Part IV, Article 750, as given below:

> Married couples shall take the name of their husband or wife, as determined at the time of their marriage.

problems addressed in this article have been raised in the courts. Thus, did this unification of the surname exist before the enactment of the present Civil Code?

The first Civil Code in Japan was promulgated in 1890, a time when the structure of the law was influenced by the French Civil Code. However, the enforcement of this law was postponed, and a new Civil Code was eventually enacted. The current Civil Code was enacted in 1896, first with the General Provisions, provisions on Property Rights and Claims, and then in 1898 with the Family and Inheritance Code, which came into force in the same year. The Civil Code adopted the German Pandekten system but was also influenced by French, English, and American legal systems, and is described as the product of comparative law.[2]

This Civil Code (hereinafter referred to as the Old Civil Code[3]) differed from the present one in that it had a strong 'family' system. Under this system, the family consisted of the head of the house, the head's relatives, and the head's spouse (Article 732 of the Old Civil Code). The head of the family had strong authority over the family's property and personnel. For example, the family could not establish a residence against the will of the head of the family (Article 749 of the former Civil Code), the head of the family's consent was required for marriage (Article 750 of the former Civil Code), and if it was unclear whether the property belonged to the head of the family or to other family members, it was presumed to belong to the head of the family (Article 748 of the former Civil Code). Concerning the surname, Article 746 of the former Civil Code provided as given below:

> The head of the family and the members of the family shall bear the surname.

In other words, the family was legally bound to take the same name as that of the head of the family. Article 788 of the Old Civil Code, which deals with marriage, states the following:

> A wife shall join her husband's family by marriage.

In addition, Article 970 of the former Civil Code stipulates that the head of the family is, in principle, inherited by legitimate senior son. So that a family was consisted by husband and wife coming into husband's clan. As mentioned above, the family was supposed to be united under the surname, that is, a wife was supposed to take the name of the family she married into.

The family system was forced to change drastically after the defeat in the Second World War and the enactment of the Constitution of Japan. First, Article 24 of the Japanese Constitution, which was the basis of these changes, provides as follows:

---

[2] Asako Hiroshi and others (eds), *Nihon Hoseishi (Legal History of Japan)* (Seirin Shoin 2016) 312–314.

[3] In Japan, it is common to refer to the Civil Code promulgated in 1890 as the Old Civil Code, but in this paper, to clarify the differences with the current provisions, the family law provisions of the current Civil Code, which came into force in 1898, are referred to as the Old Civil Code.

(1) Marriage shall be entered into solely by the consent of both sexes and shall be maintained based on mutual co-operation, with equal rights for the spouses.
(2) In matters of choice of spouse, property rights, inheritance, choice of residence, divorce, and other matters relating to marriage and family, the law shall be made based on the dignity of the individual and the equality of the sexes.

This article is the basis of marriage and other family matters in modern Japan.[4] This constitutional provision necessitated amendments to the provisions of the Civil Code. In December 1947, the 'Law for the Partial Revision of the Civil Code' was passed, which came into force in 1948. This law abolished the system of 'house' and its head, that is, the 'head of household'. Furthermore, while maintaining the principle of equal rights for married couples, as mentioned above, the law provided that 'the husband or wife shall take the name of his or her own family', implying that men and women were treated equally under the law. As mentioned above, under the Old Civil Code, wives were generally expected to join their husbands' families and take the name of their family.

Conversely, the New Civil Code (in this paper, the new provisions on the family, which came into force in 1948, are referred to as the New Civil Code or simply the Civil Code) stipulates that the husband's or wife's surname should be used. However, according to statistics from the Ministry of Health, Labor, and Welfare, 96% of those who married in 2015 chose the husband's surname, a slight decrease from the 98.8% who chose the husband's surname in 1975. However, most of couples have chosen to unify their marital status with that of their husbands.[5]

In addition, the Civil Code is not the only law that specifies the surname of a married couple. The Family Registration Act is crucial considering our point of discussion.

Family registers 'register and notarise family relationships from birth to death and are the only organized system for Japanese citizens, which also notarises Japanese nationality[6]'. It is different from the registration of residence, which is registered with the local government of the place of residence. According to the Family Registration Law, 'a family register is created for each couple whose registered domicile is within the municipality, and for each child who shares the same surname' (Article 6). In addition to the name of the domicile location, the family register must contain the

---

[4] In Japan, a marriage is entered into by submitting a marriage certificate to the city office and having it accepted (legal marriage). No ceremony is required. If a couple does not register their marriage but remains in a de facto relationship, it is called a de jure marriage. A legal marriage is different from a de facto marriage in several ways: the difference in whether a child is considered to be legitimate or illegitimate, the other party in a de facto marriage is not considered to be a legal heir in the case of inheritance, and the spouse does not have the right of representation in a de facto marriage and thus does not have the authority to give consent in the case of surgery.

[5] 'Kosei Rodosho Heisei 28 Nendo Jinko Dotai Toukei Tokubetsu Hokoku "Kon-in Ni Kansuru Toukei" No Gaikyo (Brief Report of Statistics on Family: Special Report on Statistics of Population Dynamics, 2016)', Ministry of Health, Labour and Welfare (2017), 10 <https://www.mhlw.go.jp/toukei/saikin/hw/jinkou/tokusyu/konin16/dl/gaikyo.pdf> accessed 26 September 2021.

[6] Ministry of Justice, 'Koseki (Family Register)' <https://www.moj.go.jp/MINJI/koseki.html> accessed 26 September 2021.

following information: '1. the name, 2. the date of birth, 3. the cause and date of entry into the family register, 4. the name of the biological parents and the relationship with the biological parents, 5. the name of the adoptive parents if the child is adopted and the relationship with the adoptive parents, 6. the fact that the child is a husband or a wife if the child is married' (Article 13). Furthermore, the order of entry in the family register stipulates that 'if the husband and wife take the name of the husband's family, the husband shall take the first place; if the wife takes the name of the wife's family, the wife shall take the first place' (Article 14, paragraph 1). In addition, 'a child who takes the surname of his or her parents shall enter the family register of his or her parents' (Article 18(1)). This shows that married couples are supposed to take the same surname.

In Japan, a copy of the family register is required to obtain a driver's license or apply for a passport. In other words, it is a source of the proof of identity. The official record of an individual identity is based on his or her 'family', and this is the basis for the assumption that a married couple will have the same surname when a new family register is formed for reasons such as marriage.

Thus, from the enactment of the Civil Code in 1898 to date, it has been the practice for couples to unify their surnames when they marry. However, this system has been facing problems since long. The following provides an overview of some of the problems with the current system, in particular, the legal aspects.

2.2.2 Problems with the Current System

Why is the current system of equal marital status problematic? This matter is also related to the issue of family registration in Japan.

Mr. Aono, the CEO of an IT company, chose to take his wife's surname when he married. Mr. Aono changed his name to his wife's surname, Nishibata, when they married, and he performs his normal tasks under his maiden name, Aono. He said that he thought he would have to change his name on his driving licence and passport, but they also required him to change his bank and securities accounts created based on this identity registration.[7]

It has been indicated that there is a disconnect in terms of performance records because the work accumulated before the marriage was done under the name before the marriage, so changing the surname is not seen as the work done by the same person before and after the change. In recent years, as women are increasingly advancing their careers and work in various fields, changing their surnames due to marriage causes a disconnection in their performance records.

Thus, changing one's surname can lead to practical disadvantages in daily life.

---

[7] 'Women in Japan fight for their identity—starting with their name', *The Straits Times* (20th July 2019) available at https://www.straitstimes.com/asia/east-asia/women-in-japan-fight-for-their-identity-starting-with-their-name.

Furthermore, since 98% of married couples currently choose to take the name of their husbands, it can be argued that despite the prohibition in Article 14 of the Constitution of Japan against discrimination on the basis of sex in political, economic, or social relations, many women face situations in which their personal rights are violated. In other words, women are forced to experience a greater number of inconvenient situations in their social lives. Constitutional law scholar Prof. Shigeki Matsui argues that since wives took the surname of their husbands under the family system, the provision stipulating the same surname for married couples, although seemingly neutral, effectively forced them to choose the surname of their husbands. The court should rule that the provision was unconstitutional as there was no compelling interest in forcing the same surname.[8]

Regarding women and their names, Article 16(1) of the United Nations Convention on the Elimination of All Forms of Discrimination against Women states, ‘discrimination against women in all matters relating to marriage and family relations shall be eliminated’, with subparagraph b referring to the ‘equal right to freely choose one’s spouse and to marry only by free and full consent’ and subparagraph g referring to the ‘equal rights of husband and wife’. The same personal rights apply for husbands and wives, including the right to choose a surname and occupation. Thus, the issue of names has become crucial in the consideration of the status of women internationally.

In many cases, similar to that of Mr. Aono mentioned above, the common name is used in the workplace. In other words, they united under one of their surnames at the time of marriage, and the person who has changed his or her surname uses his or her maiden name as the common name. Although this is not a fundamental solution, it is a temporary measure to avoid inconvenience. In addition, the use of a common name in the workplace is not always permitted, as it is the discretion of the management.

Given the above, various proposals have been put forward to eliminate the inconvenience of changing one’s surname upon marriage, from the viewpoint of improving the status of women. Professor Takizawa, a civil law scholar, summarizes the idea of separate surnames for married couples, which has been considered as a counter measure to the system of equal surnames for married couples, as given below:

> There is a conflict between those who say that couples can freely choose to use the same or different surnames, and those who say that in principle couples should use the same surname, but in exceptional cases they can use different surnames. The last proposal is that the maiden name should be used as a matter of common sense, and that this right should only be confirmed by the Family Registration Act. The idea of the principle of a separate surname is theoretically possible, but it is not very realistic for Japanese society.[9]

Professor Miyoko Tsujimura said that choosing the surname and changing one’s surname a requirement for marriage violates Article 24(1) of the Constitution,

---

[8] Shigenori Matsui, *Japanese Constitutional Law* (3rd edn, Yuhikaku 2007) 385–386.

[9] Takizawa Itsuyo, *Sentakuteki Fufu Besshisei: Koremade to Korekara (Selective married couples’ surname system: Retrospect and Prospect)* (Sanseido 2016) 8.

which guarantees equal rights to married couples, and infringes the right to self-determination under Article 13 of the Constitution. Furthermore, it says that the argument that the same surname would create a sense of unity is unconvincing, and if the current system violates the Constitution, the introduction of an optional surname system is necessary.[10] In the event of a divorce by mutual consent, Article 767(1) of the Civil Code states the following:

> A husband or wife who has changed his or her surname by marriage shall be restored to the surname which he or she had before the marriage by a negotiated divorce.

However, a 1976 amendment to the Civil Code added a second clause which states, 'A husband or wife who has restored his or her surname to that which it was before the marriage in accordance with the preceding clause may, within three months of the date of divorce, change the surname to that which it was at the time of the divorce by filing a notification in accordance with the provisions of the Family Registration Law'.

This implies that a woman who has changed her surname to that of her husband at the time of her marriage can continue to use the surname used by her during the marriage, although in principle, she must revert to her former surname if she gets a divorce. This is a legal recognition of the practice based on the accumulation of achievements and the continuation of social relations during the marriage.

Thus, since the change of surname is allowed without the permission of the court, it is considered possible for married couples to use different surnames by choice. In fact, since the ratification of the United Nations Convention on the Elimination of All Forms of Discrimination against Women in 1985, the demand for a system of surname separation has become more pronounced. In 1996, the Legislative Council[11] proposed a reform of the Civil Code to introduce a surname system for married couples. Although this proposal did not result in any legislation, it was one of the triggers for the subsequent debate on the surname system for married couples.

Before observing the Supreme Court's decision, which we examine in this article, we first provide an overview of the system.

---

[10] Miyoko Tsujimura *Gender to Jinken (Gender and Human Rights)* (Nihon Hyoronsha 2008) 245–247.

[11] Its role is to 'investigate and deliberate on civil law, criminal law, and other basic legal matters in response to advice from the Minister of Justice'. The Civil Law (Parent-Child Relationship), Collateral Law, and Criminal Law Sections deliberate on these matters.

2.3 Resistance to the Selective Surname System

2.3.1 *What is the System of the Separate Surname for Married Couples?*

As mentioned previously, it is difficult to accept the system of separate surnames for married couples in Japan. It is also practical to continue to use one's maiden name as a common name. However, it has become increasingly difficult to maintain the principle of the same surname for married couples, given the fact that the name is part of the individual's personality and with the increasing participation of women in society. In these circumstances, a proposal has been made for an optional system of surname reassignment.

Instead of describing the historical background of the system, we provide an overview of the different ways in which it has been proposed in the past.

As mentioned above, more than 95% of women agree to take the surname of their husbands upon marriage, but as the Ministry of Justice explains, 'against the background of the inconveniences and disadvantages that have been pointed out as a result of women's advancement in society, such as inconveniences and disadvantages in their professional and daily lives and loss of identity'. The system of selective separation of surnames has been proposed against the background of the inconvenience and disadvantages in professional sphere, daily life, loss of identity, and so on, as a result of social advancement. In 1996, the Legislative Council issued a report entitled 'Outline of a Bill to Amend a Part of the Civil Code',[12] in which the introduction of the system of selective separation of surnames was mentioned. In other words, 'the surname of the husband and wife' is defined as given below:

(1) Married couples shall take the name of their husbands or wives, or the name of their respective pre-marital names, as determined at the time of their marriage.
(2) When a husband and wife stipulate that each of them shall take his or her own pre-marital status, they shall stipulate at the time of marriage that the husband's or wife's status shall be that of the child.

In another part of the article, the surname of the child is mentioned. In the case of a legitimate child, the child shall assume the surname of his or her parents or that determined by their parents as the 'surname to be assumed by the child'. The government drew up a draft amendment to the Civil Code based on these recommendations, but there was strong opposition from within the Liberal Democratic Party (LDP), which was in power at the time, because of which it was not submitted to the Parliament.

In 2010, a new bill was drafted to amend the Civil Code and other laws, but it failed to reach Parliament. The content of this bill is almost identical to that of the 1996 bill. First, Article 750 of the Civil Code is the same as in the proposal, which

[12] The contents of this outline can be found at, Ministry of Justice, 'Minpō No Ichibu o Kaisei Suru Hōritsu-an Yōkō (Outline of the Bill to Partially Revise the Civil Code)' (26 February 1996) <https://www.moj.go.jp/shingi1/shingi_960226-1.html> accessed 22 October 2021.

states that couples may choose to take the name of their husband or wife or their former names, as determined at the time of marriage. It also states about the surnames of children and change of surname to the same (or a different) one after choosing a different (or the same) one.

Furthermore, as the issue of surnames is closely related to that of each 'family', changing the treatment of surnames from the same family system to the system of selective separation of surnames will require the compilation of family registers and thus a revision of the Family Registration Act. For example, with regard to the order of entry in the family register, under the current system, the husband is listed first when the husband's surname is used, the wife is listed first when the wife's surname is used, and followed by the spouse.[13]

Thus, the basis of the system of selective separation of surnames is as follows:

1. The right to choose at the time of marriage whether the surname of the husband or the wife should be the same, or whether each person should continue to use the surname which he or she had previously used.
2. For children, the choice of surname should be made at the time of marriage.

It is also essential that the family registration system should be modified to reflect these points. Although it would be relatively easy to introduce such a system, the fact is that twenty-five years after it was first mentioned by the Legislative Council, it has not yet become a law. Before moving on to the next section, describing the lawsuits challenging the unconstitutionality of not introducing the system, let us consider the objections that have been raised against this system.

2.3.2 *Opposition to the System of Selective Surnames*

One of the questions on the website of the Ministry of Justice regarding the system of selective separation of surnames is as follows: 'What are the reasons for your opinion in favor of or against the system of selective separation of surnames?' In response to this question, the reasons provided for the opposing opinions are that the same surname is established in Japanese society, the surname is not a matter of personal freedom but the public system, and having the same surname in the family creates a sense of unity between husband and wife and the family members, which is in the best interests of the children.

However, these objections can be criticized in the following ways.

First, the system of married couples having the same surname was established in Japanese society, and the use of surnames was not common until 1870, when commoners (farmers, merchants, etc., other than those who were members of the noble or former samurai class) were allowed to use their surnames, until the enactment of the Old Civil Code. The Meiji Government issued a proclamation stating that

[13] Ministry of Justice, 'Outline of the Revised Bill' (2010) <https://www.moj.go.jp/content/001357682.pdf> accessed 20 September 2021.

married couples were to have separate surnames, which does not necessarily mean that the system was firmly established in Japanese society.[14] However, it is also argued that even if the historically correct facts are used to refute this argument, it cannot be used to justify the surname system.[15]

Indeed, for the last 120 years, the system has been generally accepted. However, we must also consider that the reason for the introduction of this system was to cause the wife to belong to the husband's family (to submit to the authority of the head of the husband's family). As Professor Sakai indicated, it was not desirable, at least from the viewpoint of the samurai class, for a daughter to be separated from her family of origin by marriage, and both the husband's and the wife's intentions were to continue their families by continuing the separate family system. This is not a valid reason to oppose the system of separate surnames, at least not in the context of the traditions of Japanese society.

The problem with the official system seems to be that it is associated with the family registration system. As we have seen, a husband or wife is registered in a family register in which the person, whose name he or she bears, is the head. However, it is possible to introduce a surname system for married couples without fundamentally changing the current system of family registers, and the introduction of a surname system for married couples may not lead to a major collapse of the systems of family registers and official identification on which it is based. This can be observed from the fact that it was considered possible to introduce the surname system by amending parts of the Family Registration Act, even though the draft law was not submitted to Parliament in 2012.

With regard to the unconstitutionality of the system concerning the unity of husband and wife and the interests of the children, there are many countries that have introduced the system of separate surnames. This situation is more disadvantageous for the family, especially for the children.[16]

As mentioned above, there are no major disadvantages in adopting the system of selective separation of surnames. On the contrary, as the survey by the Ministry of Justice shows, more people are willing to amend the law to introduce the surname system than before.[17] Against the background of these opinions, lawsuits have been

---

[14] Ministry of Justice, 'Wagakuni Ni Okeru Uji No Seido No Hensen (Changes in his System in Japan)' <https://www.moj.go.jp/MINJI/minji36-02.html> accessed 20 September 2021.

[15] Yuichiro Sakai, *Jijitsukon to Fufu-bessei no Shakaigaku (Sociology of* De facto *marriage and Separate surname system)* (Hakutakusha 2021) 53–65.

[16] Various examples of couples who have chosen to de facto marriage, ibid 78–102.

[17] According to the results of the 2017 survey, 42.5 per cent of respondents are of the opinion that the law should be amended. It should be noted, however, that while 29.3 per cent of respondents agreed that married couples should have the same surname and that there was no need to amend the law, a non-negligible 24.4 per cent agreed that married couples should have the same surname but that the law should be amended to allow them to use their pre-marital surname as their common name. In 1996, 32.5 per cent of the respondents thought that the law should be amended to allow married couples to use their former surnames as their common names, which is a significant increase, *see* https://www.moj.go.jp/content/001271412.pdf (last accessed 22 October 2021).

filed to challenge the State's inaction in not introducing the system of selective surnames. In the next section, I provide an overview of these cases.

2.4 Judgments of the High Court and the Supreme Court on the Optional Surname System

2.4.1 2014 Tokyo High Court Judgment and 2017 Supreme Court Judgment

The Supreme Court of Japan hears cases before the Grand Bench, composed of all 15 Supreme Court judges, 'when determining whether a law, order, rule or disposition is or is not in conformity with the Constitution' or 'when an opinion on the interpretation or application of the Constitution or other law is contrary to a previous decision of the Supreme Court' (Article 10 of the Court Law). (Article 10 of the Courts Act). The Supreme Court cases discussed in this section have all been heard by the Grand Bench.

In 2017, the Grand Chamber ruled that Article 750 of the Civil Code, which establishes the system of equal marital status, violates Article 13 (the right to pursue happiness), Article 14(1) (equality under the law), Article 24 (individual dignity and equality of both sexes in family life) and other provisions of the Constitution, and the failure to take legislative action to amend or repeal it is a legislative omission. The appeal is based on a claim for damages under Article 1(1) of the State Compensation Act. In the Court of Appeal, the appellant (the plaintiff in the original case requested the introduction of the system of married couples' separate families) contested the unconstitutionality of the provision of Article 750 and that it violated Article 16 of the Convention on the Elimination of All Forms of Discrimination against Women. The Tokyo High Court, the court of appeal, ruled on these issues, as given below.

2.4.1.1 Tokyo High Court Judgment[18]

First, in order for a claim for compensation under Article 1(1) of the State Compensation Act to be recognized, the legislative acts, or omissions of the Parliament members in this case, must have illegally violated the constitutionally guaranteed rights of individuals, and the legislative work must have been performed to protect the constitutionally guaranteed rights of the people. In exceptional cases, legislative acts or omissions by members of the Parliament may be deemed unlawful in applying the provisions of Article 1(1) of the State Compensation Act, provided that the failure to do so is without justifiable reason. In order for the State to be held liable for damages under Article 1(1) of the State Compensation Act with respect to the

[18] LEX/DB25503188 (28 March 2014, High Court of Tokyo).

legislative acts or omissions of Parliament members, the existence of a 'right guaranteed to the people under the Constitution' is an essential precondition. In addition, it mentions that it judges whether the 'freedom of marriage' is a 'right guaranteed to the people under the Constitution' under Article 24 of the Constitution, and whether it is a 'right guaranteed to the people under the Convention on the Elimination of All Forms of Discrimination against Women'.[19]

Regarding the relationship between the 'right not to be compelled to change one's surname' and Article 13 of the Constitution, the Court found that a person's surname is 'conferred by the Civil Code or other laws, regardless of the individual's will, upon birth' and cannot be changed by the individual's will. However, it points out that this system is regulated by law, and various rights and interests related to the surname are not protected by law. 'It is not guaranteed by the Constitution as an innate and natural right of freedom apart from the legal system[20]'. Furthermore, it also mentions rights with regard to the 'right not to be compelled to change one's surname', although there are opinions in favor of the introduction of the system of selective separation of husband and wife, a considerable number of citizens find the system of the same surname to be positively significant, on the grounds that it 'cannot be said that it is still indispensable for the personal survival of the individual, nor that it has been fundamental to the life of the nation for a long time'. As such, it held that the 'right not to have one's surname forced upon one' could not be regarded as a fundamental right guaranteed by Article 13 of the Constitution.[21]

With regard to the appellant's argument that the 'freedom to marry' is impeded by the same surname system and violates Article 24 of the Constitution, the Court held the following: First, the Court acknowledges that the appellant's claim cannot be interfered with by the will of a third party, for example, forced marriage is not recognized as the appellant claims. However, Article 24 'establishes the dignity of the individual and the equality of the sexes in the context of marriage and family relations', and it cannot be considered to directly guarantee equal rights in each specific legal relationship. Furthermore, the Court mentions that Article 750 of the Civil Code, which provides for the system of equal surnames for married couples, does not interfere with the rights of men and women to freely and equally choose their surnames, and the legislative purpose of Article 750, which is 'to ensure the expression of community life and a sense of family unity through the use of surnames', is justified. In addition, the Court points that it is socially acceptable to use the surname before marriage as a common name, and it is reasonable to establish the same surname.

As described above, the Court held that the 'right not to be forced to change one's surname' is not a specific right guaranteed under Article 13 of the Constitution, and the 'freedom of marriage' is not a right guaranteed under Article 24 of the Constitution.[22] Thus, the court indicates that the omission to legislate for a system

[19] Ibid para 3_2(1).

[20] Ibid para 3_2(2)e.

[21] Ibid para 3_2(2)o.

[22] Ibid para 3_2(3).

of selective surnames is not illegal in terms of the application of Article 1(1) of the State Compensation Act.[23] In addition, regarding the Convention on the Elimination of All Forms of Discrimination against Women, the Court held that the Convention does not directly confer any rights on the citizens of Japan. Therefore, it cannot be said that 'the right not to be forced to change one's surname' is guaranteed to the citizens of Japan by the Convention.[24]

In the judgment of the Tokyo High Court, the right of not being compelled to change one's surname was not recognized as a constitutional right, and the legislative inaction of not introducing the system of selective surname change was not considered a violation of the Constitution. This High Court decision was appealed to the Supreme Court in the 2015 Supreme Court decision, which is discussed in the next art. The framework of the majority opinion of the Supreme Court is essentially same as this High Court decision. The following section provides an overview of the majority opinion as well as the individual opinions of the Supreme Court.

2.4.1.2 Supreme Court Judgment[25]

The Court dismissed the appeal and the plaintiff lost the case.

First, in response to the plaintiff's argument that Article 750 of the Civil Code, which stipulates that a husband and wife should have the same surname, is contrary to the right to pursue happiness under Article 13 of the Constitution. The Supreme Court ruled that although the surname constitutes one of the contents of personal rights, the content of the personal rights can be concretely understood only through the legal system, which is determined based on the Constitution. Therefore, it is inappropriate to discuss whether the change of the surname immediately infringes the personal rights, that is, whether it is unconstitutional.[26] In addition, the Court states that it is reasonable to separate the surname from the first name to remind people that they belong to the same family group by using the same surname. In addition, this is not the case in which a person is forced to change his or her surname regardless of his or her own will, but rather one in which a change in status, such as marriage, is expected to result in a change of surname. Considering the above, the Court held that 'the right not to be compelled to change one's surname' cannot be regarded as one of the constitutional personal rights and Article 750 of the Civil Code does not violate Article 13 of the Constitution.

However, the court held that the interest to maintain the credit and reputation of the individual built up before marriage is a personal interest that should be taken into account when considering the legal system of marriage and family, and that it is a

---

[23] Ibid para 3_2(4).

[24] Ibid para 3_2(5).

[25] The Judgment of the grand bench of the Supreme Court of Japan (*Supreme Court Reporters [Civil cases]* Vol. 69 No. 8) 2586–2615.

[26] Ibid 2588.

matter that should be taken into account when considering whether or not it is beyond the scope of legislative discretion recognized in Article 24 of the Constitution.[27]

Regarding the plaintiff's argument that Article 750 of the Civil Code violates Article 14 of the Constitution, the court held that the law does not discriminate on the basis of gender because it leaves it up to the parties who wish to become husband and wife to decide which of their names they wish to use. So it also concluded that there was no violation of Article 14. However, an overwhelming majority of couples have chosen their husband's surname. If this has been influenced by discriminatory attitudes and customs existing in society, it is in line with the purpose of Article 14 of the Constitution to eliminate such influences and ensure substantive equality, and this is a matter that should be taken into account when considering the legal system relating to marriage and the family. Then the Court mentions that this is in line with the purpose of Article 14 of the Constitution and is a matter that should be taken into consideration when examining the legal system concerning marriage and the family.[28]

As for the argument that Article 750 of the Civil Code infringes the 'freedom of marriage' provided for in Article 24 of the Constitution, the Court made the following observations. First, 'freedom of marriage' means that 'whether to marry or not, when to marry and with whom' must be left to the free and equal decision of the parties concerned. Article 750 of the Civil Code stipulates that a married couple shall have the same legal status as husband and wife as one of the effects of marriage and does not directly restrict the right to marry.

In addition, the construction of the system of marriage is left to the reasonable legislative discretion of the Parliament, and there is a limit to the discretion of the Parliament to observe the requirements and guidelines that should be based on 'the dignity of person and the essential equality of the sexes'. In addition to the protection of constitutionally guaranteed moral rights and the formal equality of the sexes, the Court recognizes that it is also necessary to protect personal interests and substantive equality, which are not directly guaranteed by the Constitution, and ensure that the institution of marriage does not unreasonably restrict marriage in practice. Simultaneously, it states matters relating to marriage and the family should be determined based on a comprehensive judgment, taking into account various factors in the social context, including national traditions and public sentiment, and, in particular, personal interests and substantive equality, which may vary in content. Personal interests and substantive equality are likely to be diverse in content, and their realization must be determined in relation to various matters, including social conditions and the conditions of national life. On this basis, the judgment states that the Parliament should make a multifaceted decision on what legislative measures to take in response to the requirements and guidelines of Article 24 of the Constitution. In determining whether a provision of law relating to marriage is compatible with Article 24, if it does not violate Articles 13 and 14(1) of the Constitution, the purpose of the present legal system and the effect of adopting it must be examined, and it

[27] Ibid 2590.

[28] Ibid 2591.

must be considered that Article 750 of the Civil Code is not reasonable in the light of the requirements of individual dignity and equality of the sexes, which is beyond the scope of the legislative discretion of the Parliament. The court said that the decision should be made from the perspective of whether Article 750 of the Civil Code is unreasonable in light of the demands of individual dignity and equality of the sexes and whether it is beyond the scope of the legislative discretion of the Parliament.

Given the above, the majority opinion reiterates that there is a rationality in defining a single surname as the generic name of the family, and that the use of the same surname by married couples has the function of indicating to society that they are members of a family group, and that it is easier for children to benefit from using the same surname as their parents. On the contrary, the Bench recognize that it is undeniable that there are disadvantages for the person who changes his or her name, such as the loss of identity and the difficulty of maintaining the social trust and reputation established through the use of the pre-marital surname because one of the persons who intends to become a couple always changes his or her surname. In addition, it can be inferred that, at present, a woman suffers this disadvantage after becoming the wife. However, these disadvantages may be alleviated to some extent by the widespread use of common names. Judging from the above, the Court ruled that Article 750 of the Civil Code does not violate Article 24 of the Constitution, as the system of surnames of married couples is not immediately unreasonable from the viewpoint of the dignity of the individual and the equality of the sexes.

The majority opinion also stated that the system of selective separation of surnames is not unreasonable, and the Parliament should debate and decide on this matter.

In addition to this majority opinion, there is a dissenting opinion by Justice Yamaura, a supplementary opinion by Justice Terada, and opinions by Justices Sakurai, Okabe, Onimaru, and Kiuchi. Of these, I outline the dissenting opinion by Justice Yamaura, the supplementary opinion by Justice Terada, and the opinion by Justice Okabe.

Justice Terada held that the family system, like the legal system such as the company system or the trust, was designed in a standardized way so that society views it as uncomplicated, and it was restrained from being transformed in accordance with the diverse wishes of the parties. He mentions that marriage is characterized by the system of legitimate children. However, to argue the unreasonableness of the current system in judicial review, the system should not be made more complicated, he commented. Therefore, he states that it is desirable to leave it to the democratic process to decide on a reasonable system after extensive consideration.[29] This opinion reinforces the majority opinion's view that a certain degree of unification of the family as a social institution is required.

Justice Okabe disagrees with the majority opinion on the point that Article 750 of the Civil Code does not violate Article 24 of the Constitution. First, the system of equal status of husband and wife was significant because it provided for a formal equality in that the husband and wife could decide which of their surnames they

[29] Ibid 2596–2601.

wished to use through consultation, and at the time of its enactment, it was compatible with Article 24 of the Constitution, which provides for the essential equality of the husband and wife.[30] However, she pointed out that as a long period of time has passed since the enactment of Article 750 of the Civil Code, and as women have advanced in society, the number of women who are disadvantaged by a change in their surname to that of their husband at the time of marriage has increased, and there is sufficient reason for women to use their surname before marriage.[31] In addition, even if it is based on the free will of the wife to use her husband's surname, the process of decision-making is influenced by the inequality and power equations between men and women. This system is not based on the dignity of the individual and the essential equality of the sexes'.[32]

The fact that couples have to choose their surname restricts their freedom to marry as it imposes an unreasonable requirement for the formation of a marriage. Furthermore, while acknowledging the function of the surname in identifying a person as a member of the family, the Court said that this was not a basis for making exceptions and indicated the diversity of families worldwide.[33] The use of common names is flawed in that it is only for convenience and cannot be used in official documents, and it also creates a new problem of identity between the nickname and the family register name.[34] Given the above, the rationality of Article 750 of the Civil Code has wavered with the changes in society, and it has become unreasonable in terms of the dignity of the individual and the essential equality of the sexes for married couples to take different surnames, which is beyond the scope of the legislative discretion of the Parliament and violates Article 24 of the Constitution.[35] Concurring with Justice Okabe's opinion, in an interview with a newspaper in June 2021, Justice Sakurai said that she considered it to be premature that the case was sent to the Grand Bench when there was no growing public interest and a high probability that the unified surname system would be judged constitutional. The reason for her unconstitutional decision on the surname system was that Justice Sakurai had been forced to use a common name when working as a bureaucrat, and she wanted to see the debate on the selective surname system gain momentum.[36]

Interestingly, three female judges have made such an unconstitutional decision. However, gender does not necessarily influence the decision in such case, which is shown by the fact that in the 2021 case, discussed in the next part, Justice Okamura, a female judge, ruled that the unified surname system does not violate Article 24 of

---

[30] Ibid 2601–2602.

[31] Ibid 2602.

[32] Ibid 2603–2604.

[33] Ibid 2604.

[34] Ibid 2605.

[35] Ibid 2605.

[36] '"Constitutional Judgment from the Front" 15-Year Judgment "Unconstitutional" Former Judge-Supreme Court Decision on the 23rd with Married Couple's Surname' *Jiji Press* (22 June 2021) <https://www.jiji.com/jc/article?k=2021062200718&g=soc> accessed 26 September 2021.

the Constitution, in relation to the disposition under Article 750 of the Civil Code and Article 74(1) of the Family Registration Act.

Justice Yamaura disagreed with the majority opinion and held that Article 750 of the Civil Code violated Article 24 of the Constitution, and the failure to take legislative action to amend or repeal it was unlawful, in terms of the application of section 1(1) of the State Compensation Act. Justice Yamaura said that the disadvantage of changing one's surname had increased due to changes in the social structure, and this disadvantage had been recognized by the government, especially as 'it has become a social fact that women change their surnames upon marriage, regardless of the legal framework[37]'. Furthermore, considering the background of the report of the Legislative Council on the introduction of the system of selective surname change, the Government was aware of the problems in terms of personal interests and substantive equality between husband and wife, when one of them has to change their surname. In addition, it is illegal under Article 1(1) of the State Compensation Act for the Parliament to have failed to legislate without reason to adopt the surname system for married couples, while being aware that the surname system violates the Constitution as it restricts the rights and interests protected by the Constitution without reasonable grounds. Therefore, it is illegal under Article 1(1) of the State Compensation Act.

This is the only opinion which indicates that the failure of the Parliament to legislate for the introduction of a selective surname system is illegal under the State Compensation Law.[38] It is acknowledged by both judicial precedents and academic theories that the exercise of public power by the legislature is also subject to claims for state compensation.[39] However, to make a claim for state compensation, the exercise of public power must be illegal.[40] It is difficult to state whether the absence of legislative action for a long period can be regarded as illegal, but the opinion highlights an important perspective.

2.4.1.3 Reaction in the Academic Community

A number of constitutional scholars and family law scholars have examined and commented on the judgment.[41] Some of them, except for those mentioned in the footnotes, will be introduced here. Prof. Keigo Komamura indicated a logical complication in the judgment that the surname constitutes a part of the personal rights but

---

[37] *Supreme Court Reporters [Civil cases]* (n 25) 2613.

[38] Ibid 2614.

[39] Tokiyasu Fujita, *Gyoseiho Soron* (*General Theory of Administrative Law*) (Seirinshoin 2014) 533–534.

[40] Ibid 533.

[41] For example, Yasuo Hasebe, *Chushaku Nihonkoku Kempo (Commentary of Japanese Constitution),* vol 2 (Yuhikaku 2017) 504–507; Nobuyoshi Ashibe, *Kempo (Constitutional Law)* (Kazuyuki Takahashi ed, 7th edn, Iwanami Shoten 2019) 138–139; Satoshi Kinoshita and Masato Tadano (eds), *Shin Kommental Kempo (New Commentary of Constitution)* (2nd edn, Nihon Hyoronsha 2019) 305–307; Shuhei Ninomiya, *Kazokuho (Family Law)* (5th edn, Shinseisha 2021) 51–54.

the ‘freedom not to be forced to change the surname’ is not recognized as a constitutional right. He further considered the nature of the surname, noting that the judgment referred to the nature of the surname in terms of the relevant provisions of the Civil Code, but it was unclear whether the interpretation of the nature of the surname was that of the Constitution. Moreover, it is possible to set up a new surname for each family unit, but the current law, which allows couples to choose their own surname, is potentially based on the idea that the status relationship is within the scope of kinship. Rather than the rationality of the system of surnames, that of not allowing the exception of the system of selective separation of surnames is being questioned here. The absence of a constitutional theory of the family is also questioned.[42]

Prof. Maki uses this case and the Supreme Court’s decision on the ban on remarriage as an opportunity to examine the legislative purpose of laws relating to family issues and the framework for determining constitutionality.[43] In this article, Prof. Maki re-examines the interpretation of the family in relation to the various provisions of the Constitution, stating that if we assume that the surname and marriage are self-created, we need to question the judgment that the freedom of the surname and marriage is based on the legal system. Prof. Maki introduces that the court judged that there is no constitutional restriction on the system of married couples’ surname because it considered the surname to be embodied in the system of marriage and the family system, emphasizing the significance of the embodied surname as the name of the family consisting of a married couple and a legitimate child. This idea is called ‘institution-first thinking’. In the paper, Prof. Maki discusses the concept of ‘institution-first thinking’ and how it is difficult to justify the surname system because it does not constitute marriage, nor does it take precedence over constitutional rights and interests; the system is rather a direct restriction on the freedom of marriage. It also criticizes the majority opinion on the grounds that the request for a selective surname system is made by a social minority, namely women, seeking substantive equality and should not be subjected to the democratic process of deciding by majority vote.

Other introductions to the judgment have also been critical. For example, Prof. Shibutani argues for the necessity of allowing exceptions to the uniform system of married couples’ surnames, stating that the name ‘has come to be regarded as a symbol of the individual’s personality and since ‘the dignity of the individual’ has become a fundamental principle, the same surname should not be forced on individuals against their will. The necessity of allowing exceptions rather than a uniform system of surnames is emphasized.[44]

In general, the opinion of researchers is critical of the majority opinion of the Court.

---

[42] Keigo Komamura, ‘Fufu Doshi Seido no Gokensei (Constitutionality of Same Surname System) in *Hanrei Hyakusen Kempo (Hundred Judgments of Constitution* (7th ed, vol I, Yuhikaku 2019) 66–67.

[43] Misaki Maki, ‘Kempo to Kazoku’ (Constitution and Family), *Quarterly Jurist* No.18 (Yuhikaku 2018) 86–91.

[44] Hideki Shibutani in Hideki Shibutani and Masahiro Akasaka *Kempo I Jinken (Constitutional Law I Human Rights)* (7th ed, Yuhikaku 2019) 259.

2.4.2 2021 Supreme Court Decision[45]

As mentioned above, in the 2015 decision of the Supreme Court, 5 out of 15 judges ruled that the system of unified surnames with married couples is unconstitutional under Article 24 of the Constitution. In 2021, the Supreme Court will again decide on the constitutionality of the unified surname system.

In this case, the complainant, whose marriage registration form with the husband's surname for the husband and the wife's surname for the wife had been rejected, petitioned the Family Court under the Family Registration Act to order its acceptance. The Complainant argued that Article 750 of the Civil Code, which provides for the surname system for married couples, and Article 74(1) of the Family Registration Act, which requires that the couple's surname must be written on the marriage certificate, are invalid in violation of Articles 14(1), 24, and 98(2)[46]of the Constitution.

The Supreme Court dismissed the appeal in a Grand Bench decision of 23 June 2021. First, it referred to the fact that Article 750 of the Civil Code was not considered violating Article 24 of the Constitution in the 2015 judgment, as discussed in the previous section. Furthermore, Article 74(1) of the Family Registration Act, which made the couple's surname a matter to be included in the marriage registration, did not violate Article 24 of the Constitution for the purposes of the 2015 judgment. The Court mentioned that considering the changes in social conditions and the increase in the number of those in favor of the introduction of the system of selective surnames for married couples, the decision of the 2015 judgment does not need to be changed, and the opinion that both articles violate Article 24 of the Constitution cannot be adopted.[47]

Thus, the appropriateness of a system of surnames for married couples as a matter of legislative policy is a separate issue from the examination of the constitutionality of the provisions of the current law. The Court avoided making a judgment on the issue of selective surnames, or equal surnames for married couples, stating that it should be discussed and decided upon by the Parliament.[48]

There was a joint dissenting opinion by Justices Uga and Miyazaki, a dissenting opinion by Justice Kusano, supplementary opinions by Justices Fukayama, Okamura, and Nagamine, and an opinion by Justice Miura.

In their supplementary opinion, Justices Fukayama, Okamura, and Nagamine agreed with the majority opinion that the provisions of the law in question in this case cannot be said to violate Article 24 of the Constitution. They hoped that the Parliament would have a serious discussion.[49]

In his conclusion, Justice Miura agreed with the majority opinion but held that the law's failure to provide an option for married couples to separate their surnames

---

[45] 'Reiwa 2nd Year (K) No. 102-Against the Mayor's Disposition Dismissal Appeal' (2020) https://www.courts.go.jp/app/files/hanrei_jp/412/090412_hanrei.pdf accessed 26 September 2021.

[46] Article 98 (2) provides compliance with ratified treaties.

[47] Ibid 1–2.

[48] ibid. 2.

[49] Ibid 2–7.

violated Article 24 of the Constitution. According to him, it was difficult to argue for the rationality of not allowing exceptions to the surname system for married couples, given the diversity of marriage and family forms and the current situation of women. However, based on the provisions of the Family Registration Law and other laws, refusal to accept a marriage notification is not illegal.[50]

In their dissenting opinion, Justices Miyazaki, Uga, and Kusano not only held that Article 750 of the Civil Code, among others, violated the Constitution, but also that the contested marriage certificate should be accepted. In light of Article 24 of the Constitution, which states that the state should not interfere unreasonably with the free decision-making of the parties to a marriage, the personalities of a husband and wife must be respected.[51] If the restrictions imposed by the institution of marriage are deemed to unreasonably infringe the decision of the parties considering Article 24 of the Constitution, the restrictions should be declared unconstitutional and invalid to the extent of the infringement.

They then state that making the same surname a requirement for the acceptance of a marriage registration is a direct restriction on marriage.[52] Furthermore, it requires that only one of the spouses makes the decision to accept the loss of their personal interests while making the decision to marry, which is not a free and equal decision but an oppressive one.[53]

They state that the previously mentioned oppression to the selective surname system is not justified in terms of the public welfare. In particular, it states that the idea that the surname is significant as a family designation does not have a constitutional basis, and it is difficult to use this idea as a rational basis for denying the personal rights concerning the name.[54] Therefore, 'it is reasonable from the standpoint of public welfare to suppress the decision of the parties to a marriage by making the same surname a requirement for the consummation of the marriage for those who wish to avoid the loss of the moral interest in their natural names and to enjoy the same moral interest as husband and wife, thereby infringing on their free and equal decision to marry'.[55] In addition, Article 750 of the Civil Code and Article 74 of the Family Registration Law states that it 'contradict the purpose of Article 24(1) of the Constitution in that they force married couples to use the same surname and require a single surname to be written on the marriage certificate'.[56] Moreover, they also mention that marriage is a private matter and a public notification of the privacy of a marriage is an infringement of that privacy.[57]

As mentioned above, it states that these provisions are contrary to Article 24(1) of the Constitution. Thus, Justices mention that the law cannot be said to be based

---

50 Ibid 11–17.

51 Ibid 17–21.

52 Ibid 21–22.

53 Ibid 24–27.

54 Ibid 27–29.

55 Ibid 29.

56 Ibid 29.

57 Ibid 29–30.

on 'the dignity of the individual and the equality of the sexes' as stipulated in Article 24(2) of the Constitution and must be considered unconstitutional as it is an abuse of legislative discretion.[58] The opinion states that it is unconstitutional that the law does not uniformly oblige married couples to keep separate surnames and that it does not make any exceptions to the surname system. In most cases (96%), the wife changes her surname, thus making the system incompatible with the dignity of the individual and the equality of the sexes.[59] In addition, the UN Committee on the Elimination of Discrimination against Women has issued a recommendation to revise the surname system for married couples.

Furthermore, the opinion states that as the provision that forces the married couple to use the same surname and obliges them to write a single surname is unconstitutional and invalid, the non-acceptance of the marriage notification is an illegal disposition lacking the ground rules. Therefore, the court should order the acceptance of the notification. Then lastly, the opinion stresses that the Parliament should also promptly amend the relevant provisions to ensure that all citizens can make a free and equal decision to marry, thus founding the law on the dignity of the individual and the equality of the sexes.[60]

Justice Kusano, who also delivered the dissenting opinion, considered it useful to weigh the pros of introducing a selective surname system to the public against its cons. He mentions that since enhancement of welfare from the introduction of the system is greater than its reduction, and since the negatively affected welfare cannot be regarded as a human right or a similar benefit, the failure to introduce the system of the selective surname system becomes an act of neglecting the dignity of the individual, and that Article 750 of the Civil Code, violates Article 24 of the Constitution.[61]

Comparing the 2015 decision with the 2021 decision, it can be observed that there is no significant difference in legal theory. However, since the 2021 decision did not only consider the surname system under the Civil Code but also the registration of marriages under the Family Registration Act, it provided an important opportunity to examine the relationship between the state system of family registration and the modern family.[62]

---

[58] Ibid 30–31.

[59] Ibid 32–41.

[60] Ibid 41–43.

[61] Ibid 43–49.

[62] In response to this decision, the Japan Federation of Bar Associations has issued a Chairman's Statement reiterating its call for the introduction of an alternative surname system for married couples; 'Following the Supreme Court's decision, the Chairman's statement calling for the revision of Article 750 of the Civil Code and the introduction of a selective surname system for married couples' (*Japan Federation of Bar Associations*, 25 June 2021) <https://www.nichibenren.or.jp/document/statement/year/2021/210625.html> accessed 26 September 2021.

2.5 Conclusion

As noted, the surname in modern Japan has existed not only as a means of personal identification but also as an inseparable part of the existence of the family and the family register system that officially certifies it. However, the selective surname system has been proposed as a way of mitigating the conflict between the alteration of the name, which constitutes a part of the person's dignity, and the family image, which emphasizes the family and the family registration system.[63]

The majority opinion of the Supreme Court in 2015 and the decision of the Supreme Court in 2021 both simplify the diversified image of the family in the modern age. In addition, they did not urge legislative measures to introduce an optional surname system that considered the diverse situation and the dignity of the individual, saying that they expect further debate in the Parliament.

However, in the national review of the Supreme Court judges held in October 2021, it is reported that relatively more votes of no confidence were cast for judges ruling in favor of the surname system to be constitutional in the 2021 decision than for those ruling in favor of the system as unconstitutional.[64] Although the causal link between the votes is unclear, this decision was one of the judicial decisions that received particular focus in the media coverage of the review. Therefore, this decision seemed to attract the attention of the public to the judiciary.[65]

In today's dynamic society, the nature of the family is in a state of constant flux. Thus, the appropriateness of basing constitutional judgments on a fixed image of the family needs to be further examined. The family registration system, which is based on the family, also needs to be re-analyzed to determine its appropriateness in relation to the dignity of the individual. These will be major issues for the future of the family and the state system in Japan. As a legal argument, the 2021 decision may not be substantially different from the 2015 judgment. However, given that it has attracted the attention of society, it can be a significant opportunity to comprehensively consider the aforementioned issues.

---

[63] As an examination of the nature of the surname, Prof. Noriaki Shinohara, 'Fufudoushisei to Kempo 24jo' (Same Surname System and Art.24 of the Constitution) *Hogaku Sminar (Jurisprudential Seminar)* (Hogaku Sminar (Jurisprudential Seminar) No. 79, Nihon Hyoronsha, 2021) 45–52.

[64] Available at https://www.tokyo-np.co.jp/article/140377?rct=national (1 November 2021 accessed).

[65] 'Check out the Supreme Court Judges What Have the 11 Subjects Made so Far? National Examination at the Same Time as the Lower House Election' *TOKYO Web* (28 October 2021) <https://www.tokyo-np.co.jp/article/139501> accessed 30 October 2021.

Chapter 3
Buddhist Cosmological Narratives and Hybrid Statehood in Sri Lanka and Myanmar

Punsara Amarasinghe

Abstract The rise of Buddhist nationalism in Sri Lanka and Myanmar after independence certainly caused major troubles in the post-colonial state-building processes in both countries. While the constitutional process became malleable to the influence of the growing Buddhist nationalism, this also continued to be a crucial factor in deciding the political leadership of both countries. This article argues that the conflicts emerging from Sri Lanka's and Myanmar's twisted identities weighing between modern statehood and Buddhist nationalism are rooted in the historiography of both states, which was dominated by Buddhist cosmological narratives. The article shows how the influence of Buddhist cosmology in carving a ruler who stood above mundane polity did not wither away after the British colonial experience in Sri Lanka and Myanmar. The troubled stage of constitutional practices that brought some negative impacts on the respective country's minorities has risen from the effects of Buddhist cosmological notions on the public consciousness of both Sri Lanka and Myanmar.

3.1 Introduction

Recent trends within comparative constitutional law have taken a different approach toward studying constitutional complexities from orthodox viewpoints confined to literal constitutional interpretations. In this postmodern age, we realize that simply transplanting constitutions or governance models from Western countries is not

Author wishes to thank Prof Werner F. Menski at SOAS for spending his precious time for reading this manuscript and eventually guiding me to publish this article in Indian Year Book of Comparative Law. Also, I like to thank my long-time friend Sanjayan Rajasingham at Yale University for making a constructive criticism, which helped me in improving the quality of this article. At last, but not least my sincere thanking goes to the anonymous peer reviewer who recommended this paper to publish.

P. Amarasinghe (✉)
Institute of Law, Politics and Development, Scuola Superiore Sant Anna, Pisa, Italy
e-mail: punsaraprint10@gmail.com

M. John et al. (eds.), *The Indian Yearbook of Comparative Law 2020*, The Indian Yearbook of Comparative Law, https://doi.org/10.1007/978-981-99-5467-4_3

the way forward—Afghanistan is the latest proof that indigenous, hybrid and thus deeply plural models are required, though that strategy demands new safeguards. This tectonic shift has created a certain alacrity in examining constitutions propelled by religion and other historical antecedents outside the Western world. In this context, the impact of Buddhism in constitution-making processes in South and Southeast Asia has been subjected afresh to academic inquiry. The question that comes to the fore is simply this: How would an ascetic religion, supposedly unconcerned with worldly power, be able to make benign effects in constitutional formation, specifically here applied to Sri Lanka and Myanmar? As a constitutional theorist mainly working on Buddhism and constitutional practices, Benjamin Schonthal[1] has pointed out that many modern scholars have tended to overlook Buddhism as a religion that is politically quiescent, thus an inert entity, in regimes of legal regulation.

This article revisits Sri Lanka and Myanmar's tryst with constitutional law and its discontents, as both states have grappled with various attempts to assimilate Theravada Buddhist doctrine into their post-colonial constitutional experiences. The constitutional framing of Buddhism in both Sri Lanka and Myanmar appears peculiarly hybrid. Unlike Cambodia or Bhutan, both Sri Lanka and Myanmar have not entirely embraced Buddhism as the state religion by the Constitution. Yet, the special privilege guaranteed to Buddhism by section 361 of Myanmar's Constitution and Article 9 of Sri Lanka's Second Republican Constitution has kept the Buddhist creed in those countries in a prominent place. The resulting perplexing complexities in ascertaining the respective troubled constitutional practices should be evaluated in light of the historiography of both countries, which essentially unfolds the significance of Buddhism as pervading their national consciousness.

The task of this article is threefold. First, it examines the archaic embodiment of a Buddhist ruler, whose persona was emblematic of a Cakravarti or Cakkavatti-type figure from Buddhist cosmology. The historical trajectories in both Sri Lanka and Myanmar have conspicuously shown the profound impacts of Buddhist cosmological narratives in forming a ruler akin to a universal figure who epitomizes the virtues of the Buddha (Ostensibly, this claim appears to be a reminder of the 'Divine Rights of Kings', a prevalent doctrine in medieval European political settings before it reached its ebb in the age of enlightenment. But this article unfolds idiosyncratic features embedded in the kingship of both Sri Lanka and Myanmar as the pivotal factor that firmly and uninterruptedly shaped the respective socio-political identities. Unlike Europe, where the stringent belief in the king's divine authority on earth perished in the age of reason, the Buddhist cosmological belief focused on the ruler in Sri Lanka and Myanmar did not wither even after the end of British colonial rule. When Sri Lanka and Myanmar stumbled upon the journey of Westphalian model state formation, their romance with archetypical Buddhist kingship saw a resurgence in the realm of national politics. This paved the path for ethnic strife in Sri Lanka and the troubled political dilemma in Myanmar regarding minorities.

[1] Benjamin Schonthal, Buddhism, Politics and the Limits of Law: The Pyrrhic Constitutionalism in Sri Lanka (New York: Cambridge University Press 2016).

This article also traces the robust growth of nationalism driven by the Buddhist cosmological ruler figure as an imbued concept in post-colonial state-building processes in Sri Lanka and Myanmar. In both states, the autochthonous constitutional building process, embodying multiethnic features, reached a stage of despondency as a result of continued infatuation with so-called Buddhist historical narratives. While contending how the Buddhist cosmological impact has created an indispensable footprint in both countries' state apparatus, this article illustrates the failure of constitutional experiments in Sri Lanka and Myanmar in the liminal period after independence.

3.2 The Buddhist Notion of a Ruler

Some palpable sources on understanding the Buddhist just ruler conception have derived from the canonical tradition of Theravada Buddhism, in which Buddhist discourses, named *Agganna Sutta* and *Chakkavathi Sutta*, provide some abstract thoughts on Buddhist kingship, albeit vaguely. While keeping the cardinal theme of Buddhist concepts of suffering and the impermanence of all mundane things, the *Chakkavathi Seeha Nada Sutta* evokes the concept of *dhamma* as the cosmic law which regulates the world. This text emphasizes the unbreakable thread between dhamma and kingship, portraying the ruler as a person who manifests the concept of dhamma. As shown by the Australian anthropologist Bruce Kapferer, the Agganna Sutta illustrates the Theravada Buddhist anticipation of a just ruler called *Mahasammatha* who ascends to save humankind from decadence, a concept that represents the collective consciousness of society. Kapferer writes:

> The Great Elect proceeds to establish order out of a fragmenting temporal world. The dynamic that is at the base of this inauguration of sociality as well as the possibility of a state order is the 'suffering that is integral to existence and its continual development as the differentiating entropy of existence'. The inauguration of a virtual cosmic sovereignty hence draws on a central motif in Buddhist doctrine—that suffering and dissatisfaction (dukkha) are at the root.[2]

The legitimacy of the Buddhist king and his virtuous role as the protector of dhamma in Buddhism is attributed to the void created by the death of the Buddha. The king became the person to fill that vacuum and was elevated to the status of *Cakkavatti ruler*. Stanly Tambiah argues how the mythical narrative of Mahasammatha bolsters the idea of Cakkavatti king, as he suggests a symbiotic relationship between dhamma and kingship, with the king as the wielder of dhamma, indicating how kingship becomes the functional link between the cosmological and the 'level of this world of humans'.[3]

---

[2] Bruce Kapferer, 'Sorcery, Modernity and the Constitutive Imaginary: Hybridising Continuities, Social Analysis: The International Journal of Anthropology, Vol. 46, No. 3 (2002), p. 113.

[3] S. Tambiah, The Galactic Polity in Southeast Asia, Culture, Thought and Social Action, Vol. 3, No. 31 (1973), p. 156.

The earliest and most pragmatic political manifestation of the Cakkavatti ruler concept was accomplished by the Mauryan emperor Ashoka. Comparing the sphere of influence of Emperor Constantine to Christendom and the reforms of Ashoka in Buddhist political history, the latter was more condensed in combining the temporal power with Buddhist cosmological vision, as the system of governance he introduced was an epitome of Chakkavatti ruler. Constantine's 'Edict of Milan' was little more than mere imperial acceptance of Christianity compared to the famous pillar edicts that emperor Asoka zealously erected in every nook and corner of his empire, symbolizing an explicit claim for the Buddhist idea of kingship. Moreover, the messages delivered by the pillars signified the core values of Buddha's *Chakkavathi Seeha Nada Sutta* According to Roshan de Silva-Wijeyeratne, the ritualistic traditions that emerged from Ashoka-type personalities played a crucial role in setting the path for Buddhist kingship in Sri Lankan and beyond. In this particular role of the king, he was a devotee of the Buddha, his Dhamma, and the Sangha, the Buddhist priesthood. De Silva-Wijeyeratne suggests:

> It imbued the division of space in the here and now with cosmological import, granting it a certain ontological potentiality. In the post-colonial era the rhetorical force of Sinhalese Buddhist opposition to devising a devolved cum federal constitutional structure, and a concomitant decentralization of administrative responsibilities as a means of reordering Sri Lankan space, has carried with it an ontology.[4]

This Buddhist conceptual background historically established a bulwark for the formation of a Buddhist vision of ruler in Sri Lanka and Myanmar, whose destiny drew parallels to the preservation of the Buddhist creed, an aura of defensiveness, probably fed by the ancient historical experience of being under threat from 'others'. The historical nuances of understanding the present constitutional and ethnic dilemma that has befallen both countries are rooted in this specific influence of Buddhist cosmology.

3.3 Understanding the Ashokan Persona in Sri Lanka

The military victory of the Sri Lankan government over the Tamil separatist group called LTTE in 2009 created a state beyond euphoria among the Sinhalese Buddhist society, filled with awe and a deep sense of veneration to then Sri Lankan president Mahinda Rajapaksa, whose name was raised to the level of Great King (*Maha Rajano*) by the state media. Apotheosizing the rulers of the country to Buddhist Chakravarti-type kings was not a strange occurrence in the post-colonial state machinery in Sri Lanka since its independence. A plethora of political transformations in post-independence Sri Lanka seized the moment to portray the necessity of force to consolidate political power in order to secure the Sinhalese nation and

[4] Roshan de Silva Wijeyarathne, 'Buddhism, the Asokan Persona, and the Galactic Polity: Rethinking Sri Lanka's Constitutional Present,' Social Analysis: The International Journal of Anthropology, Vol. 51, No. 1 (2007), p. 162.

protect Buddhism. This process of aggrandizing the archaic Buddhist kingship in a modern nation-state has undermined any attempt to introduce a liberal constitutional process to harmonize the multiethnic, multi-linguistic aspirations of modern Sri Lankan society.

Sri Lanka was seen as a success story of the British Empire, a model colony that could boast of high social standards compared to other South Asian colonies. Sir Ivor Jennings the architect of Sri Lanka's first Constitution in 1947, strongly believed that the country whose constitution he drafted would reach the high standards of the British Commonwealth.[5] However, subsequent events in Sri Lanka soon ruined the sanguine hopes of Jennings. In particular, though Jennings had drafted a protective clause in the constitution for the minorities under section 29(2), the first post-independence government headed by D.S. Senanayake in Sri Lanka passed a citizenship law in 1948, which systematically delegitimized the citizenship rights of the country's Indian Tamil population. Senanayake was just the first leader to dwell upon the idea of restoring ancient Sinhalese majesty at the expense of the country's minorities. Many other leaders came to power later, clinging to the same chauvinistic politics.

Sinhalese nationalism as a device to strengthen the majority ethnic group in Sri Lanka followed the main historical narrative of the *Mahavamsa*, a text written by a Buddhist monk named *Mahanama* in the fifth century AD, whose resentment toward the South Indian invaders resonated throughout the text. In the chronicle, Mahanama glorifies how the first king and the founder of the Sinhalese race, Vijaya, landed on the island on the same day when the Buddha achieved *Parinirvanna*. In his final hours, the Buddha empowered god Sakara to protect Vijaya in his voyage to Lanka, exclaiming: 'In Lanka, O Lord of the gods, will my religion be established, therefore carefully protect him with his followers and Lanka'.[6]

This historical narrative is a decisive factor in fathoming the genesis of the age-long bond between the ruler and Buddhism in Sri Lanka, wherein the symbolic allegory emanates from the Buddha's story in Mahavamsa, suggesting the gravity of Buddhism as the ruling force or domain of the island. In his analysis of the ontological impetus that carved the Ashokan persona in the kingship of Sri Lanka, Roshan de Silva-Wijeyarathne aptly describes the irrefutable connectivity between sovereign power and the Buddha, observing how, for example, building stupas to house relics of the Buddha, relics being symbolic of the cosmic order, refracted the immanence of the Buddha and suggested to the faithful the idea of the Buddha as Lord of the World.[7]

The continuation of the alliance between the kings and Buddhism intensified its momentum in the latter part of the Anuradhapura era in Sri Lankan history with the influx of the notion of venerating the king as a person who is striving to reach

[5] Sir Ivor Jennings, 'The Government of Ceylon,' India Quarterly, Vol. 4, No. 1 (1948), p. 22.

[6] Douglas Bullis (Trans), Mahavamsa: The Great Chronicle of Sri Lanka (New York: The Asian Humanities Press), p. 12.

[7] Roshan de SilvaWijeyarathne, 'Buddhism, the Asokan Persona, and the Galactic Polity: Rethinking Sri Lanka's Constitutional Present,' op.cit., p. 162.

Buddhahood (*Bodhisattva*), as de Silva-Wijeyeratne notes. The coronation of the king was organized as a galactic event with much pomp, where all the nobles and provincial leaders were supposed to show submission before the king, who would defend Buddhism from the infidels.[8]

Such ontological foundations of kingship as defender of the creed and the austere customs around kingship remained solid until the British introduced the first elements of modern statehood in Sri Lanka through the Colebrook-Cameroon constitutional reforms in 1833, which ended the prevalent feudal order in Sri Lankan polity. The centrality of power as the core element that came out of British colonial reforms in Sri Lanka since 1833 was anathema to the pre-European Sinhalese Buddhist imaginary that perpetuated a galactic position of kingship. While the ideology of imperialism was entering Sri Lanka's political scene and the British inculcated a sense of taste for Western political institutions in Sri Lanka during the colonial epoch, none of those transplanted ideas of modernity or modern statehood could entirely alter the Sinhalese ontological impulsion for Cakkavatti kingship. To a certain extent, the colonial administrators felt compelled to emulate the Sinhalese romance with kingship and Buddhist cosmological values. In fact, at the outset, the British colonial government felt obliged to preserve Buddhism by virtue of Article 5 of the Kandyan Convention, a pact between the Sinhalese chieftains in the Kandyan kingdom and the British in 1815, before the island was legitimately ceded to the British.

Nevertheless, early British governors in the nineteenth century were certainly not keen on patronizing Sri Lanka's Buddhist creed, which inevitably dismayed the Sinhalese Buddhist community. In a subtle balancing act, understanding the cardinal values of Buddhists in the state apparatus, some governors adhered to a policy of patronizing Buddhism as an aspect of public duty. For instance, Governor William Gregory (1872–1877), who was more congenial toward Buddhism, took a paternal interest in restoring the ruined Buddhist temples in the Ancient Sinhalese kingdom of *Anuradhapura.*[9] This signifies how the aura of Buddhist ontological ground pervaded the Sri Lankan state structure regardless of the sense of modernity propagated during the colonial period. In the 1920s, Governor Herbert Stanley was welcomed by Buddhist monks at a temple in Sri Lanka in a manner that invoked Stanley's status as, or at least akin to, a Cakkavatti king.

The persona of the Buddhist ruler in the Sri Lankan polity was an embodiment of the objective to lead those he ruled on the path to Nirvana (*Nibbana*), a notion that remained an integral part of Sri Lankan socio-political consciousness, regardless of the legislative changes by the British colonial rulers. From this vantage point, the political transformation process carried out by the British was little more than a modernist gesture, for modernizing demands arose from the bourgeois class in Sri Lanka to fulfill their aspirations. The British influence upon transforming the archetypical Sinhalese Buddhist majority had minimal effects, as the Sinhalese conviction remained staunchly rooted in the notion of Cakkavatti Kingship.

---

[8] Ibid., p. 168.

[9] K. Malalgoda, 'Millennialism in Relation to Buddhism,' Comparative Studies in History and Society, Vol. 12, No. 4 (1970), p. 429.

3.4 Twisted Statehood in Post-Independence Sri Lanka

The political jingoism invoked by Anagaraika Dharmapala, the most charismatic leader among the Sinhalese Buddhists in colonial Sri Lanka, left an indelible impact on Sri Lankan public opinion. When Sri Lanka became independent in 1948, the native political structure was akin to a Janus-faced reality. It was split between adherence to the British political ethos enshrined under the Constitution drafted by Jennings and continuing the ethnoreligious politics derived from Buddhist cosmological concepts.

Vehement opposition arose from the Sinhalese Buddhist fractions in the government and other pressure groups on the secular nature of the Jennings Constitution. This became already visible in the first decade after independence. The rise of the Buddhist monks as a crucial force involved in ethnopolitical discourses in post-colonial Sri Lanka further negated the young country's path from developing into a modern secular state, as the echoing voice of the Buddhist monks significantly bolstered the national(ist) political setting. A report compiled by a Buddhist commission before the *Samubuddha Jayanthi* in 1956 was a plea to the government about the grievances of the Sinhalese Buddhists. This report urged religious and political reforms that would catapult Buddhism to the forefront of Sri Lankan nationalism.[10] The pioneers of the Buddhist commission critiqued the Jennings Constitution as a colonial avatar that disdained the aspirations of the Sinhalese race and Buddhism. Apart from the Commission's recommendations, there was growing resistance among a set of Sinhalese civil officers in the bureaucracy, who called themselves *Dutugamunu Rahas Samitiya* and supported the popular leader SWRD Bandaranaike to emerge triumphant in national politics. This group took pledges in front of the Dutugamunu statue to protect Buddhism, symbolizing the cosmological metaphors that challenged the transplanted liberal bourgeois post-colonial settlement of 1948.[11]

The crescendo of events in early post-colonial Sri Lanka eventually reached its culmination by bringing Bandaranaike into power in 1956, marking the symbolic resurgence of Sinhalese longing for a *Cakkavatti*-type ruler. The grievances within the Sinhalese Buddhist majority were aptly polarized by Bandaranaike. He promised the majority Sinhalese to declare Sinhala as the official language. Bandaranaike's project left deeply detrimental impacts on the post-colonial state polity of Sri Lanka.

Indeed, they later became ground causes for the violent ethnic strife on the island. The proclivity among the Sinhalese Buddhist majority toward a ruler who would defend Buddhism continued while harmonious relations between Sinhalese and Tamils were at stake, reaching its nadir in the early 1970s. Regarding the legitimacy of the Sinhalese race to dominate the island, Sinhalese nationalist politician Prince Gunasekere remarked:

---

[10] Robert N Kearney, 'Sinhalese Nationalism and Social Conflict in Ceylon,' Pacific Affairs, Vol. 37, No. 2 (1964), p. 129.

[11] Gananath Obeyesekere, Buddhism and Conscience: An Exploratory Essay, Daedalus, Vol. 120, No. 3 (1991), p. 226.

> For over 2000 years the Sinhala people have lived in Ceylon. To them Ceylon is their motherland. This motherland was frequently invaded from South India...The history of Ceylon tells us that the Sinhala people fought incessantly against Indian invaders to keep this country for themselves...[and] the Sinhala people look upon the Tamil people now inhabiting the Northern and Eastern provinces as descendants of the invading forces whom they have been fighting to keep this country for themselves.[12]

The aforesaid statement was the echo of the common Sinhalese majoritarian belief that prevailed in post-independence Sri Lanka, while the constitutional modernity implanted by the British was least effective in deviating from the Sinhalese mindset. The ontological bent toward restoring Sinhalese *Cakkavatti* kingship virtues in the state predominantly played a dominant role in the first autochthonous constitution building in Sri Lanka in 1972. Nationalist sentiments that infiltrated into the Constituent Assembly largely outmatched the general objectives of the modern architects of the Constitution. In the 1970–1972 Constituent Assembly process, members had debated a Draft Basic Resolution on Buddhism (Draft Basic Resolution 3), which is akin in spirit to Pakistan's Objectives Resolution of 12 March 1949, reading: 'In the Republic of Sri Lanka, Buddhism, the religion of the majority of the people, shall be given its rightful place and accordingly, it shall be the duty of the State to protect and foster Buddhism, while assuring to all religions the rights granted by Basic Resolution 5(4).'

The majoritarian Sinhalese consensus emerged victorious at the Constituent Assembly on the issue of constitutionalizing Buddhism, but the recommendations from the Tamil Federal party, which had proposed that the State shall 'protect and foster all religions' received a furious response from the Sinhalese majority at the assembly. As documented in the Constituent Assembly Debates, held in the State Archives in Colombo, Sinhalese leaders like J.R. Jayewardene and V. Dahanayake brought back narratives from Sri Lankan history such as the Kandyan Convention of 1815 between the British and the Kandyan chieftains, where the British promised to safeguard and foster Buddhism.[13] The burden imposed upon the state was reflected in the stringent historiography of Sri Lanka and its rationale has gained legitimacy from the heroic nature of King Dutugamunu in the Anuradhapura kingdom, who defeated the South Indian invader Elara. The example of King Dutugamunu emboldened the Sinhalese political leaders in the aftermath of independence. This pure historical romance in the post-colonial Sinhalese Buddhist nationalism played a pivotal role even in the constitutional building process of 1971. De Silva-Wijeyeratne states: 'The Ontological ground of the Sinhalese myth of the state indicates that the virtuous Buddhist state is born of an imminent movement in which evil is overcome from within. The demonic reconstituted as a higher demonic form through the logic of the cosmic order itself.'[14]

---

[12] A. Abeyasekere, Colours of the Robe (Columbia: University of South Carolina Press) (2002), p. 20.

[13] Constituent Assembly Debates, State Archives, Colombo, 1973.

[14] Roshan de Silva Wijerathne, Republican Constitutionalism and Sinhalese Buddhist Nationalism in Sri Lanka: Towards an ontological account of the Sri Lankan state (Colombo: Centre for Policy Alternatives, 2012).

The next chapter of Sri Lanka's tryst with Buddhist ontological impetus was widely visible in the Constitutional experiment carried out by J.R. Jayewardene after coming to power in the 1977 elections, in which he secured an enormous majority in the legislature. This enabled him to centralize power with the introduction of the executive presidential system by the Second Amendment to the 1972 Constitution. His ardor regarding ancient Sinhalese kingship and the king's role as the preserver of the Buddhist Creed (*Buddha Sasana*) further propelled Jayewardene to consolidate the power around the executive presidency through the new constitution promulgated in 1978 known as the Second Republican Constitution. The new constitutional construct was an offshoot that sprang from Jayewardene's self-imaginary view of Sinhalese royalty and ancient kings, especially since he portrayed himself as a successor to the line of Sinhalese kings. The idea of Righteous Society (*Dharmishta Samajaya*) was the slogan that Jayewardene adopted in his political campaign, which intended to invoke the traditional Sinhalese Buddhist vote base at the grassroots level.[15] Building his charisma as a savior of the Sinhalese race and Buddhism made him resemble the role of a Cakkavatti Buddhist king, which aggrandized the constitution-making process of the 1978s Republican Constitution. Article 9 of the 1978 Constitution in Sri Lanka states: 'The Republic of Sri Lanka shall give to Buddhism the foremost place and accordingly it shall be the duty of the State to protect and foster the Buddha Sasana while assuring to all religions the rights granted by Articles 10 and 14(1)(e)'.

The institutional agenda that functioned in the post-colonial polity of Sri Lanka focusing on the preservation of Buddhism was not exactly just a political slogan. Concomitant with the Buddhist cosmology that elevated the status of a Cakkavatti king or Bodhisattva, the post-colonial Sri Lankan state-building process depended on these narratives. Most of the national politicians who came to power in post-independent Sri Lanka looked for the Buddhist ontology of protecting Buddhism as a paragon of virtue, and their acts gained justification from the mytho-historical narratives of ancient Sri Lankan history. Bandaranaike's association with the Five Great Forces (*Panachamaha Balawegaya*) which represented the five working classes of traditional Sri Lankan social structure, or Jayewardene's already noted fancy for Righteous Society (*Dharmishta Samajaya*) was driven by the ontological metaphors that perpetuated the Sinhalese supremacy in the island. In order to secure the rightful status of the Buddhism and Sinhalese races, acts were taken to constitutionalize those elements in the basic law. The repercussion that emerged from such acts finally resulted in creating a brutal civil war between the Sinhalese and Tamil separatists that lasted for thirty years.

[15] Benjamin Sconthal, Buddhism and the Constitution: The Historiography and Post-Colonial Politics (Colombo: CPA) (2012).

3.5 Projection of Kingship as a Karmic Bond in Myanmar

This section of the article now focuses on Burma or Myanmar, where the fervent association between Buddhism and the state apparatus has been pivotal in the emergence of a Buddhist Burmese nationalism that can be traced back almost 1000 years. The whole notion of placing Buddhism along with the state has derived from the Burmese conviction that those who ruled were destined to preserve authentic Theravada Buddhism. The Theravada cosmological view on state and politics in pre-colonial Burma referred to a self-contained framework that implied that Buddhist kings and officials used to express both the physical structure of the universe and the laws that governed existence. Regarding this power relationship, Walton states:

> It implied a natural hierarchy in which individuals were ranked according to their actions in the past and the results of those actions in the present. Explanations of the cosmology included detailed descriptions of the many realms that existed besides the human one, including hells filled with unimaginable suffering and heavenly abodes of bliss. The cosmology also legitimized the monarchical model of political rule by characterizing humans as driven to immorality by desire and craving and in need of a powerful leader whose position was justified with reference to his presumed moral conduct in past lives.[16]

According to Myanmar tradition, Buddhism was introduced to the Mons community, one of the leading ethnic communities in Myanmar, already during the lifetime of the Buddha. Further, Burmese people strongly believe that Gautama Buddha visited Myanmar and this popular belief is tantamount to Sri Lankan Sinhalese conviction of three historical visits of the Buddha to Sri Lanka. Nonetheless, much of Myanmar embraced Buddhism during the era of King Anawartha when the king united Burma into a single kingdom and founded the first Burmese empire in the year 1044 A.D. At a time when Buddhism perished in India, Theravada Buddhism began to flourish in Myanmar in the same way as in Sri Lanka.

It is interesting to observe the utmost importance of the Buddhist idea of karma (*kamma*) in the state setting of pre-colonial Myanmar, which played a catalyst role in upholding the royal statuses of Burmese kings prior to the British conquest. Stanley Tambiah's famous Mandala thesis unfolds the archaic pattern of the royal hierarchy in Myanmar, which depicts the status of the Burmese king as a supreme human being and Bodhisattva who enjoys kingship by virtue of the merits he accumulated in his previous birth. Tambiah stated:

> Perhaps the most famous of these complex schemes was realized in the Hindu Buddhist polities of Southeast Asia that employed the thirty-three-unit scheme to express and organize cosmogonies and pantheons as well as religion-political groupings. In this scheme the king as wielder of dharma (the moral law), as the Chakravarty (universal emperor) and bodhisattva (Buddha-to-be), was seen as the pivot of the polity and as the mediating link between the upper regions of the cosmos, composed of the gods and their heavens, and the lower plane

[16] Matthew Walton, Buddhism, Politics and Political Thought in Myanmar (New York: Cambridge University Press, 2016), p. 34.

> of humans and lesser beings. My thesis is that the kingdoms in question were arranged according to a galactic scheme, and that this scheme was conceptualized...[17]

In the Myanmar tradition, the king was not only a political ruler who would defend the interests of the polity. His status was alleviated to the status of a supreme being to protect the Buddhist faith, regarded as the essential task of the Burmese king. The earliest example of this role of the king as the defender of the faith can be traced to Burmese history during the era of King Anawratha in the eleventh century when he launched a campaign to eradicate tribal religious beliefs to uphold the supremacy of Buddhism in Myanmar.[18] The king was also the sole authority who appointed the chief of the Sangha (*thathanabaing*). As the Burmese public opinion was adamant in believing in the transcendental nature of the king as Bodhisattva, there were instances in Burmese history that some rulers relied on this belief to hegemoniss their authoritative rule. For example, King Bodawpaya (1782–1819) claimed to be a 'Buddhist redeemer', though he failed to convince the Sangha.[19]

When the Burmese polity of Mandalay fell into British hands in 1886, the king was exiled and Myanmar became subject to the British crown. But the subsequent events that took place in Myanmar during the colonial era convinced the British that it would be a hard process to govern Burmese people as colonial subjects, given the deep-rooted influence of Buddhism in society. A British administrator, Donald MacKenzie Smeaton observed:

> The Burman cannot conceive of a religion without a Defender of the Faith - a king who appoints and rules the Buddhist hierarchy. The extinction left the nation, according to the people's notions, without a religion. We have overthrown the king and destroyed all traces of kingly rule. Naturally they look upon this as the destruction of their nationality.[20]

The Buddhist ontological impetus that had grounded robust developments in pre-colonial Myanmar's Burmese society did not perish after the British arrival. On the contrary, the native resistance within Myanmar society gained its inspiration from the Sanghahood. Both democratic governments and military juntas that came into power in post-colonial Myanmar could not contemplate a purely secular state apparatus beyond the lenses of Buddhist cosmology. The possibilities of a straightforward transplant were foreclosed.

---

[17] S. Tambiah, 'The Galactic Polity in Southeast Asia,' Culture, Thought and Social Action, Vol. 3, No. 31 (1973), p. 189.

[18] O.H. Mootham, Burmese Buddhist Law (Oxford: Oxford University Press, 1939), p. 67.

[19] G.E. Harvey, History of Burma (London: Longman Green & Co., 1925), p. 107.

[20] Donald MacKenzie Smeaton, The Loyal Karens of Burma (London: Kabul & Company, 1887), p. 4.

3.6 *Bodhisattva* Continuity in Myanmar's Post-Colonial Constitution Building

The traditional 'protector king' figure lasted over time, dominating popular imagery also after the independence from British rule in 1948. Before independence, there had been no consensus regarding the placement of Buddhist references in the future Constitution. While some members favored recognition of Buddhism by the constitution, General Aung San, the popular leader of the Burmese nationalist movement, was said to have rejected the idea of including a special status for Buddhism.[21] Aung Sang Suki's father, General Aung San despised the Sangha's involvement in state affairs and described his organization as completely secular, a non-movement that had never existed in Myanmar (Ichikawa, 1979: 249). Though he was assassinated some months before the declaration of Independence, his ideology had significant impacts on post-independent constitutional making in Myanmar.

The country's religiously-oriented first prime minister U Nu was responsible for coining the notion of Buddhist socialism in post-independent Myanmar. U Nu's obsession with Buddhism continued to play a vitally important role in the national political setting, whereas Nu's abhorrence toward the Western democratic order urged the public to follow the old ways of Buddhist asceticism. In his election campaign in 1959, U Nu made explicit references to reviving the concept of *Chakkavathi* ruler based on the precept proclaimed by King Kyanzittha in 1099 that echoed as the yardstick of the Burmese state's Buddhist ideology.[22] His speeches were often filled with a mixture of vague Marxian expressions, Burmese folklore, and sheer political demagoguery, a mix that eventually brought him an overwhelming political victory in the 1960 election. U Nu's political campaign was a pure resemblance to SWRD Bandaranaike in Sri Lanka, who polarized the whole Sinhalese Buddhist nationalist brigade for his political triumph. Similarly to how Bandaranaike contravened the constitutional safeguards for the minorities introduced by Jennings in Sri Lanka, by introducing a discriminatory language policy to appease the Sinhalese majority, U Nu fuelled the growing anti-Muslim sentiments among Buddhists in Myanmar.[23]

The first autochthonous constitution drafted by Chan Htoon in 1947 in the advent of the country's independence from the British recognized the importance of Buddhism as the majority religion under Article 21(1), but the basic law clearly also provided for equality before the law regardless of religion and prohibited discrimination based on the faith under Articles 13 and 21(3), as Brohm identified. In fact, during the first few years after independence, Myanmar had no particular legal guidance to indicate how the privilege given to Buddhism was to be reconciled with

[21] Edmund Lech, 'Buddhism in the Post-Colonial Political Order in Burma and Ceylon, Daedalus, Vol. 102, No. 1 Post Traditional Societies (1973), p. 33.

[22] Akira Ichikawa, 'Compassionate Politics: Buddhist Concepts as Political Guide, 'Journal of Church and State, Vol. 21, No. 2 (1979), p. 249.

[23] Manuel Sarkisyanz, 'On the Place of U Nu's Buddhist Socialism in Burma's History of Ideas,' Studies on Asia, Vol. 2, No. 1 (1961), pp. 53–62.

other religions.[24] However, the partial secularity enshrined in the 1947 Myanmar Constitution faced uncertainties, as a result of the robust reforms carried out by U Nu, whose religiously-oriented state policies were antithetical to the secular nature of the Constitution. It is relevant to consider here that the circumstances that propelled U Nu were not factors that arose out of the blue. Instead, archetypical forces resonated in Myanmar's traditional attitude toward the state. As asserted in this article, the Buddhist Theravada cosmological incitement that pervaded Myanmar's history saw its natural resurgence in the aftermath of independence in the same way as it saw its steeping growth in post-colonial Sri Lanka. The revered idea of *Bodhisattva* as a transcendental figure standing above mundane politics, which stood as a relic from the country's Buddhist past, came into larger play also in Myanmar. Prime Minister U Nu was portrayed as a leader who took the Bodhisattva vow, and this popular belief among the general public gave him enormous popularity in Myanmar.

U Nu's projection of Buddhism as Myanmar's identity value in his international affairs was another notable factor that personified his role, which was venerated by the Buddhists of Myanmar. However, the provisions contained in the 1947 Constitution of Myanmar were a conspicuous obstacle, slowing down the implementation of the extremely nationalist policies of U Nu. Thus, the constitutional change appeared to be inevitable for U Nu to accelerate his strong Buddhist-centric approach, through which he created himself as a Bodhisattva before the majority of Myanmar's Buddhist population. Exactly as Bandaranaike used Sinhala language and the grievances of Buddhists for his political triumph in 1956, U Nu vociferously advocated proclaiming Buddhism as the state religion in Myanmar. In the aftermath of his electoral victory, which was mainly attributed to his political campaign focused on Burmese Buddhist nationalism, U Nu appointed a committee named 'State Religion Inquiry Committee' to consider the proposal to make Buddhism the state religion. Notwithstanding the serious opposition it received from the various minority groups, the proposal was passed in parliament with a two-thirds majority from both houses. U Nu's avidity in projecting Buddhism as the cardinal doctrine in his government was not only confined to the Constitutional Amendment, which made Buddhism the state religion of Myanmar. He made extra efforts to defend his image by including a provision that compelled the Union Government to allocate 50% of its annual current expenditures for matters connected with religion.[25] Such a provision soon took its toll on the national budget of Myanmar as a least developed state.

The question of placing Buddhism in the Constitution continued to dominate the Burmese political apparatus in its post-colonial state-building discourse. However, the status granted to Buddhism as the state religion was removed in 1962 after the military took over. Military leader Ne Win was determined to imbue Buddhism with socialist aspirations. The promulgation of the new Constitution in 1974 reaffirmed

[24] John Brohm,' Burmese Religion and the Burmese Buddhist Revival,' Ph.D. thesis, Cornel University (1957).

[25] Melissa Crouch, 'Constructing Religion by Law in Myanmar,' The Review of Faith & International Affairs, Vol. 13, No. 4 (2015), p. 27.

the secular status of the county by safeguarding the religious freedom of all communities. The rise of the military in Myanmar was a significant phenomenon that duly succeeded in fending off Buddhist nationalism as the military consolidated its power over the state.

3.7 Aung San Suu Kyi: Hybridity of Buddhist Consciousness and Western Democracy

It is a complete anomaly in how the military and the political apparatus were perceived by Myanmar's people since independence. The military, commonly known as *Tatmadaw*, was founded by General Aung San with Japanese help during the Second World War and gained fame among the people in Myanmar as an anti-imperial force.[26] But Tatmadaw's view on the state polity was an idiosyncratic one from the traditional Bodhisattva projection of the ruler. The infamous style introduced by the military during its quasi-democratic regime, known as 'Burmese socialism', consisted of traditional Buddhist beliefs and Marxist doctrine. Yet, the incompatibility of making a consensus between Sangha (*pongys*) and the military (Tatmadaw) prolonged reaching any success in the constitutional development of Myanmar.

The detention of the popular leader Aung San Suki for several decades could not uproot the Burmese nostalgia for a Bodhisattva ruler, as her detention only caused nationwide protest movements mainly led by Buddhist monks. The long period she spent in captivity under the Military Junta was viewed by the majority of Myanmar's citizens as an act similar to a Bodhisattva who faced the forces of suffering on behalf of others. Thus, her persona received great reverence both locally and internationally.[27]

Followed by the so-called Saffron revolution in 2007, the Military-headed regime in Myanmar singlehandedly drafted a new constitution in 2008, which again acknowledged a special position for Buddhism under Article 361, which states that '[t]he Union recognizes the special position of Buddhism as the faith professed by the great majority of the citizens of the union and the following article of the constitution has guaranteed the freedom for other religious practices in Myanmar.

To the biggest dismay of the Sangha, the 2008 constitution affirmed that religion cannot be abused for political gain or promote feelings of hatred among the religious or ethnic communities of the country. This provision certainly displeased the Sangha community, as they believed it was designed by the military to reduce the Sangha's political participation in state affairs, as Tin Maung has argued.[28] The constitutional development in Myanmar under military rule should be evaluated in the context of

[26] MA Myoe, 'The Soldier and the State: The Tatmadaw and Political Liberalization in Myanmar Since 2011, 'South EastAsia Research, Vol. 23, No. 2 (2014).

[27] William McGovan, 'Aung San Suu Kyi's Buddhist Problem, 'Foreign Policy (2012). https://foreignpolicy.com/2012/09/17/aung-san-suu-kyis-buddhism-problem/, accessed 3 June 2021.

[28] Tin Maung,' Myanmar in 2008: Weathering the Storm,' South East Asian Affairs, ISEAS Institute (2009), pp. 195–222.

the conflict between the Sangha and the *Tatmadaw*, in which the Buddhist monks always strived for a ruler who embodies the traditional Burmese virtues and protects Buddhism.

As this article emphasizes, the people's reverence for the ruler as an iconic figure of a Bodhisattva remained present within the political consciousness of the majority in Myanmar, which resulted in the growing hostility of the people toward the military regime. Thus, it was evident that the return of Aung San Suu Kyi in the 2015 general election, after attaining a landslide victory, was a jubilant moment for the majority of Buddhists whose aspirations remain essentially grounded on preserving Buddhism. Aung San Suu Kyi is often referred to as a female Bodhisattva (*Tara Devi*), whose compassion was ineffable for her people.[29]

But her well-wishers from the West had other concerns, as many Western states believed Suu Kyi would genuinely commit herself to restoring full democracy in Myanmar while unifying its multiethnic structure. But, contrary to the sanguine hopes of the West, the subsequent events that took place in her government unveiled she was no more than another archetypal Burmese ruler. Writing on the contemporary Myanmar political situation, Lubiana states:

> She governs like a mandate of a heaven holder, no nonsense authoritarian matriarch who preaches, declares and orders from her celestial position, who makes politics behind the closed doors in the Royal capital, who micromanages everything, who needs to consent every decision, who does not tolerate any dissident voices and does not listen to any outside ones.[30]

This damning account by a Western political scientist vividly unveils the gravity of traditional rulerhood in her political behavior, contrary to her popular depiction in the Western media as a champion of democracy. On several occasions, Suu Kyi denied acknowledging the discrimination faced by Rohingya Muslims in Myanmar and the severe state oppression against them. At the International Court of Justice, she defended the interests of Myanmar even without mentioning the term 'Rohingya', which was rather an implicit denial of this ethnic group.[31] Ostensibly, her actions appeared to have coincided with her political-strategic position to gain favor from the Tatmadaw, which remains the most powerful in Myanmar. But one should also understand that Suu Kyi's actions have gained their legitimacy from the mythical narratives of Myanmar history, filled with a romanticized notion of Bodhisattva, whose duty is to protect Buddhism. Thus, it is important to admit that the constitutional mechanism in Myanmar from its troubled post-colonial era to the twenty-first century has been a mere pretext to give a taste of modern statehood to its people, whose aspirations still dwell in the past.

---

[29] Alen Clements, 'Conversations with Aung San Suu Kyi,' Lions Roar (1997), https://www.lionsroar.com/conversations-with-aung-san-suu-kyi/, accessed 6 June 2021.

[30] M. Lubiana, The Moral Democracy: The Political Thought of Aung San Suu Kyi (Warsaw: Scholar Publishing House) (2019), p. 243.

[31] M. Simons,' Suu Kyi defends Myanmar against Rohingiya Genocide Accusations,' The New York Times, 12 December (2019).

3.8 Conclusion

The cosmological foundation propounded by Theravada Buddhist tradition in the annals of the history in Sri Lanka and Myanmar created and underpinned the identity of both states, which lasted beyond the colonial occupation.[32] The state that the British determined to build as a colonial adventure was a perplexed one, by virtue of its inability to alter the traditional concepts that existed among the people. As this article clearly shows, despite the attempts to transplant modern constitutional frameworks and components, the anatomy of the respective state built under the Buddhist ontology gave rise to both Sinhalese and Burmese nationalism, in which the ruler's role symbolized a protector of Buddhism, which was tantamount to a Chakkavathi king or a Bodhisattva. Whatsoever, it is rather relevant to admit the personification of Chakkavathi ruler or a Bodhisattva figure in the kingship in the state apparatus in both Sri Lanka and Myanmar were not primarily related to the basic tenants of Buddha, whose teachings were rooted in the idea of world renunciation. In fact, the whole projection of the kingship and its purity linked with Buddhism should be evaluated as a part of the global history of authoritarian populism. Buddha clearly saw politics not as an end itself but as an instrument that could either provide favorable conditions or harmful obstructions for an individual's personal advancement. He considered the necessity of government as a tool to provide social welfare and that its values should be consistent with *dhamma.*

Concepts of modern statehood imposed by the British during the colonial period in both Sri Lanka and Myanmar were not sufficient to crowd out the old obsession for a cosmological ruler figure. The events that led to irreversible ethnoreligious strife in both countries during their post-colonial state-building process show that the constitutional or other political experiments made by the British scarcely made any impact in transforming the political consciousness of the people in Sri Lanka and Myanmar. The efforts by Jennings and the array of expectations he reckoned with in Sri Lanka brought futile outcomes, as the constitutional safeguard guaranteed to the minorities in Sri Lanka by Article 29 (2) of the 1947 Constitution met with the furore of the Sinhalese majority.

The apotheosis of SWRD Bandaranaike as a Chakkavatti figure followed by his political triumph of 1956 eschewed the secular structure of Sri Lankan polity. Both autochthonous constitutions that came into force in post-colonial Sri Lanka could not shun the ideological predilection descended from Buddhist cosmology.

It has been the same in the case of Myanmar. The Burmese yearning for a ruler who resembles the virtues of a Bodhisattva has had inimical effects on constitution-building efforts oriented toward a modern state. Notwithstanding the special status given to Buddhism in both the 1973 and 2008 constitutions, the majority of Buddhists in Myanmar maintain allegiance to a Bodhisattva figure as their leader. From U Nu to Aung Sann Suu Kyi, the civil political realm in Myanmar has been strongly inspired by the Buddhist cosmological narratives on Bodhisattva rule. This article has shown

[32] William Long, A Buddhist Approach to International Relations (1973, Switzerland: Palgrave McMillan).

how this belief penetrated the political thoughts of both leaders. Overall, it is possible that one can argue that the state structure which the British sought to initiate in both countries could neither fathom nor alter the Buddhist cosmological impetus rooted in Sri Lanka and Myanmar.

References

Abeyasekere, A. (2002). *Colours of the robe*. University of South Carolina Press.

Brohm, J. (1957) *Burmese religion and the burmese buddhist revival* Cornell University (Ph.D. thesis).

Clements, A. (1997). Conversations with Aung San Suu Kyi, *Lions Roar*. URL (consulted 6 July 2021). https://www.lionsroar.com/conversations-with-aung-san-suu-kyi/

Crouch, M. (2015). Constructing religion by law in Myanmar. *The Review of Faith & International Affairs, 13*(4), 12–37.

de Silva-Wijeyeratne, R. (2007). Buddhism, the Asokan Persona, and the galactic polity: Rethinking Sri Lanka's constitutional present. *Social Analysis: THe International Journal of Anthropology, 51*(1), 151–164.

Harvey, G. E. (1925). *History of Burma*. Longman Green & Co.

Ichikawa, A. (1979). Compassionate politics: Buddhist concepts as political guide. *Journal of Church and State, 21*(2), 221–254.

Jennings, I. (1948). The government of Ceylon. *India Quarterly, 4*(1), 12–26.

Kapferer, B. (2002). Sorcery, modernity and the constitutive imaginary: Hybridising continuities. *Social Analysis: THe International Journal of Anthropology, 46*(3), 105–113.

Kearney, R. N. (1964). Sinhalese nationalism and social conflict in Ceylon. *Pacific Affairs, 37*(2), 120–136.

Leach, E. (1973). Buddhism in the post-colonial political order in Burma and Ceylon. *Daedalus, 102*(1), 21–33.

Lubiana, M. (2019). *The moral democracy: The political thought of Aung San Suu Kyi*. Scholar Publishing House.

Malalgoda, K. (1970). Millennialism in relation to Buddhism. *Comparative Studies in History and Society, 12*(4), 421–434.

Maung, T. (2009). Myanmar in 2008: Weathering the storm. South East Asian Affairs, ISEAS Institute (pp. 195–222).

McGovan, W. (2012). Aung San Suu Kyi's Buddhist problem. *The Foreign Policy*. URL (accessed 6 March 2021). https://foreignpolicy.com/2012/09/17/aung-san-suu-kyis-buddhism-problem/,

Mootham, O. H. (1939). *Burmese Buddhist law*. Oxford University Press.

Myoe, M. Y. (2014). The soldier and the state: The Tatmadaw and political liberalization in Myanmar since 2011. *South East Asia Research, 23*(2), 00–00.

Obeyesekere, G. (1991). Buddhism and conscience: An exploratory essay. *Daedalus, 120*(3), 219–234.

Sarkisyanz, M. (1961). On the place of U Nu's buddhist socialism in Burma's history of ideas. *Studies on Asia, 2*(1), 53–62.

Schonthal, B. (2016). *Buddhism, politics and the limits of law: The pyrrhic constitutionalism in Sri Lanka*. Cambridge University Press.

Schonthal, B. (2012). *Buddhism and the constitution: The historiography and post-colonial politics*. Center for Policy Alternatives.

de Silva-Wijeyeratne, R. (2012). *Republican constitutionalism and Sinhalese Buddhist nationalism in Sri Lanka: Towards an ontological account of the Sri Lankan state*. Centre for Policy Alternatives.

Simons, M. (2019). Suu Kyi defends Myanmar against Rohingiya Genocide Accusations. *The New York Times*. Smeaton, D.M. (1887) *The Loyal Karens of Burma*. Kabul & Company.

Tambiah, S. (1973). The galactic polity in Southeast Asia. *Culture, Thought and Social Action, 3*(31), 168–194.

Walton, M. J. (2016). *Buddhism, politics and political thought in Myanmar*. Cambridge University Press.

Chapter 4
Besmirching Honorable Men: The Defamation of Politicians in Singapore

Kevin Y. L. Tan

Abstract This paper considers the law relating to the defamation of public figures in Singapore and deals with two substantive issues. The first concerns liability for defaming politicians, and the standard to be met for a successful action in tort. The second concerns the quantum of damages awarded to the plaintiff. Since the 1980s, Singapore's politicians have resorted increasingly to defamation suits to safeguard and vindicate their reputations. It argues that the law has developed in an unsatisfactory manner over the past three decades because Singapore's courts have steadfastly refused to acknowledge any exceptions in respect of defamation, contrary to the constitutional guarantee of freedom of expression. It further argues that the law concerning the award of damages for libel against politicians and public characters is unsustainable since the quantum of damages appears to vary with the relative seniority or importance of the politician concerned rather than the actual damage caused to his or her reputation.

4.1 Introduction

In March 2021, Singapore's High Court awarded Prime Minister Lee Hsien Loong S$133,000 in damages in his defamation suit against blogger Leong Sze Hian. Leong had, in November 2018, shared a link to a defamatory article—published by a Malaysia-based social news network—on his Facebook page.[1] Leong removed

[1] Lee Hsien Loong v Leong Sze Hian [2021] SGHC 66.

An earlier version of this paper was first presented at the Association of Asian Studies in Asia Conference on 18 Jul 2014 at the National University of Singapore. It has been substantially revised for publication.

K. Y. L. Tan (✉)
National University of Singapore, Singapore, Singapore
e-mail: lawtylk@nus.edu.sg

S. Rajaratnam School of International Studies, Nanyang Technological University, Singapore, Singapore

M. John et al. (eds.), *The Indian Yearbook of Comparative Law 2020*, The Indian Yearbook of Comparative Law, https://doi.org/10.1007/978-981-99-5467-4_4

the post from his Facebook two days later after receiving a notice from the Info-communications Media Development Authority (IMDA) of Singapore. The Court held that even though Leong had posted the link without any accompanying text or commentary, he was nonetheless liable for publishing the libel.

This judgment highlights two key issues that have plagued the law on defamation of political characters in Singapore for over 30 years. The first issue concerns liability for defaming politicians, and the standard to be met for a successful action in tort. The second concerns the quantum of damages awarded to the plaintiff. Since the 1980s, politicians have increasingly resorted to defamation suits to safeguard and vindicate their reputations. This article is in two parts. The first considers the development of the law of defamation in Singapore with particular reference to libel against politicians and public characters and how the courts have steadfastly refused to acknowledge any exceptions in respect of the defamation against them. The second part considers the law concerning the award of damages for libel against politicians and public characters.

4.2 The Legal Framework of Singapore's Defamation Laws

The law of defamation in Singapore is based on the English common law which was introduced into the Straits Settlements—of which Singapore was a constituent part—via the Second Charter of Justice of 1826.[2] The first defamation case to be heard in Singapore was the case of *Miles v Abraham Logan*,[3] heard in the Court of Judicature in 1851. In this case, Abraham Logan of the *Singapore Free Press* published a libelous article in his newspaper, suggesting that the plaintiff, one William Henry Milles, had been transferred to Singapore as a felon. This statement was untrue and had been published because of Logan's carelessness. The Recorder, Sir William Jeffcott, awarded Miles $200 damages with costs.

4.2.1 The Constitutional Protection of Free Speech

Like most modern constitutions, Singapore's Constitution contains guarantees of basic freedoms and liberties, including the freedom of expression.[4] The right to the freedom of expression is, however, neither universal nor absolute. Article 14(1) of the Constitution guarantees to 'every citizen … the right to freedom of speech and expression'. Note the reference to 'citizen'. At the same time, Article 14(2)(a) provides that 'Parliament may by law impose'

[2] Letters Patent Establishing the Court of Judicature of Prince of Wales' Island, Malacca and Singapore, 1826.

[3] [1851] *Kyshe* 1.

[4] Article 14(1), Constitution of the Republic of Singapore, 1994 Reprint.

> … such restrictions as it considers necessary or expedient in the interest of the security of Singapore or any part thereof, friendly relations with other countries, public order or morality and restrictions designed to protect the privileges of Parliament or to provide against contempt of court, defamation or incitement to any offence.

A plain reading of Article 14(2)(a) makes it clear that a citizen's freedom of expression may only be curtailed if Parliament does so by a law falling within one of eight grounds, including defamation. Since Article 14(2)(a) became part of Singapore's Constitution in 1965, Parliament has not passed any specific legislation limiting the freedom of expression on the ground of defamation. Parliament did, however, pass the Protection From Online Falsehood and Manipulation Act (POFMA) in 2019[5] which does not deal with defamation per se but with online falsehoods. Three pre-independence statutes—the Penal Code, the Sedition Act,[6] and the Defamation Act—specifically curtail an individual's freedom of expression. Of these, only the Penal Code and Defamation Act are germane to our discussion.

Parliament's power to curtail a citizen's freedom of expression is limited by Article 14(2)(a) of the Constitution. Any curb on this right must be by way of a legislative enactment made in express terms. Otherwise, the court is expected to afford all constitutionally-guaranteed rights and liberties the 'a generous interpretation, avoiding what has been called "the austerity of tabulated legalism", suitable to give to individuals the full measure of the [fundamental liberties] referred to'.[7]

What about pre-independence legislation? Article 162 of the Constitution provides that 'all existing laws shall continue in force on and after the commencement' of the Constitution and shall be 'construed … with such modifications, adaptations, qualifications and exceptions as may be necessary to bring them into conformity with this Constitution.' This means that in so far as Article 14(1)(a) is concerned when the Court is confronted with a pre-independence statute limiting a citizen's freedom of expression, the Court must give primacy to the constitutional right and construe the pre-independence statute in such a manner that conforms with the constitutional guarantee.

4.2.2 *Criminal Defamation: The Penal Code*

Section 499 of the Penal Code[8] creates the offense of criminal defamation. It provides:

> 499. Whoever, by words either spoken or intended to be read, or by signs, or by visible representations, makes or publishes any imputation concerning any person, intending to harm, or knowing or having reason to believe that such imputation will harm, the reputation of such person, is said, except in the cases hereinafter excepted, to defame that person.

---

[5] Act 18 of 2019, Singapore Statutes.

[6] This Act was repealed on 5 October 2021 vide the Sedition (Repeal) Bill, No. 23/2021.

[7] *Ong Ah Chuan v Public Prosecutor* [1979–1980] SLR(R) 710, at 721, per Lord Diplock (Privy Council on appeal from Singapore).

[8] Cap 224, Singapore Statutes.

Criminal defamation is committed only where there is an *intention* on the part of the accused to harm the reputation of his victim. The requirement of intention as part of the *mens rea* of the offense would arguably justify a restriction on the constitutional right to free speech since the right to free speech ought, from a normative perspective, not be used intentionally and unjustifiably to cause harm to others in a Millian sense.[9]

Although section 499 has existed in the statute books since the Penal Code came into force in 1872, prosecutions under this provision are rare. The first reported case only came before the courts in 1898 when, one Archibald Allison was charged with defaming the Rajah of Sarawak in two books—*The Real Wreckers of a British Trade in the East*, and *How the Church Mission People are Treated in the East*—which were printed in Singapore. Allison was fined $100 for the offense. The next successful prosecution under section 499 came more than 70 years later in the case of *Harbans Singh Sindhu v Public Prosecutor.*[10]

Like the first case, this one involved two public characters—in this case, two politicians. Harbans Singh, was, at the time, a member of the opposition Barisan Sosialis (Socialist Front).[11] He was charged with defaming Prime Minister Lee Kuan Yew during an election rally in which he called Lee, among other things, a 'scoundrel', a 'gangster' and a 'kidnapper'. The High Court had no doubt that the statements were defamatory, were calculated to tarnish Lee's reputation, and had been uttered with malicious intent. Singh was sentenced to six months' imprisonment for the offense. However, there have been hardly any other successful prosecutions under section 499 since this case. In the final reported case, Leong Mun Kwai, the Secretary-General of the People's Front political party was also sentenced to six months' imprisonment in 1973 for defaming President Benjamin Henry Sheares in the party's publication, *Barisan Rakyat*.[12] The offending article had described the President as a 'puppet' and as being 'slavish'.[13]

[9] For a philosophical discussion, see Joel Feinberg, *The Moral Limits of the Criminal Law Volume 1: Harm to Others* (Oxford University Press 1987) 107–108. See also C Edwin Baker, 'Harm, Liberty, and Free Speech' (1997) 70 *Southern California Law Review* 979–1020; Daniel Jacobson, 'Mill on Liberty, Speech and the Free Society' (2000) 29 *Philosophy and Public Affairs*, 276–309.

[10] [1971–1973] SLR(R) 610.

[11] Singh would later leave the Barsian Sosialis to form his own United People's Front.

[12] See TF Hwang, 'Libel suit: People's Front man loses appeal', *The Straits Times*, 30 Aug 1973, at 5.

[13] Joseph Yeo & Gerald Pereira, 'Leong denies defaming President in article in party weekly' *The Straits Times*, 27 Oct 1972, at 8.

4.2.3 Civil Defamation and the Defamation Act

In Singapore, the civil wrong of defamation is based on the common law tort of defamation.[14] The Defamation Act[15]—which was introduced only in 1960 as the Defamation Ordinance—is not a comprehensive codification of the tort of defamation although it modifies and clarifies the operation of some of its common law elements. This Act is based on the Malayan Defamation Ordinance of 1957[16] which was itself based on the British Defamation Act of 1952.[17] The British Act was enacted to incorporate the recommendations of the Porter Committee which met between 1939 and 1948. The Act deals with topics such as unintentional defamation, defenses against a suit of defamation and qualified privilege of newspapers. The Malayan version incorporated a further provision that renders defamatory, words uttered or published which 'impute unchastity or adultery to any woman or girl'. Such a deed is actionable without the need to show special damage.[18]

The Malayan legislation was adopted in 1960 when Singapore's Legislative Assembly enacted the Defamation Ordinance[19] and repealed the old Libel Ordinance.[20] When Singapore became part of the Federation of Malaysia in 1963, the Singapore Defamation Ordinance 1960 was repealed and replaced by the Malaysian Defamation Ordinance by the Modification of Laws (Defamation) (Modification and Extension to Borneo States and Singapore) Order 1965, made under section 74 of the Malaysia Act. This move—which brought the legislation of Federation in line with the new constitutional arrangements—was largely administrative and reintroduced the law into Singapore on 22 February 1965. Substantively, the law remained unchanged. Singapore's Parliament retained this legislation after it became independent from the Federation of Malaysia in August 1965.[21] It has been amended several times—most notably in 1979—but remains fundamentally the same as when it was brought into force in 1965.

---

[14] See Doris Chia & Rueben Mathiavaranam (eds), *Evans on Defamation in Singapore and Malaysia* (LexisNexis 2008); and Gary Chan & Lee Pey Woan, *The Law of Torts in Singapore* (Academy Publishing 2016).

[15] Cap 75, Singapore Statutes.

[16] Ordinance 20 of 1957 (Federation of Malaya). See also, 'Defaming of women' *The Singapore Free Press*, 13 May 1957, at 5.

[17] On the enactment of the UK Act, see JDB Mitchell, 'The Defamation Act, 1952' (1953) 16 *Modern Law Review* 198–212; and Note, 'Reform in the Law of Defamation: The English Defamation Act of 1952' (1953) 66(3) *Harvard Law Review* 476–488.

[18] Section 4, Defamation Ordinance (Federation of Malaya).

[19] Ordinance 7 of 1960 (Colony of Singapore). See also, 'Singapore Government proposes to liberalise the law of libel' *The Straits Times* 31 Dec 1959, at 14.

[20] Ordinance No 149 (Straits Settlements). See Allington Kennard, 'Streamlining the law of libel' *The Straits Times*, 7 Jan 1960, at 6; and Editorial, 'Libel Change' *The Straits Times*, 15 Jan 1960 at 8.

[21] Under Article 162 of the Constitution of the Republic of Singapore, 'all existing laws shall continue in force' and 'shall be construed ... with such modifications, adaptation, qualifications and exceptions as may be necessary to bring them into conformity with this Constitution'.

Neither the Penal Code nor the Defamation Act defines the elements of the tort of defamation since they were enacted on the premise 'on the existence and continuation of the common law of defamation.'[22] The elements of the tort are thus to be found in decided cases. The leading case defining what constitutes defamation is the 1936 English House of Lords decision of *Sim v Stretch*[23] in which Lord Atkin famously said:

> I do not intend to ask Your Lordships to lay down a formal definition, but after collating the opinions of many authorities, I propose in the present case the test: would the words tend to lower the plaintiff in the estimation of right-thinking members of society generally?[24]

This test was first applied by the Singapore High Court in the 1974 case of *Workers' Party v Tay Boon Too*[25]—a case involving the defamation of a politician—and remains good law today. Just as the substantive rules on defamation fall to be determined under the common law, so too do the standard defenses to a defamation action—justification, fair comment and privilege (qualified and absolute).

The common law tort of defamation must thus operate in tandem with Article 14(1)(a) of the Constitution. As noted above, Article 14(2)(a) of the Constitution allows Parliament to restrict citizens' right to freedom of expression on only eight specified grounds, including defamation. Since neither the Penal Code nor the Defamation Act specifically restricts this constitutional right, and since the Constitution is the supreme law of the land, all other laws must be consonant with it. Insofar as the tort of defamation is concerned, this means that the common law rules must be read in a way that gives primacy to the constitutional guarantee under Article 14(1)(a). In practical terms, this will require the courts to construe elements of the tort and its defenses in a way that maximizes the individual's freedom of expression. However, as we shall see in the cases below, the local courts have taken a completely different approach, privileging the common law and the reputations of individuals over the Constitution.

4.3 Defamation and Free Speech: The Case Law

A quick check of the legal database reveals some 40 defamation cases in the local law reports. This is a very small number, and if we consider that several of these reports are of appeal as well, the number is even smaller. Of these, about half involve persons who might be called 'public figures', most of whom are politicians, including three successive prime ministers of Singapore: Lee Kuan Yew, Goh Chok Tong and Lee Hsien Loong. We now consider how the local courts have dealt with the tension

---

22 See *Jeyaretnam Joshua Benjamin v Lee Kuan Yew* [1992] 1 SLR(R) 791, at 812 (Court of Appeal, Singapore).

23 [1936] 2 All ER 1237.

24 Ibid, at 1240.

25 [1974–1976] SLR(R) 204.

between the constitutional right to freedom of expression on one hand, and the need to protect individual reputations on the other. Our primary focus is the Court of Appeal's 1990 decision in *Lee Kuan Yew v Jeyaretnam Joshua Benjamin* (1990)[26] which establishes many of the key principles which continue to be applied by the courts today.

4.3.1 The issues

The parties in this case were well-known politicians. Lee Kuan Yew was Prime Minister of Singapore from 1959 to 1990; Senior Minister in the Prime Minister's Office from 1990 to 2006; and Minister Mentor in the Prime Minister's Office from 2006 to 2011. He is considered by many to be the 'Father of Modern Singapore' and had, since the 1960s, been its most well-known personality inside and outside the country. Joshua Benjamin Jeyaretnam was Secretary-General of the Workers' Party from 1971 to 2001, and he founded the Reform Party in 2008, a few months before his death. A former Senior District Judge, Jeyaretnam or 'JBJ' as he is more popularly referred to, won fame by becoming the first opposition politician to win a seat in Singapore's Parliament in 14 years.

A decade earlier, these two political foes had crossed swords in court in their first defamation battle when Lee sued Jeyaretnam for intimating that Lee had abused his position as Prime Minister to enrich his family and himself.[27] In this 1990 case, Lee sued Jeyaretnam for made a speech he made in an election rally in the run-up to the 1988 general election where he referred to the suicide of Teh Cheang Wan, the former Minister for National Development who was facing charges for corruption at the time of his death. During his speech on 26 August 1988, it was alleged that Jeyaretnam, through a series of rhetorical questions, intimated that Lee had advised Teh to commit suicide so he could avoid the embarrassment of the investigations and thereby escape responsibility, and that Lee had abetted Teh's suicide. In the High Court, Justice Lai Kew Chai found 'that the speech of the defendant contained the imputations that the plaintiff had encouraged, or failed to prevent, the suicide of Mr. Teh Cheang Wan in order to cover-up wrongdoing.'[28]

4.3.2 Launching the Sullivan Defense

In his defense, Jeyaretnam argued that he was merely asking legitimate questions on matters of outstanding importance and that he did not impute nor assert that Lee nor

---

[26] [1990] 1 SLR(R) 709.

[27] See *Jeyaretnam Joshua Benjamin v Lee Kuan Yew* [1981–1982] SLR(R) 353 (Privy Council on appeal from Singapore).

[28] Ibid, at 728.

anyone else had anything to do with Teh's suicide. In any event, Jeyaretnam argued, if the speech bore the imputations alleged by Lee, he 'had made the imputations against the plaintiff as a public figure without malice'.[29] Lai J noted that Jeyaretnam's counsel, Donald Martin Thomas QC was raising a 'novel defence' in arguing that 'there is in the law of defamation of Singapore a form of "constitutional" privilege whereby a defendant who unwittingly defamed a politician or a public figure would not be liable, unless the plaintiff proved actual malice.'[30] In explaining this defense, Lai J. stated:

> Under this doctrine, which was first developed in the United States, even misstatements of facts about public officials, candidates for office and public figures would not be actionable unless made with knowledge that the statements were false or the defendant was reckless as to their truth. This principle was first laid down by the Supreme Court of the United States of America in the case of *New York Times Co v Sullivan* 376 US 254 (1964) and it has often been referred to as the *New York Times* rule. It should not be difficult to see that this rule is analogous in a sense to the traditional common law defence of fair comment and that as a matter of policy it prefers the principle that debate on public issues and on the conduct of public officials or of public figures should be uninhibited, robust and wide open than the principle that the rights of individuals (who may be public personalities), including the protection of reputation, should be respected.[31]

Thomas argued that since Article 14 of Singapore's Constitution was analogous to Article 19 of the Indian Constitution and that the latter was in turn based on the First Amendment of the US Constitution, the Singapore court should adopt the *New York Times* rule. Thomas further argued that the European Court of Human Rights (ECHR) had adopted a similar approach in the case of *Lingens v Austria*.[32]

These arguments were roundly dismissed by the court. Lai J held that Article 14 of the Singapore Constitution could not be read in the same light as the First Amendment which prohibited Congress and the states from promulgating any law restricting freedom of speech and expression. There was, he said, a clear 'divergence of public policy' between the two jurisdictions in that the framers of Singapore's Constitution had 'chosen the policy of balancing freedom of speech and expression against certain other individual rights, including not least the protection of reputation' and that the balance is achieved 'by the common law evolving certain well-known defenses, as modified by statute ... and all directed to the intent and purpose the freedom of speech must end where the rights of the individual begin.'[33] Lai J concluded that insofar as the law of defamation of Singapore was concerned, 'it has never been suggested that a privilege extends to any statements which are made to the world at large except in the case of a legal, social or moral duty' and 'there is no case law in England or in Singapore which suggests that 'public figures' fall into a special category so that anything can be said about them unless the potential plaintiff can prove malice.'[34]

---

[29] Ibid, at 730.

[30] Ibid, at 728.

[31] Ibid.

[32] (1986) 5 EHRR 407.

[33] [1990] 1 SLR(R) 709, at 732–733.

[34] Ibid, at 734.

Jeyaretnam was ordered to pay S$260,000 in damages to Lee. On appeal, he once again advanced the *Sullivan* argument. Unsurprisingly, this was again rejected. The Court of Appeal turned *Sullivan* on its head by referring to a series of cases that adopted a strict view against attacks on 'public men'. The first was the 1863 English case of *Campbell v Spottiswoode*[35] where Lord Chief Justice Cockburn held that it was necessary for the conduct of public affairs to prevent 'attacks upon public men, which if allowed would be destructive of their character and honour'.[36] The next case was the 1950 Saskatchewan Court of Appeal case of *Tucker v Douglas*[37] which held that the 'suggestion that a public man can be slandered or libeled in his public capacity is entirely without foundation', especially since his 'moral character is the same whether in private or public life and is in either case equally entitled to the protection of the law from libelous attacks.'[38] The last case referred to by the Court was the 1893 American decision of *Post Publishing Co v Hallam*[39] where the court held that if every person who offers himself as a candidate for public office must sacrifice his right to his personal reputation, it would 'do the public more harm than good.' Finally, the Court endorsed the comment in a footnote in *Gatley on Libel and Slander* that argued that the *Sullivan* rule would do more harm than good and that it would 'tend to deter sensitive and honorable men from seeking public positions of trust and responsibility, and leave them open to others who have no respect for their reputation.'[40] The quantum of damages ordered by the High Court was upheld on appeal.

It is worthwhile to note that all the authorities referred to by the Court of Appeal in justifying its rejection of *Sullivan* pre-dated *Sullivan*. There was very little discussion of public policy beyond the assertion that adopting the *Sullivan* defense would be detrimental to public politics. Neither the High Court nor the Court of Appeal dealt in depth with the public policy reasons offered by the US Supreme Court. More significantly, both the High Court and Court of Appeal side-stepped the key constitutional argument—that the Defamation Act did not restrict any rights of a citizen to the freedom of expression, and that the common law had to be read subject to the Constitution, and not the other way round.[41]

The following passage in the Court of Appeal's judgment is particularly telling and problematic:

> The terms of Art 14 of our Constitution differ materially from the First and Fourteenth Amendments of the Constitution of the United States and also from Art 10 of the European Convention on Human Rights. The First Amendment, by its express terms, prohibits Congress from making any laws 'abridging the freedom of speech, or of the press'. The

---

[35] (1863) 32 LJ QB 185.

[36] Ibid, at 200.

[37] [1950] 2 DLR 827.

[38] Ibid, at 840.

[39] (1893) 59 Fed 530.

[40] [1992] 1 SLR(R) 791, at 819.

[41] For a criticism of the two judgments, see Michael Hor, 'The Freedom of Speech and Defamation: *Jeyaretnam Joshua Benjamin v Lee Kuan Yew*' [1992] *Singapore Journal of Legal Studies* 542–556.

> Fourteenth Amendment extends the prohibition to state legislatures. No such express prohibition is found in Art 14 of our Constitution. On the contrary, *the right of free speech and expression under cl 1(a) of Art 14 is expressly subject to cl 2(a) of the same article, and the latter provides that Parliament may by law impose on the rights of free speech and expression conferred by cl 1(a) two categories of restrictions: first, such restrictions as it considers necessary and expedient in the interest of the security of Singapore or any part thereof, friendly relations with other countries, public order or morality; and second, restrictions designed to protect the privileges of Parliament or to provide against contempt of court, defamation or incitement to any offence. While the first category of restrictions must satisfy the test of necessity and expediency in the interest of the various matters specified therein, the second category of restrictions is not required to satisfy any such test. Thus, Parliament is empowered to make laws to impose on the right of free speech restriction designed to provide against defamation.* As for Art 10 of the European Convention on Human Rights, it is true that the wording in para 1 thereof is similar to cl 1(a) of Art 14. However, para 2 of Art 10 is in no way similar to cl (2) of Art 14: para 2 provides that the exercise of the freedom under para 1 is subject to 'restrictions or penalties as are prescribed by law and are necessary in a democratic society ... for the protection of the reputation or rights of others ...'. Clearly, the terms allowing restrictions to be imposed under Art 10(2) are not as wide as those under Art 14(2) [emphasis mine].[42]

4.3.3 The Court of Appeal's Problematic Logic

While Article 14 of the Singapore Constitution is not analogous to either the First or Fourteenth Amendments of the US Constitution, nor to Article 10 of the European Convention on Human Rights, it nevertheless prescribes limited and specific grounds under which Parliament may limit or restrict a citizen's right to the freedom of expression. Counsel for Jeyaretnam argued that Article 14, like all fundamental liberties provisions in the Constitution, should be 'given a generous and purposive construction' and the common law rules of defamation—which continued in force after Singapore became independent by virtue of Article 162 of the Constitution[43]—should be reformulated 'to take account of the recognition in the Constitution of the right of freedom of speech and expression.'[44] The Court of Appeal rejected this argument, holding:

> The common law of defamation as modified by the Defamation Act (then the Defamation Ordinance) was in operation at the time of commencement of the Constitution, and by virtue of Art 162 it continues in force. The question then is whether, as required by Art 162, any modification, adaptation, qualification and exception are necessary to be made to the law of defamation so as to bring it into conformity with the Constitution. We think not. The law of defamation is not inconsistent with the right of free speech under Art 14(1)(a) and

---

[42] Lee Kuan Yew v Jeyaretnam Joshua Benjamin [1992] 1 SLR(R) 791, at 815–816.

[43] Article 162 of the Constitution provides 'all existing laws shall continue in force on and after the commencement of this Constitution and all laws which have not been brought into force by the date of the commencement of this Constitution may, subject as aforesaid, be brought into force on or after its commencement, but all such laws shall, subject to this Article, be construed as from the commencement of this Constitution with such modifications, adaptations, qualifications and exceptions as may be necessary to bring them into conformity with this Constitution'.

[44] Lee Kuan Yew v Jeyaretnam Joshua Benjamin [1992] 1 SLR(R) 791, at 809.

> accordingly, no such modification, adaptation, qualification and exception is necessary to be made thereto.[45]

This is an extremely limited reading of a citizen's right to freedom of expression under Article 14. If we dissect the Court of Appeal's logic, it will flow as follows:

i. Article 162 of the Constitution requires the court to read pre-independence laws consonantly with and not in violation of the Constitution. However, Article 14(2)(a) allows Parliament to make laws to impose 'such restrictions as it considers necessary or expedient' to 'provide against ... defamation.'
ii. The Defamation Act is a post-independence law. It was enacted to modify the common law of defamation.
iii. Parliament must thus have intended to restrict a citizen's Article 14(1)(a) rights by enacting the Defamation Act—which necessarily applies the whole of the common law of defamation—to restrict a citizen's freedom of expression under Article 14(2)(a).

Thus spelt out, the logic is highly problematic. Article 14 of the Constitution came into force after Singapore became independent in August 1965. It permits Parliament to restrict a citizen's right to the freedom of expression by passing a law to 'provide against defamation'. However, Parliament has not passed any such law. The Defamation Act is not a law providing against defamation, nor does it set out the legal elements of what constitutes the tort of defamation. All it does is qualify the operation of the existing common law of defamation. Instead of dealing with the ambit of Article 14(2)(a) and the constitutionality of the common law of defamation, the Court of Appeal held that the Defamation Act was indeed legislation contemplated by Article 14(2)(b). Even if the Defamation Act operated to ensure that the law on defamation continued in force after independence, it would still be necessary for the Court to decide 'whether they need to undergo any change to comply with the requirements of the Constitution.'[46]

In doing so, the Court of Appeal gave short shrift to the constitutionally-guaranteed rights of citizens and elevated the protection of personal reputation above the Constitution. This problematic reasoning was to be repeated in all subsequent cases and has been used as a precedent for the holding that the law of defamation automatically trumps individual liberty.[47] By limiting the ambit of a citizen's freedom of association through the common law, the Court effectively made a constitutional right subject to and contingent on a common law rule. This, I would argue, is to misread and misunderstand the meaning of what constitutes constitutionally-guaranteed liberty under the Singapore Constitution. This sets a poor precedent because whenever courts deal

---

[45] Ibid, at 816.

[46] Michael Hor, 'The Freedom of Speech and Defamation: *Jeyaretnam Joshua Benjamin v Lee Kuan Yew*' ([1992]) *Singapore Journal of Legal Studies* 542–556, at 549.

[47] This holding has been followed in the High Court decisions of Lee Hsien Loong v Singapore Democratic Party and Ors and Anor Suit [2009] 1 SLR(R) 791; Lee Hsien Loong v Roy Ngerng Yi Ling [2014] SGHC 20, at [15]–[21]; and Lee Hsien Loong v Leong Sze Hian [2021] SGHC 66, at [54]–[57].

with defamation in light of Article 14, courts are not prepared to consider how the common law should be altered to maximize citizens' rights under Article 14, but simply focus on how to apply the common law rules, complete with its defenses and exceptions. In such an analysis, the Constitution and the rights it entrenches becomes redundant.

4.3.4 Subsequent Developments

The Court of Appeal had occasion to reconsider this issue in the 2009 case of *Review Publication v Lee Hsien Loong & Anor Appeal*.[48] We will consider some other aspects of this case in greater detail later, but for our present purposes, let us see how the Court dealt with the question of whether the common law acted as a restriction on a citizen's constitutional rights under Article 14.

Counsel for the appellants argued that when the freedom of speech became a constitutional right in Singapore on 16 September 1963—the date of Singapore's independence from Great Britain—Parliament did not enact the requisite legislation to restrict constitutional free speech. As the Defamation Ordinance of 1960 was a pre-independence statute, it did not amount to restrictive legislation of this nature.[49]

The Court of Appeal held that as Article 105(1) of the 1963 State Constitution (now Article 162 of the Constitution) mandated that 'all existing laws shall continue in force on and after the coming into operation of this Constitution', this provision 'itself served as a law-enacting provision, i.e. it had the effect of an enactment which expressly restricted the constitutional free speech' enshrined in the Constitution 'by continuing in force the then existing law of defamation'.[50]

This holding is highly unsatisfactory as the Court of Appeal failed to accord primacy to the Constitution. The wording of Article 105(1) of the State Constitution clearly provided for all existing laws to continue in force and require them to be 'be construed ... with such modifications, adaptations, qualifications and exceptions as may be necessary to bring them into conformity' with the Constitution. It is tautologous and illogical that the very constitutional provision requiring laws to be read in a manner that conforms to the Constitution should, at the same time, be construed to be a law that Parliament intended to enact to limit the operation of the Constitution under Article 14(2)(a). The proper reading of Article 105(1) must require the common law to must be read in a manner that brings it in line with provisions of the Constitution, including the current Article 14, not the other way round. Article 105 does not bend the Constitution to the shape of the common law as it stood when Singapore became independent.

---

[48] [2010] 1 SLR 52.

[49] Ibid, at 163–164.

[50] Ibid, at 168.

4.3.5 *Defaming 'Good Men': Beyond* Sullivan

After the Court of Appeal flatly rejected *Sullivan* and the underlying rationale of its decision, the case was not used nor argued in subsequent cases. This rejection of *Sullivan* is not altogether surprising since the doctrine has found favor in few common law jurisdictions.[51] In England, the Faulks Committee[52] rejected the *Sullivan* principle on the grounds that 'the foundation of the Supreme Court's decision was the provisions of the 1st and Fourteenth Amendments of the United States Constitution ... Here we have no written constitution to interpret; we apply the common law.'[53] In the leading British case of *Derbyshire County Council v Times Newspaper Ltd & Ors*,[54] the House of Lords came closest to affirming the underlying precepts of *Sullivan* when it declared the 'chilling effect' of civil suits by public figures to be 'very important'.[55] The House of Lords also considered the ECHR case of *Lingens v Austria* but stated steadfastly that it had come to its decision without the need to rely on Article 10 of the European Convention of Human Rights.[56]

The British common law approach in addressing this chilling effect is to focus on possible exceptions to the strict application of the law where public policy demands, such as the right to the freedom of information. This approach is not centered on the individual's right of expression as such, but rather on how exceptions may be carved out of defamation law. The freedom of the press is thus protected by the courts utilizing 'qualified privilege' as a defense to a defamation action. The line of cases on qualified privilege culminated in the case of *Reynolds v Times Newspapers Ltd*[57] which established what has now come to be called the *Reynolds* defence of 'responsible journalism'. Even the *Reynolds* defence has now been abolished under the UK Defamation Act of 2013.[58]

Sullivan did not find favor in Australia or New Zealand either. Both jurisdictions preferred a different form of qualified privilege defense on the basis of the individual's right to receive political communications. The Australian Constitution does not provide specifically for the protection of an individual's right to freedom

[51] See Adrienne Stone, 'Defamation of Public Figures: North American Contrasts' (2005) 50(1) *New York Law School Law Review* 9–32; Adrienne Stone and George Williams, 'Freedom of Speech and Defamation: Developments in the Common Law World' (2000) 26 *Monash University Law Review* 362–378; Kyu Ho Youm, '"Actual Malice" in US Defamation Law: The Minority of One Dictoriune in the World?' (2011/2012) 4(1) *Journal of International Entertainment and Media Law* 1–3; Robert D Sack, '*New York Times Co v Sullivan*: 50 Years Afterwards' (2014) 66(2) *Alabama Law Review* 273–292; and Michael S Grimsley, 'Defamation of Public Figures: Is *New York Times* Outdated?' (1995) 10(2) *Florida Journal of International Law* 293–314.

[52] Report of the Committee on Defamation, Cmnd 5909, March 1975.

[53] Ibid, paras 6.10 and 6.17.

[54] [1993] 2 WLR 449 (House of Lords).

[55] Ibid, at 457.

[56] Ibid, at 460.

[57] [2001] 2 AC 127.

[58] Eliz 2 c 26. See section 4 which creates the defence in a publication on a matter of public interest. Section 4(6) states: 'The common law defence known as the Reynolds defence is abolished.'.

of expression but the Australian High Court held that there was an implied right of individuals to receive political communication as such information was necessary for the exercise of the right to political participation since 'each member of the Australian community has an interest in disseminating and receiving information, opinions and arguments concerning government and political matters that affect the people of Australia.'[59] The mass media was thus protected by a constitutional defense of qualified privilege for defamatory material published provided the publication was reasonable in the sense that they did not believe the publication to be false and all necessary checks and inquiries had been made to verify them.[60] In New Zealand, the courts have extended this qualified privilege further to cover all publications of 'public interest' (and not just political communications) provided that the communication was responsible, with the defendant bearing the onus of proof on both counts.[61]

How did the law in Singapore develop post-1996? Two major cases call for consideration. The first is *Goh Chok Tong v Jeyaretnam Joshua Benjamin*,[62] a case that saw Jeyaretnam lock horns with Prime Minister Goh Chok Tong. The second is *Review Publishing v Lee Hsien Loong*,[63] which saw the *Far Eastern Economic Review* being sued by Prime Minister Lee Hsien Loong.

4.3.6 The Fragile Public Figure: Goh Chok Tong and Ors v Jeyaretnam

As noted earlier, the decision in *Jeyaretnam Joshua Benjamin v Lee Kuan Yew* effectively subjected the constitutional right to freedom of expression to the dynamics of the common law. The following case shows what happens when a constitutional right is trumped by a common law rule that is in turn interpreted generously in favor of the plaintiff.

---

[59] *Lange v Australian Broadcasting Corporation* (1997) 189 CLR 520 (High Court of Australia), at 571.

[60] For a discussion on the difference between the UK and Australian 'qualified privilege' test, see Andrew T Kenyon, '*Lange* and *Reynolds* Qualified Privilege: Australian and English Defamation Law and Practice' (2004) 28 *Melbourne University Law Review* 406–437.

[61] *Durie & Hall v Heta Gardiner & Maori Television Service* [2018] NZCA 278, at [58] (Court of Appeal, New Zealand).

[62] [1997] 3 SLR (R) 46 (Court of Appeal).

[63] [2010] 1 SLR 52.

4.4 The 1997 General Elections and Tang Liang Hong

In 1997, general elections were called. Jeyaretnam, who was then Secretary-General of the Workers' Party (WP), was one of six members of the WP team contesting the Cheng San Group Representation Constituency (GRC). Since 1988, the Constitution required candidates to run as a team that includes at least one ethnic minority member in designated GRCs such as Cheng San GRC. Jeyaretnam was the anchor candidate for his team that included senior lawyer, Tang Liang Hong ('Tang'). Their opponent was the PAP team led by then-Education Minister Lee Yock Suan.

In the run-up to the elections, Tang became the subject of intense scrutiny and criticism by the PAP. Prime Minister Goh Chok Tong—who succeeded Lee Kuan Yew in the office in 1990—openly called Tang an 'anti-Christian' Chinese chauvinist and labeled him 'a dangerous man'. Tang denied these charges, called Goh a liar, and filed two police reports against Goh and ten other PAP Members of Parliament (most of whom were in the Cabinet), alleging criminal defamation.

4.5 The Police Reports

At Jeyaretnam's election rally speech on the evening of 1 January 1997, Tang came up to him and placed some papers next to him. At the end of his speech, Jeyaretnam waved an envelope in his right hand and said:

> And finally, Mr. Tang Liang Hong has just placed before me two reports he has made to the police against, you know, Mr. Goh Chok Tong and his people. But just remember. Have one thing on your mind, one purpose, one will, that it is not for Mr. Tang Liang Hong or for me or for the Workers' Party that you are voting. You are voting for yourself. And the PAP have been trying desperately to win this battle. They've been trying to stop you from voting for your rights. Well, show them tomorrow and I will then be very, very proud of you people of Cheng San.[64]

Goh's solicitors wrote to Jeyaretnam on 25 January, demanding that he withdraw the statements, make an unreserved apology in specific terms, and undertake not to further publish the statements as well as compensate the victims of his attack. Four days later, Jeyaretnam replied through his lawyers, offering to give an apology on his own terms. This offer was rejected and Goh and the other 10 MPs sued Jeyaretnam for defamation.

Goh argued that Jeyaretnam's announcement that Tang had filed two police reports against him 'and his people'—was defamatory in that it suggested that they were guilty of the offense of criminal defamation and criminal conspiracy.

[64] [1997] 3 SLR (R) 46, at 57.

4.6 The Verdict

The case was heard before Rajendran J of the High Court. In considering whether Jeyaretnam's words were, in fact, defamatory, the learned judge deviated from the test in *Sim v Stretch*—which required the words to 'lower the plaintiff in the estimation of right-thinking members of society generally'. Rajendran J considered the traditional test to be unsatisfactory since the term 'right thinking' appeared to 'inject an analytical element into the test':

> Such a view would be unsatisfactory because it is clear that whether words are defamatory includes an impressionistic element. Words are defamatory if they convey a negative impression—the words spoken are not to be subjected to analysis in order to determine whether such an impression is rightly held....

Thus, that the ordinary person would have a negative first impression is a sufficient basis for an action in defamation, even though he might subsequently correct himself on that impression.[65]

Applying this test to the facts, Rajendran J held:

> Whilst the ordinary man might not think much of vague allegations made by politicians against each other and might consider them no more than mere political bluster, he might think otherwise where a prominent politician who has stepped into the limelight as Mr. Tang had, having avowed to protect his reputation and integrity, takes the serious step of reporting a matter to the police concerning his opponent's denunciation of him. By extension, where a person announces to the public that such a report has been made, I have no difficulty in concluding that such an event would give the ordinary person in Singapore a reason to pause and think. The ordinary person would consider that a police investigation into the affairs of the plaintiff might take place. However, I hasten to add that excluding all special knowledge from the mind of the ordinary person, the words complained of would not have imported any suggestion as to the subject matter of the investigation.

Does that fact alone cause the plaintiff to be lowered in the estimation of the ordinary man? I am of the view that the ordinary man in Singapore is not so steeply cynical as to shrug off a matter such as a police investigation of a public official without a second thought. And, as I have stated, even if on reflection he were to dismiss the matter because he considers it very unlikely that anything would come out of the report, the broad, negative impression left on the audience is still actionable.

I therefore find that the words spoken by the defendant are capable of defamatory meaning, not of the highest degree pleaded by the plaintiff, but of the lesser degree I have already expressed, that is, the ordinary man will come away with the impression that the plaintiff may have conducted himself in such a manner that it is possible he will be investigated for some offence or other.[66]

On the basis of these findings, the Court awarded Goh $20,000 in damages.

---

[65] Ibid, at 63.

[66] Ibid, at 77.

4.7 The Appeal

Both Goh and Jeyaretnam appealed. Goh argued that the judge erred in not holding Jeyaretnam's words to be more defamatory of his character than he did, and also challenged the quantum of damages awarded. Jeyaretnam appealed on the ground that the words complained of did not bear the defamatory meaning pleaded by Goh nor the meanings found by Rajendran J in the High Court. Jeyaretnam further argued that if they were indeed at all defamatory, Goh should only be entitled to nominal damages. After reviewing two English cases and analogizing therefrom, the Court of Appeal agreed with the trial judge in that 'the ordinary man the words would not imply that Mr. Goh was guilty of criminal defamation and criminal conspiracy or a serious criminal offense; they would not impute guilt.'[67] However, the court went on to hold that:

> But the ordinary man, having heard the statement that Mr. Tang had made police reports against Mr. Goh and his colleagues, would understand that Mr. Tang, being a lawyer and politician, "having avowed to protect his reputation and integrity" had taken a serious step and made police reports against Mr. Goh, and that it would be likely that the police would investigate into some wrong doings alleged in the reports on the part of Mr. Goh. In our opinion, that was the natural and ordinary meaning conveyed to the ordinary man, and the words bearing such meaning were defamatory of Mr Goh.[68]

The Court next considered what 'innuendo meaning' could be imputed to the crowd at the rally. It held that it was common knowledge that it was Goh who initiated the character attacks on Tang by denouncing him as an anti-Christian Chinese chauvinist and that Tang had accused Goh and his colleagues of concocting and spreading lies about him and that he publicly announced his intention to report Goh and colleagues for these accusations if they did not retract their statements.[69] Given this knowledge, the words uttered by Jeyaretnam 'bore the meaning that Mr. Goh had done something seriously wrong in launching the attacks against Mr. Tang and that Mr. Goh would be likely to be investigated for the offense or offenses alleged in the reports.'[70] Jeyaretnam's appeal failed and the Court of Appeal increased the quantum of damages awarded to $100,000.

Several important points arise from this judgment. First, because of the 1992 decision of *Jeyaretnam v Lee Kuan Yew*, the defendant did not raise the constitutional argument. It was simply assumed that the common law of defamation—or whatever the court held that law to be—applied and took precedence over any constitutional right that may well have protected Jeyaretnam. Second, the Court did not seem concerned with the fact that in their plain and ordinary meaning, the words uttered

---

[67] *Goh Chok Tong v Jeyaretnam Joshua Benjamin and Anor Action* [1998] 2 SLR(R) 971, at 985 (Court of Appeal, Singapore).

[68] Ibid.

[69] Ibid.

[70] Ibid, at 986.

by Jeyaretnam were in fact true.[71] Justification would, in this case, be a complete defense. Instead, the Court found it necessary to look for a secondary meaning—the innuendo meaning—to hold Jeyaretnam liable. Third, the whole tenor of the judgment suggests that not only should politicians be treated like all other ordinary persons, but that it mattered not that a politician as prominent as the Prime Minister had all means at his disposal to disabuse the public of any possible wrongdoing on his part.

The disturbing result of this case is the fact that a clearly ambiguous statement, uttered in the heat of an election campaign should be so readily construed as being defamatory of a politician, especially after the Prime Minister—under cross-examination—could point to no specific instance in which his reputation had been damaged by Jeyaretnam's statements. In this case, not only had the common law trumped a constitutional right, the Court altered the standard established in *Sim v Stretch* to that of an innuendo meaning, thus setting a new low bar for liability. This makes no sense when interpreting the common law in light of a constitutional right. Not only did the court not require a higher bar to be established for 'public personalities', especially in the heat of an election, but chose to subjectively lower the bar, as if applying the 'egg-shell skull'[72] principle to defamation cases.

Review Publishing Co Ltd. And Anor v Lee Hsien Loong and Anor Appeal[73]

This was a landmark decision of the Court of Appeal on the nature of freedom of expression in Singapore and how the law of defamation operates alongside it.

4.8 The Case

This case arose out of an article published in the *Far Eastern Economic Review*. Entitled 'Singapore's Martyr: Chee Soon Juan', it was written by the magazine's editor, Hugo Restall, and featured Chee Soon Juan, secretary-general of the Singapore Democratic Party. In the course of Restall's interview with Chee—contents of which were excerpted for publication—Chee alleged that former Prime Minister Lee Kuan Yew 'had accumulated enough skeletons in his closet that he knows that when he is gone, his son and the generations after him will have a price to pay.' Restall, capitalizing on this statement, then compared the running of Singapore to that of the National Kidney Foundation (NKF) while it was under its disgraced Chief Executive, TT Durai. Durai had been found guilty of abuse of the foundation's moneys with which he paid himself a princely salary, and a number of perks, including first-class air tickets. Restall added,

[71] Some years later, I actually asked Jeyaretnam if the envelope he waved did in fact contain the police reports or something else. He told me that the reports were indeed enclosed in the envelope and that he would happily have shown it to anyone who bothered to ask.

[72] See *Smith v Leech Brain & Co* [1962] 2 QB 405 (Court of Queen's Bench, UK).

[73] See *Lee Hsien Loong v Review Publishing Co Ltd* [2007] 2 SLR(R) 453; [2007] 2 SLR 453 (High Court).

> Singaporean officials have a remarkable record of success in winning libel suits against their critics. The question then is, how many other libel suits have Singapore's great and good wrongly won, resulting in the cover-up of real misdeeds? And are libel suits deliberately used as a tool to suppress questioning voices?[74]

The plaintiffs in this case were Lee Hsien Loong, the Singapore Prime Minister and his father Lee Kuan Yew (who was by then, Minister Mentor and former Prime Minister). They alleged that the impugned words 'in their natural and ordinary meaning' meant that they were 'unfit for office' because they were corrupt and 'set out to sue and suppress those who would question' them for fear that such questions 'would expose' their corruption. In the High Court, they applied and obtained summary judgment against the publisher of the *Review*, Review Publishing and against Restall.

4.9 The Appeal[75]

On appeal, appellants argued, among other things, that the disputed words did not allege that either of the Lees was corrupt and that the Judge erred in holding not applying the *Reynolds* defense of qualified privilege.

The first half of the massive 137-page judgment—by far the longest decision on any defamation case in Singapore—concerned the construction of the impugned words and their meanings to the ordinary right-thinking person. The latter half of the judgment dealt with the various defenses raised by the appellants. *Sullivan* was not raised but instead, the appellants' lawyers focused on the *Reynolds* privilege and its offshoot, the 'neutral reportage' defense. They argued that (a) the *Reynolds* privilege was and always had been, part of the common law of Singapore; and (b) if it was not part of the common law, the Court of Appeal should declare it to be such.[76] In either case, the Appellants could avail themselves of this defense in the suits filed against them.

After detailed consideration of the history of the *Reynolds* privilege in the UK and its application in subsequent cases, the Court concluded that it was based on Article 10 of the European Convention on Human Rights as well as section 12 of the UK Human Rights Act:

> Prior to the enactment of the HRA, common law free speech was no different from any other common law right (i.e., any other right which could be enjoyed at common law based on the principle that whatever conduct was not proscribed by law was permitted). After the Convention right of free speech came into existence, common law free speech became a lower order legal right in England as it did not have a 'constitutional' foundation. This change in the legal status of freedom of speech impelled the House of Lords to give greater

[74] See Review Publishing Co Ltd. and Anor v Lee Hsien Loong and Anor Appeal [2010] 1 SLR 52 (Court of Appeal), at 64.

[75] See Review Publishing Co Ltd. and Anor v Lee Hsien Loong and Anor Appeal [2010] 1 SLR 52 (Court of Appeal).

[76] [2010] 1 SLR 52, at 129.

> weight to the Convention right of free speech as compared to the protection of reputation. The law lords shifted the balance between freedom of speech and protection of reputation in favour of the former where *(inter alia)* the media was concerned because s 12(4)(a) of the HRA enjoined the English courts, where '*journalistic*, literary or artistic material (or ... conduct connected with such material)' [emphasis added] was concerned, to have '*particular regard*' [emphasis added] to the extent to which such material had or was about to become available to the public as well as the extent to which it was or would be in the public interest for such material to be published.[77]

The Court of Appeal then looked at developments in other jurisdictions and concluded that *Reynolds* had not emerged 'out of the blue' but rather against a backdrop of other common law jurisdictions—most notably Australia, New Zealand, Canada and Hong Kong—in having first 'shifted the balance between the competing interests of freedom of speech and protection of reputation in favor of the former.'[78] The Court rejected the declaratory theory of the common law—upon which stood the Appellants' first argument—and held that in a constitutional supremacy, the ultimate source of law is the Constitution and with Parliament's enactment of the Application of English Law Act in 1993, the application of the common law is subject to local circumstances.[79]

In striking the balance between free speech and the protection of personal reputation, the Court of Appeal outlined three pertinent considerations: (a) that the balance between constitutional free speech and the protection of reputation had remained unchanged since it was struck in 1963 when freedom of speech became a constitutional right; (b) there was no legislative policy (as in England) privileging journalistic material in the reporting of matters of public interest; and (c) Singapore's 'political culture places a heavy emphasis on honesty and integrity in public discourse on matters of public interest, especially those matters which concern the governance of the country.'[80]

On the first consideration, the Court maintained that the balance between free speech and the protection of personal reputation had already been struck in favor of the latter since 1963 when Singapore became independent from Britain and joined the Federation of Malaysia and thus came under the Federation of Malaysia Constitution. This balance, it opined, was still 'appropriate in the prevailing circumstances in Singapore today' and proponents of change would have to 'produce evidence of a change in our political, social and cultural values in order to satisfy the court that change is necessary so as to provide greater protection against the existing law of defamation for defendants where the publication of matters of public interest is concerned.'[81]

As for the media, its role is limited to 'the traditional activities of reporting and commenting'. There is no law in Singapore 'directing the court to have special regard, where journalistic materials are concerned, to the extent to which it is or would be

---

[77] Ibid, at 143.

[78] Ibid.

[79] Ibid, at 167.

[80] Ibid, at 177–178.

[81] Ibid, at 178.

in the public interest for the materials in question to be published.'[82] It thus has no role as a 'watchdog' of the Government. As such, *Reynolds* would not be applied to extend the scope of qualified privilege. In respect of the last consideration, the Court held that while the 'marketplace of ideas' argument for free speech made good sense for 'statements relating to *ideas or beliefs which cannot have yet to be proved with scientific certainty to be either true or false*' it was 'questionable whether the marketplace of ideas rationale is applicable to false statements' since 'society does not derive any value from the publication'.[83] The Court cited with approval, the following passage in Lord Hobhouse's judgment in *Reynolds*:

> [I]t is important always to remember that it is the communication of information not misinformation which is the subject of this liberty. There is no human right to disseminate information that is not true. No public interest is served by publishing or communicating misinformation. The working of a democratic society depends on the members of that society ... being informed not misinformed. Misleading people and ... purveying as facts statements which are not true is destructive of the democratic society and should form no part of such a society. There is no duty to publish what is not true: there is no interest in being misinformed. These are general propositions going far beyond the mere protection of reputations. [emphasis added][84]

It added that there is no place in Singapore's political culture 'for making false defamatory statements which damage the reputation of a person (especially a holder of public office) for the purposes of scoring political points' and that Singapore's political culture 'places a heavy emphasis on honesty and integrity in public discourse on matters of public interest, especially those matters which concern the governance of the country'.[85]

4.10 Damages for Public Figures

4.10.1 General

In this section, we consider how damages are awarded for political defamation in Singapore. From the foregoing discussion, it is clear that Singapore's courts are not prepared to accept a different standard for the defamation of public personalities. Indeed, the Court of Appeal made it clear that:

> Persons holding public office or politicians (we call them 'public men') are equally entitled to have their reputations protected as those of any other persons. Such persons, in the discharge of their official duties, are laying themselves open to public scrutiny both in respect of their deeds and words. In that respect, criticisms in relation to their official conduct may be

---

[82] Ibid, at 179.

[83] Ibid, at 182.

[84] Ibid, at 183.

[85] Ibid.

> 'robust' and 'wide-open' and may include 'vehement, caustic and sometimes unpleasantly sharp attacks.'[86]

Given that the test for the defamation of public officials is the same as that for all other persons, the question of damages becomes most important since large damages are more likely to deter, and huge awards are more 'chilling' than nominal ones.

Under the common law, the object of damages is to restore the plaintiff to the position the party was before the defamatory act occurred. The quantum of damages should thus be based on the extent of the injury suffered by the plaintiff. The greater the injury, the higher the quantum of damages. In cases where harm has not been suffered, nominal damages are often awarded. Depending on the circumstances of each case, factors may either mitigate or aggravate the damage, and the quantum awarded falls or rises accordingly. It is, however, not an exact science and has been described as being 'at large'.[87] The statement of the law on damages for libel in *Gatley on Libel and Slander*[88]—the standard practitioners' text on the subject—was adopted in two early cases: *Lee Kuan Yew v Jeyaretnam Joshua Benjamin* (1979)[89] and *Wu CS v Wang Look Fung & Ors* (1980).[90] The relevant paragraph from *Gatley* states:

> In an action of libel, 'the assessment of damages does not depend on any legal rule'. The amount of damages is 'peculiarly the province of the jury', who in assessing them will naturally be governed by all the circumstances of the particular case. They are entitled to take into their consideration the conduct of the plaintiff, his position and standing, the nature of the libel, the mode and extent of publication, the absence or refusal of any retraction or apology, and 'the whole conduct of the defendant from the time when the libel was published down to the very moment of their verdict. They may take into consideration the conduct of the defendant before action, after action, and in court at the trial of the action', and also, it is submitted, the conduct of his counsel, who cannot shelter his client by taking responsibility for the conduct of the case. They should allow 'for the sad truth that no apology, retraction or withdrawal can ever be guaranteed completely to undo the harm it has done or the hurt it has caused'. They should also take into account the evidence led in aggravation or mitigation of the damages. They should not take into account in assessing damages any part of the words complained of in respect of which the defendant has made out a defence or any damage done to the plaintiff's reputation or feelings by any defamatory matter for which the plaintiff is not responsible. They should not speculate on whether the defendant will be indemnified.[91]

The award of damages for libel is thus a two-step process. First, the court, having determined that a statement is libelous, will decide the extent to which a plaintiff's reputation has been harmed (if at all) and fix a sum that would set right the wrong.

---

[86] *Jeyaretnam Joshua Benjamin v Lee Kuan Yew* [1992] 1 SLR(R) 791, at 818 (Court of Appeal, Singapore).

[87] See *Cassell & Co Ltd v Broome* [1972] AC 1027, at 1071 *per* Lord Hailsham of Marylebone LC.

[88] The edition relied on was the 7th edition of this work: Sir Robert McEwen & Philip Lewis, *Gatley on Libel and Slander*, 7 ed (London: Sweet & Maxwell, 1974).

[89] *Lee Kuan Yew v Jeyaretnam Joshua Benjamin* [1979–1980] SLR(R) 24.

[90] *Wu CS v Wang Look Fung & Ors* [1979–1980] SLR(R) 528.

[91] Sir Robert McEwen & Philip Lewis, *Gatley on Libel and Slander*, 7 ed (London: Sweet & Maxwell, 1974) para 1358.

Second, the court will consider any mitigating or aggravating circumstances that would warrant it adjusting the quantum of damages already fixed.

4.10.2 Growth of Damages for Public Figures

The first case involving the defamation of public figures in independent Singapore occurred in 1967 when Prime Minister Lee Kuan Yew sued Syed Ja'afar Albar and the *Utusan Melayu* newspaper for libel.[92] The case was withdrawn after the defendants withdrew their libelous statements and apologized. In 1979, Lee sued JB Jeyaretnam[93] in respect of the latter's clearly libelous statements which intimated that Lee, as Prime Minister, had procured the grant of favors to the law firm of Lee and Lee of which Lee's wife, Kwa Geok Choo was a senior partner. Jeyaretnam further alleged that Lee had been guilty of nepotism and corruption. The High Court found Jeyaretnam's actions to have been actuated by malice and awarded Lee S$130,000 in damages. This award was affirmed by the Court of Appeal[94] and by the Privy Council.[95]

In 1984, Lee sued Seow Khee Leng, Secretary-General of the Singapore United Front for comments made during an election rally.[96] Seow had intimated Lee was corrupt and that he had covered up wrongdoing of other corrupt officials within his government. Lee's solicitors wrote to Seow, asking him if he was prepared to publish (at his expense) an apology in terms of a draft supplied, in all the national Chinese, English, Malay and Tamil newspapers; and to read the apology at the next Singapore United Front rally. If Seow agreed, Lee would be prepared to accept nominal damages of S$1,000 and legal costs of about S$500. Seow proceeded to read, in its entirety, Lee's solicitor's letter, thereby repeating the slanderous statements and offering a qualified apology at the end.

Lee decided to sue and sought aggravated damages from Seow. This was the first case in which aggravated damages for defamation was sought. The High Court, once again citing *Gatley on Libel & Slander*[97] relied on the following statement of the law on aggravated damages:

> *Aggravated damages*. The conduct of the defendant, his conduct of the case, and his state of mind are thus all matters which the plaintiff may rely on as aggravating the damages. 'Moreover, it is very well established that in cases where the damages are at large the jury (or the judge if the award is left to him) can take into account the motives and conduct of the defendant where they aggravate the injury done to the plaintiff. There may be malevolence

---

[92] Lee Kuan Yew v Syed Ja'afar Albar & Ors [1965–1967] SLR(R) 768 (High Court).

[93] *Lee Kuan Yew v Jeyaretnam Joshua Benjamin* [1979–1980] SLR(R) 24.

[94] *Jeyaretnam Joshua Benjamin v Lee Kuan Yew* [1979–1980] SLR(R) 255.

[95] *Jeyaretnam Joshua Benjamin v Lee Kuan Yew* [1981–1982] SLR(R) 353. Singapore abolished appeals to the Privy Council in 1994.

[96] Lee Kuan Yew v Seow Khee Leng [1988] 2 SLR(R) 252.

[97] Philip Lewis, *Gatley on Libel and Slander*, 8 ed (London: Sweet & Maxwell, 1981).

> or spite or the manner of committing the wrong may be such as to injure the plaintiff's proper feelings of dignity and pride. These are matters which the jury can take into account in assessing the appropriate compensation.' 'In awarding 'aggravated damages' the natural indignation of the court at the injury inflicted on the plaintiff is a perfectly legitimate motive in making a generous, rather than a more moderate award to provide an adequate solatium ... that is because the injury to the plaintiff is actually greater, and, as the result of the conduct exciting the indignation, demands a more generous solatium.[98]

The Court found that Seow's apology was neither unreserved nor sincere and instructed his lawyers to conduct the trial in a 'vexatious manner'. In view of all these factors, the Court awarded the Prime Minister damages of S$250,000.

Aggravated damages for libel were also awarded in *Lee Kuan Yew v Davies Derek Gwyn & Ors* (1989),[99] a case which saw Lee's first run-in with the *Far Eastern Economic Review*. Lee was awarded S$230,000 in damages. In another case involving the press, Lee Kuan Yew, Lee Hsien Loong and Goh Chok Tong successfully sued the *International Herald Tribune* for defamation[100] for its article, entitled 'The Claims About "Asian" Values Don't Usually Bear Scrutiny' which appeared in the *Tribune* on 2 August 1994. The article suggested that 'dynastic politics' operated in Singapore between Lee Kuan Yew and his son, Lee Hsien Loong. The Court awarded Lee Kuan Yew and Lee Hsien Loong S$300,000 each in damages, and Goh Chok Tong S$350,000 in damages.

In 1996, Lee Kuan Yew sued the *International Herald Tribune* again, this time for an article 'The Smoke Over Parts of Asia Obscures Some Profound Concerns', written by Christopher Lingle and published in the 7 October 1994 edition of the *Tribune*. Among other things, this article contained a passage that suggested that Lee had suppressed legitimate and democratic political activity in Singapore by suing his political opponents for defamation even though he had no meritorious claim and/or relying on a 'compliant judiciary' to find in his favor regardless of the merits of the case.[101] In assessing damages, Rajendran J considered the aggravating fact that while the *Tribune* had acted in a conciliatory manner but that the second defendant, Lingle had not and continued repeating the libelous comment at his book launch in Hong Kong and elsewhere. The High Court awarded Lee S$400,000 in damages, the highest amount yet. More recently, aggravated damages were awarded in the cases of *Lee Hsien Loong v Ngerng Yi Ling Roy*[102] and *Lee Hsien Loong v Leong Sze Hian.*[103]

Lee Kuan Yew and Lee Hsien Loong sued the Singapore Democratic Party[104] for defamatory articles and a photograph published in the Party's newsletter, *The Democrat*, and received aggravated damages of S$280,000 and S$330,000, respectively.

---

98 Ibid, at para 1452.

99 Lee Kuan Yew v Davies Derek Gwyn & Ors [1989] 2SLR(R) 544.

100 Lee Kuan Yew & Anor v Vinocur John & Ors and Another Suit [1995] 3 SLR(R) 38; and Lee Kuan Yew v Vinocur John & Ors [1996] 1 SLR(R) 840.

101 Lee Kuan Yew v Vinocur John & Ors [1996] 1 SLR(R) 840, at 842.

102 [2016] 1 SLR 1321 (High Court, Singapore).

103 [2021] 4 SLR 1128 (High Court, Singapore).

104 Lee Hsien Loong v Singapore Democratic Party and Ors and Anor Suit [2009] 1 SLR 642.

Politicians of the PAP were not the only public figures who succeeded in defamation actions. Veteran opposition leader Chiam See Tong successfully sued his former Singapore Democratic Party colleagues for S$120,000 in damages for libelous statements made in a press statement issued by the Party.[105] Well-known investor tycoon, Peter Lim Eng Hock also succeeded in obtaining S$140,000 in general damages and S$70,000 in aggravated damages against the owners of the Raffles Town Club in 2013.[106]

4.10.3 How Much is Your Reputation Worth?

The quanta of damages awarded to plaintiffs have ranged between S$150,000 and S$400,000. However, in the *Tang Liang Hong* case, the High Court awarded damages totalling S$8,325,000 to 11 plaintiffs. As we noted above, Tang Liang Hong was a senior lawyer who contested the 1996 general election under the Workers' Party banner. During the election campaign, he was labeled a 'Chinese chauvinist', an 'anti-Christian' and a 'dangerous man' by members of the ruling PAP, including Prime Minister Goh Chok Tong, Senior Minister Lee Kuan Yew and Deputy Prime Minister Lee Hsien Loong. This case arose out of Tang's filing of two police reports against the 11 PAP members for criminal defamation and a series of interviews Tang gave. The Court found that these actions were defamatory in that Tang had called all the plaintiffs liars and had accused them of abusing the process of the courts to paralyze him. Tang was also found to have defamed Lee Kuan Yew and Lee Hsien Loong by intimating corrupt dealings in respect of their purchase of apartments in a development known as Nassim Jade, and further saying that Lee Kuan Yew was untrustworthy.

The High Court awarded Lee Kuan Yew S$2.3 million in damages; Lee Hsien Loong S$1.3 million; Goh Chok Tong S$1.4 million; Deputy Prime Minister Tony Tan S$350,000; Minister Teo Chee Hean S$550,000 (on two counts of defamation); Ch'ng Jit Koon and Ow Chin Hock S$450,000 each; Chin Harn Tong and Ker Sin Tze S$350,000 each and Seng Han Tong S$275,000. Tang appealed the assessment of damages and the Court of Appeal varied the awards significantly. The total amount of damages was reduced from S$8.325 million to S$3.43 million.

It is not my purpose to go into the intricacies of how the Court of Appeal arrived at its computation of damages for that would require a separate discussion altogether. Suffice to say, the computation of these awards does not appear to correlate with any actual loss suffered. The only instance in which the court considered whether the plaintiff suffered any actual damage or loss as a result of the defamatory statement was in *Goh Chok Tong v Jeyaretnam Joshua Benjamin* where Rajendran J ordered general compensatory damages of S$10,000 and a further S$10,000 aggravated damages for

[105] Chiam See Tong v Ling How Doong and Ors [1996] 3 SLR(R) 942.

[106] Lim Eng Hock Peter v Lin Jian Wei and Anor and Another Appeal [2014] 4 SLR 357.

the conduct of the defense during the trial.[107] However, these were revised upwards to S$100,000 when the case went on appeal.[108] The Court of Appeal considered that Rajendra J erred in finding that there was no express malice on the part of Jeyaretnam and 'failed to give sufficient weight to some of the relevant aggravating factors; and that the award of $20,000 was 'totally disconsonant with precedent cases.'[109]

Exactly how did the court arrive at the conclusion that the damages were 'disconsonant' with those awarded in precedent cases? The Court of Appeal referred to two cases involving the veteran opposition politician Chiam See Tong. The first was the case of *Chiam See Tong v Xin Zhang Jiang Restaurant Pte Ltd*[110] where Chiam received damages of S$50,000 for the unauthorized use of his photograph in the restaurant's advertising material. The second was *Chiam See Tong v Ling How Doong,*[111] a case mentioned previously, and for which Chiam received S$120,000 in damages. While 'mindful of the differences between these two cases' and the present case, the Court nonetheless concluded:

> ... we think that the quantum of damages arrived at below must be reconsidered and the amount of damages must undergo an upward revision. In all the circumstances, we are of the opinion that a fair and reasonable sum to be awarded to Mr. Goh as damages should be $100,000. Accordingly, we increase the award of $20,000 to $100,000.[112]

The Court of Appeal proceeded to revise damages upwards notwithstanding the fact that during the trial, Goh admitted under cross-examination that his standing as a leader had not been injured and that he actually had 'a good year' in 1997, the year following the alleged slanderous remarks. He could not 'in sincerity point to a particular damage.'[113] If actual damage did not form the basis for the Court of Appeal's decision, what grounds could be offered for the upward revision of damages? Alas, the judgment offers no further analysis or guidelines. The Court appeared to be saying: 'If an opposition politician's reputation is worth between S$50,000 and S$120,000, the Prime Minister's reputation must surely be worth as much or thereabouts.' And if I am right on this, then the only basis for the assessment of damages must be the status of the defendant, nothing more.

This hypothesis is borne out by a reading of other cases involving politicians. In the earliest case, *Lee Kuan Yew v Jeyaretnam Joshua Benjamin* (1979),[114] the High Court held:

> This was a very grave slander that struck at the heart of the plaintiff's political reputation. The standing of the plaintiff is such as to mean that the injury done to him was grave. It was spoken by the principal opposition speaker and a prominent person whose words would

---

[107] [1997] 3 SLR(R) 46 at 112.

[108] Goh Chok Tong v Jeyaretnam Joshua Benjamin and Anor Action [1998] 2 SLR(R) 971.

[109] Ibid, at 998–999.

[110] [1995] 1 SLR(R) 856.

[111] [1996] 3 SLR(R) 942.

[112] Ibid, at 1000–1001.

[113] [1997] 3 SLR(R) 46 at 95.

[114] [1979–1980] SLR(R) 24.

> carry more weight than that of a lesser individual and his hearers would be inclined to believe that there must be something in the accusation he was making.[115]

This was affirmed in the Court of Appeal in the following words:

> It was a grave slander perpetrated deliberately and not only without regard to the truth but knowing that it was untrue. It was perpetrated for political gain not caring what distress it would cause and what harm it would inflict on the personal and political reputation of an incumbent prime minister.[116]

This case set the benchmark for the quantum of damages. Lee received S$130,000 on the basis that his 'political and personal reputation' had been harmed by the offending words. In *Lee Kuan Yew v Seow Khee Leng*,[117] the Court referred to this benchmark and held that the slanders under consideration were 'more serious than that in the *Jeyaretnam* case' and that in view of the fact that the award was made nine years earlier and that since 'the value of money has diminished', the award of S$250,000 'would be a fair and just compensation for this very serious slander.'

In *Lee Kuan Yew v Davies Derek Gwyn & Ors* (1989),[118] the Court held that the libelous statements 'cast serious imputations' on Lee 'as a man and as the Prime Minister of Singapore', and that this was made worse by the fact that the *Far Eastern Review* was 'not a sensational daily newspaper' but a weekly 'read generally by people in the business and financial communities and the intelligentsia.'[119] The High Court considered the *Jeyaretnam* and *Seow* cases served 'merely as illustrations of the amounts awarded' and held that it was 'fair and reasonable' for the plaintiff to be awarded S$230,000.[120] In *Lee Kuan Yew & Anor v Vinocur John & Ors and Another Suit*,[121] the High Court considered the standing of the parties and the culpability of the defendants in determining the quantum of damages. Once again, the Court considered it germane that the three plaintiffs were 'the top three Ministers of the Government' and that the defamatory attack on them 'would cause grievous harm to them in the discharge of the functions of their office and indignation on their part as it was an attack on the very core of their political credo.'[122]

Up till *Tang Liang Hong*'s case,[123] the courts have been consistent in basing the quantum of damages on the harm done to the plaintiff's political reputation and suitability for high office. But in *Tang's* case, Chao Hick Tin J (as he then was) took into consideration six factors: (a) the nature of the defamatory remark; (b) the conduct, position and standing of the plaintiff; (c) the mode and extent of the publication; (d) the defendant's conduct from the date the defamatory remarks were made right up

---

[115] Ibid, at 40.

[116] [1979–1980] SLR(R) 255, at 264,

[117] [1988] 2 SLR(R) 252, at 261.

[118] Lee Kuan Yew v Davies Derek Gwyn and Ors [1989] 2SLR(R) 544.

[119] Ibid, at 601.

[120] Ibid, at 602.

[121] [1996] 1 SLR(R) 840.

[122] Ibid, at 55.

[123] [1997] 2 SLR(R) 81.

to judgment, including the absence or refusal of any retraction or apology; (e) other aggravating or mitigating circumstances; and (f) malice.[124] After considering all the earlier cases, Chao J noted that 'substantial damages' were awarded 'against defendants who attacked the honesty, integrity or character of public figures.' He then took as his benchmark, the $400,000 damages awarded in *Lee Kuan Yew v Vinocur John* (1996)[125] and proceeded to hold that it was 'beyond doubt that the level of aggravation in *Vinocur* was nowhere near that of the present cases' and that he 'ought to take the very high level of aggravation into account in assessing quantum.'[126] On this basis, Chao J proceeded to make 25 separate awards in respect of 13 separate actions. The Court of Appeal upheld Chao J's judgment but revised the damages downwards on the grounds that Chao J had 'double counted' the aggravating factors in the case.

What is clear from our review of the cases is the fact that the courts have always considered the *status* of the plaintiff to be of the utmost importance in determining the quantum of damages to be awarded. The actual harm suffered appears to be irrelevant in this matrix. For plaintiffs of the same 'status', the amounts awarded would be similar although there is no legal basis for the baseline figure. In Singapore, that baseline was established by the first *Lee Kuan Yew v Jeyaretnam* case in 1979, revised nine years later in when Lee sued Seow Khee Leng, and incrementally added to since.

4.11 Conclusion

The law concerning defamation of politicians and public figures in Singapore is highly unsatisfactory as the courts have given short shrift to the Constitution. Instead of reading the common law in a manner that would comport with the Constitution and accordingly maximizing the guarantees of freedom of speech and expression to all citizens, the courts have subjected the Constitution to the dynamic vacillations of the common law. The balance, between individual liberty and personal reputation, has tilted completely in favor of the latter. This creates two problems.

First, the test for defamation, not being codified, nor subjected to constitutional primacy, may be varied subjectively as we saw in *Jeyaretnam v Goh Chok Tong & Ors* case. In that case, the Court would have had to absolve Jeyaretnam from all liability had it relied on the natural and ordinary meaning of the words he uttered. Instead, the court found him liable because it held that those same words carried a secondary innuendo meaning that defamed the plaintiffs.

Second, by refusing to accord the Constitution primacy, the courts have precluded any discussion on the possible exceptions and defenses that may be applied in defamation suits involving politicians and public characters. In *Jeyraretnam v Lee Kuan Yew*

[124] Ibid, at 105.

[125] [1996] 1 SLR(R) 840.

[126] [1997] 2 SLR(R) 81, at 110.

(1990), the Court of Appeal rejected the *Sullivan* defense because it was too American—that it had its basis in the First Amendment to the American Constitution which was very different from Singapore's Article 14. While this may well be true, it does not absolve the courts from taking a more serious view of the Constitution. If the courts had taken Article 14 rights more seriously, they would have tried to read the common law of defamation in a manner that would have maximized, rather than minimized citizens' rights under Article 14. This requires the courts to consider issues like raising the requirement for the tort to be established, or affording the defendant more defenses and qualified privileges.

Third, the freedom of speech and expression is further chilled by the award of huge damages by the courts since 1979. These damages, 'at large' as they are, do not in any way reflect the actual damage suffered by the plaintiffs and are based on an arbitrary baseline which the courts arrived at in *Lee Kuan Yew v Jeyaretnam* (1979), buttressed by *Lee Kuan Yew v Seow Khee Leng* (1988), and built on since. The key basis for the quantum of damages appears to be that of status, and the amounts awarded depend on who the plaintiff happens to be. The bigger his or her public reputation, the more damages will be awarded.

Thio Li-ann has posited what she calls a 'differentiated regime for defamation damages' which categorizes plaintiffs into four tiers.[127] In the top tier are political leaders 'where defamation causes injury to both personal reputation as well as the institutional reputation of government'. Next are non-political public figures 'in business, industry and the professions' who are likely to get higher damages because of 'their higher social standing and devotion to public service. The third tier comprises prominent figures 'such as businessmen who are not national leaders or involved in public affairs' but who nonetheless get higher awards on account of the 'damage done to their professional reputations.' The lowest tier comprises ordinary private individuals. Reputation, Thio asserts:

> ... is thus tied to social standing and contribution to the public welfare and the worth of one's reputation affects the quantum of damages awarded in defamation cases. The Singapore version of the public figure or public leader doctrine does not go towards enhancing the scope of free speech, but goes to a higher quantification of damages, reflecting the prioritisation or valorisation of reputation.[128]

The continued reliance on precedent cases to determine the quantum of damages for defamation is unsustainable. At some point, courts need to return to the basic principles upon which damages were awarded in the first place. It may perhaps be sobering and edifying to end with the Court of Appeal's caveat on this matter:

> ... As reflected in those precedent cases, substantial damages have been awarded for defamation. Indeed, there appears to be a trend of such damages rising steadily and significantly over the past few years, and in a few recent cases, each successive award appeared to overtop the preceding one. Such a trend should be discouraged; otherwise, damages for defamation

---

[127] Thio Li-ann, *A Treatise on Singapore Constitutional Law* (Singapore: Academy Publishing, 2012) at 837.
[128] Ibid.

> would mount and eventually become extremely high, ranking almost with the grossly exorbitant awards so often made by juries in other jurisdictions. Lest it should be misunderstood, we are not suggesting in any way that there should be a cap placed on quantum of damages for defamation.... Each case depends on its own facts and there is a great deal of factual diversity in defamation cases. However, we wish to stress that damages, even for defamation, should fall within a reasonable bracket so that what is awarded *represents a fair and reasonable sum which is proportionate to the harm and injury occasioned to the victim* who has been unjustly defamed. [emphasis mine][129]

[129] [1997] 3 SLR(R) 576, at 635.

Chapter 5
The Constitutional Value of the Guarantee Clause

Raunaq Jaiswal

Abstract The Constitutions of the United States, Australia, and India were drafted after a period of internal violence. From a historical perspective, the drafters of the constitutions in the United States, Australia, and India included this provision right in the aftermath of the Shays Rebellion, the Shearers Strike and the violence after the Partition of India. With a view to preserve the federal government, and to safeguard to prevent any future governments from resorting to tyrannical rule, the drafters included the Guarantee Clause. Conceptually, this provision confers a constitutional obligation on the Federal Union to, firstly, protect the States from external and internal dangers, and secondly, ensure that States govern according to the Constitution. The Clause, studied from a comparative perspective, reveals contradictions between the historic purpose for which it was included in the first place, and its normative utility. From a normative perspective, the Guarantee Clause has been utilized by some Executives as an enabling clause to authorize the domestic deployment of the armed force, often indefinitely and without any legislative review. This conflict between the historical and normative values cloaks the original intent of the Guarantee Clause in the Constitution—i.e., a provision meant to strengthen the institutions of the democracy, vertically and horizontally, in order to prevent their abuse at the hands of a tyrannical Government. Comparative historical and normative values of the Guarantee Clause illuminate inconsistencies in the application, and a divergence in the conceptual understanding and the contemporary utility of the Guarantee Clause, especially in the Indian context, where the armed forces have been deployed in some regions indefinitely. This indefinite deployment of armed forces domestically is inconsistent with the original intent of the Clause. Based on this, this paper argues that any deployment of armed forces for "domestic violence" and "internal disturbance" under the Guarantee Clause should be firstly, temporary in nature, and secondly open to periodic parliamentary review.

This paper is based on the author's LLM thesis submitted to the Central European University. The necessary permissions have been obtained from CEU to publish this work here.

R. Jaiswal (✉)
Jindal Global Law School, O.P. Jindal Global University, Sonipat, Haryana, India
e-mail: rjaiswal@jgu.edu.in

M. John et al. (eds.), *The Indian Yearbook of Comparative Law 2020*, The Indian Yearbook of Comparative Law, https://doi.org/10.1007/978-981-99-5467-4_5

5.1 Introduction

There have been moments in history that have been memorialized and immortalized by the Constitutions.[1] The drafters of the constitutions that follow such historic moments display a tendency to be influenced by these events and exhibit a desire to include some constitutional benefits or repair the errors of the previous constitutional system. Such an expression of intent behind including constitutional provisions of this sort can easily be understood by the references the drafters of these constitutions make during the debates in the conventions, and the essence of the constitutional provisions that follow can tacitly be retrospective introspections on averting the irrationalities of the past. The inclusion of the Guarantee Clause in the Constitutions is one such interesting symbol of retrospective introspection of the framers, and emblematic of the hope that the rights and liberties of future generations would be protected.[2] Broadly, the Guarantee Clause places a *positive* obligation on the Federal Government to protect the States from being invaded and from domestic violence. This obligation is expected to be discharged by the Federal Executive by deploying armed forces within the borders of their own country. It is telling that internal violence has been the defining moment which underlines the inclusion of Guarantee Clauses in constitutions.

The textual underpinnings of these provisions trace their lineage to the first limb of Montesquieu's famous dictum, "*that should popular insurrection happen in one of the States* (sic), *the others are able to quell it.*"[3] Before incorporating this provision in the Constitution, Madison and other drafters of the respective at their Constitutional Conventions modified this dictum so that in its present incarnation, the Guarantee Clause empowers the Federal Executive to protect the States of the Federation not only from "popular insurrections" but also from invasions and domestic violence, which the Federal Executive can suppress by deploying the armed forces under the guise of rhetorical semantics which seem to signify the gravity of the situation. Textually, the Guarantee Clause provisions in the constitutions of the United States, Australia, and India are similar, but with three main differences. *Firstly*, the Guarantee

---

[1] *See* Bruce Ackerman, "The Holmes Lectures: The Living Constitution" (2007) 120 Harvard Law Review 1737, 1762–63.

[2] In this article, the phrase Guarantee Clauses is used as a shorthand to collectively refer to Article IV Section 5.4 of the American Constitution, Section 119 of the Australian Constitution and Article 355 of the Indian Constitution. U.S. Constitution, Article IV, Section 5.4 which reads as—"The United States shall guarantee to every state in this union a republican form of government and shall protect each of them against invasion; and on application of the legislature, or of the executive (when the legislature cannot be convened) against domestic violence"; Australian Constitution, Section 119 which reads as—"Protection of States from invasion and violence—The Commonwealth shall protect every State against invasion and, on the application of the Executive Government of the State, against domestic violence"; Constitution of India, Article 355 which reads as—"Duty of the Union to protect States against external aggression and internal disturbance It shall be the duty of the Union to protect every State against external aggression and internal disturbance and to ensure that the government of every State is carried on in accordance with the provisions of this Constitution".

[3] *See* Montesquieu, *The Spirit of Laws* (first published 1752. Thomas Nugent tr, 2003) 54; *See also* James Madison, "The Federalist No. 43" in The Federalist Papers (Jacob E. Cooke ed, 1961).

Clause in the United States provides the States of the Federation with three forms of protections, namely, a republican form of government, and protection against invasion and domestic violence. The Australian Constitution provides for protection against invasion and domestic violence but does not provide for a republican form of government. The Indian Constitution for protections against internal disturbance and external aggression as well as a duty to ensure that the government of every state is carried on in accordance with the provisions of the Constitution. *Secondly,* the provision in India does not contain any mention about a request for Federal Assistance being made by States, and as such, envisages that a *suo moto* deployment is possible, as opposed to its American and Australian counterparts, which envisages that a request for federal assistance must be made by the State Government. *Thirdly,* in Australia, the request for federal assistance is made by the Executive Government of the State, while its American counterpart stipulates that the request for assistance can be made by the State Legislature in the first instance and should they be unable to convene, it can be made by the Executive of the State, while the Indian provision is however silent on this aspect.

A textual reading of these clauses does not indicate any discernible constitutional limit on the duration for which armed forces may be deployed domestically, nor do they indicate any mechanism for oversight over the actions of the armed forces. Moreover, the open-ended nature of the terms "internal disturbance", "external aggression", and "domestic violence" do not give any indication about the severity of disorder that would justify the deployment of armed forces. In particular, there is no indication in the constitutions as to what powers this constitutional provision grants to the Federation, and how is the Federation supposed to discharge its obligations to the States in pursuance to fulfilling their constitutional obligations nor is there any understanding on what were the situations which have been construed as situations of "invasion", "domestic violence", or "internal disturbance" or "external aggression". In the absence of any textual indications, it is difficult to understand the scope of these powers and what judicial safeguards may exist to review government actions when "*abuses creep in one part...*" so as to be "*...reformed by those that remain sound.*"[4]

The contemporary utility of the Guarantee Clause indicates that Executive in the United States, Australia, and India use the powers under the Guarantee Clause in a manner that is neither consistent with the purpose for which this provision was envisaged nor in its textually permissible interpretations.[5] A perfunctory glance would show that it has served merely as a constitutional justification for deploying the armed forces supposedly domestically, for a variety of reasons, which may range

---

[4] *See* James Madison, "The Federalist No. 43" in The Federalist Papers (Jacob E. Cooke ed, 1961).

[5] *See*, e.g., Khagesh Gautam, "Martial Law In India: The Deployment Of Military Under The Armed Forces Special Powers Act, 1958" (2018) 24 Southwestern Journal of International Law 177; Michael Head, "Another Expansion of Military Call Out Powers in Australia: Some Critical Legal, Constitutional and Political Questions" (2019) 5 UNSW Law Journal Forum 1, 14 (2019).

from sporadic violence, suppressing the exercise of freedom of peaceful protests,[6] or to something as drastic as turning away immigrants and refugees.[7] In effect, the contemporary understanding of this clause seems quite limited in its purpose which is not consistent with the scope of the powers of the Guarantee Clause. To support this argument, this article will rely on the contextual situations surrounding the drafting of this provision to highlight, *firstly*, that the scope of powers envisages a greater threshold of violence than what its purpose is perceived as these days, as such, the argument will be that the proper scope of the terms "domestic violence", "internal disturbance", "invasion" and "external aggression", as conceived by the drafters of this provision anticipated violence of a far greater magnitude, than mere law and order problems for which it is being used for; *secondly*, that the deployment of armed forces domestically in the exercise of the powers given by the Guarantee Clause is nothing but a de facto proclamation of emergency within a State, and as is the norm with any emergency proclamation of in a democratic country, they need to be temporary and should be open to periodic parliamentary review. As a result of these, it will be submitted that recourse to such powers should be taken in the rarest of cases subject to strict procedural safeguards to prevent the abuse of these powers.

Consequently, this paper, in the first part draws upon the debates and discussions during the drafting of the Guarantee Clause in the respective constitutions and attempts to define the scope of powers under it; the second part studies the statutory embodiments of this provision. In effect, the purpose of this article is to analyze the historical and normative values of the Guarantee Clause. It does not discuss the entire gamut of issues surrounding the deployment of armed forces, such as the situations of natural calamities, even though deployments in such situations may be justified. What it does argue is that the exercise of the powers under the guarantee clause to deploy armed forces domestically dehors the spirit of the constitution, and while they may be necessary to meet the exigencies of the situation, an exercise of this power to meet situations of "domestic violence" and "internal disturbance" should be firstly, temporary, and secondly, open to periodic parliamentary review.

5.2 The Historical Purpose of the Guarantee Clause

To understand the scope of the Guarantee Clause, a review of the debates of the constitutional convention is necessary to illuminate the intention of the framers for including this provision in their respective constitutions so as to understand the

[6] *See* Special Correspondent, "Anti-Citizenship Bill protests: Army deployed in Assam, Tripura; Internet suspended" *The Hindu* (11 December 2019) <https://www.thehindu.com/news/national/other-states/anti-citizenship-bill-protests-army-deployed-in-assam-tripura-internet-suspended/article30277108.ece> accessed on Jun. 2, 2020; Christine Hauser, "What Is the Insurrection Act of 1807, the Law Behind Trump's Threat to States?" *New York Times* (Jun. 2, 2020) <https://www.nytimes.com/article/insurrection-act.html> accessed on Jun. 2, 2020.

[7] *See, Ruddock v Vadalaris* [2001] FCA 1329; *Sarbananda Sonowal v Union of India* [2005] 5 SCC 665.

inherent constitutional limitations of this provision. This will highlight the purpose of the Clause and it will also shed light on what kind of situations amounted to "domestic violence", "internal disturbance", "invasion", and "external aggression" as envisaged by drafters of this Constitutional provisions and the inherent limitations they implicitly place on the exercise of this power.

5.2.1 United States

Under the Articles of Confederation, the Congress lacked the constitutional mandate to sanction or coerce the States to comply with the Federal Government's "desideratum". As a result, one of the things that was severely impeded was the Congress's power to maintain armed forces.[8] The Shays Rebellion, in particular, highlighted the problems this could cause, as suppressing an internal rebellion became "one of the most pressing national issues" in 1786.[9] In their response to suppress this rebellion of some roughly 1800 farmers, the Congressional Committee had to highlight the necessity for federal aid to suppress the insurgents, which if not achieved, will potentially "subvert the government" and put the United States in a civil war.[10] A resolution was slowly passed which ultimately paved the way for the Congress to begin the process of raising money to fund the military which could suppress the rebellion.[11] These difficulties in the design of the Articles of Confederation highlighted the need to include a provision to centralize the power in the Union so as to ensure the domestic tranquility of the States. Having understood that a difficulty persisted in calling the armed forces in time of exigencies which made it difficult to have troops at dispersal expeditiously, the members sought to redress this flaw by including a new provision that would cure these defects.[12] James Madison was quick to identify this issue. In his communications to Washington highlighting the vices of the political system of the United States, he highlighted the importance to include such a provision, highlighting the difficulties in centralization of the federal system in times of crisis, and the consequences which the double-edged sword of despotism

[8] *See* Editorial Note to James Madison, "Vices of the Political System of the United States' <https://founders.archives.gov/documents/Madison/01-09-02-0187> (last accessed 3 June 2020); Michael Cain and Keith Dougherty, 'Suppressing Shays' Rebellion: Collective Action and Constitutional Design under the Articles of Confederation" (1999) 11(2) Journal of Theoretical Politics, 233, 233.

[9] Michael Cain and Keith Dougherty, "Suppressing Shays' Rebellion: Collective Action and Constitutional Design under the Articles of Confederation" (1999) 11(2) Journal of Theoretical Politics, 233, 233.

[10] Michael Cain and Keith Dougherty, "Suppressing Shays' Rebellion: Collective Action and Constitutional Design under the Articles of Confederation" (1999) 11(2) Journal of Theoretical Politics, 233, 234.

[11] Ibid.

[12] *See* Jonathan Elliot, *The Debates in the Several State Conventions on the Adoption of the Federal Constitution as Recommended by the General Convention at Philadelphia in 1787*, vol 2 (1888) 521–22. For a summary on the same issue, *see* Ryan C. Williams, "The 'Guarantee' Clause" (2018) 132 Harvard Law Review 602, 645–52.

and domestic violence would trigger within the Federation without an obligation to "guaranty" the States from future "internal or external dangers".[13]

To resolve this imperfection, the framers of the U.S. Constitution sought to include a new provision in the proposed constitution, which would guarantee the States protection from insurrections, domestic violence, and internal disturbance and would ensure a "republican form of government *and* territory".[14] To do so, the members of the Convention proposed to include a new provision which would impose an obligation on the Federal Government to "*prevent establishment of governments which are not republican; protect each state against internal commotion and; against external invasion*" with the final point noting that the guarantee "*shall not operate in the last case without an application from the legislature of a state.*"[15] It was pointed out by the members of the convention that it would be antithetical to the purpose of preserving the Federation if no collateral obligation to protect the states against "…dangerous commotions, insurrections and rebellions"[16] existed. As such it would not only be dangerous to prevent the president from acting in times of necessity but also be antithetical if the Federal Government was to remain a spectator due to a perceived lack of authority to suppress rebellions *against* States, and internal subversions consequently triggered violence in between States.[17]

However, those cynical of the Guarantee Clause highlighted that the propensity to enable deployment of armed forces even in aid of civil authorities could likely result in the same sort of despotism that the framers were trying to avoid.[18] The members

---

[13] Madison to Washington—16 April 1787 "An article should be inserted expressly guarantying the tranquility of the States against internal as well as external dangers." *See* James Madison, "Vices of the Political System of the United States" <https://founders.archives.gov/documents/Madison/01-09-02-0187> (last accessed 3 June 2020). *See also* Joseph Story, *Commentaries on the Constitution* (1829) ¶1808, who notes—

> The want of a provision of this nature was felt, as a capital defect in the plan of the confederation, as it might in its consequences endanger, if not overthrow, the Union. Without a guaranty, the assistance to be derived from the national government in repelling domestic dangers, which might threaten the existence of the state constitutions, could not be demanded, as a right, from the national government.

[14] *See,* the discussions on the 5 June in Max Farrand, *The Records of the Federal Convention of 1787*, vol. 1 (1907) 121.

[15] Max Farrand, *The Records of the Federal Convention of 1787*, vol 2, (1907) 173–74.

[16] Max Farrand, *The Records of the Federal Convention of 1787*, vol 2, (1907) 47 (discussions on 18 July).

[17] Max Farrand, *The Records of the Federal Convention of 1787*, vol 2, (1907) 47 (discussions on 18 July). *See also* Alexander Hamilton, "The Federalist No. 21" in *The Federalist Papers* (Jacob E. Cooke ed, 1961) who put forward a similar line of reasoning by claiming that it was sheer good fortune for the Americans that the "despotism of Massachusetts" had not been headed by a Caesar, as then it would have been difficult to predict the collateral damage it would have had on the liberties of people living in the nearby States.

[18] *See* Jonathan Elliot, *The Debates in the Several State Conventions on the Adoption of the Federal Constitution as Recommended by the General Convention at Philadelphia in 1787*, vol 3 (1888) 417–28 (discussions on 14 June 1788).

of the Convention were also divided in their opinions as to when the president would be empowered to deploy the armed forces.[19] While a general agreement was there that it was necessary to prevent an "*insurrection*" akin to the Shays' Rebellion,[20] the members of the committee were divided in their opinions when it came to lowering this threshold for preventive federal intervention in the form of "domestic violence", and the amendment which mandated this lower threshold was agreed to by a margin of just one vote.[21] It is interesting to note that, while the term "insurrection" was used to describe the Shays Rebellion by some members of the convention,[22] the expression domestic violence remained ambiguous. By some scholarly accounts, it connoted a lower threshold for seeking federal assistance, in that, the phrase envisaged situations of "riots or disturbances within a state (as opposed to foreign attack)"[23] as opposed to situations of higher threshold implicated by the term "insurrection".

Since there were apprehensions that federal military interventions might interfere with the autonomy of the States, Madison clarified that the proper threshold justifying an intervention would be when the States comprising the Federation, and in effect, the society comprising it, are threatened by an—

> [A]*rmed hostility from another political entity not only against foreign hostility, but against ambitious or vindictive enterprises of its more powerful neighbours.*[24]

For Madison, a guarantee of a republican form of government consequently acts as one of the three layers of obligatory protections which the Union has toward the States, which explains his argument that the inclusion of a powerful executive in certain situations was necessary to prevent the risk of insurrection, rebellion, invasion, or domestic violence, which he felt would subvert the constitutional order, and therefore take away with it the order of constitutional rights.[25] In effect, according to him, protection from invasion alluded to two considerations, namely, from neighboring foreign states, which could be referred to the neighboring colonies, and from the States of the Federation themselves, which was perhaps a vague reference to

---

[19] Ibid 417–420 (John Marshall) (14 June 1788).

[20] *See* Jonathan K. Waldrop, "Rousing the Sleeping Giant - Federalism and the Guarantee Clause" (1999) 15 Journal of Law and Politics 267, 272 (1999).

[21] Max Farrand, *The Records of the Federal Convention of 1787*, vol 2, (1907) 466 (James Madison, 30 August).

[22] Kevin M. Wagner, "Rewriting the Guarantee Clause: Justifying Direct Democracy in the Constitution" (2010) 47 Willamette Law Review 67, 77–78.

[23] *See* Jack M. Balkin, *Living Originalism* (2011) 37. Some commentators have put forward the notion that the phrase domestic violence was "*interpreted to be a restricted violence of a sufficient magnitude to constitute an insurrection.*" *See also* Report of the Congressional Research Service, *The Posse Comitatus Act and Related Matters: The Use of the Military to Execute Civilian Law* (2018) 7, which relies on the definition put forward by Bennet Milton Rich in his book *Presidents and Civil Disorder* (1941).

[24] James Madison, "The Federalist No. 43" in *The Federalist Papers* (Jacob E. Cooke ed, 1961).

[25] Ibid. "It will be much better that the violence in such cases should be repressed by the superintending power, than that the majority should be left to maintain their cause by a bloody and obstinate contest." *See also,* ibid "...and that it is a sufficient recommendation of the federal Constitution that it diminishes the risk of a calamity for which no possible constitution can provide a cure."

what Hamilton had previously warned about, i.e., had the rebellion of 1787 been led by a Caesar, the liberties of the people of neighboring states would have been trampled upon.[26] As for the threshold of intervention in times of domestic violence, Madison was of the view federal intervention would be justified only in such situations which are likely to produce a "bloody and obstinate contest".[27] Hamilton however envisaged a narrower view. According to him, the duty of the federation to repel "domestic dangers" connoted violence that threatens the existence of the State Government and renders them powerless spectators of the violence besieging the States.[28] It is clear that the purpose which Madison envisaged this Clause would be serving as a constitutional embodiment of Montesquieu's dictum—

> [T]*hat should popular insurrection happen in one of the States, the others are able to quell it. Should abuses creep in one part, they are reformed by those that remain sound.*[29]

Concerns and fears were raised by some members, highlighting that the powers of the Guarantee Clause and the way it seeks to operate bear an inherent propensity to be abused.[30] Concerns were also raised as to the necessity to have an armed force at all, chief among them by Governor Randolph who questioned the necessity of having an armed force rather than a defensive armed force. Madison in his speech at the Virginia Ratifying Convention, sought to dispel the fears of other members, by highlighting that the necessity of having an armed force will be protected from abuse by their military discipline.[31] According to him, a disciplined militia under the control of the Congress could function *only* in times of "obvious necessity", and as

---

[26] Alexander Hamilton, "The Federalist No. 21" in *The Federalist Papers* (Jacob E. Cooke ed, 1961).

[27] James Madison, "The Federalist No. 43" in *The Federalist Papers* (Jacob E. Cooke ed, 1961).

[28] Alexander Hamilton, "The Federalist No. 21" in *The Federalist Papers* (Jacob E. Cooke ed, 1961).

[29] James Madison, "The Federalist No. 43" in *The Federalist Papers* (Jacob E. Cooke ed, 1961).

[30] *See*, e.g., The Federal Farmer, "The Antifederalist No. 18" in *The Anti-Federalist Papers* (Ralph Ketcham ed, 1986) ("*it may be proper to add, that the militia of any state shall not remain in the service of the union, beyond a given period, without the express consent of the state legislature.*"). *See also* Jonathan Elliot, *The Debates in the Several State Conventions on the Adoption of the Federal Constitution as Recommended by the General Convention at Philadelphia in 1787*, vol 3 (1888) 378–98 (Speech of Mr. Mason), wherein it is noted that—

> unless there be some restrictions on the power of calling forth the militia...we may very easily see that it will produce dreadful oppressions. It is extremely unsafe, without some alterations...This would harass the people so much that they would agree to abolish the use of the militia, and establish a standing army...If gentlemen say that the militia of a neighbouring state is not sufficient, the government ought to have power to call forth those of other states, the most convenient and contiguous...But in this case, the consent of the state legislatures ought to be had. On real emergencies, this consent will never be denied, each state being concerned in the safety of the rest.

[31] Jonathan Elliot, *The Debates in the Several State Conventions on the Adoption of the Federal Constitution as Recommended by the General Convention at Philadelphia in 1787*, vol 3 (1888) 84–85.

such, their domestic role would be required only in times of necessity, to provide for the "*execution of laws, suppressing insurrections and repelling invasions...without [which]...liberties might be destroyed by domestic factions...and domestic tyranny be established*."[32] In effect, these powers granted the federal government the power, to call forth the *aid of the militia* to quell rebellions on the application of the legislature of any State, which was subsequently codified by the Congress.

5.2.2 Australia

Some scholars have indicated that the catalyst for including this provision was the Sheep Shearer's Strike of 1891.[33] According to them, the Sheep Shearers went on strike to protest against the Pastoralists' Agreement, which had a severe impact on the working conditions of the shearers.[34] In response, the labor from other colonies was called in, which resulted in the shearer's picketing railway stations. After receiving reports which "*suggested that the conflict could escalate*"[35] the Premier of Queensland, Samuel Griffith, who by some accounts is also credited with including the Guarantee Clause in the draft Constitution,[36] decided to deploy the armed forces "for special service in the aid of civil powers."[37] This **aid**, by one account, has been described as comprising of "permanent artillerymen armed with field pieces and Gatling Guns, mounted infantry of the Defence Forces and mounted infantry of the Defence Forces, besides armed police…".[38] While some have authors have claimed that Griffith's role was key to toning done the measures to be employed against the shearers,[39] Griffith's justification for deploying these armed forces on them are particularly revealing—

> It is all very well for the pastoralists to demand largely increased protection from the government. It appears to me that they wish to settle all the preliminaries of a war between classes to be carried on at the expense of the government. *The must understand that the forces of the government will not assume the position of being allies of one class only.*[40]

[32] Ibid 90.

[33] *See*, e.g., Michael Head and Scott Mann, "*Law in Perspective: Ethics, Society and Critical Thinking*" (UNSW Press, 2005) 357–59; Peta Stephenson, "Fertile Ground for Federalism - Internal Security, the States and Section 119 of the Constitution" (2015) 43 Federal Law Review 289, 293.

[34] Ibid 294.

[35] Ibid.

[36] Ibid 293.

[37] Ibid 294.

[38] Geoffrey Bolton and Helen Gregory, "Commemorative Address: The 1891 Shearers Strike Leaders: Railroaded?" (1992) 62 Labour History, 116, 116.

[39] R.B. Joyce, "S. W. Griffith: Towards the Biography of a Lawyer" (1974) 16 Historical Studies 235, 247.

[40] Ibid 247–48 (relying on Griffiths" telegram from 16 March 1889).

Griffith had called in the assistance of the armed forces of 1442 troops,[41] purportedly to *prevent* any escalation of the confrontation between the two groups in Queensland. By his understanding, the necessity for calling out federal troops could be based on providing *increased* protection, but it cannot be deployed to settle disputes between two groups of people, with the assumption that the armed forces will be expected to remain partial to a class of people. The necessity to provide "increased protection" could have possibly made him push forward for the inclusion of the guarantee clause in the Australian Constitution, which was initially not present in Andrew Inglis Clark's initial draft, despite it drawing several inspirations from the US Constitution.[42]

Sir Samuel Griffiths is also credited with introducing the Clauses into the draft Constitution in 1891.[43] In its original version, the clause read as —

> *The Commonwealth shall protect every state against invasion and, on the application of the Legislature of a State, or when the Legislature cannot be convened, on the Executive Government of a State, against domestic violence.*[44]

Doubts were raised as to what the proper scope of the word "invasion" connoted, and whether it was inclusive of the word "attack".[45] As such, an attempt was made by a member to lower the threshold of the Guarantee Clause in order to cover attacks. It was asserted by the members that the scope of the word "invasion" covered the word "attack" and given the geographical location that Australia enjoyed, they deemed it improbable that they will ever be attacked.[46] Members of the Convention were also quick to distinguish the fact that an invasion is preceded by an attack, and the meaning of the Clause incorporated attack as well.[47] One reason for this line of thought could be to understand whether any failure of the Federation to protect member states would give rise to claims against the Commonwealth for their failure to discharge their obligations.[48] An understanding between the members was ultimately arrived at, when it was pointed out to Mr. Gordon, that in times of necessity (or when the guns are booming), the categorial differentiations of attacks and invasions would be trivial. Apart from this, another issue that was discussed was the question of who

[41] Michael Head and Scott Mann, *Domestic Deployment of Armed Forces* (2009) 38.

[42] Peta Stephenson, "Fertile Ground for Federalism - Internal Security, the States and Section 119 of the Constitution" (2015) 43 Federal Law Review 289, 293.

[43] Ibid 293.

[44] Ibid.

[45] *See* Mr. Gordon's proposed amendment on Clause 112 of the draft Constitution, dated 8 February 1898, at <https://parlinfo.aph.gov.au/parlInfo/search/display/display.w3p;adv=yes;orderBy=customrank;page=0;query=%22domestic%20violence%22%20Dataset%3Aconventions;rec=1;resCount=Default> (last accessed 21 November 2021).

[46] Ibid.

[47] Ibid Mr. Barton's speech.

[48] Ibid. *See* Mr. Gordon's reply to the objection on debates on Clause 112 of the draft Constitution, dated 8 February 1898, at <https://parlinfo.aph.gov.au/parlInfo/search/display/display.w3p;adv=yes;orderBy=customrank;page=0;query=%22domestic%20violence%22%20Dataset%3Aconventions;rec=1;resCount=Default> (last accessed 21 November 2021).

would be the competent authority to invoke the powers of the clause, i.e., whether it shall be the Governor-General or whether the power should lie with the States or legislative.[49] A move was also made to include a clause that sought to empower the Governor-General to take recourse to these powers if he was of the opinion that a pressing necessity to preserve public peace existed, which was also negatived.[50]

In effect, instead of replicating the American provision, the members instead adapted the Clause with a slight variation, which made it possible for the State Executive to request the federal intervention at the first instance, rather than the state legislature, as it may not be possible for the legislature to convene during times of violence.

5.2.3 India

The reason which would explain the exclusion of the Governor's power and the inclusion of the Guarantee Clause in India could be understood from the context of the prevalent political situation in the princely state of Hyderabad where the Nizam had raised armed militia with a view to secede. As such, the Governor-General of India at that time, C. Rajagopalachari was compelled to declare a state of emergency due to "internal disturbance" on 13 September 1948,[51] and the Indian military proceeded to suppress the militia of the Nizam in less than a week.[52] While the terminology of "Police Action" was used to describe the federal intervention, it was nothing less than a military action to quell an armed rebellion.[53] and the mobilization of armed forces was made possible only due to the Governor-General's proclamation of emergency. On 3 October 1948, in the aftermath of the Police Action in Hyderabad, the Drafting Committee discussed the functional purpose of the guarantee clause in the United States and Australia and the need for conferring an obligation on the

---

[49] Ibid. Mr. Gordon's objection noting that the Governor-General is not a resident of the State.

[50] Ibid.

[51] *See* Emergency Proclamation by C. Rajagopalachari, Gazette of India, Pt. II sec 5.1 (13 September 1948) under the Government of India Act, 1935, 9 & 10 Geo. 5 c. 101, § 102. The said proclamation read—

> In pursuance of section 102 of the Government of India Act, 1935, I, Chakravarti Rajagopalachari, Governor-General of India, being satisfied that there is **imminent danger of the security of India being threatened by internal disturbance**, do by thus Proclamation, declare that a grave emergency exists whereby the security of India is threatened by internal disturbance.

[52] *See* Taylor C. Sherman, "The Integration Of The Princely State Of Hyderabad And The Making Of Postcolonial State In India, 1948–56" (2007) 44 The Indian Economic and Social History Review 489, 495–96.

[53] Sunil Purushotham, "Internal Violence: The 'Police Action' in Hyderabad," (2015) 57(2) Comparative Studies in Society and History 435, 440.

Federal Government to protect the States from domestic violence and invasion. This duty was entrusted to the Federal Executive to protect the States, as a situation, like in Hyderabad, may arise wherein the Governor of a State, when faced with the threat of imminent invasion or violence, may not be inclined to protect the State. However, the earlier drafts of the proposed constitution had empowered the **Governor of a State** to declare a 2-week state of emergency. It was not until the constituent assembly debates on the 3 August 1949,[54] Dr. Ambedkar moved a series of amendments to remove the Governor's power to declare an emergency from the draft constitution.[55]

Some scholars have been of the view that Dr. Ambedkar feared that the "*intense uncertainty and unprecedent violence…*,"[56] in Hyderabad threatened to replicate the violence of the partition.[57] It was a fear shared by other founding fathers.[58] To change this, Dr. Ambedkar moved two key amendments on the 3 August 1949. The first one was to repeal the power of the Governor of a State to declare a state of emergency for a period of two weeks. The second one was proposed to include draft Article 277-A (later Art. 355)[59] which according to Ambedkar, bore some resemblance to the American and Australian Guarantee Clause.[60] This provision, according to him, would be nothing more than a "pious declaration", would *not be* used to provide the Federal Government to make any law for the "peace, order and good government of States", the power for which would still reside within the powers allocated to the State.[61] From his understanding, any justification for interfering with

---

[54] Dr. Ambedkar Speech 3 August 1949—at volume 9, document number 110, paragraph 17, <https://www.constitutionofindia.net/constitution_assembly_debates/volume/9/> (last accessed 11 June 2020). Subsequent references to the Constituent Assembly Debates of India in this paper will not bear a link, but just the volume number, document number, date, and paragraph.

[55] *See* Dr. Ambedkar Speech 3 August 1949—at volume 9, document number 110, paragraph 21.

[56] Sunil Purushotham, "Internal Violence: The 'Police Action' in Hyderabad," (2015) 57(2) Comparative Studies in Society and History 435, 438.

[57] Ibid 439.

[58] *See* Selected Works of Jawaharlal Nehru, vol. 7 (S. Gopal ed. 1988) 185–86 (Letter to Lord Mountbatten, 3 July1948, informing him of Hyderabad's plans to invade Indian Union); ibid 206–7 (Letter to V.K. Krishna Menon, 15 August 1948, informing him of violence in the State of Hyderabad committed by the Razakars); and lastly, *see* ibid 222–223, Letter to V.K. Krishna Menon (29 August 1948).

> I am myself convinced that it is impossible to arrive at any solution of the Hyderabad problem by settlement or peaceful negotiations. Military action becomes essential; we call it, as you have called it, police action. We certainly do not call it here or elsewhere war, though soldiers will be involved. The question then limits itself to the time and manner of doing it. Any marked delay would have, as it is having, a very bad effect on our people and a feeling of desperation, and utter frustration will seize hold of them.

[59] As Members will see, Article 277-A says that it shall be the duty of the Union to protect every unit, and to maintain the Constitution. So far as such obligation is concerned, it will be found that it is not our Constitution alone which is going to create this duty and this obligation. Similar clauses appear in the American Constitution.

[60] *See* speech of Dr. Ambedkar on 3 August 1949—volume 9, document 110 paragraph 31.

[61] Constitution of India Sch. 7, List II Entry 1, 2.

the State's autonomy must flow from the authority placed by the Constitution on the Federal Government, and any interference by the Federal Government with the State's autonomy cannot be *"an invasion which is wanton, arbitrary and unauthorised by law..."*.[62]

This proposed amendment came under severe criticism from some members of the Assembly, who felt that the proposed amendment not only stripped away the autonomy of the States but also the vagueness of the phrase "internal disturbance" and the normative threshold which could justify a federal intervention.[63] Kamath, in particular, highlighted the Delphic nature of the proposed amendment, noting that Ambedkar on the one hand proposed to protect the States from undefined situations of internal disturbances which justified federal intervention and at the same time, provided the States the explicit power to preserve public order. Another criticism leveled against the text of the proposed amendment was the lack of clarity in the phrase "union" which lacked the clarity as to which branch of the Union Government could intervene,[64] and the presence of the conjoiner "and" between the situations of external aggression and internal disturbance, which was textually envisaged a situation of both external aggression and internal disturbance to be present before a federal intervention action could be justified. Other criticism that was levelled against the article related to overlapping powers conferred by concurrent emergency provisions, i.e., Art. 352 (draft articles 275) and 356 (draft article 278); the likelihood of emergency powers resulting in excessive federal intervention in State's domestic affairs, like in the times of colonial rule, and the withering effect it had on democracy.[65]

In his reply, Ambedkar explained that federal intervention would be on two grounds. Firstly, it can be at the request of the State, i.e., should the police be incapable or unequipped to do so, the first step would not be to invoke the powers under this provision, but to take recourse of the armed police (not the armed force); should this measure not succeed in quelling violence, then recourse may be taken to the armed forces. Secondly, it can be the Federal Government taking *suo moto* cognizance of the violence in the State and deploying the armed forces. In this situation, it is understood that the Federal Government cannot be a bystander as the violence erupts in a state. However, before taking recourse to the powers under this clause, the procedure as envisaged in the debates, stipulates that first a notice be issued to the erring state, *then* a plebiscite to let the people elect their own leader, and only then can the powers under Art. 355 be exercised.[66] Despite the criticism leveled, Ambedkar's persuasive arguments held more weight in the assembly, and none of the criticisms against the

---

[62] *See* Dr. Ambedkar's Speech during the Constituent Assembly Debates on 3 August, 1949—volume 9, document 110 paragraph 31. ("Therefore, in order to make it quite clear that Articles 278 and 278-A are not to be deemed as a wanton invasion by the Centre upon the authority of the province, we, propose to introduce Article 277-A.").

[63] *See* H.V. Kamath's speech on 3 August 1949—volume 9, document 110 paragraph 31.

[64] *See* speech of Hriday Nath Kunzru—3 August 1949—volume 9, document 110 paragraph 113.

[65] Naziruddin Ahmed—3 August 1949—volume 9, document 110 paragraph 127.

[66] *See* speech of Dr. Ambedkar, 3 August 1949—volume 9, document 111 paragraph 49.

proposed amendment to the article of the draft constitution was admitted, and the draft article passed as per the wording it was tabled on, one week later.

It is perceivable that the Hyderabad incident was fresh in the minds of the members of the Drafting Committee when they sought to include a new draft provision on the 3rd of October.[67] The timing of the introduction of the Clause and the chronology of events, and the references to Dr. Ambedkar's understanding of the U.S. Constitutions all seem to allude to countless speculations, but it is not improbable that he was mindful of the historical context which led the United States to include this provision in their own constitution, in order to prevent any future occurrences of violent riots and armed rebellions, he placed an obligation on the Union to protect the States.[68] It is imperative to highlight how the Madisonian idea of the guarantee clause has seeped through in the Australian and Indian constitutions. It is essential to remember that the situations of necessity as envisaged by Madison relied heavily on the corrective remedies and obligations of the States on the State affected, "*in all for one, one for all*" manner, and the primacy of the onus is not necessarily falling solely on the President to ensure this, but only when the gravity of violent situations so demand, that he may resort to the domestic deployment of the armed forces to prevent further bloodshed.[69] A review of the drafting history of s 119 of the Australian Constitution illuminates other things that *suo moto* federal intervention at the behest of the Governor-General is not possible, as a state executive has to make a request for federal assistance. A review of the drafting history of Article 355, and documents which highlight the procedure of how this provision takes shape normatively illuminates that the provision was primarily meant to counter extreme violence which the police have been incapable of handling. While the draft article in the United States went through a lot of deliberations and a lot of criticisms and was revised several times to bear the text it bore ultimately, the clause was scarcely debated in Australia and India, and the provisions were essentially passed as proposed.

5.3 Contemporary Utility of the Guarantee Clause

By including the Guarantee Clause provision in their respective Constitutions, the benefits which the framers of the constitutions of United States, Australia and India were pursuing was that of preserving the new federation of States from crumbling in the face of adversity which could come in form of insurrections, invasions, rebellions and other acts of domestic violence. By including these provisions, the framers were also trying to avoid the ills that the lack of such provision would entail, namely the

[67] *See* B. Shiva Rao, *The Framing of India's Constitution: A Study*, vol 4 (1968) 368. The draft provision read as—"Duty of the Union to protect States against external aggression and domestic violence: It shall be the duty of the Union to protect every State against external aggression and domestic violence." The decision by the Committee was taken on 3rd October 1948.

[68] *See* Sunil Purushotham, "Internal Violence: The 'Police Action' in Hyderabad," (2015) 57(2) Comparative Studies in Society and History 435, 438–39.

[69] James Madison, "The Federalist No. 43" in *The Federalist Papers* (Jacob E. Cooke ed, 1961).

federal government's lack of authority to intervene in state matters when faced with situations of violence, the constitutional conundrum of how to protect the States, when their capabilities have been overrun.[70] At the same time, they were also trying to preserve the federation against rebellions that could come in the form of State Governments rebelling against the Federal Government.[71]

In spite of the intentions that the framers envisaged it will have on the Federation, and the role they presumed it would serve in the Constitution, and the repeated assurances which the framers had to offer that these provisions were above and beyond from being abused, textual ambiguities have provided some flexibility to the Constitutional Courts to put forward some controversial opinions,[72] which interpret the provisions of the Guarantee Clause without taking into account the proper purpose for which it was included in the constitution.[73] As we shall see in this section, the modern understanding which this Clause serves seems oriented toward only deploying the armed forces domestically, sometimes for routine law and order infractions, it is not consistent with the scope of the powers envisaged by the drafters of the Guarantee Clause.

5.3.1 United States

The Guarantee Clause, as envisaged, did not have any scope for unilateral federal intervention. The State Legislature had to make a request for Federal assistance, and, when the Legislature of the State was unable to convene, the State Executive had the capacity to request the assistance. Unilateral intervention while hotly debated has only been impliedly made possible on the grounds of extreme necessity at which point it would amount to a dereliction of duty owed by the Union to States to not intervene. The earliest statutory embodiment of the Constitutional obligation to protect States from domestic violence and insurrection came in the form of the Calling Forth Act, 1792, which enabled the President of the United States to mobilize the militia for a maximum period of 30 days "*whenever the laws of United States...in any*

[70] Jonathan K. Waldrop, "Rousing the Sleeping Giant - Federalism and the Guarantee Clause" (1999) 15 Journal of Law and Politics 267, 272 (1999); Amanda L. Tyler, "The Forgotten Core Meaning Of The Suspension Clause" (2012) 125 Harvard Law Review 901, 965–68;Michael Morea, "Guaranteeing Republics to the Confederate States: A Guarantee Clause Justification for Lincoln's Response to Civil War" (2014) 42 Pepperdine Law Review 59, 62.

[71] *See* Stephen I. Vladek, "Emergency Power & The Militia Acts" (2004) 114 Yale Law Journal 151, 160–63.

[72] *See*, e.g., *Ruddock v Vadalaris* [2001] FCA 1329; *Sarbananda Sonowal v Union of India* [2005] 5 SCC 665, 725–27. *See also* J. Andrew Heaton, "The Guarantee Clause: A Role for the Courts" (1985) 16 Cumberland Law Review 477, 514–16.

[73] Sarbananda Sonowal's case is particularly revealing in this aspect, as a panel of three Supreme Court judges lead by Justice Mathur, held that illegal immigrants are a cause of external aggression. To reach this conclusion, the learned judge relied on the US Supreme Court judgement in *Chae Chan Ping v United States*, [1889] 130 U.S. 581. *See Sarbananda Sonowal v Union of India* [2005] 5 SCC 665, 720–27.

State...by combinations too powerful to be suppressed by ordinary course of judicial proceedings...or...the marshals....the same being notified to the President of the United States, by an associate justice or the district judge."[74]

It is interesting to note that this statutory provision was enacted following on the heels of the US Constitution, and perhaps capturing the spirit of Art. IV §4 the best too, provided for sanctions, in terms of temporary deployment of militia, when the Federal laws faced an opposition of such nature that judicial remedies and penalties for breach of law became difficult to implement, or in other words, it became impossible to hold the violators of the law accountable to justice, and, in such situations, a judge, a notification had to be issued by a judge to the US President. Subsequent versions of this act and their numerous amendments have completely obliterated these minimal safeguards and enlarged the grounds for deploying armed forces considerably. The current version of the Statute empowers the President, to *firstly*, at the behest of the State legislature or executive, deploy the armed forces to suppress insurrections[75]; *secondly,* to deploy the armed forces *suo moto* if the implementation of laws and recourse to judicial remedies become "impracticable"[76]; *thirdly*, (and most stunningly) to use the armed forces, to suppress insurrections, domestic violence, "*unlawful combination, or conspiracy*" which "hinders the execution of laws of that State..." which tramples upon the constitutional rights, privileges, immunities, which the authorities of that State are either "*unable, fail or refuse to protect...*"[77]; and, *fourthly*, prior to the deployment of the armed forces, the President has to, by a proclamation, order the "insurgents to disperse...to their abodes...*within a limited time.*"[78]

In order to understand how these provisions work in practice, a reference must be made to the recently declassified Field Manual of 1945 which notes that the military can be called out, *inter alia*, for the purposes of "*aiding the civil authorities at the request of the State,... [or an] emergency unexpected invasion, insurrection, or riot endangering the public property of the United States...so imminent as to*

[74] *See* Calling Forth Act of 1792s 2. *See also* Report of the Congressional Research Service, "The Posse Comitatus Act and Related Matters: The Use of the Military to Execute Civilian Law" (2018).

[75] *See* Federal Aid for State Governments 10 USCA 2016, s 251 which reads as—Whenever there is an insurrection in any State against its government, the President may, upon the request of its legislature or of its governor if the legislature cannot be convened, call into Federal service such of the militia of the other States, in the number requested by that State, and use such of the armed forces, as he considers necessary to suppress the insurrection.

[76] *See* Use of Militia and Armed Forces to Enforce Federal Authority 10 USCA 2016, s 252 which reads as—Whenever the President considers that unlawful obstructions, combinations, or assemblages, or rebellion against the authority of the United States, make it impracticable to enforce the laws of the United States in any State by the ordinary course of judicial proceedings, he may call into Federal service such of the militia of any State, and use such of the armed forces, as he considers necessary to enforce those laws or to suppress the rebellion.

[77] *See* Interference with State and Federal Law 10 USCA 2016, s 253.

[78] *See* Proclamation to Disperse 10 USCA 2016, s 254—Whenever the President considers it necessary to use the militia or the armed forces under this chapter, he shall, by proclamation, immediately order the insurgents to disperse and retire peaceably to their abodes within a limited time.

render it dangerous to await instructions from the War Department"[79] firstly at the behest of the State, in which case, the provisions of the guarantee clause will operate, i.e., the request should originate at the behest of the State Legislature or with the State Executive if situations require make it impossible for the legislature to convene,[80] and if an intervention is made at the behest of the President, the provisions of the Insurrection Act will be applicable, as such, intervention requested for any purposes apart from emergency measures and measures to protect public property, a proclamation demanding the "insurgents" to disperse has to be published before any action can be taken.[81]

5.3.2 Australia

In Australia, the Guarantee Clause provisions have been codified in the Defence Act of 1903. Since the Sydney Olympics, and the attack on the Twin Towers in New York, the penal provisions and justifications for mandating the deployment of armed forces have been steadily and surreptitiously increased without little public debate.[82] The scope of powers to deploy military domestically has been enlarged considerably after these two pieces of legislation.[83] The concept of domestic violence is mentioned in prospective terms, i.e., "domestic violence that is occurring or is likely to…"[84] occur or affect, and it is quite alarming to witness that the Act provides for the deployment of armed forces even if there is no visible indication as to the existence or imminence of a threat. The armed forces may be deployed for several reasons, such as to protect the property of the Commonwealth,[85] or critical infrastructure.[86] The most recent amendment, coming out in 2018, and purportedly in response to the recommendations of the State Coroner's Report,[87] further enhanced the ability of the Authorizing Ministers to advise the Governor-General to deploy the defence forces domestically for several broadly defined prospective or pre-existing threats, such as the threat of domestic violence or threat to public safety, both defined in broad vernacular encompassing both preventive actions, and, reaction to a threat or

[79] War Department, *The Field Manual of 1945*, (1945) 4.

[80] Ibid 5.

[81] Ibid 5–6.

[82] Michael Head, "Another Expansion of Military Call Out Powers in Australia: Some Critical Legal, Constitutional and Political Questions" (2019) 5 UNSW Law Journal Forum 1, 1.

[83] Peta Stephenson, "Fertile Ground for Federalism - Internal Security, the States and Section 119 of the Constitution" (2015) 43 Federal Law Review 289, 301.

[84] The Defence Act 1903, s 34 (Australia).

[85] Ibid s 33(1)(a)(i). *See also* Michael Head, "Another Expansion of Military Call Out Powers in Australia: Some Critical Legal, Constitutional and Political Questions" (2019) 5 UNSW Law Journal Forum 1, 4.

[86] The Defence Act 1903, ss 51H, 51 J, 51L (Australia).

[87] Michael Head, "Another Expansion of Military Call Out Powers in Australia: Some Critical Legal, Constitutional and Political Questions" (2019) 5 UNSW Law Journal Forum 1, 4.

perceived threat. Under this Act, an order to deploy armed forces can be issued by the Governor-General on the advice of the Authorizing Minister, if it is necessary to protect Commonwealth interests or the interests of the State and Territories. Such a deployment can be either a deployment to meet either a contingency or a real situation or instance, not limited to those of domestic violence.[88] Any such deployment of armed forces domestically occurs for a period of 20 days,[89] but the Governor-General has the power to prolong the order beyond this period if the Authorizing Ministers recommend it.[90] Under this Act, the armed forces have the power to search private properties without a warrant,[91] use force to the extent of causing a person's death. Apart from the safeguard of duration, the other safeguard that this act has is in form of review by the Independent National Security Legislation Monitor Act, every five years.[92]

5.3.3 India

One key area where the Guarantee Clause provision in India differs from its counterparts in the United States and Australia rests in the fact that it does not provide the State to request federal aid explicitly, highlighting that the Federal Government can intervene *suo moto*. To recall, the debates at the assembly highlights that Dr. Ambedkar was of the view that should it ever be imperative that recourse needs to be taken to Art. 355 by the Government, the Government must first issue a warning, then, dissolve the State Government, presumably by taking recourse to Art. 356, and should these measures fail, then only can recourse be taken to this provision. The Government has interpreted this provision as a source of power to enable the domestic deployment of armed forces in some regions for perpetuity.

The powers mentioned in the Indian version of the Guarantee Clause find their statutory embodiment in the Armed Forces Special Powers Act (1958).[93] When it was passed in the parliament, it was only deliberated upon for two hours,[94] and

[88] Ibid 1.

[89] The Defence Act 1903, s 37 (Australia).

[90] Ibid.

[91] Ibid s 51A.

[92] Ibid s 51 ZB.

[93] The Act was first passed as an ordinance in 1942, allowed to lapse shortly after independence, then promulgated as an ordinance from 1948 to 1957, and codified as a Statute in 1958. As such, the relevant portion of the "Objects and Reasons" clause to the Act reads as—"...*Keeping in view the duty of the Union under Article 355 of the Constitution...to protect every State against internal disturbance, it is considered desirable that the Central Government should also have the power to declare areas as 'disturbed', to enable its armed forces to exercise the special powers.*" *See* generally, *Naga People's Movement for Human Rights v Union of India* [1998] 2 SCC 109.

[94] *See* Gautam Navlakha, "Internal Militarisation: Blood on the Tracks" (1997) 32(6) Economic and Political Weekly 299, 306.

there were assurances that the legislation will only be a temporary measure[95] and shall be allowed to lapse after a year.[96] The Act conferred concurrent powers to the federally nominated State Governor and to the Federal Government to declare any or all part of a State where the Act extends as being a "disturbed area",[97] which is meant to serve as a justification for the domestic deployment of armed forces in that particular region. Once deployed in a "disturbed area" the armed forces have special powers, i.e., powers which are not prescribed or governed by the regular law provisions, but extraordinary powers outside the regular framework, such as using force "necessary…for the maintenance of public order"[98]… "even to the causing the death"[99] of any person who is acting in contravention of "any law and order for the time being in force in a disturbed area,"[100] and, the arresting a person without any warrant; and entering private premises without a search warrant.[101]

The absence of any textual limitations, or indications of constitutional limitations, or statutory limitations on the Executive, or the Legislature as to *how long* armed forces can be deployed in aid of civil authorities ensured a departure from the ethos of constitutionalism, as recourse was taken to these statutory provisions, when the appropriate action, according to some scholars, laid under the provisions of Art. 356,[102] which would have provided time-bound restrictions as well as the oversight of the Legislature in terms of periodic parliamentary review of the de facto emergency proclamations, which only the semantics classified as "internal disturbance". Some aspects of how these provisions work in practice have been clarified by the Reddy Commission, which, while being rejected by the Central Government in 2005, is nonetheless illuminating. The President, the report notes, is also empowered to act unilaterally, rather than wait for a request to be made by the State executive. In their opinion, the Committee Report notes that the Federal Government has flexibility in terms of the manner they choose to discharge their obligation toward the States, and as such, has the discretion to provide suggestions and assistance, initiate measures to prevent recurrence or may deploy the armed forces in aid of state police and magistracy. The Committee also suggested that when the armed forces are deployed, it is **implicative** that the State authorities have to cooperate and coordinate the forces, and should they lack such cooperation, the Federal Government can take further actions under Arts. 257 & 355. However, the most interesting point that the report

---

[95] Ibid 302.

[96] Ibid (Quoting from the debates from 1958 to highlight among other things that the nature of the powers they conferred were visible to all the members of the legislature, as the Home Minister GB Pant mentioned that "a regulation more or less on the lines of this bill was applicable to that area. It's a simple measure. It does not create any new offences. It only provides for the protection of the army when it has to deal with hostile Nagas.").

[97] Armed Forces Special Powers Act, 1958, s 3 (India).

[98] Ibid s 3(a).

[99] Ibid.

[100] Ibid.

[101] Ibid ss 3(a), 3(b).

[102] Surabhi Chopra, "National Security Laws in India: The Unravelling of Constitutional Constraints" (2015–2016) 17 Orlando Review of International Law 1, 15.

highlights is the issue pertaining to how a disturbed area notification may be revoked. According to the representation of the Home Minister, the armed forces would be "progressively withdrawn" from the regions once the capacity and standards of the police have reached the requisite levels.[103]

5.4 Limitations on the Utility of Guarantee Clause as Peacetime Emergency Power

5.4.1 Problems with Defining Internal Disturbance

The primary justification for the deployment of armed forces domestically in all the three countries under review is that of controlling "domestic violence" and "internal disturbance". The elements of what the phrases "disturbed area" or for that matter "internal disturbances" demand has not been objectively described by either the statute or the judicial opinions but has been left to the subjective prudence of the Government. The terminology itself is a child borne out of the politics of national security legislation, and as such, the definitions are as illuminative to understanding the situations of necessity as a rhetorical palindrome would be. The Defence Act, 1903, for instance, defines "domestic violence" as "domestic violence has the same meaning as in s 119",[104] while the Armed Forces Special Powers Act defines a disturbed area as "disturbed area means an area which is for the time being declared by notification to be a disturbed area."[105] The definitions provided by Australia and India in their respective legislations are indicative of this problem.

The problems with the lack of clarifications on the definitions here give rise to a plenitude of circumstances under which armed forces can be deployed without any safeguards to prevent their abuse. The fluidity of the definitions has been mitigated to some extent circumscribed by the secondary sources, which illuminate the practices. In Australia for example, the Government recently rejected the demands made by the Parliamentary Inquiry Committee which asked them to define the scope of "domestic violence".[106] Scholars have drawn on the history of the exercise of this power, to note that the term "domestic violence" encompasses "industrial disputes, protests, demonstrations, riots and many traditions forms of political opposition,

[103] It is a discussion for another day that the funding levels for the police modernization in the North-East have fallen by more than 50% over the past five years. *See* Parliament of India's Standing Committee Report on Security Situation in the North-Eastern States at page 30 (2018).

[104] The Defence Act 1903, s 31 (Australia).

[105] Armed Forces Special Powers Act, 1958, s 2(b) (India).

[106] Michael Head, "Another Expansion of Military Call Out Powers in Australia: Some Critical Legal, Constitutional and Political Questions" (2019) 5 UNSW Law Journal Forum 1, 4.

which may threaten the existence or institution of the states."[107] In the United States, a declassified Field Manual issued by the War Department on controlling domestic disturbances defines domestic disturbances as—

> manifestations of civil unrest or tension which take the form of demonstrations or rioting...[of] such proportions that civil authorities cannot maintain law and order by usual methods. Such disturbances may be caused by agitators, racial strife, controversies between employees and employers concerning wages or working conditions, unemployment, lack of housing or food, or other economic or social conditions. Looting of areas ravaged by storms, fires, floods, or other catastrophes may become so pronounced as to constitute a domestic disturbance. Public revulsion to serious crimes and feeling against suspected criminals may prompt groups of persons to attempt to take the law into their own hands, thereby creating a civil disturbance.[108]

Similarly, the Sarkaria Committee Report attempted to demystify what the term "internal disturbance" connotes. According to the Report, the phrase "internal disturbance", was differentiated in terms of the heightened degree of public disorder, which is widespread in nature, and also "endangering the security of state."[109] In such situations of widespread public disorder which threaten the security of India, the President is empowered to take action under Art. 355, which is to say, deploy federal armed forces *in aid of civil power*.[110] Similar observations were made by the Reddy Committee, which defined "internal disturbance" as representing very serious, large scale and sustained chaotic conditions over a large area of the State.[111] It is imperative to say that the classifications of violence here envisage a far lower threshold than the kind of violence and disorder which compelled Madison, Griffith and Ambedkar to include the guarantee clause within their constitutions. What is notable about all these definitions is that some of these can very well be law and order infractions rather than national security concerns.

This circularity in definitions has resulted in litigations. In the United States, in 1997, the State of California made a claim before the federal circuit court, stating that the Federal Government's inability to prevent swathes of immigrants crossing the federal borders unlawfully, constituted a violation of their obligation toward the States to protect them from invasion. The Court rejected their claim on the basis that the remedies they asked for, do not envisage judicially manageable standards. They also took the pains to elaborate that the word "**invasion**" as envisaged by Madison in Federalist No. 43, construed as **protections** in situations where a State is exposed to "*armed hostility from another political entity*".[112] On a different note, a two judge bench of the Indian Supreme Court in Sonowal's case took a different view,

---

[107] Peta Stephenson, "Fertile Ground for Federalism - Internal Security, the States and Section 119 of the Constitution" (2015) 43 Federal Law Review 289, 298 (relying on the definition laid out by Michael Head).

[108] War Department, *The Field Manual of 1945*, (1945) 14.

[109] *See* R.S. Sarkaria, *Report of The Sarkaria Commission* (1988) 7.03.04.

[110] Ibid 7.03.06.

[111] B.P. Jeevan Reddy, *Report of the Committee to Review the Armed Forces Special Powers Act* (2005) 68.

[112] California v. United State 104 F. 3d 1086, 1091 (C.A. 9) (Cal.) (1997).

noting that Government's inability to "illegal migration of Bangladeshi nationals" amounts to "external aggression and internal disturbance".[113] Similarly, in *Ruddock v Vadalaris,* the Australian High Court invoked a variation of the plenary powers doctrine, in order to permit the use of armed forces to turn away asylum seekers.[114]

5.4.2 Military Acting in Aid of Civil Authorities

The drafting history of the three countries indicates that the rationale for adopting these provisions was to protect the states from riots, rebellions, and insurrections, and from attacks and invasions from neighboring states. The provisions themselves did not presume an attack of the scale of war but an armed rebellion from within the State itself. The framers of this clause did not impose any constitutional limits, nor did they stipulate any time limit when the intervention period has to be allowed to lapse. The history of the political situations of these countries at the time these constitutions were being drafted, and the debates themselves highlight that the mechanism through which the Federation was supposed to fulfil this obligation was that of domestic deployment of armed forces in *aid* of civil authorities. The deployment of armed forces domestically, even if it is in aid of civil authorities is an indication that situations are of such gravity that situations of necessity exist which warrant recourse to these drastic measures, without a proclamation of a state of emergency.

The contemporary utility of the Guarantee Clause highlights that the scope of the clause has been predominantly confined to deploying armed forces to purportedly suppress situations of domestic violence, internal disturbances.[115] The use of the armed forces under the cover of the guarantee clause in the USA, Australia, and India bear testament to this fact.[116] In the context of using the Guarantee clause

[113] Sarbananda Sonowal's case.

[114] *Ruddock v Vadalaris* [2001] FCA 1329. *See* also Michael Head and Scott Mann, Domestic Deployment of the Armed Forces: Military Powers, Law and Human Rights 135 (2009).

[115] *See* e.g., William M. Wiecek, *The Guarantee Clause in the U.S. Constitution* (1972) 85; Michael Head and Scott Mann, *Domestic Deployment of the Armed Forces: Military Powers, Law and Human Rights* (2009) 50–51; Louise Weinberg, "Political Questions and the Guarantee Clause" (1994) 65 University of Colorado Law Review 887, 902; Jarret A. Zafran, "Referees of Republicanism: How the Guarantee Clause Can Address State Political Lockup" (2016) 91 New York University Law Review 1418, 1435. It is pertinent to note that this measure is different from a formally declared state of emergency.

[116] *Instances of recent import include the deployment of air force pilots to fly commercial airplanes to break a strike by the Union. See* Peta Stephenson, "Fertile Ground for Federalism - Internal Security, the States and Section 119 of the Constitution" (2015) 43 Federal Law Review 289, 291; The deployment of armed forces in India in perpetuity without declaring a state of emergency in India—*See* Gautam Navlakha, "Internal Militarisation: Blood on the Tracks" (1997) 32(6) Economic and Political Weekly 299; and invoking the Insurrection Act to dismiss peaceful protests. *See* Christine Hauser, "What Is the Insurrection Act of 1807, the Law Behind Trump's Threat to States?" *New York Times*, Jun. 2, 2020 <https://www.nytimes.com/article/insurrection-act.html> (last accessed 21 November 2021).

as a source for the domestic deployment of armed forces, all three countries have one or more form of such legislation, which arguably ousts parliamentary review in some manner.[117] It is therefore unsurprising that the Guarantee Clause provisions in their present-day incarnation have been reduced for the mere purpose of the domestic deployment of armed forces. It is not necessary for the domestic deployment of armed forces to be accompanied or preceded by a declaration of a state of emergency. While the invocation of a state of emergency confers on the executive with discretionary powers that would otherwise have been unavailable to him, such as the power to suspend access to fundamental rights, the domestic deployment of armed forces is conferring upon the military the power to restrict liberties and work outside the normal procedural rules.

Essentially, the goalposts of riot, insurrection and rebellion have been shifted dramatically, in that the threshold for invocation of a situation as such has been lowered to the extent that peaceful protests or protests with sporadic non-life-threatening violence have been suppressed by the Executive by resorting to the deployment of armed forces. Similarly, the test for whether an emergency exists or not is no longer a bright-line test to be determined under "laboratory conditions" and by looking into the official gazettes and other sources of informational media for proclamations of emergency. Frankenberg offers some evidence for this assertion, highlighting how the culture of justifications for invoking a state of emergency has gone out of vogue. Instead, according to him, constitutional prolegomenon bear indication that the thresholds of state of emergency have transgressed, as such states of emergency have gone from being instances of foreign armed aggressions, wars, and insurrection, to being declared to suppress instances of civil unrest, riot, and terrorist attacks,[118] which in essence seems to have "devoured the rules and benchmarks of normality."[119] This raises the question of what limitations are there on the use of guarantee clause powers?

[117] In the USA, there is the Insurrection Act, the Posse Comitatus Act, and until recently, there was the US PATRIOT Act. For a brief account, *see* Antonios Kouroutakis and Sofia Ranchordás, "Snoozing Democracy: Sunset Clauses, De-Juridification, and Emergency" (2016) 25 Minnesota Journal of International Law 29, 54–56. For a brief account from the Australian Defense Act 1903, §51A– §51Y *see* Michael Head and Scott Mann, *Domestic Deployment of the Armed Forces: Military Powers, Law and Human Rights* (2009) 130–31. In India, there is the Armed Forces Special Powers Act which allows the domestic deployment of armed forces. For an account of the same, *see generally* Khagesh Gautam, "Martial Law In India: The Deployment Of Military Under The Armed Forces Special Powers Act, 1958" (2018) 24 Southwestern Journal of International Law 177.

[118] Günter Frankenberg, *Between Magic and Deceit* (2017) 264–67.

[119] Ibid 290.

5.4.3 Implied Limitations on Guarantee Clause

The drafting history of these clauses does not stipulate express limits as to how long the armed forces can be deployed domestically. The courts in the three jurisdictions have afforded significant deference to the executive when it comes to reviewing the legitimacy of domestic deployment of armed forces. In the United States, the principle laid out in *Debs* stating that "*The entire strength of the nation may be used to enforce in any part of the land the full and free exercise of all national powers and…if the emergency arises, the army of the nation and all its militia are at the service to compel obedience to the laws…*"[120] is still held to be a valid law. In Australia, in R v. Sharkey, the High Court noted that since maintenance of order is primarily the responsibility of the States, federal intervention is not justified unless the federal interests are infringed by such a situation of domestic violence,[121] a principle which was reiterated in Thomas v. Mowbray where the High Court of Australia upheld the constitutional validity of a counter-terrorism legislation that permitted the domestic deployment of armed and naval forces.[122] In the *Naga People's* case, the Indian Supreme Court upheld the constitutional validity of the Armed Forces Special Powers Act. Importantly, they read a sunset clause into the Act, noting that the structure of the Indian Constitution's emergency provisions do not envisage recourse to emergency powers above a period of six months and therefore, the judges stipulated that disturbed area notifications have to be reviewed by the Executive every 6 months before being renewed.[123] Whether the Executive branch has "periodically reviewed" and declared areas to be manifestly "disturbed areas" is not the same thing as allowing the legislature to review, which incidentally is what the Emergency provisions mandate, and therefore, does not constitute a sufficient ground for excluding it outside the Legislative purview. Nineteen years later, Justice Lokur expressed similar concerns, highlighting how prolonged use of such legislations to has been unravelling the democratic fabric of the Nation. Taking exception to the fact that normalcy had still not been restored in the State, even after sixty years, the Court remarked that, "*normalcy not being restored cannot be a fig leaf for prolonged, permanent or indefinite deployment of the Armed Forces…as it would mock at our democratic practice and would be a travesty of the jurisdiction…to normalize a situation.*"[124]

It is asserted that while the constitutions of the United States and Australia do not contain any express emergency provision like the constitution of India, the deployments are nonetheless bound by the same principles of temporality and the deployments are subject to periodic review by the Legislature. The reason for assertion lies in the fact that the Guarantee Clause, which as noted above, is a constitutional

---

[120] In Re Debs [1895] US 564, 582.

[121] H.P. Lee, *Emergency Powers in Australia* (2nd edn, 2018) 227–28.

[122] *Thomas v Mowbray* [2007] HCA 33. *See also* Michael Head and Scott Mann, Domestic Deployment of the Armed Forces: Military Powers, Law and Human Rights 128 (2009).

[123] *Naga People's Movement for Human Rights v Union of India* [1998] 2 SCC 109, 155–56.

[124] *Extra-Judicial Execution Victim Families Association v Union of India* [2016] 14 SCC 536, 597–600.

embodiment of Montesquieu's dictum, and the conferment of powers of dictatorship in times of emergencies, also places limits on their exercise, as a consequence of which, by necessary implication, the exercise of these powers had to be temporary.[125] It is a testament to the influence that Montesquieu's work had on the drafters of the American constitution that when the powers envisaged by the Guarantee Clause first embodied by the Legislature, the provided the deployment of armed forces domestically can be for a period of 30 days.[126] Such an interpretation of the guarantee clause would stand in conformity with the principles of constitutionalism as by a corollary extension of the interpretation also envisages a ratification by the Legislature of every declaration of a state of emergency and periodic parliamentary review of subsequent renewals, which serves as a check on the inherent power of the Executive to override these structural safeguards, that can only be permitted in times of necessity.

It is a common denominator across the three countries that legislations bestowing extra-ordinary, and sometimes extra-constitutional powers to the military are often passed by the Parliament with minimal deliberation and are allowed to continue without any further deliberation.[127] The Indian Armed Forces Special Powers Act is emblematic as well as illustrative of this disturbing phenomenon. Australia, which as noted above, has been credited with "hyper-legislation" when it comes to legislating on federal counter-terrorism measures, has come up with an innovative mechanism to review such legislations. In Australia, the Parliament passed the Independent National Security Legislation Monitor Act in 2010 which provides for the composition of an independent body to review the necessity for continuing counter-terrorism legislations, their effectiveness and their impact on the individual rights. As per the provisions of the Act, any counter-terrorism legislation may be reviewed on the "own motion" of the INSLM, or if the Prime Minister recommends its review, or if the Sunset clause of the legislation mandates such a review.[128] These provisions guarantee both a high degree autonomy to review extra-ordinary legislations, as well as the safeguards to protect the prolongation of emergency legislations. The absence of any similar mechanism in the Indian context has therefore left the judiciary with filling in the wide gaps left by parliamentary inertia and the unenviable task of reviewing the feasibility of emergency measures. For example, in Surinder Bhardwaj v. Union Territory of Chandigarh,[129] the High Court of Punjab and Chandigarh took cognizance of the fact that normalcy had returned to the Union Territory of Chandigarh. Yet as the notifications under the Disturbed Areas Act continued to operate in a wholly unjustified manner, though normalcy had returned, the Court quashed the notifications issued under the Disturbed Area Act. Similarly, time and time again, the Indian

[125] Montesquieu, *The Spirit of Laws* (first published 1752. Thomas Nugent tr, 2003) 12.

[126] James D. Richardson, *A Compilation of the Messages and Papers of the Presidents, 1789–1897,* vol 1, (1896) 158–60 (Washington's order calling up the Militia).

[127] *See* David Bonner, *Emergency Powers in Peacetime* (1985) 41; Surabhi Chopra, "National Security Laws in India: The Unraveling of Constitutional Constraints" (2015) 17 Orlando Review of International Law 1, 34–35; *See also ibid.* at footnote 159.

[128] See the summarization of the statutory functions of the INSLM listed at <https://www.inslm.gov.au/statutory-functions>.

[129] CWP 499 of 2012 (Decided on 19 September 2012).

Court has condemned the prolonged deployment of the armed forces in the designated disturbed areas, and time and time again the Executive has failed to heed to these judicial pronouncements. This indefinite deployment of armed forces domestically, without a proclamation of emergency is inconsistent with the original intent of the Clause, and the evidence from comparable jurisdictions highlight the same, where any deployment of armed forces for "domestic violence" and "internal disturbance" under the Guarantee Clause are firstly, temporary in nature, and secondly open to periodic parliamentary review as any ordinary emergency proclamation is.

5.5 Conclusion

This inquiry began with a simple question, namely, to understand how the background of the Guarantee Clause has defined its contemporary purpose. Madison and other members of the Constitutional Convention perceived the Guarantee Clause provision as one of the symbols commencing the new era, which stemmed not only from the need to quell insurrections and rebellions but also from the need to ensure that despotic governments do not usurp the liberties of the people. The purpose of this provision as envisaged was to empower the Union of the States as a collective to assist another State which faced the demands of suppressing insurrections. In order to ensure protection against future recurrences, the drafters of the respective constitutions included this provision in their respective constitutions.

If the historical value of the Guarantee Clause lay in ensuring the perpetuity of the Federation, its normative value lay in exposing the faults of the systems and mitigating the faults within the constitution to ensure that the provision falls into desuetude. The normative values of this provision reveal the vernacular categorization of domestic violence has been eroded significantly by changes after changes, as such, there is no one understanding of when the Federal Executive may abuse this power which has been quite the case in India. The hierarchical categorization of the vernacular of insurrection, invasion and armed rebellion, has been significantly lowered at the time of the framing of the constitutions, suggesting that the intent of the framers was to prevent the escalation of situations which had the propensity to tear the federation apart. In the absence of any constitutional safeguards against the use of these powers, the erosion of liberties has all the Guarantee Clause has yielded. The vernacular of "military-acting in aid of civil authorities" may just become another justification for intruding on the fundamental rights of the people, and semantics notwithstanding, it is a proclaiming a state of emergency and should be subject necessarily provide for the same constitutional limitations as a declared state of emergency would. If originalists intention is to be held valid then, the benefits that the framers had the intention of conferring was in the form of a reassurance and an obligation, that a State in distress can count on the assistance of other States. Collective exercise of these powers they felt, would bring the States closer to each other and combine to form a more perfect union. It is only a limited imagination that has constrained the scope of powers for domestic deployment. Abolitionists saw it as a source of power to emancipate the people, and progressives saw it as a source of power to provide for education reforms. Whether these goals can confer a new meaning to the guarantee, would be a moment more remarkable to be memorialized and immortalized than the history of violence its current incarnation has given.

Acknowledgements The author would like to thank Renata Uitz, Arun K. Thiruvengadam, Khagesh Gautam, and the editors of this book for comments on earlier drafts of the paper. All errors are his own.

Chapter 6
Beyond Friend and Enemy: The Stranger as a Political Category in Colonial Modernity

Moiz Tundawala and Salmoli Choudhuri

Abstract This piece is a book comment on Jon Wilson's "The Domination of Strangers: Modern Governance in Eastern India 1780–1835." Center-staging early colonial Bengal as an innovative site of practice in the history of modern law and constitutionalism, the book moves beyond the political distinction between friends and enemies and introduces the category of the "stranger" as an essential ingredient of state formation in South Asia and the modern world. It convincingly shows how the British colonial enterprise in India broke away from pre-colonial relations of concrete familiarity and intimacy to govern a distant and inscrutable society through the detached rule of a mechanistic, bureaucratic, and positivist state. However, Wilson does not reckon seriously with the constitutive role of ideas and ideology and misses out on intellectually engaging with the question of whether colonial practices were determined by the strangeness of the colonized other, or whether abstract estrangement was a product of colonial rule itself. More than an empirical or sociological phenomenon, we argue that strangeness is a conceptual and psychical category crucial for a renewed subjectivity, and promises rich dividends for the discipline of Indian political thought looking past the framework of imperialist and nationalist historiography.

6.1 The Colonial Officer and His Incomplete Sovereignty

In what has now become a classic essay, George Orwell wrote revealingly about his encounter with a domestic elephant while serving as an imperial sub-divisional police officer in colonized Burma. The elephant in a fit of "must" was ravaging a bazaar in the lower Burman town of Moulmein. Orwell, who was called upon to attend to the

M. Tundawala
Jindal Global Law School, Sonipat, India
e-mail: mtundawala@jgu.edu.in

S. Choudhuri (✉)
National Law School of India University, Bengaluru, India
e-mail: salmoli.choudhuri@nls.ac.in

M. John et al. (eds.), *The Indian Yearbook of Comparative Law 2020*, The Indian Yearbook of Comparative Law, https://doi.org/10.1007/978-981-99-5467-4_6

matter as a law officer, felt impelled by the expectations of a pressing crowd of two thousand onlookers to shoot it down, although he cognized that the animal no longer posed a threat having already overcome its temporary frenzy. At this moment, even a mighty essayist like him struggled to make sense of the incoherence of his situation precisely because it was beset with paradoxes. While Orwell was supposed to be invincible as a confident white masculine sahib, he seemed impotent before a jeering crowd of "yellow faces". So much so, that he undermined his rational assessment and killed the perfectly composed elephant only in order to keep his authority intact. Much more than the fear of violence either from the crowd or the elephant, what unnerved him was the inscrutability of the colonial racial 'other', which was simultaneously both an object of sympathy and revulsion. The brutal killing of the elephant then was not so much a self-assured exercise of power as it was a desperate act of putting an end to his own anxiety.[1]

The extraordinary feeling of anxiety that animated Orwell as a colonial official, forms the binding premise of Jon Wilson's extremely thoughtful and rigorously researched work, *The domination of strangers: modern governance in eastern India, 1780–1835*.[2] While Wilson studies the early colonial state in India, he center stages this uncanny mood of anxiety as not only utterly common and a crucial part of everyday reality of the colonizers but also as the very generative impulse for their constitutional and administrative practices. With such a novel theoretical framework, he jettisons the Manichean dualisms of imperialist and nationalist historiographies and focuses on the category of the stranger in the study of the colonial enterprise.

Wilson's core argument is that far from being a confident imposition of a coherent political ideology rooted in European intellectual history, at least in its initial phase from 1780 to 1835, colonial rule was marked by a deep sense of insecurity about a distant and aloof Bengali society. It is this lack of certitude that gave rise to one of the first institutionalizations of a liberal regime of governmentality, which was subsequently generalized as a powerful model for the modern state form elsewhere in the nineteenth and twentieth centuries. The book must be commended for attempting to decentre a derivative understanding of European political thought as the primary intellectual source of the material historical developments in the colonial world. Rather, the South Asian subcontinent emerges as a site for powerful innovations in practices of modern law and constitutionalism. In making this intervention, he joins a growing body of historical and philosophical scholarship which is now showing how modern political institutions and concepts were produced out of interactions with the wider imperial world and not merely transmitted from factories of metropolitan high theory.[3]

---

[1] George Orwell, *Shooting an Elephant*, http://orwell.ru/library/articles/elephant/english/e_eleph (accessed on March 13, 2022).

[2] Jon Wilson, *The domination of strangers: modern governance in eastern India, 1780–1835*, New York: Palgrave Macmillan, 2008.

[3] Susan Buck-Morss, *Hegel, Haiti and Universal History*, Pittsburgh: University of Pittsburgh Press, 2009; Kris Manjapra, *Age of Entanglement: German and Indian intellectuals across Empire*, Massachusetts: Harvard University Press, 2014.

6.2 From Concrete Familiarity to Abstract Estrangement as a Mode of Governance

Prior to the inception of colonial modernity in India, the practices of governance in the eighteenth-century Bengal shared a stark resemblance with the extant political culture in Britain, as both were based on concrete relations of familiarity and face-to-face interactions between the rulers and the ruled.[4] Wilson however argues that following the initial decades of Company rule in Bengal, despite London's insistence on persisting with India's ancient constitution, colonial officials in Calcutta increasingly felt the need to bring about a rupture from the past since the 1780s. Apart from military-fiscal crises faced by the East India Company, influence of British ideas such as primitivism and oriental despotism, and metropolitan politics of property, all of which have figured in previous literature, he importantly directs our attention to the changing structures of the Company service and the attitude of colonial officers toward social life in India as contributing to their self-professed disavowal of pre-colonial governmental legacies.[5] According to Wilson, this break however took at least three constitutional moments encapsulated in the Permanent Settlement of 1793 and the Charter Acts of 1813 and 1833 to be actually materialized on the ground, with its origins remaining shrouded in uncertainty because of the ineliminable feelings of anxiety and estrangement under which it was produced.[6] It is these ambivalent conditions which were behind the increasing engagement with a perceivably distant and inscrutable society through abstract categories of rule, such as "the Hindu family" and "the Bengali landholder", and the eventual establishment of a mechanistic bureaucratic state supplemented by a culture of legal positivism in colonial Bengal by the first few decades of the nineteenth century.[7]

There is not much to contest in this dialectical assessment of break and continuity insofar as it unearths a cognitive dissonance among colonial officials required to govern a people whom they could not comprehend through frames of reference more familiar to them. Wilson cites the late Mughal administrator-cum-chronicler, Ghulam Hussein Tabatabai, who precociously perceived the turn away from concrete familiarity to abstract estrangement with the onset of British colonialism. In a complete departure from prevailing ethical relations of intimacy and proximity between the governors and the governed, Tabatabai remarked that colonial officials treated the natives merely as objects of governance like "pictures on a wall".[8] But there remains a minor quibble regarding Wilson's ambiguity on the period before the first signs of a purported dramatic change emerged in the 1780s. Does he presume that a moment of break is to be traced merely through official intentions? If so, how would he explain the continued reliance of the colonial regime on Mughal and local royal ritualistic

---

[4] Wilson, *The domination of strangers*, Chap. 2.

[5] Wilson, *The domination of strangers*, pp. 55–56.

[6] Wilson, *The domination of strangers*, Chap. 6.

[7] Wilson, *The domination of strangers*, Chap. 3,4,5.

[8] Wilson, *The domination of strangers*, p. 5.

ceremonies till its very last days in India? If not, how are we to make sense of the fact that the juridical techniques of domination which he has so carefully scrutinized were to be found even in the initial decades following Bengal's conquest in 1757 as is clear from Tabatabai's historical work of 1784?

6.3 Ideology Versus Practice

A major discomfiture with Wilson's argument is that he appears to be working with too sharp a separation between ideology and practice. While his inclination towards the latter makes perfect sense as an oppositional response to the Cambridge historian Quentin Skinner's contextualist methodology which only takes into account linguistic and discursive surroundings of a text to be central to history writing,[9] this binary does not exhaust the possibilities of a creative and critical engagement with the history of law and politics in India. The discipline has made considerable progress since the days of a defined methodological dichotomy between the Marxian emphasis on transforming the concrete material order of the world and a Weberian insistence on interpreting it solely through the abstraction of ideas alone. For instance, twentieth-century theorists like Cornelius Castoriadis and Claude Lefort have shown us the generative potential of working with the notion of a "social imaginary", understood as constituted through symbolic representation and furthermore sustained and transformed by social contexts even if not entirely determined by them.[10] But Wilson completely moves beyond the question of ideology and instead engages with what are taken as practices in their purity inexplicable conceptually or cognitively, to unravel the chaos and instability underlying colonial imagination. In doing so, he erroneously accords only a justificatory role to ideology and not a constitutive one.

Ideology does not merely obfuscate power relations of domination and subordination, but in a more fundamental sense, structures social reality as a whole. When Wilson ascribes primacy to practices, he misses how they are always mediated by ideas and ideology.[11] There is certainly a close connection between the condition of estrangement and the institution of colonial governmentality; yet, this does not tell us if colonial practices were entirely determined by the strangeness of the colonized 'other', or whether abstract estrangement was a product of colonial rule itself. While India had pre-colonial empires that were radically cosmopolitan in their constitution where foreign antecedents of the rulers never became a political question, it is only with British colonialism that we see the emergence of liberal modernity and a state-sponsored capitalist civil society. When understood in such a manner, the colonial apprehension of the indigenous as a strange society is inconceivable without the abstract technologies of rule that liberal capitalist modernity generated in India.

---

[9] Wilson, *The domination of strangers*, p. 9.

[10] Samuel Moyn, "Imaginary Intellectual History," in *Rethinking Modern European Intellectual History*, ed. Darrin M. McMohan and Samuel Moyn, Oxford: Oxford University Press, 2014.

[11] Slavoj Zizek, *The Sublime Object of Ideology*, London and New York: Verso, 1989.

6.4 Strangeness and Anxiety

For sure, Wilson must be appreciated for bringing the figure of the stranger to the forefront of intellectual enquiry in a refreshing move away from much of historical and political thought which has generally remained preoccupied with the question of state formation through the self/other and friend/enemy distinctions. However, strangeness is not merely an empirical or sociological category defined by fixed identities; more germinally, it is a conceptual and psychical category that has the potential to unsettle any given consensus and open up the possibilities for a renewed subjectivity. This perhaps explains why MK Gandhi and other Indian nationalists singularly left out the issue of the foreignness of the colonizers even while resisting their pervasive intrusion and violent domination of indigenous society. BR Ambedkar observed that India was not a nation, but a society of strangers segregated by caste and community, and so no political unity was possible over here without taking this precolonial and primary fact of estrangement seriously. Equally, Rabindranath Tagore recasts foreignness in his poems and plays as a source of creative energy and subjective regeneration for a caste-ridden introverted society. Thus, the category of strangeness promises rich dividends in the study of Indian political thought, if only one is willing to look past conventional frames of imperial and national histories.

While studying the British enterprise in India as a domination of strangers, Wilson borrows his framework from the Subaltern Studies historian Ranajit Guha and especially the latter's rendering of anxiety as one of the formative experiences of colonial life.[12] However, he does not follow Guha all the way through. Inflected with Heideggerian existentialist and Lacanian psychoanalytic insights, Guha distinguishes anxiety as an "indefinite and pervasive" state of mind from fear that is always directed to a particular object. In a way, his phrase "not at home in empire" coined to describe the mental condition of a few colonial officials precisely captures what Wilson's project is all about. Yet, we see that Wilson's account starkly departs from Guha's on two very important counts: first, anxiety features in his work as a prolonged and permanent condition of the British empire, and secondly, as a statist phenomenon it is made amenable to historicization. But Guha on the other hand retrieves anxiety as a momentary rupture in the routine performance of imperial duties from the slippages and involuntary admissions of colonial officials driven by their personal experiences. Conceived in this way, anxiety resists seamless absorption in a linear historical narrative that is predicated on the state as the arch-political actor. What Wilson can at best help us understand is the fear of the colonial state under perpetual threat of sedition and insurgency. For the anxiety of the colonial officials, we would have to supplement state-centric histories of law and politics with literary studies and psychoanalytic investigations of subjectivity.

[12] Ranajit Guha, "Not at Home in Empire," *Critical Enquiry*, 23:3 (Spring, 1997).

Chapter 7
The European Social Model Facing the Economic and the COVID Pandemic Crises

George Katrougalos

Abstract The article explores the constitutional identity of the European Polity, regarding its social dimension, in comparison with the American one and the fundamental principles of its member states. It finds that there is an initial asymmetry, yet to be overcome, between the market-oriented character of the European project and the more socially oriented national constitutional orders. Subsequently, it explores the reaction of the European Union to the economic crisis of 2008 and the crisis of the COVID-19 pandemic. It concludes with the assertion that the crucial issue of the European Union remains the reconciliation of social rights with the logic of market integration.

Keywords EU polity · Social rights · Social state · American polity · European Polity · Welfare State · Memoranda · Economic crisis · COVID crisis · Recovery fund

---

The article draws heavily from the below mentioned previous works of mine. Its added value is the repositioning of the analysis on the new institutional and economic situation framework of the COVID-19 pandemic, which shows some qualitative mutations vis-à-vis the reaction to the economic crisis of 2008. George S. Katrougalos, The (Dim) Perspectives of the European Social Citizenship, Jean Monnet Working Paper no. 05/2007, https://jeanmonnetprogram.org/paper/the-dim-perspectives-of-the-european-social-citizenship/; Katrougalos, G. (2012). The Greek Debt, under the light of Constitutional and International Law. CADTM Publications. https://www.cadtm.org/The-Greek-Debt-under-the-light-of.

G. Katrougalos (✉)
Democritus University, Komotini, Greece
e-mail: gkatroug@sp.duth.gr

M. John et al. (eds.), *The Indian Yearbook of Comparative Law 2020*, The Indian Yearbook of Comparative Law, https://doi.org/10.1007/978-981-99-5467-4_9

7.1 The Distinct Constitutional Qualities of the American and European Polities

The European social model is the distinct institutional signature that distinguishes European polities from the American one. European "social states" have a defined constitutional ethos, which determines their entire legal culture,[1] including also the conceptualization and the functions of the traditional rights and freedoms. Therefore, a clear dividing line is still discernible between the European and American legal cultures, despite important osmotic procedures between them, which lead some authors to speak of a "European–Atlantic constitutional state."[2]

This differentiation goes beyond the divergent political economy of the two continental cousins, the "liberal capitalist" system of the United States and Britain and the "social market" capitalism of northern Europe.[3] As R. Aron has remarked, in Europe *"the concept of State and law is not anymore merely negative, but also positive, in the sense that the law is considered to be not only the juridical foundation but also the source of the material conditions for its fulfillment.*[4]" On the contrary, the functions of the liberal state are essentially negative. They consist of the removal of arbitrary legal impediments, not to the provision of positive means for the exercise of rights and liberties. In consequence, there is an eclipse of positive rights, even as guarantees of traditional liberties[5] and a complete vacuum of constitutional social rights.[6] For this reason, for many scholars, the concept of the "State" itself in Europe is closer to the Anglo-American notion of the Welfare State or even of the "administrative state".[7] There is not only "a European culture of social justice",[8] in the sense of

---

[1] I use the term legal culture broadly, in the sense that includes every aspect of institutional and legal setup, including the particular ethos of a polity. For the concept of the "common european legal culture," *see* P. Häberle (1991), "Gemeineuropäisches Verfassungsrecht," *EuGRZ* (1991), p. 261, 274.

[2] See G. Katrougalos (2008) "European 'Social States' and the USA: An Ocean Apart?" *European Constitutional Law Review*, 4: 225–250, from which I draw for the analycf. S. Fabrini (2004), "Transatlantic constitutionalism: comparing the United States and the European Union," 43 *European Journal of Political Research* p. 547, M. Rosenfeld (ed.) (1994), *Constitutionalism, Identity, Difference and Legitimacy*, Durham, Duke University Press.

[3] See J. Pontusson (2005), *Inequality and Prosperity: Social Europe Vs. Liberal America,* Cornell University Press.

[4] R., Aron, (1972) Etudes Politiques, Paris: Gallimard, p. 242.

[5] Cf. the cases Harris v. MacRae, 448 US 297 (1980), Deshaney v. Winnebago County Department of Social Services, 489 US 189 (1989).

[6] See, for instance, R. Bork, (1979), The impossibility of finding welfare rights in the Constitution, Washington University Law Quarterlym, p. 695, cf. G. Scoffoni, (2006) Observations comparatives sur la place des droits sociaux constitutionnels deans les systèmes de common law et de droit mixte in L. Gay, et al. Les droits sociaux fondamentaux, Paris, Bruylant,167–184.

[7] See, for instance, G. Casper, (1989) "Changing Concepts of Constitutionalism," S Ct Rev 311, 318–399, M.A. Glendon, (1992) "Rights in the Twentieth Century Constitutions," U Chi L Rev 59, 519.

[8] C. Fabre, (2005) "Social Rights in European Constitutions," in G. De Búrca and B. De Witte, Social Rights in Europe, Oxford: Oxford University Press, 15–28, p. 16.

a distinct ethos vis-à-vis the Anglo-Saxon legal systems, but essentially a different polity.

This fundamental division of European, "social" and Anglo-American "liberal" states cannot be reduced only to the legal differences between the common law and continental legal traditions.[9] It reflects much more profound political, moral, and societal choices.[10] This happens because one of the functions of the Constitution is to ensure social integration, by presupposing and promising the common values that constitute the foundations of the political community.[11] This is a two-directional process, because the Constitution crystallizes already embedded social values, but, on the other hand, it contributes to their consolidation into an objective system, which can have normative repercussions. So, the normative and axiological elements are closely and mutually underpinned.

The empirical studies of Alberto Alesina reaffirm the deep clash of values between Europe and America[12] with regard to the redistributive functions of the state. In the former, in the words of Abba Sieyès, the citizens feel they have a right to demand from the state everything it can do for them.[13] In the latter, the belief that individual talent and effort determine income, that all have a right to enjoy the fruits of their effort, in tandem with the traditional mistrust toward the state result in a much more individualistic, Lockean Weltanschauung and, especially, a fundamentally different conceptualization of equality. As Slaughter remarks, the American concept of equality tolerates a lot of inequality, as it focuses on starting points, not endpoints. The idea that everybody is created equal, but opportunity and individual effort can make a difference is deeply embedded in the American dream.[14] That's why many poor people are for tax cuts for the wealthier, hoping that one day they will be rich, too.[15]

In order to define this new type of polity, German legal theory has developed the concept of the "Social State" ("Sozialstaat"). Usually, the terms "Welfare State" (Wohlfahrtstaat/Etat-Providence) and "Social State" (Sozialstaat/Etat social) are

---

[9] See K. Dyson, (1980), *The state tradition in Western Europe*, Oxford: Martin Robertson, cf. Kahn-Freund, O., (1978) "Common Law and Civil Law—Imaginary and Real Obstacles to Assimilation," in Mauro Cappelleti (ed), New Perspectives for a Common Law of Europe-, London: Sijmoff.

[10] Cf. B. Markezinis, (2001), "Unity or Division: The search for similarities in contemporary European Law," Current Legal Problems, 51, 591–617, p. 612.

[11] N.Walker,, (2006) "European Constitutionalism in the State Constitutional Tradition." Current Legal Problems, 57, 51–89, p. 63, Grimm, D. (2005) "Integration by Constitution," ICON 3, 193–208, cf. Smend, R., (1956) "Integrationslehre", in Handwörterbuch der Sozialwissenschaften, 5, 299–310.

[12] A. Alesina,, Angeletos, M., (2002) "Fairness and Redistribution: US versus Europe," Harvard Institute of Economic Research Working Papers 1983, Harvard Institute of Economic Research.

[13] "Il suffit de dire que les citoyens en commun ont droit à tout ce que l'Etat peut faire en leur faveur." Abba Sieyès, "Des droits de l'homme et du citoyen," lu les 20 et 21 juillet 1789 au comité de la Constitution, Hermann, 1939, p. 70.

[14] A.M. Slaughter, (2007), *The idea that is America*, Cambridge, MA: Basic Books, p. 80, 105.

[15] According to a World Values Survey, 71 percent of Americans versus 40 percent of Europeans believe that the poor could become rich if they just tried hard enough. See A. Alesina, Angeletos, M., (2002) "Fairness and Redistribution: US versus Europe," op. cit.

used interchangeably. However, there is a qualitative distinction between the two; the first term (Welfare State) describes the universal type of state which evolved in all industrialized countries during the twentieth century. The emergence of the welfare state responds to a functional necessity of the modern capitalist economy, related to the reproduction of a well-educated working class, as "a problem of industry."[16]

On the other hand, the Social State is a normative, prescriptive principle, which defines a specific polity, which undertakes the constitutional obligation (a) to assume interventionist functions in the economic and social spheres and (b) to guarantee fundamental social rights to all citizens. In this sense, the USA or Australia are "welfare" but not "social" states, as social policy therein has no constitutional foundation. In contrast, countries such as India or South Africa, although lacking the basic infrastructure of a mature welfare state, can be considered as social states, due to their constitutional arrangements regarding the protection of social rights.

While the concept of the Social State has its origins in German legal thought, it is now widely accepted throughout Europe as a fundamental normative and general organizational principle of the Constitution, on a par with the Rule of Law. Nearly all countries in Europe—with the most notable exception being the United Kingdom—are social states, either comprising an explicit "Social State" clause in their Constitutions,[17] or an analytical enumeration of social rights,[18] or both. It is broadly accepted that the principle can be deduced from the overall corpus of constitutional legislation, even without explicit reference to it. Therefore, the explicit inclusion of social rights in the Constitution is not a prerequisite for a polity to be a Social State.

The archetypical social states of Germany and Austria, for example, do not have such rights in their constitutional charters and the Nordic Constitutions—with the exception of Finland—contain only minimal provisions.

The constitutional recognition of social rights after the First World War in a number of European countries implied a change in the functions of the State: instead of regulating the market only on the basis of norms that derive from the private law of contract, property and tort,[19] the European state uses, in addition, "political power to supersede, supplement or modify operations of the economic system in order to achieve results, which the economic system would not achieve on its own ... guided by other values than those determined by open market forces."[20]

---

[16] W. Beveridge, *Unemployment: A Problem of Industry,* London, Longmans, 1909.

[17] As in article 20 para 1 of the German Fundamental Law, art. 1 of the Constitution of France, art. 1 para 1 of the Constitution of Spain, art. 2 of the Constitution of Portugal, the Preamble of the Constitution of Bulgaria and Art. 1 para 1 of the Constitutions of Croatia and FYR of Macedonia, 2 of Slovenia, 6 para 1 of Russia.

[18] See, e.g., the Constitutions of Belgium (art. 23), Italy (art. 2–4, 31, 32, 35–38, 41, 45, 46), Luxembourg (11, 23, 94), Netherlands (19, 20, 22) Greece (21, 22), Spain (39–52, 129, 148, 149), Portugal (56, 59, 63–72, 108, 109, 167, 216).

[19] Cf. F.A Hayek, Law, *Legislation and Liberty: A New Statement of the Liberal Principles of Justice and Political Economy* (London, Routledge 1980) p. 141.

[20] T.H. Marshall, *Social Policy* (London, Routledge 1975) at p. 15. Marshall was referring to social policy in general, but his description defines very precisely also the basic functions of the social state principle.

What is interesting is that this different understanding of the state's role, social justice, and equality is not limited to "old Europe" but characterizes also the new democracies of Central and Eastern Europe. Hence, according to Eurobarometer surveys,[21] a vast majority of citizens of these republics agree with the proposition that "*there is a need for more equality and social justice even if this means less freedom for the individual*".[22]

However, all this concern the national member states, not the European Union per se.

7.2 The Constitutional Asymmetry Between the Social Member States and the European Polity

Paradoxically, the legal order of the European Union seems closer to the American archetype than to the European social states,[23] as the European integration had at the beginning the character of an economic, not a social project.[24] Integration's social objectives have served merely as an auxiliary and European rights were tailored according to the functional requirements of the internal market.[25] As a consequence, the fundamental constitutional principle of "Social State", enshrined in almost all national constitutions of its member states, is not embodied in the Treaties, although the Treaty of Rome contained some social provisions, especially the programmatic clause of Article 117, by which the member states agreed to improve working conditions and living standards for workers, "*so as to make possible their harmonization while the improvement is being maintained.*"[26] However, this goal was not to be achieved by interventionist redistributive measures, but spontaneously, by the formation of the common market, which would promote wealth and, consecutively, welfare.

---

[21] Poll carried out between 6 September and 10 October 2006, by TNS Opinion & Social, a consortium createdcbetween Taylor Nelson Sofres and EOS Gallup Europe, accessible at http://ec.europa.eu/public_opinion/archives/eb/eb66/.

[22] Sometimes, more predominantly than the EU average, for instance, in Slovakia, where 66% of citizens agree with this proposition, as against 64% in the EU25.

[23] For a more analytical discourse on that see Katrougalos, G. (2007), *The dim perspectives of the European social citizenship*, NYU Jean Monnet Paper 7, New York, New York University.

[24] See, among others, Scharpf, F. (2002), "The European Social Model" Journal of Common Market Studies, Vol. 40, pp. 645–670, 2002 Moravcsik, A. (1998) *The Choice for Europe: Social Purpose and State Power from Messina to Maastricht* Ithaca, NY: Cornell University Press).

[25] Cf. Everson, M. (1995) "The legacy of the market citizen," in: J. Shaw and G. More (Eds), New Legal Dynamics of European Union Oxford: Oxford University Press, ibidem.

[26] The Court of Justice considers that such a provision "is essentially in the nature of a programme" although "an important aid, in particular for the interpretation of other provisions of the Treaty and of secondary legislation in the social field." See Case 149/77 *Defrenne v. Sabena III* [1978] ECR. 1365, Case 170/84 *Bilka / Weber von Hartz* [1986], ECR 1607, Case 126/86 *Giménez Zaera v Instituto Nacional de la Seguridad Social and Tesorerva General de la Seguridad Social* [1987] ECR 3697.

In this framework, social policy has always been the "step-child" of the European integration,[27] as its basic goal was to facilitate free movement, especially through the aggregation of eligibility and social security benefits for EU migrants and standardization of the interfaces between national systems.[28] This is why, contrary to its traditional function at the national level, European social policy is not of the "market breaking" but of the "market-making" variety.

Advocate General P. Maduro has shown the clear relation between the process of constitutionalization of the Treaties and the rules of market integration[29]: The functional result of negative integration in the form of judicial review of divergent state regulations restricting trade was the emergence of a European economic constitution, with only two Grundnorms: free movement and competition rules.[30] Consequently, any national interference with market freedoms, even if it derives from constitutional provisions, reflecting "a deeply held national societal more or value",[31] or even if it concerns matters that do not fall directly within the scope of application of EC law, is contrary to European Law and prohibited, unless if it falls under its derogation clauses.

Moreover, the Court of Justice of the European Union (CJEU), based on international law sources as inspirational guidelines and the "constitutional traditions common to Member States"[32] has recognized many fundamental rights as general principles of European law and among them the protection of the rights to property and economic freedom. However, the language of rights has been used selectively.

---

[27] See Flora, P. (1993), The national welfare states and the European Integration, *in:* L. Moreno (Ed.), *Social Exchange and Welfare Development*, Madrid: Consejo Superior de Investigaciones científicas, Instituto de Estudios Sociales Avanzados.

[28] Through Community Regulation 1408/71, which has recently been substantially reformed with the adoption of Regulation 883/2004. Cf. Streeck, W., (1996) "Neo-Voluntarism: A new European Social Regime?" in F. Snyder (Ed.) Constitutional Dimensions of European Economic Integration, London: Kluwer Law International, 229–268, p. 258, Mosley, H. (1990), "The Social Dimension of European Integration," International Labour Review, 129 (2): 147–64.

[29] Maduro, M.P., (1998), We The Court, *The European Court of Justice and the European Economic Constitution*, Oxford: Hart Publishing,, pp. 61 ff., the same, (1999) "We Still Have Not Found What We Have Been Looking For. The Balance Between Economic Freedom and Social Rights in the European Union," Faculdade de Direito da Universidade Nova de Lisboa Working Paper 4/99,, accessible at www.fd.unl.pt/web/Anexos/Downloads/185.pdf, p. 6, cf. Davies, P., (1995) "Market Integration and Social Policy in the Court of Justice," 24 Industrial Law Journal 1995, 49, p. 51.

[30] On the concept of the European economic constitution see, among others, Sauter, W. (1998), "The Economic Constitution of the European Union," 4 Columbia Journal of European Law 1998, p. 27 ff., Jorges,S., (1997), The market without the state? The "Economic Constitution" of the European Community and the rebirth of regulator policies, European Integration online Papers (EioP), v. 1, 19, Behrens, P. (1994), "Die Wirtschaftsverfassung der Europäischen Gemeinschaft," in G. BRAGGERMEIER (Hrsg.), Verfassungen für ein ziviles Europa, Baden-Baden: Nomos, p. 7 ff, Boscowits K., (2001) The European Judge and the Economic Constitution: The Contribution of ECJ to the formulation of a constitutional economic model of the European Community, ToS, 2, (in Greek).

[31] Weiler, J.H.H. (1999), Fundamental Rights and Fundamental Boundaries, in Weiler, J.H.H.(ed.), The Constitution of Europe, Cambridge: Cambridge University Press, Chap. 3, p. 121.

[32] See, for example, Case 4/73, *Nold*, [1974] ECR 491 and Case 44/79, *Hauer*, [1979] ECR 3727.

Although the Court has sporadically referred to general sources of social rights protection such as the European and Community Social Charters,[33] it is very reluctant to recognize any social rights as general principles,[34] much less as fundamental rights.[35]

The social rights, although enshrined, one way or another, in the majority of the national Constitutions, have never been considered by the Court as part of the common constitutional tradition of member states. (It is true that the Britannic delegate at the European Convention of the Constitutional Treaty has argued that the social rights do not exist in English law, at least not with the same meaning as in continental law.[36] However, the fact that such rights and an entire Chap. 4 on Solidarity have been included in the Charter of Fundamental Rights of the EU is an irrefutable proof that there is, after all, a European common denominator regarding them). This reluctance of the Court to recognize social rights at the European level is probably explained, as De Búrca remarks, by the "fear of giving strong legal recognition and priority to particular social values in the face of competing economic interests.[37]" Evidently, social citizenship's rights make the market less free.[38]

This economic constitution, developed as a function of economic efficiency and with the basic aim of protecting market freedom from public power,[39] is clearly in conflict with the essence of the Social State principle. Of course, economic freedom,

---

[33] The first references by the ECJ to the European Social Charter were in the Case 149/77 *Defrenne III* [1978] ECR 1365 and in Case 24/86, *Vincent Blaizot and others against the City of Liege* [1988], ECR 379, cf. also Case C-246/96 *Magorrian and Cunningham v. Eastern Health and Social Service Board and the Department of Health and Social Services* [1997] ECR I-7153, Case C-191/94 *AGF Belgium* [1996] ECR I-1859.

[34] Cf. Witte de, B., (2005)"The trajectory of fundamental social rights in the European Union" in G. De Búrca and B. De Witte, Social Rights in Europe, Oxford: Oxford University Press, 153–168 Witte de, B., "The trajectory of fundamental social rights in the European Union" in G. De Búrca and B. De Witte, Social Rights in Europe, Oxford: Oxford University Press, 153–168, Ponthoreau, M.-C. (2003), "Le principe de l'indivisibilité des droits: l'apport de la Charte des droits fondamentaux," Revue Française de Droit Administratif, p. 931. The initial proposal of the Commission was also referring to rights of citizens.

[35] With most notable exception the gender equality, which is, however, primarily a civil, not a social right.

[36] See Braibant, G. (2001), *La Charte des droits fondamentaux de l'Union européenne*, Paris: Seuil, p. 40, cf. Molinier, J. (dir.) (2005), *Les principes fondateurs de l'Union européenne*, Paris: PUF, pp. 271–272.

[37] De Búrca, G., (2005) "Introduction", in G. De Búrca and B. De Witte, Social Rights in Europe, Oxford: Oxford University Press, 1–14, p. 14, cf. Sciarra, S. (1996) "Building on European Social Values: an analysis of the multiple sources of European social law," in F. Snyder (Ed.) Constitutional Dimensions of European Economic Integration, London: Kluwer Law International, 1175-206.

[38] Streeck W. (1995), "From market making to state building? Reflections on the political economy of European social policy" in S. Leibfried and P. Pierson (Eds) European Social Policy: Between fragmentation and integration, Washington: The Brookings Institution, 389–431, p. 413Lehning, P, (1997) "European citizenship: A mirage?" in P. Lehning, and A Weale, Citizenship, democracy and justice in the new Europe, London, New York: Routledge, 175–199, p. 180.

[39] Maduro, M.P. (1999), "We Still Have Not Found What We Have Been Looking For. The Balance Between Economic Freedom and Social Rights in the European Union,". note 30, p. 1.

efficiency, and even competition and consumer choice are also part of the national constitutions of social states, but in harmonized co-existence with opposing general principles, such as human dignity, social justice, substantive equality, and solidarity. These latter are absent or, at least underdeveloped in the European law.[40]

As EU welfare law remained in "embryonic state",[41] the repercussions of this clash of values are mostly felt domestically.[42] (European social policy is developing simultaneously at two levels, but predominantly at national and only residually at a supranational one.) According to the Court, "Community law does not detract from the powers of the Member States to organize their social security systems",[43] but only insofar as they conform to it. Hence, the negative integration of the common market had immediate de-regulatory consequences on national social rights,[44] especially where protective national social regulation was above the European average.

It is true that the gradual demise of the European nation-state's Keynesian capacity[45] is a very complex process, triggered by the general trends of globalization. Still, it is certain that European law has played also an important role therein. On the one hand, many national social rights or arrangements have been challenged under the freedom of movement or competition rules.[46] On the other, even when it was not normatively imposed on member states to change their social legislation, the imperatives of the stability pact and the general political orientation of the Community

---

[40] Cf. Fitzpatrick, B. (2000) "Converse pyramids and the EU social Constitution," in J. Shaw (Ed.), Social Law and Policy in an Evolving European Union, Oxford, Portland: Hart Publishing, 304–324, who describes how the respective underpinning values are reversed in the economic and social constitutions of the member states and the Union.

[41] O' Leary, S., (2005) "Solidarity and Citizenship Rights in the Charter of Fundamental Rights of the European Union," in G. De Búrca, EU Law and the Welfare, In Search of Solidarity, Oxford: Oxford University Press, 40–88, p. 54.

[42] Streeck, W., (1996) "Neo-Voluntarism: A new European Social Regime?" in F. Snyder (Ed.) Constitutional Dimensions of European Economic Integration, London: Kluwer Law International, 229–268, p. 230.

[43] Case 238/82 *Duphar v Netherlands* [1984] ECR 523 para 16, Cases C-159 and C-160/91 *Poucet and Pistre* [1993] ECR I-637, para 6, Case C-158/96 *Kohl v. Union des Caisses de Maladie* [1998] ECR I-1931, para 17, see Hervey, T. (2000) "Social Solidarity: A buttress against internal market law?" in J. Shaw (Ed.), Social Law and Policy in an Evolving European Union, Oxford, Portland: Hart Publishing, 31–47, p. 33 ff.

[44] In areas so diverse as the working hours of workers (see Case 145/88, *Torfaen Borough Council*, [1989] ECR 3851, or prices regulations (Case 65/75, *Tasca,* [1976] ECR 291; Case 13/77, *ATAB,* [1977] ECR 2115. See Maduro, M.P., (1999) "We Still Have Not Found What We Have Been Looking For. The Balance Between Economic Freedom and Social Rights in the European Union," op. cit., note 30.

[45] Streeck, W., (1996) "Neo-Voluntarism: A new European Social Regime?" in F. Snyder (Ed.) Constitutional Dimensions of European Economic Integration, London: Kluwer Law International, 229–268, p. 262.

[46] Maduro, M.P. (2003) The Double Constitutional Life of the Charter of Fundamental Rights of the European Union, in T. Hervey and J. Kenner, Economic and Social Rights under the EU Charter of Fundamental Rights-A legal perspective, Oxford-Portland Oregon: Hart Publishing, 269–298, p. 286.

have, de facto, subjected their policies to a more or less neoliberal reasoning leading to reduction of public social expenditure.[47]

This ideological and institutional mismatch between the European and the national polities could, potentially, undermine the project of deepening of political integration. Several attempts have been made to introduce a "social dimension" into the Community, since the Treaty of Amsterdam, which added a new, fourth recital to the Preamble of the EC Treaty that confirms the attachment of member states to fundamental social rights, as defined in the European Social Charter and the 1989 Community Charter of the Fundamental Social Rights of Workers. Article 117 (now 136) of the Treaty has also been reformulated accordingly. Most of these changes have been more rhetorical than substantive.[48]

In 2016, the European Commission has lanced a new initiative, called the European Pillar of Social Rights (EPSR),[49] with very ambitious aims; to bring back the social dimension of the EU, rebalance economic policies with social considerations, reconnect with European citizens, while at the same time addressing key issues related to changes in the world of work and society more generally, promoting higher social standards. However, the Pillar is basically a pious declaration of good intentions and an exercise of public relations. It does not give the European Union new competences, but aims to be a tool to promote social rights with joint collaboration and responsibility of the European institutions together with member states, civil society, social actors, and social partners.[50]

7.3 The EU Under Pressure of the Twin Crises of the Twenty-First Century

It seemed initially that the economic crisis of 2008 would have an inverse effect than the oil crisis of the 1970s, which triggered the contestation of the welfare state. There was a hope for a reversal of the neoliberal flux, toward a reinforcement of public responsibility in social affairs, through policies like the Obama plan on health

---

[47] See, among others, Panic, M. (2005) "The Euro and the Welfare State" in E. Spaventa, M. Dougan, Social Welfare and EU Law, Oxford and Portland: Hart Publishing, 25–44, p. 161 ff.

[48] Cf. Shaw, J., (1994) "Twin-Track Social Europe –The inside track" in O' Keefe and Twomey (Eds) Legal Issues of the Maastricht Treaty, 295–311, p. 298: "Since the Paris Summit in 1972, the Member States have been concerned to promote a public rhetoric in which social affairs are accorded equal status with 'pure' economic integration. The rhetoric (…) indicates that it is 'neo-liberal business as usual', with these provisions (of the TEU) aping those which have long stood largely unheeded in the Treaty of Rome.".

[49] For a description of the Pillar see (2027) European Platform for Rehabilitation, The European Pillar of Social Rights & Service delivery for persons with disabilities, at http://epr.eu/wp-content/uploads/EPSR-Analytical-Paper-1.pdf.

[50] See K. Lörcher (2016), New Tensions over Social Europe? The European Pillar of Social Rights and the Debate within the European Parliament, European Trade Union Institute (ETUI) Research Paper - Report 139, P. Vesan, F. Corti (2019), The European Pillar of Social Rights: Critical Legal Analysis and Proposals, Journal of Common Market Studies, Vol. 57, Issue 5.

reform and the Abenomics in Japan. In the European Union, it had become evident, even before the crisis, that the Maastricht criteria have failed to fuel real economic convergence, as they were based on the fallacy of tricking down policies.

The crisis of 2008–2010 was more than everything else a crisis of the imbalance between economic integration and monetary union in the European Union. Economic Monetary Union (EMU) was just monetary, not economic. It brought together countries with diverse institutional and economic conditions, without any strategy for convergence. The project was grounded in the faith that countries would eventually converge upward, relying on financial market integration to mitigate the inability of participating states to autonomously adjust nominal exchange rates.

In the reality, strong and weak economies diverged after Maastricht. The reason is simple. A single currency, by definition, does not allow national fluctuation, even when individual countries in the monetary union would benefit from changes in relative values. Therefore, all other things being equal, in a time span and due to the inability of devaluation, a product produced by the weaker economy is becoming more expensive than a similar one produced by the stronger. In consequence, the trade deficit between the respective states is increasing. (This happens not only in monetary unions with single currency but any time a weaker economy pegs its currency to a stronger one, as in the case of Mexico's and Argentina's peso vis-à-vis the US$). For this reason, economists, such as M. Feldstein, have from the beginning warned that the Euro would inevitably lead to persistent trade imbalances between the more competitive core countries—especially Germany—and the less competitive countries of the South. Therefore, the deficits of the latter are just the other side of the coin of the surpluses of the former.

Hence, the economic imbalance of the Union is an externality, not imputable to the national politics of the "profligate" southern states but, instead, one imposed on them by the inherent dynamics of the single currency and the monetary union. The same trend is occurring in a federation: There is a flux of capital from weaker to stronger subnational economies, e.g., from Wyoming to New York. But then, at the end of the economic year, the fiscal union mechanisms ensure through taxes and transfers a partial compensation of Wyoming's losses. The structural funds in the EU could play a similar role, but they cannot, due to their limited resources.

As a result, as previous stark macroeconomic imbalances have already built up within the euro area over a number of years, when the economic crisis hit the European Union, the weakest economies have been more severely hit, Greece first among them. It had the worst combination of huge public debt and high budget deficit among the EU states. In similar situations, a default, combined with reconstruction of the debt and protection of social state structures and more vulnerable would be the most rational solution. Yet Greece's euro area partners were not willing to let it take that decision, in fear that the Eurosystem could not withstand the market turbulence.[51] Moreover, the Maastricht Treaty contained a "no bail-out" provision, which didn't

[51] Buckley, R. (2010) "The Bankruptcy of Nations: Let the Law Reflect Reality." Banking and Financial Services Policy Report, Vol. 29, No. 6, pp. 1–17.

allow for rescuing a failing state member (Article 125 of the Consolidated EU Treaty, formerly Article 123 TEC).

The austerity programs imposed on the peripheral states of Europe (Greece, Portugal, and Ireland) by a series of "Memoranda", have been by many aspects a remedy more lethal than the crisis.[52] They called for horizontal reduction of all public expenses, primarily of social expenditures, a thorough deregulation of labor law legislation, and a massive transfer of wealth from the public to the private sector through privatizations of public enterprises. These privatizations were to take place regardless of the strategic nature of public enterprises, their social contribution, or their financial utility for the budget. In this framework, the Memoranda could be seen as just one more episode of the prevailing "Sado-Monetarism"[53] of the EU economic orthodoxy, reflecting the neoliberal Washington consensus, imposed by the International Monetary Fund (IMF) so far to many countries of the Global South.

Was there an alternative? A monetary union deprives member countries of independently making adjustments to economic shocks, by undervaluation of its currency or other monetary means. This inherent defect could be remedied only through the existence of some kind of mutualization of risk, by risk-sharing mechanisms within the European Union. However, from the beginning of the crisis Germany has precluded a collective European crisis response with pooled resources, based on mutualization of the risk. As former German foreign minister J. Fischer has critically argued, in "the financial crisis this logic (of a European Germany…) has been replaced by the domination of the creditors on the debtors".[54] Germany's adherence to austerity has not solved the crisis but rather moved it into the political realm, hindering the process of deeper integration.

Only a decade after the eurozone sovereign debt crisis that almost led to the break-up of the monetary union, the euro area had to face another threat, with the COVID-19 pandemic leading to the most severe contraction of output ever recorded. Given the global and exogenous nature of the pandemic, imposing a new wave of austerity in exchange for ESM support was unthinkable.

On the contrary, a Franco-German initiative announced on May 18, 2020, has adopted a much more rational position, contrary to the traditional prejudices against mutualization of risk. It called for the development of a recovery fund, in the form of transfers financed by common long-term European debt issuance. Despite the initial opposition by the so-called "frugal four" governments (i.e., Austria, Denmark, the Netherlands, and Sweden), the European Council agreed on July 21, 2020, to develop, for the first time, countercyclical fiscal transfers financed by common debt issuance, in the form of a Recovery Fund.

---

[52] See Katrougalos, G. (2013), Memoranda: Greek exceptionalism or the Mirror of Europe's Future in A. Trianafyllidou et al., *The Greek Crisis and European Modernity*, Parlgrave Macmillan, New York, pp. 89–109.

[53] M. Perelman, (2012). "Sado-Monetarism: The Role of the Federal Reserve System in Keeping Wages Low," Monthly Review, 63, p. 11.

[54] J. Fischer (2014), *Scheitert Europa?*, Kiepenheuer&Witsch, Cologne, p. 39.

This Recovery Fund used allocation criteria linked to infection rates and past economic performance. More than half of these funds (€390 billion) have been allocated as grants to EU countries, in effect introducing debt-financed cross-country transfers in the EU for the first time, while the reimbursement of the joint debt was to be serviced by the general EU budget, in consideration to the country size and the adverse economic impact of COVID-19. In addition to this new ESM credit line, euro area finance ministers also agreed to create a temporary new EU instrument, entitled "Support to mitigate Unemployment Risks in an Emergency" (SURE). This additional borrowing facility could provide up to €100 billion in loans to EU countries to fund short-term work schemes that have been heavily relied upon since the beginning of COVID-19 lockdowns in March 2020. As for the ESM, the main advantage of SURE is that it can rely on the AAA rating of EU institutions to borrow cheaply and pass these interest savings on to member states.[55]

Although the 750 billion Euros allocated to the fund fell behind the almost three times bigger stimulus package of the USA, its importance should not be underestimated. It is a first, timid step toward the mutualization of the risk in Europe. For the first time in its history, the EU will borrow from capital markets to finance member states expenditures throughout the Union. Although it would be an exaggeration to speak already for a "Hamiltonian moment" for Europe, this move not only increases the stability of the monetary union but also opens a window of opportunity for a more social future for the EU.

7.4 Conclusion

The initial "constitutional asymmetry"[56] of economic and social elements in the Community Treaties and between social member states and the EU is yet to be overcome.[57] EU citizenship is still defined by a link not to a demos but to a market.[58] When social rights are measured against the common market interests, the former, they almost never win.[59] A new balancing in the judicial and political construction

[55] See A. Camous, G. Claeys (2020), The evolution of European economic institutions during the COVID-19 crisis, European Policy Analysis, Volume 6, Issue 2, December 2020, pp. 328–341.

[56] See Scharpf, F. (2002) "The European Social Model: Coping with the Challenges of Diversity," Journal of Common Market Studies, vol.40, n°4, 645–669, p. 646.

[57] Wendler F. (2004) The paradoxical effects of institutional change for the legitimacy of European governance: the case of EU Social Policy, European Integration on line Papers (EIoP), vol. 8, 7, Scharpf, F. (2002) The European Social Model: Coping with the Challenges of Diversity, in: Journal of Common Market Studies, 40, 645–70.

[58] Maduro, M.P. (2000), "Europe's Social Self: 'The sickness unto death'" in J. Shaw (Ed.), Social Law and Policy in an Evolving European Union, Oxford, Portland: Hart Publishing, 325–349, p. 340.

[59] Lorber, P. (2004), "Labour Law" in S. Peers and A. Ward, The European Union Charter of Fundamental Rights, Oxford and Portland Oregon: Hart Publishing, 210F-230, p. 225, Gijzen, M. (2001) "The Charter: A milestone for social protection in Europe" 8 MJ 1, 33–48, p. 45.

of the European Economic Constitution is necessary. The crucial issue is how to reconcile social rights with the logic of market integration, so as to "transnational governance would not encroach of fundamental social values (…) which go to the very self-understanding of the European citizen".[60] This will be the central issue for the future of the European Polity.

George S.-P. Katrougalos is a Professor of Public Law at Democritus University of Thrace, former Minister of Foreign Affairs of Greece. He has published extensively on comparative constitutional law, law and globalization, and social rights. He has lectured as visiting professor or invited speaker at New York University, Columbia, Oxford, Humboldt, London School of Economics, Dublin College University, Tilburg, UNAM, New Delhi Law School, and others. He has served as a member of the Greek Parliament and the European Parliament, State Minister for European Affairs, Minister of Labor and Social Security, and State Minister for Administrative Reforms of Greece.

[60] Weiler, J. H.H., (1995), "Fundamental rights and fundamental boundaries: On standards and values in the protection of human rights," in N. Neuwahl and A. Rosas (Eds), The Hague, Boston, London: Martinus Nijzhoff Publishers, 51–76, p. 53, 54.

Part II
Administrative Law

Chapter 8
Administrative Justice in Iran; Oscillating Between Monism and Dualism

Moslem Aghaeitogh

Abstract The history of administrative justice in Iran can be divided into two periods. Before the Islamic Revolution of 1979, Iranian administrative justice belonged to the British monist model and the Supreme Court had the jurisdiction over administrative disputes. The constitution of the Islamic Republic of Iran (1979), however, has accepted the French dualist model and created the Court of Administrative Justice which has the responsibility to review the administrative acts and regulations. But, in some aspects, there are deviations from this dualist model. More precisely, cases concerning bilateral administrative acts and administrative liability are dealt with by ordinary courts. Thus, it can be argued that the Iranian legislature has accepted a modified version of the French system of administrative justice and combined it with the British system. This paper uses analytic and doctrinal approaches to discuss the effects of this oscillation.

8.1 Introduction

Iran has a long history of modern administrative law which dates back to the last decades of the *Qajar* Dynasty (1789–1925). After the Constitutional Revolution of 1906, the first steps have been taken to build a modern public administration in Iran, and over the successive years, different legislative acts have been passed, various events occurred and significant milestones have been reached. As one of the notable developments in the area of administrative law, the constitution of the Islamic Republic of Iran (1979) has created the Court of Administrative Justice (hereinafter CAJ) which has the responsibility to review the administrative acts and regulations and to investigate the complaints, grievances, and objections of the people against administrative authorities as well as administrative regulations.

Despite this constitutionalization of administrative justice in Iran and its subsequent notable developments, there are some debates about this court's position in the

M. Aghaeitogh (✉)
University of Judicial Sciences and Administrative Services, Tehran, Iran
e-mail: moslemtog@gmail.com

M. John et al. (eds.), *The Indian Yearbook of Comparative Law 2020*, The Indian Yearbook of Comparative Law, https://doi.org/10.1007/978-981-99-5467-4_7

judicial system of Iran.[1] The main question is that if the CAJ should be considered as a special court belonging to judicial courts with limited jurisdiction in administrative law matters or should be counted as an administrative court separate from judicial courts and with inherent jurisdiction over generally all administrative law matters. In other words, it is questionable whether the Iranian administrative justice system is among the dualist, continental or French model of administrative justice or should be considered monist, common law, or Anglo-Saxon model of administrative justice. Whether the Iranian administrative justice belongs to the monist or the dualist model has a direct effect on determining the jurisdiction of CAJ.

This paper theoretically is based on the dichotomy between dualist and monist models of administrative justice that is best presented by Guy Braibant.[2] My thesis is that the Constitution of the Islamic Republic of Iran has accepted a modified version of a dualist system of administrative justice and accordingly, the CAJ should be considered as an administrative court distinct from ordinary and special judicial courts with its inherent jurisdiction in administrative disputes.

8.2 The Dichotomy Between Monism and Dualism in Administrative Justice

The establishment and the evolution of the systems of administrative justice "is the fruit of history and national traditions."[3] As a result, all legal systems around the world choose different ways of judicial review of administrative acts or resolving conflicts arising out of relations between administration and citizens. There are at least two main questions that each legal system should respond to; who resolves the conflicts of citizens and administrative bodies and on what basis? In other words, it should be determined that if it is necessary to establish a new order of special courts to resolve administrative conflicts or not and ordinary courts can do this task. There is another important question: is there a need for specific legal rules or ordinary common rules is enough?

Based on the responses of national judicial systems to these two essential questions, scholars have classified the systems of administrative justice in different ways.[4] For example, according to the classification presented by Jesus González Pérez, there

[1] On this debate see for example, Moslem Aghaei Togh and Hasan Lotfi, *Administrative Law*, vol 1 (Sherkat Sahami Enteshar 2020) 295. Reza Mousazadeh, *Administrative Law* (13th edn, Mizan Publication 2010) 314–317.

[2] Guy Braibant, "La Juridiction Administrative En Droit Comparé" (1999) 52 La Revue administrative.

[3] Bernard Stirn and Yann Aguila, *Droit administratif français et européen* (Paris, Presses de sciences po et dalloz Fraga 2014) 525.

[4] There are other classifications that are based on different questions or variables. For example, Michael Asimow identifies five models of administrative justice based on four key variables, namely, combined function agencies or separate tribunals, adversarial or inquisitorial procedure, open or closed judicial review, and judicial review by generalized or specialized courts. See: Michael

are three models of administrative justice around the world. In the first model, there exist special administrative tribunals separate from judiciary such as in France and Colombia. In the second model, ordinary courts deal with administrative matters such as common law systems. In the third model, special judicial organs have been created inside the judiciary to handle administrative cases such as in Spain.[5] Morand-Deviller presents a similar classification and names the third model as mixed or German model.[6] Stirn and Aguila also provide a detailed classification of four models of administrative justice which is originally based on monist and dualist dichotomy.[7]

The classification that is provided by González Pérez is very similar to that of Guy Braibant, who has stated almost two decades ago in one of his speeches on comparative administrative justice. According to Braibant, although there is no uniform system at all and there are even very big differences among national systems in terms of administrative justice,[8] the responses of different legal systems to these preliminary questions could be classified into two models: dualism and monism.

In the dualist model, also known as the continental or French model, they accept the necessity of the establishment of new bodies to review the administrative acts. In their opinion, administrative acts and the disputes related to these acts are not similar to private disputes and ordinary courts which "obey radically different principles,"[9] could not handle these types of problems. Also, these new bodies need access to new rules governing administrative action. So in this model, there are two fundamental pillars: "*dualisme juridique*" which means a different "body of rules regulate the relationships of the administration or of the administrative authority towards private citizens"[10] and "*dualisme juridictionnel*" which means there are two distinct hierarchies of courts and judicial activities, one concerns administrative litigations and other, private traditional disputes.

This is generally summarized as autonomy or independence of administrative law which is the main feature of French administrative law. At least since the law of 16–20 August 1790, the separation of administrative and judicial authorities is announced with absolute prohibition for the latter "to disturb in any way the operations of the administrative bodies or to summon administrators because of their functions."[11] This dualism has its roots in the historical distrust of French revolutionists on judicial power. Historically, the courts had constituted a redoubt of the aristocracy and in the years immediately prior to the Revolution they had come

Asimow, "Five Models of Administrative Adjudication"(2015) 63 American Journal of Comparative Law 3.

5 Jesus Gonzales Perez, *Manual de derecho procesal administrativo* (Civitas 2001) 100.

6 Jacqueline Morand-Deviller, *Droit administratif* (10th edn, Montchrestien 2007) 14.

7 Strin and Aguila (n 3) 525–528.

8 Braibant (n 2) 234.

9 Armando Rizo Oyanguren, *Manual Elemental de Derecho Administrativo* (Universidad Nacional Autónoma de Nicaragua 1991) 123.

10 AV Dicey, *The Law of the Constitution* (JWF Allison ed, Oxford University Press 2013) 378.

11 Strin and Aguila (n 3) 524; Gabino Fraga, *Derecho Administrativo* (Manuel Fraga ed, 24th edn, Editorial Porrúa 1985) 447. See also, Georges Dupuis, Marie-José Guédon and Patrice Chrétien, *Droit administratif* (10th edn, Dalloz 2007) 4–5.

to hinder the application of essential economic and social reforms, agreed by the King.[12] As a result of this distrust, disputes between individuals and administrative authorities are heard in administrative tribunals headed by *Conseil d'Etat* separate from the ordinary civil courts and where different rules applied.[13] In this system of specialized administrative tribunals, parties have access to a set of judges who have more expertise in resolving administrative law disputes than their colleagues in ordinary courts.[14] These two pillars distinguish the French model from the so-called monist or Anglo-Saxon model, in which there are the same legal rules governing public administration and private activities and ordinary courts settle all the disputes arising.

In the monist model, also known as the common law model, there are countries that reject the necessity of the establishment of new bodies to resolve administrative disputes. Their view is that administrative authorities as well as individuals are within the bounds of the Rule of Law and administrative disputes conceptually and essentially are not different from ordinary disputes and fall within the jurisdiction of ordinary courts. Furthermore, administrative bodies and their relations with citizens are subject to the rule of general law and there is no need to produce the new set of laws, different from ordinary law. Anglo-Saxon administrative law falls within this category. Albert Venn Dicey, the most important figure in this picture has summarized the monist tradition of administrative justice in writing that:

> any official who exceeds the authority given him by the law incurs the common law responsibility for his wrongful act; he is amenable to the authority of the ordinary courts.[15]

Some scholars, however, argue that the dichotomy between dualism and monism in the administrative justice is outdated and "was actual in a period that has now past and in the framework of legal systems not so in communication between them."[16] I think that this dichotomy has not lost its importance and as I will discuss, does affect how an administrative system works.

---

[12] Miguel Sánchez Morón, *Derecho administrative: Parte General* (Tecnos 2014) 34.

[13] Jamie Grace, *Constitutional and Administrative Law: Key Facts and Key Cases* (Routledge, 2016) 25.

[14] Asimow (N 4) 25.

[15] Dicey (N 10) 389. For the historical basis of this dichotomy according to Dicey, see: Francesca Bignami, "Regulation and the Courts: Judicial Review in Comparative Perspective" in Francesca Bignami and David Zaring, *Comparative Law and Regulation* (Edward Elgar Publishing 2016) 277–278.

[16] Mario P Chiti, "Monism or dualism in Administrative Law: A True or a False Dilemma?" *(2000) 53 La Revue administrative* 56.

8.3 Administrative Justice After the Constitutional Revolution of 1906

Historically, Iran's modern legal system dates back to the Constitutional Revolution of 1906. Prior to that, there was a scattered set of customary rules and royal decrees in addition to sharia law, and there was no clear process for judicial review of public administration. If anyone wanted to object to the public administration or to complain about the actions of public officials, they would go to the administration itself and there would be no special court. There is no clear evidence on the scale and the nature of these complaints as well as the administrative reactions to them.

The first Constitution of Iran that is ratified in a post haste way after the Constitutional Revolution of 1906 has not mentioned the judicial system of the country.[17] So, there are not any special rules about the duties and activities of the courts or judicial branch. The issue of judicial review of the public administration was also not mentioned in this constitution. One year later, the newly established parliament of Iran enacted a supplementary constitution which contained the bill of rights and designed the overall system of government which was a constitutional monarchy based on the separation of powers.

Article 27 and Sect. 8.7 of this supplementary constitution, "were the first laws on judicial affairs introduced after the Constitutional Revolution."[18] In article 27 (2) of this act, a dual system of the judiciary was accepted: judicial power "belongs to the ecclesiastical (sharia) courts in matters of Islamic law and civil courts in matters of customary law." So, there were two distinct hierarchies of courts: on the one hand, there were civil courts headed by the Supreme Court of Justice, and on the other hand, ecclesiastical courts were responsible to settle conflicts on religious matters. In the side of civil, non-religious matters all conflicts and litigations belong to the civil courts headed by the Supreme Court of Justice (divan-e 'edalat-e 'ozma) or the Court of Cassation, whose powers and attributes were mentioned in article 71 of the supplementary constitution: "the Supreme Court of Justice and the courts of the judiciary are the official authority for public petitions…".[19]

In the area of administrative law, the approach of the supplementary constitution was not generously and its approach was narrow. Because of this, some scholars

[17] The constitution of 1905 was incomplete in many ways. For example, there was not any rule concerning the rights of the people, especially the principle of equality, and separation of powers. See: Mostafa Rahimi, *Iran's Constitution and Principles of Democracy* (4th edn, Niloufar 2010) 80–81. One of the reasons of this incompleteness was that the king was not eager as the constitution was about to confine his powers. See: Mohammad Moghadamfard, "Critical Analysis of Judicial Review of Administrative Actions in Iran" (2018) 23 *The Malaysian Journal of Law and Society* 27.

[18] Hadi Enayat, *Law, State, and Society in Modern Iran: Constitutionalism, Autocracy, and Legal Reform, 1906–1941* (Palgrave Macmillan 2013) 64.

[19] Baldwin provides a short introduction to judicial system of Iran in this pre-Islamic Revolution era. See: Gordon Baldwin, "The Legal System of Iran" (1973) 7 The International Lawyer 497–500.

believe that in the supplementary constitution, there was no judicial review of administrative action.[20] But this is not the case. All conflicts of administrative authorities with each other concerning their competences as well as some types of administrative law cases, especially disputes arising out of public employment, fall within the general jurisdiction of the Supreme Court of Justice. Article 88 of the supplementary constitution illustrated, "arbitration in the cases of dispute as to the limitations of the functions and duties of the different departments of government shall, agreeably to the provisions of the Law, be referred to the Court of Cassation." This article that accepted the jurisdiction of the Supreme Court in administrative acts could be recognized as the cornerstone of the Iranian administrative justice system in the constitutional era. Since the constitution had delegated the jurisdiction of administrative disputes to the Supreme Court and did not establish another administrative body for this purpose, it is accepted among scholars that the classic model of administrative justice of Iran was a monistic model.[21]

This monistic approach to the administrative justice system, however, is not respected by ordinary laws in subsequent years. Deviations from this monistic approach appeared very soon after the supplementary constitution was passed. The first deviation was the establishment of different administrative tribunals in the number of ministries, reinforced, especially with the ratification of the Jurisdiction on Disputes between Government and People Act in 1928 by the parliament.[22] Some scholars had mentioned this deviation and pointed out that the creation of these tribunals is unconstitutional and must be eliminated.[23] Editorial of the Iranian Bar Association's influential magazine, which was written in 1949 on the occasion of this magazine's first anniversary, regarded the establishment of these tribunals "at the forefront of all defects and disadvantages" of the judicial system and criticized this situation:

> the proliferation of various specialized administrative courts based on the unprecedented foundations within the Ministry of Justice and its subsidiary departments and even other ministries, is a major disadvantage that has diminished the authority of the judiciary.[24]

Criticisms of this kind were effective and put pressure on the government to dissolve administrative tribunals. As a result, an act was passed by the Mossadegh government in 1952 abolishing almost all administrative tribunals. Article 5 of this act clearly emphasizes the general jurisdiction of the judiciary and reaffirms the general jurisdiction of the judicial courts to hear administrative law cases: "all disputes between government and individuals except tax disputes in general, like

[20] Moghadamfard (n 17) 27.

[21] Javad Mahmoodi and Hoda Ghaffari, "Judicial Oversight of Administration in the Constitutional Legal System" (2008) 5 Constitutional Law Review 224.

[22] Mohammad Farnia, "Administrative Tribunals" (1948) 1 *Iranian Bar Association Magazine* 2.

[23] See generally: ibid 1–8; Arsalan Khalatbari, "The Necessity of Unification of Judicial Organizations and Laws" (1952) 2 *Iranian Bar Association Magazine* 1–3; Arsalan Khalatbari, "Authorities of Legislative and Judicial Powers" (1952) 1 *Iranian Bar Association Magazine* 36–39.

[24] Majidi, "After One Year" (1952) 1 *Iranian Bar Association Magazine* 1–4.

other disputes shall be settled down in judicial courts according to general laws and regulations."

The second major deviation from the monistic approach of the constitution to the administrative justice system was related to the efforts to establish the Council of State as an administrative court. From the very beginning of the constitutional era in Iran, the creation of this council has been promised in different acts of the parliament. First of all, article 28 of the Public Finance Act (1911) and then article 71 of the Public Finance Tribunal Act (1912) should be mentioned here. Ten years later, in 1921, when Ahmad Qavam wanted to present his program as prime minister to the Parliament he declared his will to establish the Council of State. In 1922, the resolution of public employment cases was assigned to this council by article 64 of the Public Employment Act. This article declared that as long as the Council of State has not been established, the Supreme Court will have jurisdiction in civil service and public employment cases.

In 1960, a bill was introduced by the Minister of Justice, Mohammad Ali Hedayati, as a part of his liberal reforms to establish the Council of State.[25] Consequently, the Council of State Act was enacted by parliament, and for the first time, duties and structure of this council as an independent administrative court have been determined by the legislature. Council was under the supervision of the Minister of Justice and had five chambers, all located in the capital city of Tehran. Each chamber consisted of one president and two associate judges. All three members were appointed by the King (*shah*) upon the proposal of the Minister of Justice. All petitions against administrative acts and regulations in matters of *ultra vires*, abuse of power, and illegality were within the jurisdiction of the council.

Despite this council's appearance in legislative acts from the very beginning of the constitutional era, it was not a constitutionally acceptable institution. Its existence was explicitly contrary to the constitution. As mentioned above, the judicial review of administrative actions was within the jurisdiction of the Supreme Court and creation of another court was unconstitutional and unnecessary. Possibly because the constitutionality of the Council of State was highly questionable, designers of the council limited its jurisdiction to the annulment of administrative unilateral acts, and administrative contracts and administrative liability cases remain on the jurisdiction of ordinary courts and the Supreme Court.[26]

Efforts of the parliament to create an unconstitutional institution occurred because, in the constitution of 1906, there was not any official mechanism for constitutional review of legislative action[27] and history showed that, in that era, there is nothing to guarantee the constitution and impede this kind of irregularities. It seems that, because of this unconstitutionality and tremendous effects and burdens of creating

---

[25] Enayat (n 18) 178.

[26] Moslem Aghaei Togh, "A Historical Analysis of the Duality of Litigation Process in matters of Responsibility of State in Iran" (2019) 20 Quarterly Journal of Public Law 252.

[27] Baldwin (n 19) 500.

an unconstitutional judicial institution with such a vast authority, the government refrained from enforcing the act of 1960 and this council was never established.[28]

8.4 Administrative Justice After the Islamic Revolution

The Islamic Revolution of Iran took place in 1979 and changed deeply political, judicial, and administrative structure of Iran.[29] In the constitution of the Islamic Republic of Iran which was ratified in 1979 and amended 10 years later, judicial power like other political powers of the state, underwent profound changes and reforms[30]; the ministerial classic judiciary changed first to the council-based Latin American model which originally "came with the promise of independent,]and[better functioning judiciary."[31] In 1989, after 10 years of unsuccessful experiences with council-based judiciary which allegedly was so inefficient and slow, this model changed to a new and unprecedented centralized managerial model in which judicial power is headed by a high cleric appointed by the Supreme Leader for 5 years—with the possibility of re-appointment—who is responsible for the "establishment of the organizational structure" of the judicial system.[32] The Head of Judiciary is deemed to be "the highest authority of the judiciary" and has the power to appoint and dismiss judges, define their jobs, make promotions and transfers of judges, and make other administrative decisions. The Head of Judiciary also appoints the Prosecutor General and President of the Supreme Court, both of whom also must be clerics.[33]

According to Article 160 of the Constitution, "the Minister of Justice owes responsibility in all matters concerning the relationship between the judiciary, on the one hand, and the executive and legislative branches, on the other hand. He will be elected from among the individuals proposed to the President by the head of the judiciary branch." Although "the Head of the Judiciary may delegate full authority to the Minister of Justice in financial and administrative areas and for the employment of personnel other than judges," but this does not mean that the Minister has the power over the judiciary.

---

[28] Some authors believe that "although the bill was passed by parliament, it was opposed by the shah and the institution was never established." Enayat (n 18) 179.

[29] For more information on the legal and judicial system of Islamic Reupublic of Iran, see generally Adineh Abghari, *Introduction to the Iranian Legal System and the Protection of Human Rights in Iran* (British Institute of International and Comparative Law 2008).

[30] See: Sahar Maranlou, *Access to Justice in Iran: Women, Perceptions, and Reality* (Cambridge University Press 2015) 64–68.

[31] Michal Bobek, and David Kosař, "Global Solutions, Local Damages: A Critical Study in Judicial Councils in Central and Eastern Europe" (2014) 15 German Law Journal 1258.

[32] Article 157 of the Constitution of the Islamic Republic of Iran.

[33] Ronda Cress, Catherine Kent and Mohammad Nayyeri, "*Rule of Law in Iran: Independence of the Judiciary, Bar Association, Lawyers and Iran's Compliance with International Human Rights Obligations*" [2014] Human Rights in Iran unit, University of Essex 12.

The constitution called the judiciary to be "an independent power," and charges it with "investigating and passing judgments on grievances; ...supervising the proper enforcement of laws; ... uncovering crimes; prosecuting, punishing, and chastising criminals;" taking "suitable measures" to prevent crime and reform criminals.[34] These functions of the judiciary are performed by courts which are vested with the authority to examine and settle lawsuits and protect the rights of the public.[35]

The constitution shares judicial authority between two main categories of courts: judicial courts under the supervision of the Supreme Court or Court of Cassation on the one hand and the CAJ, on the other hand. Judicial courts deal with classic conflicts and disputes of people between themselves and are divided into two categories: ordinary or general courts and special courts. Ordinary courts which are more numerous and are widely spread across the country have a general jurisdiction in civil and criminal cases and are organized in two levels: preliminary courts and appellate courts. Preliminary courts consist of Civil Courts, Criminal Courts, and Family Courts. The Appellate Court which has provincial jurisdiction hears appeals from preliminary courts and has civil, criminal, and family branches. Alongside these ordinary courts, there are also some special courts which include Revolutionary Courts, Military Courts, and Clergies' Courts. All these judicial courts, ordinary as well as special courts are under the supervision of the Supreme Court which is "formed to supervise the correct implementation of the laws by the courts" and "to ensure the uniformity of judicial procedure."[36]

Although civil and criminal cases are heard by judicial courts, petitions and complaints of the people against administrative organizations and agencies are dealt with by the CAJ. Article 173 of the constitution for the first time in the history of Iran, established a special judicial order to review the administrative acts and regulations. According to this article, which has constitutionalized administrative justice in Iran,[37]

> in order to investigate the complaints, grievances, and objections of the people against governmental officials, units, and protocols, and in order for the people to restore their rights, a court, named the Court of Administrative Justice, will be established under the supervision of the head of the judiciary. The law shall determine the responsibility and the mode of operation of this court.

The current law determining the structure and the procedure of the court is ratified by the Council of Expediency in 2013. According to this law, the CAJ is

---

[34] The Constitution of the Islamic Republic of Iran, article 156.

[35] The Constitution of the Islamic Republic of Iran, article 61.

[36] The Constitution of the Islamic Republic of Iran, article 161.

[37] According to Tom Ginsburg, "constitutions engage with administrative law through the designation of administrative court systems. These are found in countries from Mexico to Mongolia, though they are not always constitutionalized (only about 2% of cases in our sample include them). Even the French Constitution makes only incremental reference to the Conseil d'Etat, which is not properly speaking a creature of the political constitution." Tom Ginsburg, "Written Constitutions and the Administrative State: On the Constitutional Character of Administrative Law" in Susan Rose-Ackerman, Peter Lindseth and Blake Emerson, *Comparative Administrative Law* (Edward Elgar Publishing 2017) 123.

located in the capital city of Tehran and deals with administrative law cases. This court consists of primary chambers, appellate chambers, specialized boards, and the plenary session.[38] The head of the court is appointed by the head of the judicial power. Each primary chamber consists of one judge and appellate chambers consist of three judges. Specialized boards consist of at least 15 judges[39] and the plenary session is composed of all the judges of the court.[40] The quorum for the appellate chambers is two judges and for the plenary session is at least two-thirds of the members.

Chambers, first instance as well as appellate, have jurisdiction over complaints, grievances, and actions against two types of administrative actions. First, they have the jurisdiction over the complaints against decisions and actions of administrative units including ministries, governmental institutions, state-owned companies, municipalities, Social Security Organization, and revolutionary institutions and their affiliated organizations. Second, they have the jurisdiction over decisive judgments rendered by administrative tribunals or quasi-judicial bodies. In addition to this, civil servants and judges could file their complaints about their employment in these chambers. Thus, it is conceivable that all cases heard by the chambers of the CAJ are related to the unilateral individual administrative acts, and these chambers lack the jurisdiction over general administrative acts that fall within the jurisdiction of the plenary session of the Court which deals with appeals against regulations enacted by governmental bodies (ministries, governmental institutions, and state-owned companies), municipalities, and non-governmental public institutions.

The constitutional fathers of the Islamic Republic of Iran had in their mind to create an independent and separate judicial body to deal with all administrative acts, individual as well as general, and unilateral as well as bilateral. This original intent is understandable from the text of article 173 of the constitution, where investigation of all complaints, grievances, and objections of the people against government officials and units and restoration of their rights are vested to the CAJ. But, this original intent of the constituent power to create a dual judicial system has not been respected by the parliament. It seems that the ghost of the pre-Islamic Revolution monist model of judicial review lurking behind the numerous laws that are enacted after the Islamic Revolution has affected directly or indirectly the jurisdiction of the Court, especially the Court of Administrative Justice acts of 1981 and 2006 and the current law of 2013. Despite the tremendous changes in the political and judicial structure of the nation after the Islamic Revolution and the substitution of the dualist model of administrative justice with monist model, some important aspects of the judicial review of administrative actions follow the arrays of monist model.

The deviations from the dualist model have affected the jurisdiction of the CAJ. As a result, some areas of administrative law and some cases that theoretically belong to the administrative law, especially bilateral administrative acts, litigious cases, and administrative liability cases are not in the jurisdiction of CAJ and are dealt with by ordinary courts.

---

[38] The Organization and Procedure of the Court of Administrative Justice Act of 2013, article 2.

[39] The Organization and Procedure of the Court of Administrative Justice Act of 2013, article 84.

[40] The Organization and Procedure of the Court of Administrative Justice Act of 2013, article 8.

8.5 Bilateral Administrative Acts

In one category, administrative acts are divided into unilateral and bilateral or plurilateral acts. A unilateral administrative act may be defined as an expression of will emanating from administrative authority or authorities which produces legal effects and imposes changes in the legal situations of citizens in conformity with the law.[41] Unilateral acts are divided into two major forms: regulations and individual decisions.[42] The regulations are ratified and promulgated by administrative authorities and like legislative acts, are of general character. Individual decisions, however, don't have general character and consider the legal situation of a certain person. In contrast, the bilateral administrative act refers to an act that involves the consenting wills of at least two parties and produces legal effects. The bilateral administrative acts or contracts may be private or public.[43] Private contracts of administration are regulated by private law but public contracts or administrative contracts are regulated generally by public law.[44]

In the majority of civil law countries, litigations concerning administrative contracts are dealt with by administrative courts. In French administrative law, when a contract is qualified as an administrative contract (contrat administratif), disputes and conflicts arising from it will be dealt with by administrative tribunals (tribunaux administratifs). This results from the fact that, in French administrative law, administrative contracts are considered somehow different from civil law contracts,[45] and thus, litigations concerning administrative contracts are dealt with through appeals of full jurisdiction (plein contentieux) in which administrative tribunal decides about the case such as an ordinary civil court.[46] That is, in cases involving administrative contracts the remedy is not limited to the annulment of the administrative action or an injunction but it extends to all judicial remedies available in the ordinary courts. In Spanish administrative law too, cases concerning public contracts of the administration are settled down by administrative courts.[47]

In Iranian administrative law, the disputes arising from the contracts of administrative authorities, both public and private, generally are excluded from the jurisdiction of CAJ and are dealt with by the ordinary civil courts.[48] All three legislations enacted

---

[41] Jean Waline, *Droit administratif* (22nd edn, Dalloz 2008) 377.

[42] Dupuis, Guédon and Chrétien (n 11) 229.

[43] Some authors, however, argue that all contracts of administration are of administrative nature and "there are no private contracts of administration." See for example Agustín Gordillo, *Tratado de Derecho Administrativo: Parte General*, vol 1, (Fundación de Derecho Administrativo 2003) 327.

[44] Dupuis, Guédon and Chrétien (n 11) 263.

[45] Dupuis, Guédon and Chrétien (n 11) 506.

[46] Dupuis, Guédon and Chrétien (n 11) 497.

[47] Enrique Arnaldo Alcubilla, y Rafael Fernández Valverde (eds.) *Jurisdicción Contencioso-Administrativa*, 3ª Edición, (Wolters Kluwer Espana, S. A., 2007), 76.

[48] Manoochehr Tabatabai Motamani, *Administrative Law* (16th edn, SAMT 2011) 484; Aghaei Toghand Lotfi (n 1) 326–328; Mohammad Jalali, Mohammad Hasanvand, and Ayob Miri, "Differentiation between the Jurisdiction of the Administrative Justice Court and the Public Court over Claims for Civil Responsibility against the Government" (2017) 81 Judiciary Law Journal 98.

after the Islamic Revolution about the CAJ, limit the jurisdiction of this court to unilateral acts of administration. From among administrative contracts, only public employment contracts fall within the jurisdiction of this court.[49] This limitation has been recognized and asserted in different decisions of both the Supreme Court of Iran and the CAJ. The plenary session of the CAJ in a number of its judgments for the unification of jurisprudence such as judgment number 59 (21 July 1992),[50] judgment number 33 (18 May 1996),[51] judgment number 130 (12 September 1998),[52] judgment number 197 (10 September 2000),[53] judgment number 1329 (3 February 2008), and judgment number 228 (29 July 2012)[54] has asserted that disputes arising from contracts and transactions including foreign exchange contracts are considered as civil disputes and fall within the jurisdiction of the civil courts.

8.6 Litigious or Entre Partes Cases

In procedural law, litigation is a term used to describe the dispute between two or more parties. The opposing parties want to protect and enforce their subjective rights against each other. The majority of cases before courts, especially civil courts, are made up of litigious actions filed by one party against another. Besides these litigious lawsuits, there are some non-litigious cases in which there are no opposing sides. Similar to civil courts, in administrative courts, there might be litigious as well as non-litigious cases.

Concerning Iranian administrative law, some scholars argue that the jurisdiction of the CAJ is limited to non-litigious cases. Both the Supreme Court and the CAJ confirm this approach in their long-standing jurisprudence. Supreme Court in the number of its judgments for the unification of jurisprudence such as judgment number 47 (7 January 1985)[55] and judgment number 558 (28 May 1991),[56] affirmed this approach. Also, CAJ in some cases such as judgment number 59 (21 July 1992)[57] and judgment number 228 (29 July 2012) rejected its jurisdiction over litigious cases.

The limitation of court's jurisdiction to non-litigious cases stems from the fact that the jurisdiction of the CAJ is limited to the classic annulment of administrative acts

---

[49] Some authors, however, argue that in the Iranian administrative law, public employment is not the matter of administrative bilateral act or contract. See, Morteza Nejabatkhah, and Farhang Faghih Larijani, "The Jurisdiction of Administrative Justice Court in Connection with the Complaints Arising from the Public Employment Contracts" (2016) 46 Public Law Studies Quarterly 244.

[50] Official Gazette of I.R. of Iran, 5 March 1994, no. 14275.

[51] Official Gazette of I.R. of Iran, 30 September 1996, no.15024.

[52] Official Gazette of I.R. of Iran, 6 January 1999, no. 15692.

[53] Official Gazette of I.R. of Iran, 31 December 2000, no. 16269.

[54] Official Gazette of I.R. of Iran, 11 August 2012, no. 19643.

[55] Official Gazette of I.R. of Iran, 31 July 1985, no. 11139.

[56] Official Gazette of I.R. of Iran, 7 July 1991, no. 13491.

[57] Official Gazette of I.R. of Iran, 5 March 1994, no. 14275.

and as Édouard Laferrière (1841–1901) has discussed in his magnum opus, *Traité de la juridiction administrative et des recours contentieux*, actions for annulment are actions against administrative act itself and not against persons.[58] In this meaning, actions of annulments are non-litigious actions and fall beyond the jurisdiction of the CAJ which is limited to the complaints against the administrative actions. This conception of Iranian administrative justice is similar to the Spanish classic conception of the "*contencioso- administrativo como revisora*" by which what was intended was to review the legality of administrative acts and not to address the subjective rights of the individuals vis-á-vis the administration.[59]

8.7 Administrative Liability

When an individual suffers from loss or harm because of an administrative act, we face the problem of administrative liability which can be defined as the obligation for the administration to repair the damage it causes to others. Non-contractual liability of administration for damages incurred to an individual by breach of a legal obligation is an important part of the administrative law today. The administrative liability regarding its various foundations and standards could be divided into two main categories: liability for fault or fault-based liability and liability without fault or strict liability, which understood in the sense of a liability untied and independent of any concept of fault or negligence and is based mostly on two foundations, risk and the breach of equality before public charges.[60] These foundations are the principles that justify the imposition on administrative authorities of the obligation to repair certain prejudices. In addition to this, in each liability case, three elements should be considered by the judge. These necessary elements of liability include the generating event, damage, and the causal link between the two.[61] For example, in case of damage, the judge has to find out if the damage is special, abnormal, and certain or not. Finally, after considering these three elements, the administrative judge will announce upon the monetary evaluation of the damage suffered and will choose the amount of the compensation.

In France, as well as some other civil law countries such as Spain, Portugal, and Greece, administrative liability cases generally fall within the jurisdiction of administrative courts and these courts announce upon all elements of the case.[62] For example, in France, most of the administrative liability cases fall within the

[58] Strin and Aguila (n 3) 599; Andre de Laubadère, Jean-Claude Venezia and Yves Gaudemet, *Traité de droit administrative* (15th edn, LGDJ 1999) 497.

[59] José Antonio Moreno Molina and others, *Procedimiento y proceso administrativo práctico*, vol 3 (La Ley 2006) 189.

[60] Waline (n 41) 473; Stirn and Aguila add two other founadations for this type of responsability. See, Strin and Aguila (n 3) 467–472.

[61] Ibid 452.

[62] Ibid 477.

jurisdiction of administrative courts. Regarding the role of administrative courts in administrative liability law in France, it is famously accepted that the rules of this branch of liability are mostly originated from *Conseil d'Etat*.[63] Indeed, administrative liability actions are an important part of the full litigations in French *droit de contentieux administratif*.

In Iranian administrative law, claims concerning administrative responsibility are dealt with in two different courts. Administrative liability cases generally fall within the jurisdiction of ordinary civil courts and only some questions of these cases may be processed in the CAJ.[64] More precisely, all strict liability cases, like liabilities dictated by explicit legislative rules or liabilities based on risk theory, don't go to administrative jurisdiction and are dealt with by civil courts.[65] Only in case of fault-based liabilities, the CAJ decides on the legality of the administrative action that is alleged to have caused damage. In these cases, the CAJ merely declares the validity of the administrative action and does not punish the wrongful action of the administration and does not announce anything about the compensation of the damage.

Supreme Court in her judgment number 747 for the unification of jurisprudence dated 19 January 2016 has reaffirmed the duality of judicial procedure in administrative liability cases. According to this judgment:

> given that one of the conditions for civil liability is the existence of a fault, so in such cases as a prelude to the issuance of a judgment by the civil court to the compensation, the existence of fault and violation of rule of law must be established and after this, the amount of damage and compensation should be determined by the civil court... It is obvious that in cases where the owners of the lands which are seized and owned by the municipality demand the price of those lands without claiming the violation and infringement of the legal rules by the municipality, the case is out of the jurisdiction of CAJ and the civil court must hear the case and issue the appropriate rule.[66]

This duality in judicial procedure in administrative liability cases is the relic of the Law on the State Council approved in 1960, which seemed logical given the constraints of that institution, which was contrary to the constitutional rules. However, the CAJ is identified in the Constitution of the I.R.I. as part of the country's judiciary and article 173 of the Constitution grants jurisdiction over complaints, grievances, and objections of the people against the State. Accordingly, this duality is not compatible with the current judicial structure of the country and it aggravates the slowness of the judicial process, and increases the complexity of the judicial system and its costs, without any clear necessity.

---

[63] ibid 456.

[64] See generally: Ayat Mulaee, and Hasan Lotfi, "Critical Analysis on How to Prove the Elements of the Civil Liability of the Administration in the Framework of the Article 10 of the Administrative Justice Court Act" (2019) 10 Journal of Legal Studies 189–218; Javad Kashani, "The Competence for Hearing to Responsibility Case against State" (2016) 21 Judicial Law Views Quarterly 127–162.

[65] Aghaei Toghand Lotfi (n 1) 328.

[66] Official Gazette of Islamic Republic of Iran, no 20691, 15 March 2016.

8.8 Conclusion

Iranian administrative law belongs to the French dualist system of droit administratif. Both Iranian and French administrative law have accepted two kinds of duality: legal duality which means the existence of different rules governing relations between administration and individuals, judicial duality which means the existence of two distinct judicial orders; administrative courts for administrative matters and ordinary courts for classic disputes of the people between themselves. But, there are numerous deviations from this original model, especially in the case of judicial duality. In this paper, we discussed these deviations and their effects on Iranian administrative justice. More precisely, we argued that bilateral administrative acts, litigious cases and the most important part of the administrative liability cases are not in the jurisdiction of CAJ and are dealt with by ordinary courts.

Theoretically, it seems that the CAJ should be counted as an administrative court with general jurisdiction in administrative law cases. Article 173 of the Constitution of the Islamic Republic of Iran recognizes such a prominent role for this court in entrenching the rights of the people in relation with public administration. In some cases, however, it seems that this court is treated as a special court belonging to an ordinary judicial order and not as an administrative court. This erroneous approach to the position of the CAJ produces some problems in legislative as well as judicial level. In the legislative level, it resulted in underestimating the role and position of CAJ in settling administrative law cases. As a result, some administrative law disputes are not dealt with in CAJ and fall within the jurisdiction of ordinary civil courts. Similarly, in the judicial level, the vague position of the CAJ in the judicial system produces different jurisdictional disputes among the judicial system which in some cases need the Supreme Court's intervention to settle the dispute.

Chapter 9
Administrative Adjudication in the Common Law: A Comparison of Setups and Legal Tensions with India

Dinesh Singh

Abstract The system of administrative adjudication has not faced legal tensions in India alone, rather the system has evolved across the common law with similar issues. Largely the issues revolve around the traditional doctrines of Common Law, more prominently the doctrine of the Rule of Law upon which the concept of Independence of Judiciary is based. From the Common Law world, Australia, the United Kingdom, the United States of America, and Canada have been studied to find out such legal tensions and functionality of the system in the present form. Australia has a unique aspect of administrative adjudication through "merits review". That unlike judicial review could go beyond the limitation of review within four corners of law. Hence, under merits review the adjudicator could decide upon factual and even policy aspects. Further, the bodies performing the administrative adjudication in Australia are considered as part of the executive's domain. In the United Kingdom, the agency that manages the Courts and Tribunals remains same, i.e., the Her Majesty Courts and Tribunal Service (HMCTS). Further, the tribunals are not considered as part of the executive. Though there remains dispute on this proposition, the broad demarcation criteria for classification of a body as part of judicial structure remains the exercise of the "judicial power of the state" and the applicability of contempt law for its decisions. The "New Deal" and the politics behind it in the United States of America germinating the circumstances for creation of the Federal Administrative Procedures Act or "APA" leading various states enacting similar legislations have been discussed. The salient procedural features of APA have also been discussed. The Canadian trend of treating tribunals as creatures of statutes and outside the judicial domain has been discussed with the cases leading the legal position. Then some recommendations based on the comparative study have been proposed with regard to the system of Tribunals in India.

D. Singh (✉)
National Law University, Delhi, India
e-mail: dineshnlud@gmail.com; dinesh@nludelhi.ac.in

M. John et al. (eds.), *The Indian Yearbook of Comparative Law 2020*, The Indian Yearbook of Comparative Law, https://doi.org/10.1007/978-981-99-5467-4_8

9.1 Introduction

There have been debates as well as legal tensions across the globe regarding the adjudicating powers being exercised by some bodies mostly as the part of executive wing of the government, thereby trespassing upon the traditional judicial functions of the judicial wing.[1] The administrative *rulemaking* by the regulators laying down regulations could also be classified as an overlap of the legislative functions belonging to the legislative wing of the traditional government. Such delegated overlap, to an extent, is recognized for providing functional freedom for the implementation of legislations providing broad skeleton guidance.

Administrative adjudication is necessarily a fundamental and most important part of the Administrative Law.[2] It might be performed as a daily unconscious activity being incidental to administration but sometimes this process might also entail judicial functions.[3] The word "adjudication" comprises various meanings according to the context in which it is used. Generally, it connotes dispute resolution using a well-defined legal method or a decision arrived using the judicial method.[4] The phrase "Administrative Justice" includes adjudication among other things in its framework. The reference of justice in "Administrative Justice" falls within the domain of certain established legal principles like natural justice to be adhered to by the administration in its activities having civil consequences. The principles so established have evolved certain mechanisms that facilitate in effectuating "Administrative Justice". Apart from traditional courts, certain bodies with nomenclatures like ombudsmen, regulators, commissions, tribunals, etc., depict institutions that are part of this mechanism. There exist processes *inter alia* based primarily on principles of natural justice or procedural fairness that play a fundamental role before these forums.

The adjudicatory role of these bodies particularly of those bodies classified generally as "Tribunals" in India has been under challenge on various grounds. Some of these grounds inter alia include composition, uniformity of appointment processes as well as qualifications, powers, functions performed, administrative control, the methods used for them, etc.[5] But broadly, the challenge to the establishment as well

---

[1] See, Bernie R. Burrus & Harry Teter, "Antitrust: Rulemaking v. Adjudication in the FTC", (1966) 54 Georgetown Law Journal 1106. In this paper a discussion between the merits and demerits of the rulemaking and adjudicatory process has been performed with specific reference to Federal Trade Commission or FTC. The idea of the paper evolved from the public statement made by the Commissioners at FTC regarding more suitability of rulemaking process over the adjudicatory process in decision-making.; See also, David L. Shapiro, "The Choice of Rulemaking or Adjudication in the Development of Administrative Policy", (1965) 78 Harvard Law Review 921 (1965).

[2] Id.

[3] See, M.P. Jain & S.N. Jain, *Principles of Administrative Law* (LexisNexis, 6th Edn. 2007; Reprint, 2010) 642.

[4] Garner Bryan A. ed., *Black's Law Dictionary Ninth Edition* (West Thomson Reuters 2009) 47.

[5] See, *Union of India* v. *R. Gandhi, Civil Appeal No. 3067 of 2004* with *Madras Bar Association* v. *Union of India* (2010) 11 SCC 1; *Madras Bar Association v. Union of India* (2014) 10 SCC 1; *Madras Bar Association* v. *Union of India* (2015) 8 SCC 583; *Gujarat Urja Vikas Nigam* v. *Essar*

as the vires and functioning of these bodies intertwined with the concepts like separation of powers, rule of law, independence of the judiciary, power of judicial review, and the inherent limitations, etc., also pose issues.

Post-forty-second constitutional amendment,[6] the "Tribunals" were thought of as an "*alternative institutional mechanism*"[7] providing speedy administrative justice.[8] These bodies were envisaged to exclusively deal to the extent of replacing even the High Courts for disputes placed within their jurisdiction. Had the ability to have original and appellate jurisdiction, not necessarily bound by the adversarial procedural codes. Thus, with the freedom to regulate their procedure with limitations subject to principles of natural justice (hereinafter "PNJ").[9] But continuously, the system has been marred by one or the other hiccup particularly but not limiting to their organizational structure, legislative issues, process and procedure, leadership, organizational culture, and political commitment.[10]

Though, these legal tensions[11] are not native only to the Indian scenario but rather have been felt in different legal cultures at different times as part of the process of the development of their legal systems.[12] Another reason for the legal tensions to emerge

---

Power Limited (2016) 9 SCC 103; *Rojer Mathew* v. *South Indian Bank Ltd,* (2020) 6 SCC 1; *Madras Bar Association* v. *Union of India* 2020 SCC OnLine SC 962, etc.

[6] The Constitution (Forty-second amendment) Act, 1976 inserted Part XIV-A to the Constitution of India. See also, H.S. Saxena, *Central Administrative Tribunal* (Deep & deep 1996) 42. The author while discussing and quoting from the parliamentary debates argues regarding 44th amendment bill (that ultimately resulted into forty-second amendment act) that the main reason behind the insertion of this part was to create "election tribunals" (Article 323-B(2)(f) of the Constitution of India) to the exclusion of high courts as desired by the then incumbent Prime Minister.

[7] The status is at a higher pedestal than the normal statutory tribunals as rendered by the amendment is such that illustratively whenever a tribunal is created under Article 323B it gets power even to decide the constitutional validity of the Act. See, Arvind P. Datar, *Commentary On The Constitution Of India Volume II* (2nd Edition, 2007) 1799.; See also, K.C. Joshi, "Service Tribunals under Administrative Tribunals Act", (1986) 28 JILI 207.

[8] See (n 3), M.P. Jain & S.N. Jain at 648–655. *See for more*, Arvind Datar, "Tribunalisation of Justice in India", 2006 Acta Juridica 288.

[9] See, *Kamal Kanti Dutta v. Union of India* (1980) 4 SCC 38.

[10] See, Rachel Bacon, "Amalgamating tribunals: a recipe for optimal reform", Ph.D. Thesis, Sydney University (2004) available at http://ses.library.usyd.edu.au/bitstream/2123/621/1/adt-NU20050104.11271602whole.pdf (last assessed 12th November 2021). Rachel on the similar lines argues that amalgamation of tribunals into one should only be followed by proper appreciation of the five factors mentioned above such as people, law, context, culture, and organization.

[11] See, Dinesh, "The Administrative Tribunals Conundrum: A Fig Leaf for Executive Adjudication?", (2021) 8 Journal Of The Campus Law Centre 129.

[12] In the context of United States of America *see*, Christopher J. Walker, "Constitutional Tensions in Agency Adjudication", (2019) 104 Iowa Law Review 2679. Professor Walker refers the decisions in the *Lucia* v. *SEC* related to Presidential control in the appointment of Administrative Law Judges or ALJs at Securities and Exchange Commission (SEC). The control was exercised by deciding ALJs status as inferior officers and subjecting them to the "Appointments Clause" without approval of the Senate through its advisory or consensus role under Article 2, S.2 to the US Constitution and as per the dictum in *Oil States Energy Services* v. *Greene's Energy Group, LLC.* In the latter decision, the Court approved certain forms of administrative adjudications. In the paper, Professor Walker discusses the chances or possibility in the American legal system where such tensions

with the regulators' adjudication is the apparent integration of the *implementation agency*, the *investigator*, and *prosecutor* with the *adjudicator* within the single institution.[13] This appears to violate the legal principle of *Nemo judex in causa sua* that bars a person or institution from adjudicating the case in which the personal or institutional interests are involved. The questions also arise pertaining to the observance of *due process* aspects in such adjudicatory processes as well as regarding the violation of individual rights and rights available to legal personalities as ordained through the mandate of constitutions or the magna carta unique to different countries.

The *regulator* as a specialist body when also adjudicating along with regulating, when not independent of the executive government, could be assumed to be more interested in preserving the actions and decisions arrived at by the executive government or by itself as the original decision-maker, as the case may be. Thus, the legal necessity of separation of adjudicative and regulatory functions or availability of the statutory provisions guaranteeing adjudicative independence cannot be ignored for maintaining fairness and justice. Hence, Administrative Codes adopted by various countries[14] may ensure that the minimum basic independence for the administrative adjudicators, irrespective of the fact that they may or may not be part of the executive, is preserved.

The expansion of adjudicatory aspects of the Administrative State through these bodies (i.e., boards, regulators, agencies, councils, committees, commissions, authorities, tribunals, etc.)[15] requires a solution in terms of settling the legal position of these bodies.[16] This is necessary so that the rights of the persons (both natural and legal) and

---

could be resolved either by referring to Article III powers of the Court and rejecting the idea that such reference could be of any help with the broadened functioning of regulatory state or by making the agencies as part of the system of Courts.; *See also*, Emily S. Bremer, "Reckoning with Adjudication's Exceptionalism Norm", (2020) 69 Duke Law Journal 1749. Discussing the USA's Administrative Procedures Act's shortcoming in enacting the norm of exceptionalism in favor of specialized agencies' power to adjudicate relaxing the evidentiary rules as against the constitutional order of uniformity available with all courts in adjudication of matters.; *See also*, Christopher Jon Springman, "Congress's Article III Power and the Process of Constitutional Change", (2020) 95:6 New York University Law Review 1781. In this recent article, Christopher calls for a harmonious interpretation of Article III of the US Constitution for protection of constitutionalism as well as the judicial review between the Congress and the Judiciary. The discussion majorly revolves around the Congress's power under Article III to take away jurisdiction and the power as well as limitations of the Courts to judicially review these acts of Congress. He gives example of the recent case *Patchak* v. *Zinke* 138 S. Ct. 897 (2018) where the Federal Court declared that any attempt by the Congress to take away the power of judicial review of a statute would not be constitutionally valid.

[13] *Mahindra Electric Mobility Ltd. v. Competition Commission of India* 2019 SCC OnLine Del 8032.

[14] *For illustration*, United States of America in 1946; Germany in 1960; Japan in 1960, 1962 & 1993; France of recently in 2015; etc.

[15] See, Robin Creyke, "Administrative Tribunals", in Matthew Groves and HP Lee (eds), *Australian Administrative Law: Fundamentals, Principles And Doctrines* 77–99 (Cambridge University Press 2007), 77. These bodies have developed into many comparative jurisdictions known with different names but performing the task of administrative adjudication. In the Chapter the Author Robin Creyke discusses the features and characteristics of these bodies in Australian context.

[16] It would be better if such solution is devised before the dockets of these bodies further expand and become comparable to the judicial dockets and thus creating tensions as now observant with the US

the accountability of these bodies and their procedural fairness in decision-making could there of be established.[17]

For the current discussion, the legal systems under the study have been chosen among the Common Law-based Legal Systems, namely, the Commonwealth of Australia, the United Kingdom, the United States of America, and Canada. The Commonwealth of Australia is chosen because of the peculiar feature of "Merits Review" uncommon to other nations in the Common Law World. The system in the United Kingdom being chosen because of its major effects on the development of the Indian Legal System due to the latter's colonial past. The United States of America has been a pioneer in developing an Administrative Procedure Code in response to the similar Separation of Powers (SoP) tensions contemporarily faced in the Indian Legal context. The system in Canada stands at a different footing in the Common Law World where Tribunals are considered creatures of statute and extent of their independence depending upon the parent statutes. One common thread that runs through all the selected Common Law countries with slight exception of the United Kingdom is the presence of a Federal Structure. The presence of similar polity acts as an aid for the comparative discussion among the nations.

On the methodology part, pertaining to the Comparative aspects of the present discussion, it is to be noted that no isolated legal aspect of one system could be successfully transplanted into another.[18] Every legal system and the aspects involved, work in synchronization with the whole system hence isolated transplants might not work. There have been scholastic discussions on the point of finding permanent solutions to the legal issues through the Comparative method instead of opting for

---

legal system. For better understanding of the US legal tensions please see, Christopher J. Walker, "Charting the New Landscape of Administrative Adjudication", (2020) 69 Duke Law Journal 1687.

[17] *Id.* at 1693. Citing the vast number of Administrative Law Adjudicators outside the Article III jurisdiction adjudicating the vast number of matters and thus looking at them from the vantage point of Article III becomes little cumbersome.

[18] *See*, Joseph Minattur, "French Administrative Law", 16(3) Journal Of The Indian Law Institute (July–September 1974) 364- - 376, 375 available at, http://14.139.60.114:8080/jspui/bitstream/123456789/16330/1/010_French%20Administrative%20Law%20%28364-376%29.pdf (Last Accessed 20th November 2021). Professor Minattur expresses his doubts on the adoption of any civil aspect of the French administrative Legal setup in Indian setup because of latter being too much cluttered with the common law obstructions. With this the recommendation comes closer to adoption of the mechanisms that United Kingdom is adopting for the betterment of legal system and mitigating the tensions arising because of administrative adjudication by the executive based bodies.; On the import and export of the comparative aspects from one legal system to the other.; *See also*, Ran Hirschl, *Comparative Matters-The Renaissance Of Comparative Constitutional Law* (OUP 2014) 148–150.

temporary transplants.[19] There may be certain jurisdictions where the judicial determinations by these bodies are honored as precedents and in others they may not. It creates enough curiosity in the mind of a researcher on finding the method to compare these jurisdictions with each other and on what parameters?[20] The comparison may arise numerous linguistic problems, as one particular term in one jurisdiction may not have a parallel linguistic word or phrase in another, or translation difficulties may arise.[21] As happened during the present study as most of the major legal literature in Canada is in the French language, causing the present research to be limited to available English language legal resources from these nations.

9.2 The Australian System

The Australian System is noted as the one, based on the legal systems in England and Canada.[22] But as the discussion shall proceed, it shall be observed that there are subtle features that are unique to this system.[23] The most modern features[24] of the system are mostly developed through the Kerr, Bland, and Ellicott committees' suggested reforms starting the 1970s.[25] One among many distinguishing features

---

[19] *See*, John C. Reitz, "How to Do Comparative Law", (1998) 46 American Journal of Comparative Law 617; *See also*, Catherine Valcke, "Global Law Teaching", (2004) 54 Journal of Legal Education 160; *See also*, Rodolfo Sacco, "Legal Formants: A Dynamic Approach to Comparative Law", (1991) 39 American Journal of Comparative Law 1. The articles describe the pitfalls as well as approaches that need to be adopted during the course of research in comparative systems and the elements that need to be noted by the researcher so as to be able to imbibe as well as cull out the relevant extract for the purpose of the study.

[20] *Id*. Rodolfo Sacco at 21.

[21] *Id*. at 10–20.; *For example*, most of the substantial academic legal discussions in French (French), Germany (German), Japan (Japanese), Canada (Canadian French) systems are in the local languages and not in English.

[22] *See*, *Rojer Mathew* v. *South Indian Bank* (2020) 6 SCC 1. Majority judgment at ¶ 25, page 12 available at, https://www.sci.gov.in/pdf/JUD_4.pdf (last accessed 12th July 2020).

[23] *See*, Garry Downes, "Speech by the President of the Australian AAT on Structure, Power and Duties of the Administrative Appeals Tribunal of Australia on how the modern system has evolved", *Supreme Administrative Court of Thailand*, 21st February 2006 at ¶¶ 13–17 available at https://www.aat.gov.au/AAT/media/AAT/Files/Speeches%20and%20Papers/StructurePowerDutiesFebruary2006.pdf (last accessed 13th November 2021).

[24] *See*, MP Jain, "Reform of Administrative Law in Australia", (1973) 15(2) JILI 185. Discussing the comparison of reforms proposals as they were made before the Australian system adopted these reforms.

[25] *Supra* (n 15), R Creyke at 81–82. Though Australia initially adhered to the UK like setup but left the same, placing the tribunals at a sui generis place but within the common executive setup. Though Professor Creyke in her work suggests referring to the celebrated study on *New Separation of Powers* by Professor Bruce Ackerman published in Harvard Law Review that these bodies could be placed as the fourth place after the Legislature, Executive and Judiciary in the traditional setup of Separation of Powers.; *See also*, Bruce Ackerman, The New Separation of Powers, (2000) 113 Harvard Law Review 633.

uncommon to ancient Common Law is the system of Tribunals for Administrative Adjudication not Courts. In the Commonwealth of Australia, Tribunals are part of the Executive branch unlike those in the United Kingdom where they are commonly managed by the common body that manages the Judiciary. Another distinguishing feature is the exercise of broad "Merits Review" by these bodies unlike limited "Judicial Review" while administering administrative adjudication.

The Commonwealth comprised of six states has tribunals, at both the States' as well as at the Central or the Commonwealth level. The leading tribunal at the Commonwealth level is the Administrative Appeals Tribunal [hereinafter "AAT"]. Certain other notable tribunals at Commonwealth Level are the Veterans' Review Board [VRB],[26] National Native Title Tribunal [NNTT],[27] Superannuation Complaints Tribunal [SCT],[28] etc. Though, the functionality of SCT is transferred to a non-governmental independent not-for-profit organization named as Australian Financial Complaints Authority [AFCA].[29] The cases pending erstwhile with the SCT have not been transferred to the AFCA and even the fresh cases arising out of disputes on or before a designated date shall be dealt with by the SCT itself.[30]

Despite existence of other tribunals as well, the Commonwealth law relating to the bodies adjudicating the administrative justice, mostly revolves around AAT. The AAT was created through 1975 legislation and can even review the government policy matters under its jurisdiction.[31] This *review* feature unlike "*Judicial Review*", but as another form of *review,* is known more popularly as the "*Merits Review*". And the AAT being at the apex of all tribunals is also known popularly as *"Merits Review Tribunal"*.[32] The jurisdiction of AAT is so unique and vast that it spans over more than four hundred different statutes.[33]

[26] For more about this tribunal please visit the website of the VRB at http://www.vrb.gov.au (last accessed 30 November 2021).

[27] For more about the tribunal please visit the website of the NNTT at http://www.nntt.gov.au/aboutus/Pages/default.aspx (last accessed 30 November 2021).

[28] For more about the tribunal please visit the website of the SCT at https://sct.gov.au/pages/about-us/about-the-tribunal (last accessed 30 November 2021).

[29] For more about the AFCA please visit the website of the AFCA at https://www.afca.org.au/about-afca (last accessed 30 November 2021). It has been claimed at the website of SCT that all the matters that arise after 31st October 2018 shall be dealt with by AFCA. The SCT shall cease to operate after it disposes all the pending matters.

[30] Ibid. See the website of SCT.

[31] The Administrative Appeals Tribunal (AAT) Act, 1975 (Act 91 of 1975) was the result of the recommendations of the Kerr Committee named upon Justice John Kerr, also known as the *Commonwealth Administrative Review Committee* recommending a form of review that goes further than the judicial review. Based on reasons of inadequacy and lack of broadness of judicial review in Administrative Matters. Though the Bland Committee or the *Committee on Administrative Discretions* that constituted after the Kerr Committee recommended three bodies but within a single structure in the form of AAT. Leading the constitution of modern day AAT with three wings.; See also supra (n 23), Garry Downes.

[32] Supra (n 15), R Creyke at 77.

[33] Id at 80.

9.3 The System of Merits Review

The features of "*Merits Review*"[34] are significant in terms of the functions and powers that AAT exercises in the Commonwealth and are distinctive in nature that creates a need for them to be discussed.[35] The merits of "*Merits Review*" lay in the fact that the tribunal examining a decision under that system is free to go into the aspects that even courts cannot go into. Courts under "*Judicial Review*" are barred due to the doctrine of Separation of Powers from going into the specific merits[36] of a policy decision unless certain exceptional legal conditions exist.[37] Aspects like fact-finding and the examination of facts are also something that the Courts do not entertain while exercising *judicial review* as this review is based on the "questions of law" and not the "questions of fact" that are left to be decided by the original decision-maker.[38]

For illustration, if a particular state government in India is providing electricity subsidy through a policy decision based on certain logical reasoning, then courts cannot go into the aspect of why a particular policy is preferred over another available one, or how the available circumstances for choosing that policy are different from the present circumstances until the change in circumstances brings legality of the policy in question.[39] As going into such aspects requires consideration of non-judicial policy aspects that Courts are neither best suited nor created for. But, illustratively,

---

[34] See, S.43 of the AAT Act, 1975.

[35] Supra (n 15), R Creyke at 84. The Merits review in the context of AAT stems from the S.43(1) of the AAT Act, 1975 that confer the decision-maker's all powers over the AAT while undertaking the review of that decision. Similar provisions are found in various statutes creating the tribunals.

[36] Though a trend is observant in Common Law courts after the decision in *Anisminic Ltd.* v. *Foreign Compensation Commission* [1969] 2 AC 147, regarding broad and expanding interpretation of any "*error of law*" under the "*collateral fact doctrine*" as well as strict interpretation of any exclusionary or privative clause.; *See also*, Christopher Forsyth, "Error of Fact Revisited: Waiting for the 'Anisminic Moment'", (2018) 23 Jud. Rev. 1, 1–10.

[37] The conditions like the *policy decision* being 'arbitrary' or taken with 'mala-fide intention' or not having any 'reasonable principle' behind it or being disproportional to the ends it seeks to meet are very limited conditions for exercise of '*judicial review*'. Thus, making the power of *judicial review* limited based on the principle of '*Separation of Powers*'. The reasoning behind such non-interference by judiciary with the executive decisions is to exercise restraint on its powers by not encroaching the executive's territory so as to maintain *balance of vires* as well as to signal the executive to keep same level of restraint, to not to impinge upon judiciary's territory thus maintaining the same balance.

[38] See the opinion of Mason, CJ in *Australian Broadcasting Tribunal* v *Bond* (1990) 170 CLR 321 at 341. Mason, CJ while referring AAT and ADJR Act specifically elucidated the judicial review limitations with regard to the findings of fact. As including the findings of fact within the ambit of judicial review would lead to an ever-expansive review of administrative decisions. This would entangle the relationship of executive and judiciary with the issues pertaining limits and extents of such power. The judgment is also available here, https://www.ato.gov.au/law/view/document?DocID=JUD%2F170CLR321%2F00002 (last accessed 14th August 2020).; *See also*, Bill Lane, 'The 'no evidence' rule', in Matthew Groves and HP Lee (eds), *Australian Administrative Law: Fundamentals, Principles And Doctrines* 233–252 (Cambridge University Press 2007) 234.

[39] *For example*, please see the decision and judgment of the Delhi High Court (India) in *Shailendra Kumar Singh* v. *Govt. of NCT of Delhi and Anr.* W.P. (C) No. 4621/2020 (28th July 2020), rejecting similar plea while referring another decision of the Supreme Court of India in *Villianur Iyarkkai*

in the course of the *merits review* the tribunal can even question that aspect of a policy and the government would have to defend deeper into the merits of the policy decision taken. The adjudication under merits review could be exercised afresh based on the facts and circumstances that may not be available to the decision-maker whose decision is being reviewed.[40]

Hence, in the case of *judicial review,* the courts are bound to exercise restraint regarding the choice of policy that the policymaker has decided irrespective of the *most suitability* of the alternative policy available, though not chosen to be implemented. Here the words like "*most suitability*" provide a discretionary element to the policymaker executive. The merits review does not take away that aspect but just makes scrutiny of that discretion, unlike courts, available with the original decision-maker. The *Becker's Case* of AAT could be of reference here.[41] Wherein the AAT decided that government policy is not binding for AAT during its review. Though the procedure adopted by AAT was initially very formal and documented but later diluted with some informality, bringing a flexible ratio of both.[42]

Another salient aspect that needs special mention here is the co-existence of the *merits review* along with the constitutional acceptability of the Separation of Powers doctrine in the Australian Westminster model.[43] Though comparably the applicability of the Separation of Powers is not in strict sense, like in India.[44] The question that thus, becomes salient here, is that whether like India, the Australian setup, does also face legal tensions owing to the doctrine of Separation of Powers (SoP) in the creation of administrative adjudicatory bodies?[45]

9.4 The Separation of Powers and the Merits Review

The answer to the query raised above could be answered by understanding the demands of the doctrine of SoP, and by understanding the true nature and meaning of the power that it vests with the particular organ. Though attempts have been made in the Australian context to define the "*Judicial Power*" by attempting to define its scope

---

Padukappu Maiyam v. *Union of India* (2009) 7 SCC 561. The judgment of the Delhi High Court is available at, https://indiankanoon.org/doc/48566010/ (last accessed 12th August 2020).

[40] Supra (n 15), R Creyke at 85.

[41] *Becker v. Minister for Immigration and Ethnic Affairs* (1977) 1 ALD 158.

[42] *Supra* (n 23), Garry Downes.

[43] M Groves and HP Lee, 'Australian administrative law: the constitutional and legal matrix', in Matthew Groves and HP Lee (eds.), *Australian Administrative Law: Fundamentals, Principles And Doctrines* 1–14 (CUP, 2007) 6.; *See also, NSW v. Commonwealth* (1915) 20 CLR 54. Also popularly referred as 'Wheat case'.

[44] Id, Groves & Lee at 6–7.

[45] This needs to be seen in light of the fact that the Constitution of Australia (The Commonwealth of Australia Constitution Act, 1901) specifically denotes separate primary three chapters on defining the Parliament, the Executive and the Judiciary *inter alia* out of total eight chapters. The phenomenon of Separation of Powers thus has been respectfully accepted in the Commonwealth Constitution.

and nature.[46] Still, it has been considered an exercise in futility by some legal scholars unless the attempt is made rather to gain an understanding of the aspects for which the need and requirement of judicial power could be justified.[47] The entrenchment of the judicial power of the High Court through Section 75(v)[48] in the Commonwealth's Constitution makes judicial power and resultant jurisdiction to review administrative action vested with the High Court as inviolably immune to the exclusion by statutes without a referendum.[49]

The SoP doctrine demands that the judicial power be vested with the organ designed to perform the function of the judiciary. Thus, prohibits the vesting of the judicial power of the state in any other organ, other than the judiciary.[50] On similar lines, the doctrine also demands that the interpretation of, *discretionary power* and its exercise by the executive, could be provided by the judiciary but it cannot undertake the capacity to use that *discretionary power* by itself replacing the executive.

Following the same restraint as above, the courts in Australia were not vested with the power of "Merits Review".[51] The power is considered as part of Chapter II that defines "the Executive Government"[52] and not as a part of Chapter III that defines "the Judicature"[53] under the Australian Constitution.[54] This indicates that the AAT's jurisdiction is under the authority ordained to the Executive as per the Commonwealth Constitution.[55] Hence, strict adherence to the principle of "Rule of Law" is claimed in the setting of the authorities like AAT that came into existence as part of the reform proposal.[56] In the Indian setup, the jurisdiction erstwhile vested in the traditional courts had and is being shifted to the tribunals thus creating the legal tensions owing to the doctrine of SoP.

---

[46] In the Australian context please see the opinion of Griffith, CJ in *Huddart Parker & Anr. v. Moorehead* (1909) 8 CLR 330. Attempting to define '*judicial power*' as a secondary review of the binding decision by some authority or tribunal.; See also supra (n 43), M Groves and HP Lee at 7.

[47] See, P Cane, 'Understanding Judicial Review and Its Impact', in M Hertogh and S Halliday (eds), *Judicial And Bureaucratic Impact* (CUP 2004) 26.

[48] The relevant portion of S.75(v) of the Commonwealth Constitution, 1901 reads, '75. Original jurisdiction of High Court: In all matters- (v) in which a writ of Mandamus or prohibition or an injunction is sought against an officer of the Commonwealth; the High Court shall have original jurisdiction'.

[49] *Supra* (n 43), M Groves and HP Lee at 12. Referring the S.75(v) of the Commonwealth Constitution and the High Court's interpretation of the same in *Re Minister for Immigration and Multicultural Affairs* [2003] HCA 30, as the provision that creates weighty hindrance for any statutory exclusion of judicial review of administrative action.

[50] Supra (n 23), Garry Downes at ¶¶ 10–11.

[51] See, Anthony Mason, 'Administrative Law Reform: The Vision and the Reality', (2001) 8 Australian Journal of Administrative Law 135 at 138–141.

[52] See, Chapter II, Ss.61–70 of the Commonwealth of Australia Constitution Act, 1901.

[53] Id, Chapter III, Ss.71–80.

[54] Supra (n 43), M Groves and HP Lee at 13.

[55] Id.

[56] Id. at 14. It has been claimed that the Kerr as well as the Bland committee's reform proposals in their implemented shape had a single common feature. That was regarding the adherence to the principle of 'Rule of Law'.

The jurisdiction of the AAT or the other tribunals is not shifted from the traditional judiciary rather they act in the exercise of the executive power of the state reviewing the administrative decisions. The tribunal apparatus have emerged from the modern reform proposals proposed by the reform committees like Kerr, Bland, and Ellicott Committees. There have been questions regarding the independence of bodies that are part of the executive and them still exercising the review of executive actions.[57] But the answer to such questions could only be suggestive as the legal irritations regarding such aspects persist throughout the legal systems in the world. Though such a setup of "*Merit Review*" could be preferred for establishing these administrative adjudicatory bodies as the fourth branch of the government.[58]

9.5 The Composition and Appointments Process to the Tribunals

The provisions regarding the composition and appointments could be analyzed from the vantage point of the most prominent tribunal in the Commonwealth, i.e., AAT. The reason for such analysis is that the AAT is the lead tribunal and the 1975 statute that created the AAT acts as the foremost guiding light in setting up other tribunals across the Commonwealth. Another reason for the analysis is the understanding of the structure of AAT shall aid in assimilating the institutional functioning of the AAT. The factors like the design of an institution pertains salience as this determines the structure, functioning as well as the independence of the body.

The comparing ground for the discussion shall be the provisions ensuring the independence and competence of the persons manning the AAT. The need for independence from the executive arises from the doctrine of Separation of Powers. Independence from the private parties or the third persons is required so that the decision-maker could not be influenced and remain impartial. The need for competence arises to protect the rights of the persons seeking to secure justice from the AAT. Competence ensures the ability of the decision-maker to properly weigh the balance of facts in the proceedings according to the principles of law. The AAT consists of four categories of persons to be appointed as the position holders, i.e., the president, deputy presidents, senior members, and other members.[59]

The president is appointed among the sitting judges of the Federal Court of Australia with the guarantee of the preservation of their tenure and service conditions

[57] See, Gabriel Fleming, 'Administrative Review and the "Normative" Goal-is Anybody Out There?', (2000) 28 Federal Law Review 61–86 at 65. Available at, http://classic.austlii.edu.au/au/journals/FedLawRw/2000/3.pdf (last accessed 21st November 2021).

[58] *See*, B Ackerman, 'The New Separation of Powers', (2000) 113 Harvard Law Review 633; See also, Supra (n 15), R Creyke at 82. Refer for a methodological study arguing for creation of new setups and branches.

[59] S.5A of the Administrative Appeals Tribunal (AAT) Act, 1975.

as judges.[60] The status of the Federal Court could be understood from the fact that appeal from the decisions of the Court could only be at the High Court of Australia.[61] The deputies are appointed among the judges of the Federal Court or the legal practitioners with certain specific standing at the bar or among the persons having requisite specialized knowledge or skills.[62] Though the "skills and knowledge" part is the one that opens a subjective window to be decided by the Governor-General with the advice of the Council.[63] Also, the political interferences in the appointment process cannot be denied, as such allegations tend to affect justice delivery by these bodies.[64] Allegations of favored appointment of members with known sympathy to the government policies, do raise questions on the impartiality of their decisions.[65] Like India, there have been recommendations for unifying the tribunal structure with the judiciary for better independence and improving the public faith in the impartiality of decisions.[66] Though the tribunals in the Commonwealth are broadly accepted to retain the public trust regarding their impartiality and independent decision-making.[67]

Since all the appointments are to be made by the Governor-General with the advice of the Council either as full-time or as part-time, the decision rests with the executive wing, with no interference in the appointment process from the federal judiciary. Though the protocol for such appointments is devised that largely revolves around the Attorney General and the office.[68] But the Attorney General herself/himself is the political appointee as per the Commonwealth setup. Thus, the possibility of executive picking persons of their choice could not be denied. This distinguishes the Australian appointments from the counterparts in India where the judiciary plays a prominent role for the sake of ensuring independence and maintaining the Separation of Powers.[69]

---

[60] Id, Ss.7 & 7A.

[61] See, Ss.33 & 33ZD of the Federal Court of Australia Act, 1976. Though the jurisdiction of the Federal Court in the Nine National Practice Areas is based on statute but its status is either equivalent or greater than the Supreme Courts of federal states.

[62] See, S.7 of the AAT Act, 1975. It is to be noted that the changes with regard to the qualification have been amended vide the Administrative Appeals Tribunal Amendment Act of 2005. The amendment act vide S.15 amended the qualifications for President and the Deputy including the Federal Judges and the legal practitioners with certain specific minimum standing at the bar. Whether the judge of the Federal Court is appointed as the President or the Deputy President of AAT this appointment shall not affect their initial tenure as a judge. Them are collectively called as Presidential member and the tenure is secured via S.7A of the AAT Act, 1975.

[63] Id.

[64] Gabriel Fleming, 'Chapter 4-Tribunals in Australia: How to achieve Independence', in Robin Creyke (ed), *Tribunals In The Common Law World* 86–103 (The Federation Press 2008) 96. Available at, https://books.google.co.in/books?id=Opvn1CiM7zwC&printsec=frontcover&source=gbs_ge_summary_r&cad=0#v=onepage&q&f=false (last accessed 12th November 2021).

[65] Id.

[66] Id at 97.

[67] Id. at 103.

[68] See, Commonwealth of Australia, 'Protocol for Appointments to the Administrative Appeals Tribunal' (2015). Available at, (Last accessed 12th August 2020).

[69] Supra (n 11), Dinesh at 137.

Another important aspect is the reappointment eligibility of the members of AAT after their tenure of seven years is over.[70] The sitting judges shall hold office until the expiry of their term of seven years or until they remain as judges.[71] The members can resign from their position through their written resignations submitted to the office of the Governor-General.[72]

The accountability features such as the disclosure of interests by the members that could affect the work that they perform[73]; their recreational leaves and the conditions thereon to be determined by the Remuneration Tribunal[74]; termination of their appointments in case of established misbehavior, inability to perform duties on account of any mental or physical disability, indulgence in corrupt activities and certain other conditions as mentioned[75]; partial restriction on acquiring any gainful conflicting employment unrelated to the duties to be performed as a member without permission of the president in case of full-time member and complete restriction in case of part-time member[76]; etc., exists in the setup so that the members could not take advantage of the positions that they are holding.

The support staff and the Registrar to the AAT are appointed through the mechanism established under the Public Service Act of 1999 and not under the AAT Act. Thus, distinguishing the nature of their appointments from the members of AAT.[77] Though the Registrar can engage other persons for seeking their services to the AAT.[78] The role of the Registrar[79] has been made pivotal through statutory means in administratively managing the AAT though she/he has to perform those functions in consultation with the president.[80] The Registrar is aided by registries at central as well as district levels. Such registries exist in each Commonwealth State's Capital as well as Canberra.

9.6 The Procedural Standards Before the Tribunal

Since the vantage point of the discussion has been AAT hence the procedural aspect shall be seen in contrast with the procedure adopted before AAT. As already discussed, the majority of the tribunals in the Commonwealth follow AAT in the most significant forms of their structure and functioning. Another significance of AAT

70 S.8 of the Administrative Appeals Tribunal (AAT) Act, 1975.

71 Id.

72 Id, S.15.

73 Id, S.14.

74 Ibid. AAT Act, S.12.

75 Id, S.13.

76 Id, S.11.

77 Id, S.24N.

78 Id, Ss.24D read with 24PA-24Q.

79 Id, S.24B.

80 Id, Refer Divisions 2, 3 & 4 to the Act.

could be assessed from the fact that its formation, structure, jurisdiction, powers as well as functioning, make it one of the most interesting tribunals in Common Law systems. The AAT's Merits Review and the standards adopted for the same are not visible in any other jurisdictions of the Common Law world.

The redressal procedure adopted by AAT is equally interesting as once a party applies for the redressal, except the cases related to security division, AAT provides a time limit of 28 days to the decision-maker to rely on the reasoning aspects of the decision with pertaining documentation to be supplied to AAT.[81] The tribunal then assesses the matter and the possibility of Alternative Dispute Resolution (ADR) through a discussion with the party. In case a solution is not reached the tribunal then conducts the hearing and renders a decision.

The hearing process before AAT is inquisitorial in nature.[82] Though like AAT, most of the tribunals in the Commonwealth adopt informal redressal procedures.[83] This nature stems from the powers ordained to the tribunals.[84] Though the degree of digression from the ordinary procedural rules of law pertaining to evidence depends on the adherence to the merits of the case as well as the procedural fairness adhered by the tribunal.[85]

This type of setup aids in a visible sense of justice for the affected stakeholders as the decision gets reviewed with an obligation on the reviewing body to act fairly. Also, the decisions do not remain a closed secret and the person(s) affected could seek review on the merits of the decision. Though the body is part of the executive arm of the government still the statute under which it has been constituted provides sufficient safeguards as the prominent decision-makers remain part of the judicial wing.[86]

For example, in case the decision of the tribunal considers *inter alia* the evidence which would have been ordinarily inadmissible before the court of law then the legality of such admission would largely depend on whether in the conduct of such "*inquiry*" the tribunal adhered to fairness, equity, and principles of natural justice. And also, on the probative force of the evidence considered. Contrastingly when the Courts decide a case based on statutory principles then they sometimes might also entail the exclusion of some natural justice principles that are to be strictly followed by these tribunals and no divergence therefrom is allowed.[87]

It is to be made clear that the nature of proceedings being inquisitorial does not shift the burden of proof on the tribunal for investigating or finding the truth by

---

[81] See, S.37 of the AAT Act, 1975.

[82] Id, Ss.33(1), 34, 37(1) & (2), 38, 40(1A), etc. providing that the procedure adopted to be little formal though adhering to the most legal aspects ensuring utmost fairness, preliminary conferences, seeking statement of reasoning from decision-maker, power to seek additional documents as well as statements, summoning any person for evidence, etc.

[83] Supra (n 15), R Creyke at 90 & 91.

[84] Id.

[85] Id.

[86] See, Part II of the AAT Act, 1975. The section on Composition and Appointments standards above could also be referred.

[87] Id.

searching the facts.[88] The Common Law dual standards of rigor, regarding proof, is based on the notions of the *nature of proceeding* being *criminal* or *civil.* Under the Common Law generally observing, the evidentiary burden of being *beyond a reasonable doubt* in criminal and based on the *preponderance of probabilities* in civil proceeds, is followed. Out of this duality, the latter civil standards generally apply to the proceedings before these tribunals though proper weightage is given to the seriousness of each matter and the facts involved.[89] These dual standards might prove short of the requirements needed for Merits Review as it sometimes entails, assessment of the future consequences of a decision or action taken by the decision-maker, leaving discretion with the tribunal.[90]

9.7 Nature of Decision and Extent of Intervention by Courts

The appeals from the decisions of AAT arise only on the questions of law before the Federal Court of Australia.[91] Thus, the appeals are permitted only on such "questions of law" not involving any issue regarding facts or mixed issues of facts and law.[92] The route of appeal opened from the decision of AAT is very narrow. The appeal could be preferred only on limited statutory terms and in case it is available.[93] As commonly known that in Common Law there is no inherent right to appeal. Similarly, from every decision of the AAT or the other tribunals in the hierarchy, there is no right to appeal unless the statute under which the matter was decided, provided such right.[94] Though certain state tribunals have an alternative to the judicial review in the form of an additional tier to their hierarchical structure within the tribunal setup.[95]

The judgment of *Drake*[96] marked an important point at the initial stages about the nature of review that tribunals offer in policy matters as after the provision providing for "Merits Review", "policy matters" did not remain a pious-no-touch category where lawyers cannot challenge the decision simply based on the reasoning until

---

88 Supra (n 15), R Creyke at 95.

89 id. Prof. Creyke cites *Minister of Immigration and Ethnic Affairs* v. *Wu Shan Liang* (1996) 185 CLR 259 at 282 as the reason for the proposition.

90 Id.

91 See, 'The scope of jurisdiction of the Federal Court of Australia', available on the official website of the Court at https://www.fedcourt.gov.au/law-and-practice/national-practice-areas/aclhr (last accessed 24 November 2021).

92 See, *Birdseye* v. *Australian Securities and Investment Commission* (2003) 76 ALD 121.

93 Supra (n 15), R Creyke at 96.

94 Id.

95 Supra (n 64), G Fleming at 95.

96 See, *Drake v. Minister for Immigration and Ethnic Affairs* (1979) 46 FLR 409.

it doesn't follow the law. Though certain states in Commonwealth tried to bind the state tribunals with the policy and based decisions but in vain.[97]

The decisions by the tribunals do not operate as binding precedents though the earlier decisions are looked at for consistency.[98] This again distinguishes the tribunals from the Common Law courts where the doctrine of precedent acts as the primary creature and developer of the legal system. The decisions rendered operate with a persuasive value in similar kinds of policy and factual issues.[99] Though the tribunal like AAT is capable to punish up to twelve months for its contempt.[100] As seen in India many state tribunals are not only financially connected and dependent on the parent body whose decisions are reviewed by them.[101] Some of them, like India, are also geographically located within the same place as the parent body itself.[102]

The judicial review of the tribunal decisions exists but as already discussed on very limited aspects. There have been similar questions regarding the independence of these bodies in India, as well as in the Commonwealth of Australia.[103]

9.8 The Amalgamation and Service Body Aspect

From May to July 2015, as part of the "*Smaller Government Reforms*" the Migration Review Tribunal (MRT), Refugee Review Tribunal (RRT), and Social Security Appeals Tribunal (SSAT) were merged with the Administrative Appeals Tribunal (AAT). This was also done as part of budget, like the finance bill route taken in India to bring better value for money for the exchequer.[104] Reforms also disbanded the Administrative Review Council (ARCu)[105] a policy-recommending body and one of the key recommendations of the Kerr Committee.[106] The functions performed by ARCu were vested within the Attorney General's Department.[107] The Council

---

[97] Supra (n 15), R Creyke at 98.

[98] Id. at 98.

[99] Id.

[100] See, S.63 of the AAT Act, 1975.

[101] Supra (n 64), G Fleming at 94.

[102] Id.; This phenomenon in Indian context is more common with Banking tribunals like Debt Recovery Tribunals.

[103] Id., Gabriel Fleming at 95.

[104] Parliament of Australia, Moira Coombs, 'Amalgamation of merits review tribunals Budget Review' (2014–15). Available at, https://www.aph.gov.au/About_Parliament/Parliamentary_Departments/Parliamentary_Library/pubs/rp/BudgetReview201415/Tribunals (last accessed on 30 November 2017).

[105] See Part-V, Ss.47–58 of the AAT Act, 1975.

[106] Parliament of Australia, 'Report of the Commonwealth Administrative Review Committee' (1971). Available at https://trove.nla.gov.au/work/9491948 (last accessed 24th November 2021).

[107] Government of the Commonwealth of Australia, 'Smaller Government—Transforming The Public Sector' (Ministry of Finance, 2015), available at, https://www.financeminister.gov.au/media-release/2015/05/11/smaller-government-transforming-public-sector (last accessed 12th August

was proposed as a major reform so that a permanent body could be established that could review the functioning of the AAT as well as the Administrative bodies and the procedures involved for suggesting organic continuing reforms for the betterment of the system.[108] With this budget-cutting reform, the "proposed reforms structure" by various reform committees and the idea of research about them shall remain at the mercy of the already very busy Attorney General's Department.[109]

In 2014, the Australian State of Victoria developed a body called Court Services Victoria (CSV) through the statute.[110] Unlike the AAT that is generally managed through the Registrar and the support staff, the CSV acts as a common setup for administratively aiding all the Tribunals in the state of Victoria. The CSV is run by an executive-appointed officer who facilitates administrative needs and services of certain administrative adjudicatory bodies in Victoria.[111] Thus, making these bodies free from the administration, of rulemaking and other administrative tasks that they earlier carried with the help of the executive. This could be taken as an illustration, for setting up combined assistance services for cluster of different bodies that need similar administrative aids. This combined assistance service could work better for tribunals instead of establishing separate registry and the staff below for each tribunal. This shall also reduce the cost as well as provide efficient vacancy filling and budget management.

Commonwealth's AAT is part of the executive, as discussed, and not the judiciary, unlike the United Kingdom where the legislation passed in the first decade of the twenty-first Century (i.e., the Tribunals, Courts, and Enforcement Act of 2007), has made Tribunals part of the combined judicial hierarchy. The discussion on this constituted combined tribunals and courts service pertains salience for understanding the modern English administrative adjudication mechanism.

9.9 United Kingdom System

It is widely remarked that development or rather a miss to it, of tribunals in England in its earlier stages, influenced by Dicey's theory of rejection of tribunals being part of the "un-existing" field of administrative law. Them according to him being the adjudicating executive bodies, against the theory of *rule of law,* the theory that

---

2020).

[108] Id.

[109] To know more about the Attorney General Australia's Department and its functions please visit the official website. Available at, https://www.ag.gov.au/about-us (last accessed 24th November 2021).

[110] The Court Services Victoria Act, 2014.

[111] Namely, Victorian Civil and Administrative Tribunal (VCAT) and the Judicial College of Victoria (JCV). For more information is available at, https://www.courts.vic.gov.au/about-csv (Last accessed on 30 November 2017).

acted as a protection for the Englishmen from the arbitrary exercise of power.[112] Dicey's exposition was widely criticized[113] for being short-sighted to the increasingly extensive state intervention for public welfare and public functionaries being exposed to the evolving executive bodies instead of only being bound by the ordinary statutes and courts.[114] Even Dicey's approach for *Rule of Law* from the supremacy of the ordinary law, as he understood initially in his work [i.e., *the Law of the Constitution* (1885)], changed to the supremacy of an "*ordinary legal method*" in the final version of his same work underplaying the ideas proposed regarding the ordinary law.[115]

Mentioning Dicey's work is important, as him not only was a prominent English scholar but also his work influenced various inquiry committees [i.e., Donoughmore Committee (Report 1932) and Franks Committee (Report 1957)] formed initially in the United Kingdom. Both the committees accepted the existence of tribunals in the English legal system but the report of the latter, post-II-World War, led to the enactment of legislation.[116] The foundations of the legislation were based upon the application of universal fair procedural standards emerging from the workings of Courts to the decision-making process conducted by administrative agencies by establishing a recommendatory Council on Tribunals.[117] This recommendatory limited role of the Tribunal Council led to the formation of another committee headed by Sir Andrew Leggatt on the recommendation of which and followed by a white paper, the 2007 statute reforming the structure of these bodies was enacted.[118]

Later, it was much popularly remarked by Prof. W.A. Robson in his work on *administrative law* that the committees started with the "*dead hand of Dicey lying frozen on its neck*".[119] Later, many scholars did not agree with the view taken by

---

[112] *See*, Michael Adler, 'From Tribunal Reform to the Reform of Administrative Justice', in Robin Creyke (ed), *Tribunals In The Common Law World* 153–174 (The Federation Press Australia 2008) 156.; See also, Nick Wikeley, 'Burying Bell: managing the judicialization of social security tribunals', 63(4) Modern Law Review 475–501 (2000). Discussing the fundamental structural changes in the system of tribunals at UK that started happening in the beginning of the twenty-first century that made the tribunals (in the light of changes made to Social Security Tribunal) more closer to the system of courts and then in 2007 they were merged with the courts leading to creation of HMCTS.

[113] Martina Kunnecke, *Tradition and Change in Administrative Law-An Anglo German Comparison* (Springer 2007) 16.

[114] *See*, Mark D Walters, 'Public Law and Ordinary Legal Method: Revisiting Dicey's Approach to Droit Administratiff', 66(1) The University of Toronto Law Journal 53–82 (Winter 2016) 56–58. While criticizing Dicey's critique of French Administrative Law and appreciating the same Harold Laski wrote a letter to OW Holmes Jr. and referred it as 'muddleheadedness' by Dicey.

[115] Id at 57.

[116] The Tribunals and Enquiries Act, 1958. The act was amended in 1992 for the causes involving the independence as well as fairness and impartiality.

[117] H. W. R. Wade, 'Tribunals and Inquiries Act 1958', 16(2) The Cambridge Law Journal 129–134 (Nov. 1958) 129. Available at, https://www.jstor.org/stable/4504507 (Last accessed 22 November 2021).

[118] M.P. Singh, *Administrative Justice in India: The Urgency of Reforms,* (2013) 1 SCC J-65–80, 68.

[119] Chantal Stebbings, *Legal Foundations of Tribunals in 19th-Century England* (CUP 2007) 330–331.; See, AV Dicey, *The Development of Administrative Law in England,* (1915) 31 L.Q.R. 148.

Dicey.[120] This was remarkable in the report of the Franks Committee, where the Committee palpably hesitatingly recommended that the *lis* should be left to the jurisdiction of ordinary courts unless its reference to a tribunal and creation of the same is warranted by a special reason like specialization, cost-effectiveness, etc.[121] The Franks Committee recommended that tribunals be considered as adjudicatory bodies with a kind of legal or judicial character different from the past understanding of them being part of administrative apparatus.[122] That proposal was also agreeable to the majority of legal practitioners and academicians.[123] The recommendation of tribunals being considered as a body and part of the machinery of dispute resolution though was not in resonance with courts exercising the judicial power but was accepted out of considerations involving growing regulatory governance and utilitarianism, without much protest.[124]

One of the primary utilitarian considerations requiring the creation of this adjudicatory character with tribunals was the triviality and large number of specialized disputes arising between subjects. This is with ever-increasing activities of the welfare-government burdening the already overburdened legal setup.[125] But despite having that character, the tribunals like earlier were not made part of the judicial setup. This dispute resolution exercise by the tribunals out of the hierarchy of regular courts was to create legal tensions in the coming years.[126]

Professor Stebbings in her seminal work calls this arrangement of tribunals in the previous centuries as "*appendages*".[127] In the nineteenth century as the "*appendages of government*" and a shift in the twentieth century as "*appendages of courts*".[128] According to Stebbings,[129] the development of these bodies was largely contributed by the new regulatory regime and the industrial revolution and the existence of

Though Professor Dicey later himself acknowledged the development of administrative law in England as part of the welfare state.

[120] For more discussion please see, Joseph Minattur, 'French Administrative Law', 16(3) Journal of the Indian Law Institute 364–376 (July–September 1974) available at, http://14.139.60.114:8080/jspui/bitstream/123456789/16330/1/010_French%20Administrative%20Law%20%28364-376%29.pdf (last accessed 20th November 2021).

[121] Ibid (n 119), Chantal Stebbings at 331.

[122] Id. at 332.

[123] Id. at 333.

[124] Id.

[125] Id.

[126] Id. at 332.

[127] Id. at 334.

[128] Id.

[129] See also, Wraith and Hutchesson, *Administrative Tribunals* (George Allen and Unwin 1973); JA Farmer, *Tribunals and Government* (Weidenfeld and Nicolson 1974) and; Peter Cane, 'Judicial Review in the Age of Tribunals', (2009) 3 Public Law 479–500. Apart from Chantal Stebbings all of these mentioned authors have discussed in detail the origin as well as the reasons behind the origins of the Administrative Tribunals in England.

disputes that were considered too trivial but involving questions of complex specialized facts and law.[130] The disputes apart were also very large in quantity and the expensive, as well as complex court procedures, were considered inappropriate for the redressal of them as a forum without affording the clogged dockets.[131] Further, according to academic discussions these bodies in the UK might owe their origins to the disputes generated under the Railway and Canal Traffic Act of 1854.[132] Under the Act, the judges were hesitant to deal with the abstruse subject-specific factual disputes. This increased discontent among the litigants on the decisions rendered due to lack of expertise. The inexperience of the adjudicators on the subject matter, inter alia, was the main reason for the establishment of a special body of Commissioners in 1873. That further led to the creation of the Railway and Canals Commission in 1888 having judicial as well as the expert members or lay members.[133]

The above situation explains the need for advent of the adjudicatory bodies, not part of the judicial wing of the state,[134] in their modern form like tribunals.[135] Though, it shall be seen that adjudicating bodies that were not part of Common Law courts existed much before the nineteenth century.[136] Another reason for the growth of tribunals could be ascribed to the informality in a procedure like evidence, no requirements of representation through a pleader, etc.[137] This aided the less educated to seek justice through the resolution of their disputes without much spending and hassles.[138] Thus, the scholars call the advent of these bodies unsystematic till their large structure was studied, organized, and mapped in the Leggatt Commission's report.[139]

---

[130] *Supra* (n 119), Chantal Stebbings at 333.

[131] Id.

[132] Gavin Drewry, 'The judicialization of 'Administrative' tribunals in the UK: From Hewart to Legatt', (2009) 28 Transylvanian Review of Administrative Sciences 45–64, 47. Available at, https://rtsa.ro/tras/index.php/tras/article/viewFile/27/23 (last accessed 20 November 2021).

[133] Id.

[134] In today's scenario, the assumption of existence of these wings of the state could be easily made but the polity of modern states have evolved from the times where there were no fixed criteria for classification of a body into one wing of the state or the other. In the past history of most of the modern nation states there have existed the periods where autocrats have exercised despotic powers and states have learnt from such experiences. The situation changed after the scholarly classifications were proposed and were actually followed and accepted in large by the people. This has been discussed in detail in the section related to the 'Separation of Powers' as part of this Section in this Chapter.

[135] Ibid, G Drewry at 48.

[136] Please see the section on 'Separation of Powers' below in this chapter.

[137] Supra (n 132), Gavin Drewry at 48.

[138] Id, The vulnerable people from less educated sections settled their claims for old age pensions and un-employment benefits. Post first world war the injured and disabled sought their compensations and pensions through the settlement tribunal formed for that purpose.

[139] Id.

Then came the criticism from the then Chief Justice Lord Hewart,[140] on which a Committee popularly known as Donoughmore Committee[141] was set up in 1929 to examine the criticisms raised in the book.[142] But the Committee so constituted in principle supported the idea of tribunals by welcoming the exercise of adjudicatory powers by the Tribunals though accepting the idea with a caution that there should be a presumption for courts as the primary adjudicatory body.[143] Also, certain cautionary principles were proposed by advising the tribunals for reasoned decisions and certain other procedural recommendations. Though the proposal of Professor William Robson[144] was not accepted by the committee that suggested the creation of administrative courts on the line similar as in France.[145] Since the proposals of the committee were in the nature to maintain the status quo, they had little or no impact on the reformatory proposals about the existing system.[146] Then came the period before the Franks Committee report in 1957 where the judicial response of the courts was hesitant in reviewing against the administrative decisions because of many reasons owing to the structure of the judicial remedies and various principles laid down earlier.[147] The Franks Committee though limited by the terms and mandate it got, supported the idea of independent tribunals. It did not consider them as part of the government, leaning toward, them being part of the judicial structure but refraining from calling them so in clear words.[148] The Committee gave a tripartite test for the tribunals in the form of their openness in decisions, fairness in the procedure adopted for reaching those decisions, and conduct governed by impartiality in the

[140] Id., Lord Chief Justice Hewart of Bury in his work titled, 'The New Despotism' (Cosmopolitan Book Corp., 1929) criticized the practice of taking away of the legislative and judicial powers by the executive through enhancing the rule making powers of bureaucracy and creation of bodies in the nature of tribunals respectively.

[141] United Kingdom, 'The Committee on the Power of Ministers' (1929–1932).

[142] Supra (n 132), Gavin Drewry at 49.

[143] Id.

[144] W. Robson, *Justice and Administrative Law* (London, Stevens 1928).

[145] Supra (n 132), Gavin Drewry at 50. Though Lord Hewart later in his biography written by Jackson regretted his sharp criticism that he noted in his book written earlier in 1929. R Jackson, *The Biography of Lord Hewart* (Harrap 1959); *See also*, First Law Commission of India, 'Reform of Judicial Administration' (Report Number 14, volume 2, 1958) 687–689, 694. Available at http://lawcommissionofindia.nic.in/1-50/Report14Vol2.pdf (Last accessed 20th November 2021). Based upon the Franks Committee proposals and the study conducted by Professor Hamson of Trinity College.

[146] Ibid, G Drewry at 50.

[147] Id.

[148] Id. at 50–51. The Franks Committee was formed against the criticism of the government after the 'Chrichel Down Affair' Case where the certain decisions of the bureaucrats against a landowner, who gave his land for a specific use, were considered unfair due to which the even the minister had to resign from his office. The decisions were in the nature putting the ministry in the bad light owing to the profit making purpose it depicted by extraordinarily increasing the price of the land it took from the owner for a particular purpose and after that purpose was served post World War II then using the land for another purpose, subsequently increasing the price of the land so as to make impossible for the previous owner to reoccupy the same.; See also, P. Chandrasekhar, *Tribunal System: The Indian Perspective*, (2015) 7 SCC J-10, 10.

whole process of decision-making.[149] Though the committee did not pay much attention to certain prefixes used as an adjective before these tribunals like "ministerial" or "administrative" that among themselves contained ascribed meanings.[150]

It was the Franks Committee that for the first time suggested an advisory body in the form of Tribunals Council to monitor the whole system of Tribunals and their functioning so that any creases could be streamlined. [151] Professor Robson's proposal to establish a general appellate court for dealing with the appeals on these administrative matters from all tribunals did not get houseroom with the recommendations of the Committee.[152] The silver lining that could be undertaken from the recommendations of the Franks Committee was the consideration of Tribunals by the Committee as the "adjudicators" and not as simple decision-makers.[153] But, this was to be meant in some other terms for the executive and the tribunals kept increasing in numbers as the replacement of courts in the jurisdictions that erstwhile were exercisable by the judiciary.[154] The Leggatt Committee was set up in the year 2000 and its report was presented next year, i.e., 2001. The Committee led the baton for certain pathbreaking reforms in the justice system in the United Kingdom. The reforms inter alia also proposed the unification of tribunals as their chaotic growth was lacking coherence and many tribunals were functioning with overlapping jurisdictions.[155] The recommendations of the Leggatt Committee were fairly comprehensive and led to the enactment of the Tribunal, Courts and Enforcement Act in 2007 by the

[149] Ibid, G Drewry at 51.

[150] Id.

[151] Id. at 52. This monitoring body later translated in to the Administrative Justice and Tribunals Council (AJTC) in 2007 and then into the Administrative Justice Forum (AJF) in 2012.

[152] Id; See also supra (n 144). This was marked later by the remarks of Professor Robson noted by Chantal Stebbings in her work on Tribunals (2009) that the premise of the committee's inquiry was deeply influenced by the Dicey's work making it incapable to perceive any further ideas open to the query.

[153] Id, In simple terms the consideration of Tribunals as adjudicators pertains salience as an adjudicating authority has certain basic procedures to follow to reach upon a decision. Though even a decision-maker reaches the decision based upon rules and law through which his discretion is governed. But the reasoning of the discretion could be based on different policies of the decision-maker herself and can be partisan under certain conditions leaning towards the maximization of the good for the decision-maker or her organization. The Adjudicator or the Adjudicating Body on the other hand has the responsibility to give equal weightage to the adversarial arguments raised and reach the decision in a non-partisan way. Though the rules of Natural Justice are equally applicable on both.

[154] See, C Harlow et al. (eds), *Law and Administration* (Butterworths, 2nd ed, 1987) 31–33.

[155] See, Andrew Leggatt, 'Tribunal for users: One system, one service: Report of the review of Tribunals' (March 2001). Available at, https://webarchive.nationalarchives.gov.uk/+/, http://www.tribunals-review.org.uk/leggatthtm/leg-00.htm(Last Accessed 20th November 2021).

Parliament.[156] The Committee proposed that the tribunals must have unimpeachable independence. That could be achieved by insulating them from the department against which they take appeals. Further, the unification shall enhance the quality of the decisions by streamlining the setup. The flexibility would also increase accessibility by allowing self-representation to applicants. Laying the expected standards of the justice that could be reasonably expected by the users, such as the time taken for decisions, procedures involved, etc.[157]

Though after the enactment of the 2007 legislation and HMCTS in 2011, these bodies largely form part of the judicial structure with the judges mandatorily being legally qualified to have similar protections to Courts for independence. It was necessary to understand the evolution of these bodies in their present framework to understand the issues that came through this process of evolution. This becomes salient as Indian law also traces major background from the Anglo system as well as the Common Law. Hence, to understand a familiar legal system as well as the challenges and the methods adopted by that system to overcome those challenges the discussion was necessary.

9.10 The Overview of the Existing Tribunals

In the United Kingdom or the UK post the Tribunals, Courts, and Enforcement Act, 2007 (TCEA) presently exists a two-tiered *unified* structure for the tribunals. This two-tiered structure is further divided into seven lower chambers[158] and four upper chambers[159] having jurisdiction in the English-Welsh region but in certain specific jurisdictions at Scotland and Northern Ireland also.[160] The Her Majesty Courts and

---

[156] See, United Kingdom, 'Transforming Public Services: Complaints, Redress and Tribunals' (Department of Constitutional Affairs, July, 2004). The white paper released, recommended the niceties based on the outer framework provided by Sir Leggatt Committee's Report the establishment of an administrative agency to support the newly formed unified tribunals and also the setting up of annual review mechanism by publication of annual appraisal report of the tribunals and their functioning. The White paper is available online at https://webarchive.nationalarchives.gov.uk/20040722024356/http://www.dca.gov.uk/pubs/adminjust/transformfull.pdf (Last Accessed 20th September, 2020).

[157] Ibid, Leggatt's Report.

[158] The seven Chambers are: I. 'General Regulatory Chamber' GRC, II. 'Health, Education and Social Care Chamber' HESCC, III. 'Immigration and Asylum Chamber' IAC, IV. 'Property Chamber' PCh, V. 'Social Entitlement Chamber' SECh, VI. 'Tax Chamber' TC and VII. 'War Pensions and Armed Forces Compensation Chamber' WPAFCC.

[159] The four Chambers are: I. 'Administrative Appeals Chamber' hearing appeals from GRC, HESCC, SEC and WPAFCC; II. 'Immigration and Asylum Chamber' hearing appeals from IAC only, III. 'Lands Chamber' hearing appeals from PC, IV. 'Tax and Chancery Chamber' hearing appeals from TC.

[160] This is to be made clear that there exist tribunals outside this two-tiered structure, unified by the TCEA statute of 2007, as well like the Employment Tribunals but are managed by the HMCTS under the aegis of Ministry of Justice (MoJ).

Tribunals Service manned by career bureaucrats also known as HMCTS, performs the functions of managing and supporting these two-tiered tribunals along with Courts in an organized manner.[161] The supervisory role is performed by the Administrative Justice Forum (AJF) that under the aegis of the Ministry of Justice (MoJ) analyzes the performance of these bodies and provides suggestions for improving the system. The AJF is the result of the replacement of the AJTC (Administrative Justice and Tribunals Council) that itself was the result of the abolition of the Council on Tribunals (CoT).[162] The AJTC was abolished using the vires under the Public Bodies Act of 2011 for reasoning that the newly constituted HMCTS (2011) had sufficient monitoring and oversight powers necessary for governance.[163] Another reasoning given by the government against the criticism of removing the oversight body (i.e., AJTC), was that the government would be benefitted most if the system is burdened less. Thus, any attempt to dilute oversight functionality would harm the government first and then any other institution.[164] The AJF particularly works under the support of the Ministry of Justice and is not a statutory body.

Despite all these attempts of unification, there exist many tribunal bodies that are outside this tiered and monitored structure. They function independently of this, such as Employment Tribunals, Anti-trust bodies, Special Immigration Appeals Tribunals, Pathogens Access Appeal Tribunal, Gang masters and Labour Abuse Authorities, etc. Hence, the reform introduced in 2007 through TCEA statute and the unification of the Tribunals and Courts Service in 2011, has unified the structure to some extent but not completely. The unification could be seen as the efforts in the directions of convergence of the English and the Continental (particularly France) traditions though in peculiar English style by according legal status to the Tribunals within the judicial hierarchy.[165]

The Employment Tribunals though managed by the HMCTS but are going through a lot of hiccups post-COVID-19 scenario.[166] They still exist outside the unified structure of the tribunals. There exist controversies regarding the inexperience of the

---

[161] While the Lord Chief Justice remains the head of judiciary there also exists a position with nomenclature as Senior President of Tribunals (SPT) who possess similar functions with respect to management of Tribunals whether Tier I or Tier II and some other like EAT.

[162] The AJTC was established under S.44 of the TCEA, 2007 with a larger mandate than the body it replaced, i.e., CoT.

[163] *See*, Lord McNally, 'Speech of the Minister of State for the motion to approve the Public Bodies (Abolition of Administrative Justice and Tribunals Council) Order', *House of Lords*, 22nd July 2013. Available at, https://www.theyworkforyou.com/lords/?id=2013-07-22a.1125.0 (Last accessed 14th February 2020); *See also*, Michael Adler, *The Rise and fall of Administrative Justice—A Cautionary Tale*, 8(2) Socio-Legal Rev. 28 (2012). Adler criticizes the abolition of AJTC citing various benefits it posed for development of '*rising from the shadows*' administrative justice in UK.

[164] Ibid, Lord McNally.

[165] See, Bernardo Sordi, 'Révolution, Rechtsstaat, and the Rule of Law: historical reflections on the emergence of administrative law in Europe', in Susan Rose Ackerman et al. (eds), *Research Handbooks In Comparative Law* 23–36 (Edward Elgar 2010) 35.

[166] Dominic Kennedy, 'No Experience necessary to be a judge in hearings free-for-all by', *The Times*, 1 February 2021.

adjudicators, clogged dockets as well as the power grab[167] by the adjudicators of these tribunals.[168] Hence, apparently, the Tribunal system still has some issues that need to be addressed through the reforms. An approach of unification and integration with courts of the other tribunals though seems to be working fine with certain minor institutional issues.

9.11 The Composition and Appointments Process to the Tribunals

The Lower tier appointments are made on the recommendations of the Lord Chancellor and Upper-tier ones are being regulated by the Judicial Appointments Commission[169] having mixed Quorum. There still exist certain tribunals like the Employments Appeal Tribunal (EAT) and the Competition Appeal Tribunal (CATr) that were the formation of their respective statutes[170] and accorded the status equivalent to that of a High Court (i.e., of a superior Court of Record).[171]

9.12 "Court" and "Tribunal" Are Different?

The differentiation between a "court" and a "tribunal" has raised legal questions and tensions not only in India[172] but also in the United Kingdom.[173] The key differentiation between a "*Tribunal*" and a "*Court*" from the catena of decisions could be understood as the body that is established to exercise the judicial power of the state and not for exercising any administrative or legislative functions, could only be classified as "*Court*".[174] Then, irrespective of whatever nomenclature that body be established, it may be called and understood as "*Court*".

---

[167] Id.

[168] Id.

[169] This body was setup under the Constitutional Reform Act, 2005.

[170] *See*, The Employment Tribunals Act, 1996 and The Enterprise Act, 2002.

[171] *Ibid* (n 169), Gary Slapper et al., at 235.

[172] For more on the Indian legal debates in this respect please see the chapter on 'Background' as part of this work.

[173] The issue of difference between what could be considered as '*court*' and what to be considered as '*tribunal*' has been part of various decisions. For reference the *Attorney General* v. *British Broadcasting Corporation*, [1980] 3 All ER 161 can be the case in which the House of Lords decided the 'Court' to be understood as a body adjudicating and exercising through the judicial power of the state. It was held that the purpose for establishment of a body is needed to be seen to decide whether it is established for exercising judicial power of the state or for other purposes incidentally performing duties of judicial character.

[174] R Huxley and J Martin, *Unlocking The English Legal System* (Routledge, 4th ed, 2014) 228.

To identify the judicial power of the state it becomes necessary to understand the purpose for which that body is established and the powers granted to it for the fulfillment of the same. As the Court of Appeal held in the *General Medical Council* case[175] that a body performing regulatory functions to regulate the medical profession for maintenance of professional standards cannot be classified as "*Court*", as it does not act in the exercise of the judicial power of the state. Rather the adjudication, though statutory, performed is for maintenance of standards and is self-regulatory in nature.[176] This aspect of having the "*judicial power of the State*" for a body exercising contempt jurisdiction has now been statutorily recognized in the Contempt of Court Act of 1981.[177]

Though it is stated in many documents including the Franks Committee Report,[178] judgment in *Bakers case*,[179] etc., that the tribunals are a mere extension of the executive functionality as administration and are not adjudicators like courts but part of administrative decision-making.[180] In many other documents also, pertaining the Her Majesty Courts and Tribunal Service (HMCTS) as a managing agency, the HMCTS is mentioned as an executive agency of the Ministry of Justice.[181] But the distinguishing factor comes while looking at the contempt jurisdiction. As discussed in the previous paragraph, the Contempt of Court Act of 1981 clarifies this position of differentiation of "Court" from any other institution owing to the "*judicial power of the state*" vested with the former. This issue was raised in *Liverpool Daily Post and Echo Newspapers Case*[182] where the erstwhile Metal Health Review Tribunal[183] was

---

175 *General Medical Council* v. *British Broadcasting Corporation* [1998] 3 All ER 426.

176 *Ibid.* (n 175), Huxley & Martin at 228.

177 *See*, S.19 of the Contempt of Court Act, 1981 [United Kingdom]. The section reads, "*court' includes any tribunal or body exercising the* ***judicial power of the State****, and 'legal proceedings' shall be construed accordingly*'. The legislation can be accessed at, https://www.legislation.gov.uk/ukpga/1981/49/1999-01-31/data.pdf (Last accessed 12th November 2021).

178 Government of United Kingdom, 'Franks Committee Report' (1957). The Report at ¶ 40 read the tribunals, '.....[A]s part of the machinery of administration...'.

179 *Baker v. HMRC* [2013] UKFTT 294 ¶ 86. In this case the First Tier Tribunal while rejecting a relief claimed under S.727 of the Companies Act ostensibly stated that it does not possess the vires as vested with the court and thus since it is not a court it cannot grant the relief claimed. Text Available at, https://www.bailii.org/uk/cases/UKFTT/TC/2013/TC02790.html (Last Accessed 20 November 2021).

180 Supra (n 169), Gary Slapper et al., at 627.

181 Please see, the progress report presented before the Public Accounts Committee of House of Commons titled, '*Transforming Courts and Tribunals: progress review*' 'Introduction' (II Report of 2019 session) 5th November 2019 at 4. Available at, https://publications.parliament.uk/pa/cm201919/cmselect/cmpubacc/27/27.pdf (Last Accessed 20th November 2021). The report as like many other similar previous reports clearly categorizes HMCTS as an executive agency of the Ministry of Justice of UK Executive Government.

182 *Pickering v. Liverpool Daily Post and Echo Newspapers* [1991] 2 AC 370.

183 Later due to reorganization in 2008 after TCEA 2007 its jurisdiction was transferred to first tier Health, Education and Social Care Chamber.

held to be court since its proceedings were subject to the Contempt law.[184] But even after the above decisions the nature of tribunals and their status, when compared to courts is not clear and is often recognized as one inferior, to the courts.[185]

The questions like India regarding the independence of "Tribunals" have emerged in the English Legal System as well. As the nineteenth century was dominated by the doctrine of separation of powers.[186] The Indian legal setup, mostly, has followed and inherited the English legal system in most parts of its legal affairs hence its issues as well. Though these bodies were considered part of the executive decision-making until the reforms in the twenty-first century. This despite them performing dispute resolution functions which were considered as part of executive decision-making method rather than these functions being considered judicial in nature involving adjudication.[187]

The "Tribunals" are often appreciated for their merits of informal procedures, cost-effectiveness, and more appropriately the field specialization that they demonstrate by often inculcation of experts' opinion as part of the adjudicatory body.[188] The system of tribunals has evolved more and more from the proposed informal procedures to adversarial procedures and from cost-effective to expensive.[189]

9.13 The Procedural Standards Before the Tribunal

Generally, a tribunal proceeding is comprised of a judge trained in law and the two other lay members who are non-legal experts[190] appointed according to the field of the tribunal.[191] The Quorum for lay members depends also on the nature of dispute. For example, in the Employment Tribunal one of the lay members shall belong to the party raising the dispute and the other against whom the dispute has been raised.[192] Further, as part of the series of reforms the Senior President of Tribunals was provided with the authority to restrict the number of lay members in the first-tier tribunals to one in case not otherwise required.[193]

184 Id. Hence it was held that the contempt jurisdiction was rightly applied by the High Court for finding the contempt of an order of the Mental Health Review Tribunal.

185 Supra (n 169), Gary Slapper et al., at 627.

186 Supra (n 119), Chantal Stebbings at 106.

187 Id. at 107.

188 For a critical discussion on this aspect please see another 'Chapter-5' of this work titled, 'Towards more Robust System'.

189 *See generally supra* (n 132), Gavin Drewry. For further discussion on this aspect please see the chapter on 'Towards more robust system' as part of this work.

190 *Supra* (n 166). Doubts have been raised on the expertise level of such members and is a controversial issue.

191 R Huxley and J Martin, *Unlocking The English Legal System* (Routledge, 5th ed, 2017) 262.

192 Id.

193 *Supra* (n 169), Gary Slapper at 638.

The Judicial Appointment Commission or JAC is the body responsible for the selection of judges for the Tribunals. The focus is *not on the Conflict but the Conciliation,* thus, increasingly Alternative Dispute Resolution process is advised to be adopted by the 2007 legislation.[194] The hearings at these forums are also *informal* to the extent that parties do represent themselves without the need of a trained legal counselor and thus reducing the litigation cost for the parties.[195] The inquisitorial nature of the procedures, is also proposed to be litigant centric as against the adversarial methods where the proceedings are left to the parties and the judge just act as the umpire. This aids the litigant self-represented as in case the litigant is unfairly dominated by the other party using the pleader to represent then the judge could perform an active role and set the balance in the proceedings. This also aids in obtaining the necessary evidence that parties otherwise would not have disclosed.[196]

Here, it is important to mention that the nature of judicial review available before the courts in the United Kingdom is much different from what is offered by the countries having the written Constitution like India. To understand the same, the discussion on the famous *GCHQ Case*[197] is necessary. *GCHQ is* named upon the *Government Communication Head Quarters,* which is a premier agency of the government of the United Kingdom providing security and intelligence services at various levels to different departments of the government. The facts of the case involved a ban on the formation or joining of any trade union by the employees of *GCHQ* through the usage of the royal prerogative by the issuance of an order in council by the Thatcher Government. The House of Lords rejected the argument that royal prerogative when used is not subject to judicial review as against the traditional understanding in this regard. The decision of the court clarified that the application or non-application of judicial review upon a decision of the government would depend on the nature of the decision and not upon the nature of authority or its source through which the decision

---

[194] Ibid (n 192) at 263. This is done so that the mandate of the TCE Act, 2007 could be fulfilled. As the statute under S.2(3)(d) suggests the '*proportionate dispute resolution*'. The Ministry of Justice operates various programs to facilitate this cause further in the right direction.

[195] *Id*. This has proved to be a double-edged sword for the litigants as the parties representing in person have been seen to have less chances of succeeding in their claims as against the parties represented by a counselor. There has been research based evidence for this claim.; *See also*, Hazel Genn & Yvette Genn, 'The Effectiveness of Representation at Tribunals' (London: Lord Chancellor's. Department, 1989). For reference this research could be seen. Though as the year of the study indicates it was based on the previous system where tribunals were not integrated. But since the representation and the procedures for same have not changed drastically the same could be taken as an indication of the scenario.

[196] *Id* at 264. Though it has been seen that not in all the cases the Chairperson of the Tribunal perform as active role as is expected from the Chair in case of inquisitorial proceeds.

[197] *Council of Civil Service Unions v Minister for the Civil Service* [1985] AC 374 [United Kingdom].

is made.[198] The case remarks a significant authority in delineating the limits of the *judicial review* or the *Common Law review* in the context of the United Kingdom.[199]

9.14 Amalgamation Aspect

The amalgamation of tribunals as done[200] in India through the Finance Act in 2017, could be traced analogously in the context of the United Kingdom also. At the beginning of the twenty-first century, four tribunals, namely, Child Support Appeals Tribunal, Disability Appeals Tribunal, Medical Appeals Tribunal, and Vaccine Damage Tribunal were merged with Social Security Appeal Tribunal (SSAT).[201] Still, when Leggatt's Committee took up the review of the administrative tribunals in the UK more than 70 such bodies were existing in different jurisdictions that it recommended to be brought together into a single but separate system.[202] The system proposed by the Committee was Appellate tribunals throughout were to be made part of the appellate division to be able to take appeals from the lower tier tribunals that led to the creation of the Tribunals Courts and Enforcement Act, 2007.

9.15 United States of America System

In the USA the federal Administrative Procedure Act, 1946[203] or "APA" regulates the administrative adjudicatory process. The APA also governs the appeal as well as jurisdictional issues pertaining to different adjudicatory agencies as well as federal courts. The APA is fairly comprehensive in dealing with all the procedures as well as their meaning thus bringing greater clarity about the power and functions of the bodies regulated under it. It is considered to be a pioneer legislation across the Common Law world, streamlining the administrative procedures when the Commonwealth

---

[198] The House of Lords in its decision applied the doctrine of Legitimate Expectation for reviewing the ban upon the rights of the employees to form or join unions. The case also delineates the limits of the common law review.

[199] *id.*

[200] See, Schedule IX to the Finance Act, 2017.

[201] This was done through the Social Security Act, 1998 and The Social Security and Child Support (Decisions and Appeals) Regulations, 1998.; *See also*, Hartley Dean, 'Losing appeal? The changing face of redress', (2004) 12(1) Benefits: a journal of poverty and social justice, 3–7.

[202] *Id.*, Hartley Dean at 3–4.; *See also*, Robin Creyke, 'Tribunals and access to justice', (2002) 2(1) Queensland University of Technology Law and Justice Journal 64–82, 69.

[203] The Administrative Procedure Act, 1946 (Public Law 404, 79th Congress). Available at, https://www.justice.gov/sites/default/files/jmd/legacy/2014/05/01/act-pl79-404.pdf (last accessed 20th November 2021).

was still struggling with Dicey's dilemma[204] of questioning the legality of French *droit administratiff*.

In USA-based model doubts have been raised regarding the application of the "Independence of Judiciary" *strictu* sensu to such administrative bodies, though the APA streamlines the procedure followed in such bodies.[205] It has also been argued in the context of the USA that the nature of functions performed by administrative adjudicatory bodies must be kept in mind before assigning any random independence akin to the mainstream judiciary.[206] The division of powers and the existence of commissions has been part of curious study among legal scholars, only them to be considered as "headless fourth branch".[207]

9.16 The Evolution of the System in the Present Form

Such Bodies akin to modern Tribunals did evolve and exist in the American Jurisprudence as early as Nineteenth-Century like ICC or the Interstate Commerce Commission manned by the Commissioners.[208] The ICC in 1987 had certain adjudicatory powers apart from its administrative powers.[209] Certain bodies similar to the United Kingdom counterparts did also establish like Railway Commission in 1873.[210] The purpose of the establishment of these agencies is said to be a lack of trust in the

---

[204] *See*, A.V. Dicey, *Introduction To The Study Of The Law Of The Constitution* (Macmillan, 10th ed, 1959) 345–348. Professor AV Dicey did not like the idea of insulation of the decisions of the officials of the Conseil d'etat from the review by ordinary courts' jurisdiction and he considered such arrangement to be outside of the Rule of Law doctrine as well as against the principle of Separation of Powers.; *See*, H. W. Arthurs, 'Rethinking Administrative Law: A Slightly Dicey Business', (1979) 17 Osgoode Hall Law Journal 1, 6. The article discusses the legality of tribunals and them being adopted though with a caution that certain transcendental values ought to be followed by them. It also discusses the shortcomings in the Dicey's application of Rule of Law to other jurisdictions.; *See also*, James E. Pfander, 'Dicey's Nightmare: An Essay on the Rule of Law', (2019) 107 California Law Review 737, 744. The article discusses more on the aspects that AV Dicey elaborated with respect to the Rule of Law and the Common Law's beneficial universal application of the same.

[205] *See*, James E. Moliterno, 'The Administrative Judiciary's Independence Myth', (2007) 27 Journal of the National Association of Administrative Law Judges 53.

[206] *Id.*, James E. Moliterno at 96.; *See also*, Frank B. Cross, 'Thoughts on Goldilocks and Judicial Independence', (2003) 64 Ohio State Law Journal 195–218. Here the author argues that random unfettered judicial independence would prove detrimental for not only the judiciary but also for citizenry at large rather an empirical study is required based on the roles and functioning of the particular branch of the judiciary and the role performed by the body in adjudication, nature of cases involved, complexities of issues involved, etc.

[207] *See*, Peter L Strauss, 'The place of agencies in Government: Separation of Powers and the fourth branch', (1984) 84 (3) Columbia Law Review 573.

[208] Peter Cane, *Administrative Tribunals and Adjudication* (Hart 2009) 48–49.

[209] *Id.*

[210] *Id.* This could be signified by comparing this evolution of the UK's the Railway and Canal Traffic Act, 1854 that was the result of increasing industrialization and pertinent activities and discussed by Professor Cane.

archaic court system in dealing with and in understanding the systematic issues with these new fields of industrialization.[211]

The Federal Constitution of the USA is a document heavily influenced by the Montesquieu theory of Separation of Powers. Thus, the Governmental setup is divided in the Constitution itself into three broad categorizations.[212] Though like India, the judges forming part of the judicial hierarchy do enjoy the independence that is entrenched in the Constitution.[213] The Supreme Court of the USA allowed the creation of the legislative-powered courts in 1828[214] as different from Article III Courts, having the adjudicatory powers but this view was modified later in the middle of the nineteenth century itself. Where the creation of such bodies was allowed but the determination by them was subject to review before Article III established Courts.[215]

For illustration, the functions of the bodies like ICC or Interstate Commerce Commission included the finding of appropriate facts before the determination. Further, with increasing dockets, the "Commissioners" delegated the power to chaff out the facts to the "hearing examiners" (i.e., another entity with the institution). Thus, these examiners becoming significant in deciding on the factual aspects of the case and the usual basis their recommendations being accepted by the Commissioners.[216] The final decision-making remained with the Commissioners but the practice gained acceptance by the time Federal Trade Commission (FTC) was established in 1914.[217] This practice was later deprecated by the Supreme Court[218] by holding that the person who hears the case must be the decision-maker. This decision by the Court laid the foundation of the criticism of the functionality of these bodies as it became uncertain that how much of the functions regarding the hearings that these bodies can delegate to the entities, like hearing examiners.[219]

The much popular, President Roosevelt faced the crisis of the *economic depression* and that involved dealing with the socio-economic issues that emerged because

---

[211] *Id.*, The difference in the ideology of Courts from the dispenser of justice from these bodies having the psychology of not only regulating but also promoting the economic activity developing through these new emerging industrial fields is also said to be the factor promoting trust on these bodies as against the Court's system.

[212] The Articles I, II and III divide the government into Legislative, Executive and Judicial compartments having their powers in their specified domains.

[213] The protection with regard to salary, tenure, decisions, etc. are certain provisions among others that enshrine the independence of the judiciary in USA. The judges that are protected through such protection are known and referred as the 'Article III judges' popularly.

[214] The decision in reference being *American Insurance Co v. Canter* (1828) 1 Pet 511. The decision allowed the bodies akin to the modern Tribunals who could exercise the adjudicatory powers which could be difficult to distinguish from the power exercised by the local inferior courts at different federal levels.

[215] *Supra* (n 209), P. Cane at 50.

[216] *Id.* at 51.

[217] *Id.*; *See also*, The Government of United States of America, 'The Report of the President's Committee on Administrative Management' (Washington, 1937) 209–214.; *See also*, RE Cushman, *The Independent Regulatory Commissions* (OUP 1941).

[218] *See*, *Morgan v. United States* (1936) 298 US 468.

[219] *Supra* (n 209), P. Cane at 51.

of the same in the 1930s. But at the same time, criticism against the administrative adjudicatory process and the threat they posed to the regular court system was increasingly being criticized in the United Kingdom as well as the United States of America.[220] President Roosevelt wanted a robust executive system that could provide concerted solutions to the crisis. For the existence of this type of system, the regular interventions by the Courts, in the form of review of administrative actions were the big hurdles.[221]

The Committee[222] appointed by the President in 1936 to review the rapid growth of these agencies, in its report presented in 1937 referred to these agencies as the "*Headless Fourth Branch of the Government*".[223] The reference of the Committee was in the nature that these regulatory bodies in their policy governance aspect ought to be accountable to the President but are usually not and should be independent in their adjudicatory aspects.[224] The recommendations of the Committee involved the restructuring of these bodies making their policy aspects accountable to the President and the adjudicatory aspects independent though administratively they may be attached to the executive.[225] Though, the Committee's suggestions did not find much houseroom considering the support they required in the Congress for their implementation, was not available.[226] The New Deal proposals starting the year 1933 included the policies, legislations, and measures to set straight the crisis and re-establish the golden era of the American economy. But they also faced challenges from *ABA* or the *American Bar Association* as well as Courts. But these challenges shifted their directions from disbanding these agencies in the form of "*Administrative Courts*" to their restructuration. That involved making these bodies more accountable in their procedure and also subjecting their decisions to Article III courts.[227] This

---

[220] Id., P Cane.; Please see the discussion in this Chapter's section pertaining the UK's Legal System and the book written by Lord CJ Hewart criticizing the taking away of judicial power that lead to the genesis of Donoughmore Committee to review the same.; Even the ABA, i.e., American Bar Association categorically criticized this practice of executive bodies exercising the adjudicatory functions. The criticisms involved the issues like maintenance of Separation of Powers, protection of independence of judiciary, rule of law and the individual's right to have the judicial review by independent courts.

[221] Id, P Cane at 51–52.

[222] *Supra* (n 218), The Report of the President's Committee at 39–40. The Committee while referring the '*independent regulatory commissions*' called their growth as random and unplanned and their accountability to none except Courts but only on the legality aspect of their decisions.

[223] *Supra* (n 209), P. Cane at 52.

[224] *Id.*

[225] *Id.* at 53. Thus, through such exercise the control of the President on these bodies shall be re-established and the adjudicatory functions can be prevented from the criticism regarding the independence aspects.

[226] *Id.*

[227] *Id.* at 54. This was done through a proposal of a legislation in the form of the Walter Logan Bill, 1938 drafted by a special committee of the American bar Association.

shift was responded to in the form of the creation of the Committee on Administrative Procedure led by the Attorney General in 1939.[228]

The post-Second World War phase saw the salience of the functionality of these agencies in mitigating the effects of the wars and thus the criticism was not as stringent as in the phase before the War.[229] The reform agenda led to the creation of the fairly concise act[230] as part of the historical compromise known in the form of the Administrative Procedures Act, 1946,[231] as the New Deal supporters wanted to gain something post Roosevelt's death and the uncertainty that persisted thereafter. Further, the conflict with judiciary was much less due to long and strong presidency of Roosevelt in comparison to the earlier phases of the New Deal policy and thus judiciary was not seen as that great a hurdle as seen in the earlier phases of the New Deal. Thus, "the APA" as based on the proposals of the decade-old Committee on Administrative Management was enacted.[232]

The APA led to a major change in the thinking of the critics of administrative adjudication as it led to a complete paradigm shift from retaining the three compartments and the Separation of Powers toward procedural fairness, openness, and due process.[233] There exist the comparative difference between the system adopted by the United State of America with that of Australia. As in the latter's context, the Separation of Powers doctrine was kept intact and inviolable by considering the tribunals clearly as part of the executive based on practical reasons having no or little procedural controversies.[234]

---

[228] *Id.*, The creation of this Committee was to cause the failure of the draft bill of 1938. But despite this the bill was passed by the Congress only to be defeated later by the Veto of the President which sustained through the Congress by a narrow margin.

[229] *Id.*

[230] The Act contained twelve sections only defining various procedural constraints while conducting the procedures before the agencies and departments covered.

[231] *See*, McNollgast, 'The Political Origins of the Administrative Procedure Act', (1999) 15(1) Journal of Law Economics & Organization 180–217, 182, 183. Refer for an intriguing discussion on the politics behind the creation of such a significant Act. According to the Article, this compromise led by the democrats shattered by the death of their great leader proposing stronger procedural control on the administration's power was based on the belief that firstly, the speculated chances of Truman's retaining the Presidency were bleak through it proved that he retained the same till 1953 and secondly, the New Deal's reforms could be preserved through these procedural controls on the upcoming Republican Government's power.

[232] *id*, The creation of this bill has been referred as a compromise between the demand for radical change in disbanding these bodies altogether towards the acceptance of these bodies through the procedural modifications gained from the legislation of 1946.

[233] *Supra* (n 209), P. Cane at 54. A similar shift of focus on procedural fairness and due process before these bodies was seen through the Frank Committee's report in the context of United Kingdom as discussed in this Chapter above.

[234] *Id.*, For more on this See, to the Kerr Committee's recommendations and the reasons for evolution of these bodies in Australian context discussed above in this Chapter.

The APA applies to all administrative agencies whether departmental or independent, whether part of executive or independent of it. In APA there lies a difference between the adjudicatory regulation and regulation through rulemaking.[235] The former is a broad term combining all aspects that do not fall in the category of the latter. In case the statute under which an appeal is being procedurally regulated through the APA, provides for an opportunity for hearing, then the case would be heard by the Administrative Law Judges or ALJs.[236] This type of adjudication is known as formal adjudication, different from informal adjudication where no such requirement is there according to the parent statute.[237]

9.17 Composition and Appointments

The appointments of these ALJs are through an open competitive procedure by an independent agency, the Office of Personnel Management, or the OPM. The accountability of these ALJs is established through the independent Merit System Protection Board or MSPB. Their salary, tenure, seniority, removal, etc., is protected, unless the MSPB finds a substantial reason for interference with the same after affording a hearing to the concerned personnel.[238] The cases are also allotted to them through the rotation-based policy and APA ensures that they are not made subordinate or accountable to the personnel conducting the prosecuting or investigating functions for the agency.[239]

9.18 Procedural Elements and the APA

The decisions of the ALJs are subject to two forms of reviews, i.e., the external and the internal review. The former external review being in the nature of judicial review before Article III established Courts. The judicial review could only be of the determination of the agency and not the decision of the ALJ. The latter, i.e., internal review before Agency, reviews the decision of ALJs, within the agency itself. The Agency Review could render de novo decision, as during the process, the

[235] Please see, Ss.4 & 5 of the act that broadly separates these functions and the S.6 that defines the ancillary matters remaining thereto.

[236] The name evolved from the Hearing Examiners in the year 1972 so as to increase the stature of the office and provide a formal nomenclature to adjudicators as part of the process of juridification of these agencies by the APA.

[237] The Informal adjudication happens in the nature of in chamber negotiations, or the inspections conducted, or the conferences for the purpose of decision-making where no such formal hearings take place.

[238] *Supra* (n 209), P. Cane at 55.

[239] Under S.5 of the APA this separation is proposed so that the adjudicator do not get influenced from the conduct of these personnel.

agency has a wide amplitude of powers, had the decision not being taken by the ALJ. Thus, the agency could review the factual aspects as well as the legal aspects.[240] The decision of ALJ is not subjected to direct judicial review as it is considered as the act of the agency, not of an individual entity as ALJ. In case the decision is not appealed internally, i.e., within the agency as Agency Review but is appealed externally before Article III Court then such appeal is considered as the review of the act of the agency and not the decision of the ALJ.[241] The APA existing at the Federal Level is reproduced with certain amendments or peculiarities by the states. Such form adopted by states keeps a broad structure of State's APA similar to the federal APA. Thus, appointing their own ALJs for the agencies under the aegis of different states governed by the State's APA.[242]

The parties are allowed to make representations through their counselors or lawyers in the hearing before these bodies. The ALJs are required to provide reasoned decisions with the onus to have cogent reasons based on evidence. The parties are also allowed to cross-examine the witnesses but in case the chances of parties getting prejudiced are less or none, the cross could be in the written form or through forms similar to interrogatories in the Indian context.[243] Though the APA is not as comprehensive as the civil codes of procedures regulating the conduct of proceedings before the civil arm of the judicial wing of the government but the demands for such code in the US administration have been there with debates on its merits[244] and demerits.[245]

---

[240] *Supra* (n 209), P. Cane at 56.

[241] *id.*

[242] See, National Conference of Commissioners on Uniform State Laws, 'Revised Model State Administrative Procedure Act' (Chicago, Illinois, July, 2010). The National Commissioners on Uniform State Law, USA, a body similar to the Law Commission of India, constituted to advise on the changes needed in its functions advised in 2010 in favor of the need for the Uniform Model State APA. Available at, https://www.uniformlaws.org/HigherLogic/System/DownloadDocumentFile.ashx?DocumentFileKey=3ab796d4-9636-d856-48e5-b638021eb54d&forceDialog=0 (Last Accessed 20th November 2021).

[243] *See*, the decision of the first circuit court in, *Citizens Awareness Network* v. *United States* 391 F.3d 338. In the case where the agency exercising adjudicatory powers decide against allowing the formal cross examination the party must approach the hearing officer and convince her on the essentiality of the formal cross examination. For concept of Interrogatories under Indian Law please refer S. 30 and Order XI of the Code of Civil Procedure, 1908.

[244] M Asimow, 'The Administrative Judiciary: ALJs in Historical Perspective', (2000) 20 Journal of the National Association of Administrative Law Judges 157, 163. Available at, https://core.ac.uk/download/pdf/71933703.pdf (Last accessed 20th November 2021). Professor Asimow goes to the extent of claiming that the APA proved to be magna carta for the state's administrative rulemaking and adjudication in the sense that there was no major change in it for a very long time gaining wide acceptance.; Michael Asimow, 'Five Models of Administrative Adjudication', (2015) 63 American Journal of Comparative Law 3. Later Professor Asimow classified five 'models' of administrative adjudication.

[245] *Supra* (n 209), P. Cane at 236–238. Professor Cane discusses the difficulty in application of a general comprehensive code with uniform prescriptions due to varied nature of these forums. As tribunals are generalists as well as specialized bodies, applying one set of rules to all these bodies might make the things difficult for the latter except few uniform procedural standards. Professor Cane provides the example of UK where the TCE Act, 2007 provided for a Procedural Committee for Tribunals and thus this body decides the procedural aspects and requirements for these bodies.

Later in the history of the USA, the idea of the establishment of administrative courts was also mooted upon during the times of President Nixon.[246] But, the idea did not receive much support and was dropped later.[247]

The nature of proceedings before these bodies in stark contrast to the United Kingdom's counterpart, is the acceptance of adversarial method in the conduct of the proceedings rather than having the inquisitorial methods for the same.[248]

This shift toward the adversarial model lies in the fact that at the time of the draft of the APA in 1946, the focus was much more on the adjudicatory function of these agencies due to conflict of the same with the judicial functions. This led, the APA to have more provisions securing the court-like procedural aspects within the statute than having the inquisitorial approach toward the adjudication. This could also be seen as having the inquisitorial approach that requires the judge or the adjudicator to play a more proactive role that sometimes falls a little short of the role played by the prosecutor. The focus of the APA as part of the compromise[249] was itself to secure the adjudicators or the ALJs as they were later referred from the prosecutor or the investigative wing and this is clearly noted within the mandate of APA.[250]

Thus, the role of the ALJs in the proceedings before them is limited to the briefs submitted by the lawyers and the witnesses and evidence produced. The decisions of the ALJs could be seen as the draft of the recommendations based on the

---

Though the major debates on the Tribunals procedures converge on the aspects of them being 'inquisitorial' or 'adversarial' but according to Professor Cane this is not the right method, due to uncertainty about their meanings, for describing the Tribunal procedures and according to him the roles played by the adjudicator and the parties need to be focused more.

[246] As like his predecessor from the Republican Party, i.e., President Eisenhower, Nixon also appointed an advisory council on the Executive Organizations that was also popularly referred to as the 'Ash Council'. The Council recommended the establishment of administrative courts particularly for the review of decisions of some of the significant commissions and agencies so as to bring them within a unified structure and act as a separate adjudicatory body instead of one agency with both the functions of rulemaking and adjudication.

[247] *See*, Harold H. Bruff, 'Coordinating Judicial Review in Administrative Law', (1992) 39 UCLA Law Review 1193, 1231. The author favors the broad jurisdiction to be vested in an administrative court for it to function properly unlike that proposed in the Council setup by Nixon. The specialization argument is countered by the fact that broader the jurisdiction of the court, the broader would be the relief it would be able to render without limiting it to certain narrow specific field. Also an administrative court with wider powers to review the decisions of inferior agencies would help bring uniformity in the nation-wide legal decisions, would be inexpensive as against the system of multiple specialist courts, etc. Hence according to the author, the benefits of broad administrative court outweighs the benefits of having multiple specialist adjudicators.

[248] *See*, Michael Asimow, 'Chapter 5- Inquisitorial Adjudication and Mass Justice in American Administrative law', in Laverne Jacobs et al. (eds), *The Nature Of Inquisitorial Processes In Administrative Regimes: Global Perspectives E-edition* (Routledge 2013).

[249] *Supra* (n 232), McNollgast, the discussion regarding the compromise reached between the Democrat supporters of New Deal after the death of Roosevelt and how the power dynamics played part in the compromise securing much accountability of the agencies through the enactment of APA for preserving the New Deal policies from these agencies in case Democrats lose support.

[250] See, S.5 of The Federal APA, 1946.

briefs presented and the final decision is made by the agency heads.[251] As already discussed during the review of the agency decisions by Article III Courts the decision that is reviewed is of the Agency head and not of the concerned ALJ on whose recommendation finality was accorded to the determination by the agency head.

Another interesting facet about the procedural guarantees established by the APA, Federal or State, is that they do not apply to many agencies as these agencies do not use ALJs as an adjudicator. Though the proceedings before these agencies exist in the nature similar to the one provided under the APA. Instead, the determination is made by the agency officers presiding over the hearings in the similar fashion as conducted by the ALJs.[252] The application of APA requires statutory provision providing for requirement of formal agency hearing. In case statutorily provided agency hearing is missing then the APA procedures are left only directory and least mandatory in nature.[253]

9.19 Canadian System

Canada like India has a strong influence of the United Kingdom's legal setup upon its institutions, it being part of the Commonwealth. Though it is interesting to note that certain aspects of the French setup in their nitty–gritty are also seen, obviously owing to its French roots. Hence, the Canadian setup makes an interesting case to see and observe among the Common Law. The factors that are most interesting to note are that Tribunals or the administrative adjudicators in Canada are categorically part of the Executive Branch. They enjoy independence depending upon the statute under which they were created but not the inherent judicial independence accorded to the judiciary as per the Canadian Constitution.

9.20 Composition and Structure

The tribunals in Canada's polity are considered as part of the executive government and the degree of independence that they enjoy, depends on the parent statute.[254] The Canadian Courts have been cautious about any delegation of judicial power to non-judicial bodies whether named as tribunals or not.[255] The Courts had laid the

[251] These heads also look after other agency functions such as the prosecutions, rulemaking, investigatory process, etc.; *See supra* (n 249), Michael Asimow.

[252] *Supra* (n 249), Michael Asimow. Under; *See also*, Michael Asimow, 'The Spreading Umbrella: Extending the APA's Adjudication Provisions to All Evidentiary Hearings Required by Statute', (2004) 56 Administrative Law Review 1003, 1004.

[253] *Id.*; *See also*, S. 554(a) of the Administrative Procedures Act, 1946.

[254] John D. Richard, 'Judicial Review in Canada', (2007) 45 Duquesne Law Review 483, 491.

[255] *Re Residential Tenancies Act, 1979* [1981] 1 S.C.R. 714.

"triple-step" test to analyze the existence of such delegation.[256] The persons manning these bodies have not conferred the title of "judges" though they may be performing the adjudicatory determination in several administrative disputes.[257] The structure here appears, somewhere similar to the one in the United Kingdom where the usual composition of the body consists of a chair and two members. These multifarious bodies occupy the structure that could also be comparable to the UK's quangos or NDPBs mostly performing regulatory but also adjudicatory functions.[258] The existence of these bodies is at both Federal as well as at the level of the states having their parent statutes. The difference that is seen from the counterpart in the USA is that unlike the USA's system there is no uniform procedural code that applies to these bodies and they rather are regulated through the language of their parent statutes.

The persons holding the adjudicatory positions are not always the ones with legal training though they are also expected to have certain specialized knowledge of the field of the respective tribunal they have been appointed.[259]

9.21 Procedural and Evidentiary Aspects

The evidentiary structure is also close to what is seen with the tribunals in the UK and is largely informal. The shreds of evidence that could not be produced before the courts of law due to strict admissibility standards could be produced before these bodies. These bodies enjoy certain powers similar to ordinary civil courts such as the power to enforce the attendance of the witnesses, summon for documents, take evidence under oath, etc. One difference that is seen from the UK's position is that some of the tribunals hold and exercise these extraordinary powers akin to the powers of the Superior Court of records.[260]

Many procedural aspects depend on the nature of the statute under which the Tribunal is constituted and the "*procedural leeway*" that statute allows to the Tribunal. Hence, many times, it is seen that the Tribunals determine their procedural standards. That *in absentia* of a uniform central procedural code regulating the same, could be adversarial or inquisitorial or a mixture of both depending on the statute and the powers ordained thereunder.[261]

The procedural aspects, unlike USA's APAs, are not regulated through a uniform code of procedure rather the applicability of procedural standards depends on the parent statute of the body.[262] These standards can be explicit or implicit but in the

[256] Id.

[257] Ibid., John D. Richard at 492.

[258] Sasha Baglay, *Introduction To The Canadian Legal System* (Pearson 2016) 158–162. A comprehensive list of these bodies has been provided by Baglay.

[259] *Supra* (n 255), John D Richard at 492.; *See also supra* (n 259), Sasha Baglay at 167.

[260] *id.*, JD Richard.

[261] *ibid.*, Sasha Baglay at 167.

[262] *Id.* at 163.

case of implied standards the intention of the legislature is seen to interpret the extent of vires vested with the tribunal.[263]

One minor similarity between the Indian counterpart[264] of these tribunals is in the authority to interpret the statutory provisions.[265] The tribunals can interpret the statutory provisions to the extent that they may be inconsistent with Canada's Constitution but only to the extent that due to such inconsistency the provision becomes inapplicable to the proceedings before the tribunal.[266] Though there is a limitation on their ability to interpret the Constitutional Charter and pertinent questions but can apply the charter interpretations already rendered by the judiciary to the matters they are *seisin of*.[267] Also, this authority to some extent depends on the vires ordained through the parent statute of the tribunal. When the parent statute grants authority to interpret statutory validity of certain provisions then the tribunal could be understood to be capable of interpreting the constitutional legality of the same.[268] The absolute limitation akin in comparative perspective to the Indian scenario is on the declaration of the constitutionality of the statutory provisions.[269]

9.22 The Adjudication and the Extent of Independence

The importance of the due process clause as seen with the US administrative procedure, as part of the compromise achieved through the APA in 1946, is also seen in Canada's system. The two aspects of the fair decision-making process are followed in Canada's Administrative setup.[270] First, the appellate procedure or the availability of the same from the decision of the Tribunal and second, the adjudicator is regulated

[263] *Supra* (n 255), JD Richard at 498.; See also, *Nova Scotia (WCB)* v. *Laseur* 2003 SCC 54 [Canada]. The case discussed the question of the interpretative vires vested with these bodies and held that it is the intention vested in the parent statute that must be seen for the purpose.

[264] *See, L Chandra Kumar* v. *Union of India* AIR 1997 SC 1125 [India].

[265] *Supra* (n 255), JD Richard at 498.

[266] *id.*

[267] *id.* at 499.

[268] *id.*

[269] *id*; This must be read with the interpretive leeway granted by the Supreme Court of India in the *L Chandra Kumar* v. *Union of India,* AIR 1997 SC 1125 [India] through the seven judge bench decision in which these quasi-judicial bodies were vested with the powers of similar nature but limiting their ability to declare the provision of a statute as unconstitutional.

[270] *Supra* (n 259), Sasha Baglay at 164–165. The aspects being the right of fair hearing and the right of independent forum following the two iconic maxims, i.e., *Audi alteram partem* and *Nemo judex in causa sua,* i.e., the doctrine against bias signifying both the principles. Both these rights as students of the discipline of Administrative Law be reminded, are assisted and aided by many other rights such as the right to have counsel, to call support witnesses, etc.; *See also*, the decision of the Canadian Supreme Court in *Baker v. Canada (Minister of Citizenship and Immigration)* [1999] 2 SCR 817 [Canada]. Available at, https://scc-csc.lexum.com/scc-csc/scc-csc/en/item/1717/index.do (Last Accessed 2nd March 2020). In the decision the Court directed certain contextual aspects to be considered for determination of the fairness of a particular decision like the nature

by the parent statute that has constituted the tribunal.[271] Though the judicial review by the Courts of law is also open.[272]

One significant decision of the Supreme Court of Canada in the *Ocean Port Hotel* Case[273] is worth mentioning on the doctrine of the independence of adjudicators in Canada.[274] The factual matrix of the case consists of the decision of the "British Columbia Liquor Appeal Board" (BCLAB) or "the Board" against the Hotel suspending the license of the hotel for violations of the applicable legal standards. The Hotel challenged the decision, more on the aspect of lack of competency of the Board owing to the lack of independence and thus affecting the fairness of the hearing it accorded to the Hotel. This is due to *uncertain service tenures* of the members of the Board and also their dependability on the *privilege* of the executive branch for retaining them. Though, no such precedence occurred where the executive exercised such privilege against the members of the board.[275] Though the decision against the Hotel was remitted back to the Court of Appeal in the final decision but during the course of reasoning, the Court made certain pertinent observations.

The Court held that the tribunals have the majority function of the implementation of the policy of the executive and are creatures of the Parliamentary statutes for that purpose unlike Courts of Law. The principle of independence from executive interference that is constitutionally entrenched for the courts does not apply for these bodies for the same reason. Though they do exercise some level of freedom in the exercise of their functions but according to the Court such freedom, the extent, depends largely on the statute that has created the body and the objectives for which

---

of legislation under which the decision is made, decisional conditions, consistency of procedure chosen for making it and its effect on the parties.

[271] *Supra* (n 259), Sasha Baglay at 175–177.

[272] Id. The reviewability standards include the extent of the decision of the tribunal and the obedient exercise of the same within the powers vested in it through the parent statute. The author in the book provides readers with an example of a case of *Johnstone* v. *Canada* [2014] FCJ No 455 in which though the court while reviewing a decision of the Tribunal on Human Rights upheld the major part of the decision but remanded the decision back providing certain areas where the tribunal exceeded its authority.

[273] *Ocean Port Hotel* v. *B.C. (GM, LQ)* 2001 SCC 52. Available at, https://scc-csc.lexum.com/scc-csc/scc-csc/en/item/1891/index.do (Last Accessed 2nd March 2020). The decision is worth reading on many aspects like Canadian legal understanding of the 'Tribunal' and 'Court'. Emphasis is supplied through the decision of then Chief Justice McLachlin who as part of her decision in ¶ ¶ 23–24 clarifies this distinction.

[274] *See also*, David J. Mullan, 'Ocean Port Hotel and Statutory Compromises of Tribunal Independence', (2002) 9 Canadian Labour & Employment Law Journal 193. The much celebrated and revered author of this paper Professor Mullan discusses how the decision has the potential of impacting the future independence of various other adjudicators of the similar nature. As the decision appears to be granting importance to the statutory mandates over the common law principles required for the independence of adjudicators.

[275] This has to be seen in the light of the *Dewar's* and *Hewat's* decision [*Dewar* v. *Ontario* 1998, 156 D.L.R. (4th) 202 (C.A.); *Hewat v. Ontario* 1998, 156 D.L.R. (4th) 193 (C.A.)] where the interference in the form of removals of the members of the *Ottawa-Carleton Police Services Board* and *Ontario Labor Relations Board* respectively were invalidated by the Court as they were before the expiry of their terms.

the body was created. These independence aspects (or absence of them) as the will of the Parliament get embodied in the statute creating the Tribunal.[276] Thus, the tribunals according to the decision do not fall within the domain of the judiciary exactly unlike the provincial subordinate courts.[277]

Another issue raised and negated by the Court was regarding the overlap of the functionality of these bodies performing investigating, regulation related and adjudicatory functions. But the Court while referring to another decision[278] called such convergence as necessary to the Tribunals and also owing to the saving of some taxpayers' penny by the exchequer.[279]

The Canadian Professor Mullan did not agree with the decision of the Court.[280] According to him, the tribunals were constituted for implementation of the policies of the executive government but the exclusion of jurisdiction that they enjoy replacing the jurisdiction of the regular courts require a certain degree of independence.[281] Though he agrees that the domains of the doctrine of Separation of Powers have not been the same in Canada as in the Australian or the United States of America's legal setup. Raising doubts on the Courts being the sole arbiter for the exercise of the judicial power in the Canadian setup.[282] Even historically, the concerns regarding the independence of Tribunals as administrative adjudicators have existed in Canadian Legal Setup.[283] With Scholars recommending long-pending implementation of various recommendations for the independence of regulators and their decision-making in the Canadian setup.[284] Also, the concerns regarding the lack of constitutionally validated and supported status of the Administrative process have been the part of scholarly discussions.[285]

---

[276] Ibid. *Please see the discussion starting ¶ ¶ 23 to 24 in the judgment cited above.*

[277] *Supra* (n 275). This view taken by the Court is vehemently criticized by Professor Mullan in his paper by calling it oversimplification of the understanding of the administration of tribunals and the process.

[278] *Newfoundland Telephone Co v. Newfoundland (Board of Commissioners of Public Utilities)* [1992] 1 SCR 623 [Canada].

[279] Id, Please see ¶ 41 of the decision.

[280] Ibid; *See also*, David J. Mullan, 'Ocean Port Hotel and Statutory Compromises of Tribunal Independence', (2002) 9 Canadian Labour & Employment Law Journal 193.

[281] Id. at 203.

[282] Id.

[283] *Please see*, H. N. Janisch, 'Independence of Administrative Tribunals in Canada: In Praise of Structural Heretics', (1988) 8 Journal of the National Association of Administrative Law Judiciary 75.

[284] Id; Please see the '*Conclusion*' section of the article referred.

[285] David J. Mullan, 'The Future of Canadian Administrative Law', (1991) 16 Queen's Law Journal 77, 87–89. This discussion assumes much importance after the enforcement of the Canadian Charter of Rights and Freedoms in 1982.

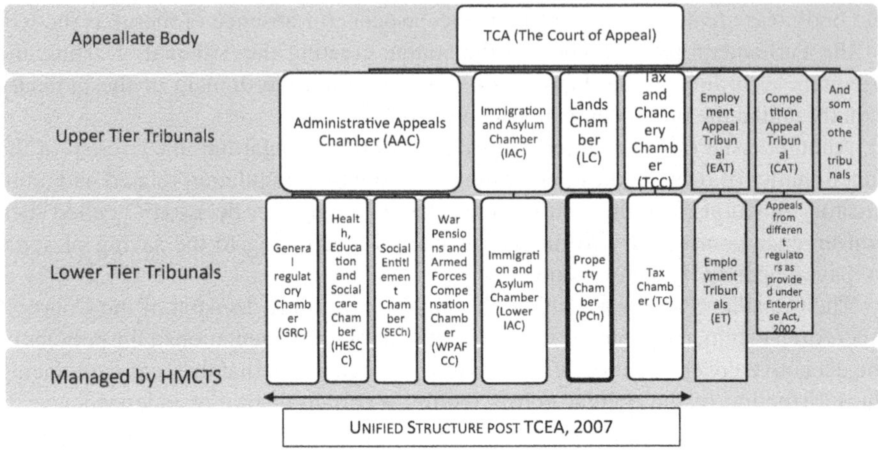

Fig. 9.1 Unified Tribunal Structure with certain Tribunals still functioning outside this structure, in UK

9.23 Conclusion

One common factor that could be seen throughout the Common Law world, is the existence of legal tensions across the institutions due to adoption of administrative adjudication by the means of encroachment upon the traditional judicial functions. Despite these tensions the system of administrative adjudication in the form of tribunals has a peculiar significance that justifies dabbling with them for acceptance of certain best characteristics of this alternative system within the traditional setup. The Australian administrative adjudicator has this characteristic in the form of the *merits review.* Under which the policy matters and abstruse factual decisions could also be reviewed by the adjudicator. The merits review is sui generis in the sense that it is uncommon in Common Law for the courts to judicially review the reasons or merits behind the enactment of a particular policy beyond legal validity of the same. It is to be reminded that Australian adjudicators are considered as part of the executive and not judiciary. Though certain safeguards have been provided for ensuring the independence of the determination that they make. For India, being the developing economy, policy-making is increasingly salient but due to limitations of the traditional courts of their ability to judicially review the policy decisions the setup for merits review would offer much relief for litigants significantly affected by the policy decisions.[286]

[286] In India when policy decisions are arbitrary, *mala-fide, per incuriam*, etc. them could be successfully judicially reviewed before the courts under the doctrine of substantive and procedural ultra vires. But this review has certain limitations based upon non-intervention in the factual position or non-appreciation of the facts or the alternative available to the policy challenged. Since policy-making is considered as expertise of the executive, the courts do not intervene in the merits of such decisions following the norms of Separation of Powers doctrine and exercising self-restraint.

The United Kingdom's administrative-legal and constitutional setup, recently, in the past fifteen years, has undergone significant changes. One of them, is the integration of the tribunals within the judicial hierarchy offering the same parameters for ensuring the independence for these bodies as available to the traditional Common Law Courts in the United Kingdom. Thus, sorting certain legal tensions as well issues that this setup faced in terms of administrative support, streamlining the appointments, independence of the administrative adjudicator, etc. The Indian legal setup is highly motivated by the UK's setup. Justifying the reliance of India upon the institutional aspects of this polity, as the Tribunals in the UK are administered by an agency also common to Courts, i.e., HMCTS. This is under the common supervision of the Senior President of Tribunals or SPT and overall supervision of the Lord Chancellor. Their appeal system is also streamlined with the proper role of each institution in the appeal process. Apart from that, the appointments are also ensured through the independent *Judicial Appointments Commission* or *JAC*.[287] But there are still some issues that need redress as observed in the case of employment tribunals in the pertinent discussion. Another noteworthy and interesting observation from UK's legal position for India is the contempt jurisdiction. In India, though many tribunals[288] exercise jurisdiction erstwhile vested with the courts but lack the power to punish for contempt of their order. The position in the UK is governed by the Contempt of Court Act[289] that includes tribunals exercising the judicial power of the state to possess the contempt jurisdiction. This position was further strengthened by the judgment in *Liverpool Daily Post and Echo Newspapers Case*.[290]

The system of the United States of America provides various learning outcomes. The historical compromise in the form of APA or the Administrative Procedures Act of 1946 was achieved in that system based upon the legal tensions that were created by the administrative adjudication outside the setup of regular courts. The basis of the compromise was the dispute caused by the legal tensions caused by the executive or agency adjudication outside the scope of the traditional doctrine of Separation of Powers. The *New Deal* (1933) supporters after the death of their Leader and popular Democrat President Roosevelt in 1945, were keen on preserving the crucial elements of the deal providing leeway to the executive government. The compromise in the form of *APA* served the twin goals. *First*, of securing the due process, fairness, etc., in the agency adjudication. *Second*, keeping this adjudication amenable to judicial review before Article III courts in case it violated these procedural principles. This

---

[287] *Supra* (n 169), Gary Slapper at 636–638.

[288] For example, The tribunals like Debt Recovery Tribunal (DRT), Income Tax Appellate Tribunal (ITAT), National Company Law Tribunal (NCLT), etc.; *See also*, Joshi Kashyap, 'Tribunalisation In India: Where We Are Lacking?' *LiveLaw Online Legal Magazine Column*, 15th Sep. 2020. Available at, http://www.livelaw.in/columns/tribunalisation-in-india-where-we-are-lacking-162949www.livelaw.in/columns/tribunalisation-in-india-where-we-are-lacking-162949 (Last accessed 20th November 2021).

[289] *See*, S.19 of the Contempt of Court Act, 1981 [United Kingdom]. The legislation can be accessed at, https://www.legislation.gov.uk/ukpga/1981/49/1999-01-31/data.pdf (Last accessed 20th November 2021).

[290] *Pickering v. Liverpool Daily Post and Echo Newspapers*, [1991] 2 AC 370.

secured both the purposes of required leeway for administrative adjudication as well as judicial control over the whole process in case the process goes outside the overall scope mandated through the APA. The proposals for a similar procedural code as APA were also made in India but were not given houseroom by the state.[291]

The setup in Canada provided peculiar learnings in the way such bodies have been designed and seen in the legal system. The observations of the Chief Justice of the Canadian Supreme Court concerning tribunals in the *Ocean Port Hotels Case*[292] pertains to larger salience. The observations referred to these tribunals or agencies as the statute-based bodies created by the Parliament for implementation of the policies of the government and left the limits of the required independence for these bodies to be chosen by the Legislature. This approach differentiated these bodies from the courts exercising the judicial power of the state in Canada.

This approach broadly separates Canada from the Indian Position[293] where the same constitutional safeguards as available to the judicial wing are applied[294] for these adjudicatory bodies. In case Parliamentary law creating these adjudicatory bodies in India falls short in those safeguards then the law is amenable to successful judicial review before the supervisory puisne courts based on the Rule of Law as Independence of Judiciary is an essential facet of the same, more apparently after Second Judges case.[295] In India, the recent proposal to set up National Tribunal Commission (NTC) falls short of the requirements based upon which the HMCTS was formed in the UK, as HMCTS is a setup serving common administrative needs for both judiciary and tribunals in the UK. Though the NTC on the other hand is proposed to be enacted as a separate body for the Tribunals alone. This adds the expenditure for creating the parallel structure outside judicial hierarchy in the form of tribunals. The specialization feature of the tribunals has also given way for the generalist tribunals after amalgamation in India.[296] It is also not the case that these bodies have been instrumental in reducing the pendency[297] to justify their parallel creation to courts.[298] Hence, it is advisable that Tribunals form part of judicial

---

[291] *See*, IP Massey, *Compulsions and Constraints of Administrative Justice Against the Backdrop of the Swaran Singh Committee Report,* (1976) 3 SCC J-9,14. Far back and during the time of the paradigm shift in administrative justice in India, i.e., in 1976, Professor Massey recommended APA [USA] or the Tribunal and Enquiries Act, 1958 [United Kingdom] like code in India for ensuring the minimum standards in administrative procedure and particularly in Administrative Justice.

[292] *Supra* (n 274), *Ocean Port Hotel, 2001 SCC 52* [Canada].

[293] *Supra* (n 5), *Rojer Mathew* ¶ 158 at pages 87–88. Available at, https://www.sci.gov.in/pdf/JUD_4.pdf (Last Accessed 20th November 2021).

[294] Id.

[295] *Supreme Court Advocates-on- Record Association v. Union of India* (1993) 4 SCC 441.

[296] *Supra* (n 201).

[297] At the inauguration of the Armed Forces Tribunal in 2009 the nine thousand cases relating army matters were pending with the judiciary that got handed over to the tribunal. See, Press Note of the Ministry of Defense, 'Armed Forces Tribunal to be inaugurated tomorrow' *Press Information Bureau*, 7th August 2009. Available at, https://pib.gov.in/newsite/erelcontent.aspx?relid=51613 (Last accessed 30th January 2022).

[298] See, Bhadra Sinha and Amrita Nayak Dutta, 'Armed Forces Tribunal has 19,000 pending cases, but here's why this is least of its problems' *The Print E-Edition*, 18 March

hierarchy with separate Administrative Procedure Code (APC) to cater the requisite flexibility of procedure. The herculean challenge, now posed after recent judicial decisions in India, to set up tribunals parallel and outside judicial hierarchy but with same standards of independence as applicable to judiciary, justifies this conclusion more. The vast subordinate but higher judicial cadres available could facilitate judges for these bodies after some training in the judicial academies across the country. This not only resolves the persistent issue of vacancies at the tribunals in India but also makes tribunals geographically more accessible preserving the judicial review with the puisne judiciary.[299]

2021. Available at, https://theprint.in/judiciary/armed-forces-tribunal-has-19000-pending-cases-but-heres-why-this-is-least-of-its-problems/624020/ (Last accessed 30th January 2022).

[299] For a more detailed and comprehensive chart on the hierarchy of these bodies and the complete structure please visit the Official Website of the Judiciary of the United Kingdom. Available at, https://www.judiciary.uk/wp-content/uploads/2020/08/tribunals-chart-updated-May-2020-1.pdf (Last Accessed 20th November 2021).; *See also*, Gary Slapper, et. al., *The English Legal System* (Routledge, 2017) 633, 637. The Table is also inspired from the one provided in this book.

Part III
Private Law: General Themes

Chapter 10
Intellectual Property and Investment Treaties: Comparing Newest Indian and Australian Treaty Practices

Prabhash Ranjan

Abstract This paper discusses the interface between intellectual property (IP) rights and the protection of foreign investment under bilateral investment treaties (BITs) and investment chapters in free trade agreements (FTAs). Foreign investors have used BITs or FTA investment chapters to enforce their IP rights in host States. BITs are treaties aimed at protecting foreign investment. This paper, undertaking a comparative approach, contrasts the provisions in the Indian Model BIT with select Australian investment treaties to determine the interplay with IP, foreign investment protection, and the host State's right to regulate in the public interest. It studies those provisions in the investment treaties of both countries that can be employed to safeguard the host State's regulatory power in the event a foreign investor uses the BIT to protect its IP rights. The paper aims to contribute to the rising literature in the field of IP and international investment law by comparing the practices of India and Australia—two important trading partners.

10.1 Introduction

Over the years, the interface between intellectual property (IP) rights and protection of foreign investment under bilateral investment treaties (BITs)[1] and investment chapters in free trade agreements (FTAs) has intensified. Foreign investors have used BITs or FTA investment chapters to enforce their IP rights in host States. BITs are treaties aimed at protecting foreign investment. They protect the foreign investment by imposing conditions on the State's regulatory power thus, prevent undue interference with the rights of the foreign investor. These conditions include confining the state from expropriating investments, barring for public interest with

[1] Till the end of 2020, 2943 BITs have been concluded. See, UNCTAD (2021) 'World Investment Report 2021: Investing in Sustainable Recovery' (2021) (New York and Geneva, United Nations) 123.

P. Ranjan (✉)
Faculty of Legal Studies, South Asian University, New Delhi, India
e-mail: pranjan1278@gmail.com

M. John et al. (eds.), *The Indian Yearbook of Comparative Law 2020*, The Indian Yearbook of Comparative Law, https://doi.org/10.1007/978-981-99-5467-4_10

adequate compensation and following due process; imposing obligations on States to accord fair and equitable treatment (FET) to foreign investment and not to discriminate against foreign investment; etc.[2] Investment chapters in FTAs perform similar functions.

A defining characteristic of BITs is that they empower foreign investors to directly bring claims against the State for alleged treaty breaches through a mechanism known as investor-State dispute settlement (ISDS) before international arbitral forums often without exhausting local remedies. All these years, there has been a proliferation of ISDS claims against host States covering a wide range of regulatory measures of host States such as monetary policy, taxation, environment protection, and public health.[3]

Typically BITs and FTA investment chapters contain a broad assets-based definition of investment specifically including IP rights within it.[4] In the famous *Eli Lily v Canada*[5] case, where an American pharmaceutical company brought a claim against Canada under the North American Free Trade Agreement (NAFTA) challenging the invalidation of its patent by a Canadian federal court on the ground of "inutility",[6] the tribunal had no hesitation in accepting that patents are protected investments in investment treaties.[7] Recognizing IP rights as part of the definition of investment implies ISDS tribunals have jurisdiction over host State's regulatory measures that affect the foreign investors' IP rights. In other words, a foreign investor can challenge such IP-related regulatory measures as a treaty breach before an ISDS tribunal. This makes the ISDS mechanism an attractive pathway for multinational pharmaceutical companies to implement their IP rights and, if successful, claim monetary compensation from the host State.[8]

Indeed, in the last few years, foreign investors have challenged the host State's IP-related regulatory measures before ISDS tribunals. For example, as already pointed out, in *Eli Lily v Canada*, Eli Lily argued that the invalidation of its patents by

---

[2] For a general discussion on BITs see R. Dolzer, U. Kriebaum and C. Schreuer. 2022. Principles of International Investment Law. Oxford: Oxford University Press; A. Newcombe and L. Paradell. 2009. Law and Practice of Investment Treaties. Bedfordshire: Kluwer Law International, pp. 1–73; Jeswald Salacuse. 2015. The Law of Investment Treaties. Oxford: Oxford University Press.

[3] As of 1 January 2021, the cumulative number of known ISDS cases stands at 1104, see UNCTAD 2021, 129.

[4] See Pratyush Nath Upreti, 'Enforcing IPRs through Investor-State Dispute Settlement: A Paradigm Shift in Global IP Practice' (2016) 19 The Journal of World Intellectual Property 53.

[5] *Eli Lilly and Company v The Government of Canada* ICSID Case No UNCT/14/2, Final Award, 16 March 2017.

[6] See also Valentia S Vadi, 'Towards a New Dialectics: Pharmaceutical Patents, Public Health and Foreign Direct Investments' (2015) 5 New York University Journal of Intellectual Property and Entertainment Law 113.

[7] *Eli Lily v Canada*, para 167. Also see Daniel Gervais, 'Intellectual Property: A Beacon for Reform of Investor-State Dispute Settlement' (2019) 40 Michigan Journal of International Law 289, 299.

[8] Peter K Yu, 'The Pathways of Multinational Intellectual Property Dispute Settlement in Christopher Heath and Anselm Kamperman Sanders (eds), Intellectual Property and International Dispute Resolution (Kluwer 2019), 123–141.

Canadian courts amounts to a breach of the expropriation and the fair and equitable treatment (FET) provisions of NAFTA's investment chapter.[9] Although Eli Lily lost the dispute, the case exhibited the ability of foreign investors to employ BIT's ISDS mechanism for enforcing their IP rights in the host State. Likewise, in another case known as *Philip Morris v Uruguay*,[10] a tobacco company called Philip Morris contested Uruguay's trademark measures under the Switzerland-Uruguay BIT.[11] Uruguay won the dispute.[12]

Notwithstanding the outcomes in these cases, there are concerns globally that domestic IP-related regulatory measures such as issuance of compulsory licenses (CLs) or revocation of patents for public purposes could trigger ISDS claims against States. This concern, in turn, has triggered a process of new treaty practices of countries striving to insulate their IP-related regulatory measures from the purview of ISDS claims. Important to bear in mind that CLs are considered a very important flexibility in the IP regime that allows countries to adopt measures for the public interest such as increasing the supply of a patented drug.[13]

Against this global background, the purpose of this paper is to compare the Indian and Australian practices on IP in investment treaties. The paper will endeavor to decipher whether the two countries have been able to carve-out their IP-related regulatory measures from the ambit of ISDS or not. This comparative study will enable us to comprehend the similarities and divergences between India and Australia on this important issue. It is significant given the fact that India and Australia recently signed an interim FTA, known as Economic Cooperation and Trade Agreement (ECTA).[14] Although the ECTA does not contain a chapter on investment protection, it is possible that the two sides might decide to legalize their international investment relations in the future. The analysis, in this paper, thus, might prove to be useful in this regard.

---

[9] *Eli Lily v Canada*, paras 181 and 183.

[10] *Philip Morris Brands Sàrl, Philip Morris Products S.A. and Abal Hermanos S.A. v Oriental Republic of Uruguay*, ICSID Case No ARB/10/7, Award (8 July 2016).

[11] See also *Philip Morris Asia Limited v The Commonwealth of Australia*, PCA Case No 2012–12 Award on Jurisdiction and Admissibility (17 December 2015).

[12] See also *Apotex Holdings Inc and Apotex Inc v United States of America (Apotex III)* ICSID Case No ARB(AF)/12/1, Award (25 August 2014); *Les Laboratoires Servier, S.A.A., Biofarma, S.A.S., Arts et Techniques du Progres S.A.S. v The Republic of Poland* UNCITRAL Award (14 February 2012). For more discussion on ISDS and IPR see Bryan Mercurio, 'Awakening the Sleeping Giant: Intellectual Property Rights in International Investment Agreements' (2012) 15 Journal of International Economic Law 871.

[13] For the significance of CL in the Indian context see Jodie Liu, 'Compulsory Licensing and Anti-Evergreening: Interpreting the TRIPS Flexibilities in Section 10.84 and 10.3(d) of the Indian Patents Act' (2015) 56 Harvard International Law Journal 207.

[14] India-Australia Economic Cooperation and Trade Agreement (INDAUS ECTA) between the Government of the Republic of India and the Government of Australia. https://commerce.gov.in/international-trade/trade-agreements/ind-aus-ecta/.

As part of the methodology, the comparison between the two country's investment treaty practices is restricted to assessing India's 2016 Model BIT[15] and the subsequent ones that India has signed based on the 2016 Model[16] and Australia's recent BITs and FTA investment chapters. This is because India's investment treaty practice has undergone a complete overhaul and is now based on the 2016 Model. Likewise, there has been some re-think in Australia about investment treaties.[17] Thus, the paper will study the recent BITs and FTA investment chapters signed by Australia, i.e., Australia-Uruguay BIT,[18] Australia-Hong Kong Investment agreement,[19] and the investment chapter in the Australia-Indonesia FTA[20] that are representative of its investment treaty practice. The paper will compare the Indian and Australia investment treaty practice on the issue of IP under the following heads. Part II discusses IP as part of the definition of investment in the Indian and Australian BITs. In part III, the paper contrasts the exclusion of IP-related regulatory measures especially the issuance of CL from the ambit of expropriation. Next, in part IV, the paper deliberates the issue of IP-related regulatory measures in the context of performance requirements on foreign investment. Part V offers the concluding remarks.

---

[15] Model Text for the Indian Bilateral Investment Treaty <https://dea.gov.in/sites/default/files/ModelBIT_Annex_0.pdf> accessed on 27 February 2022.

[16] Treaty between the Republic of Belarus and the Republic of India on Investments (signed 24 September 2018, entered into force 5 March 2020) ('India-Belarus BIT'); Agreement between the India Taipei Association in Taipei And The Taipei Economic and Cultural Center in New Delhi on The Promotion and Protection of Investments (signed 18 December 2018, entered into force 14 February 2019) ('India-Taiwan BIT'); Bilateral Investment Treaty between the Government of the Kyrgyz Republic and the Government of the Republic of India (signed 14 June 2019) ('India-Kyrgyzstan BIT'); Investment Cooperation and Facilitation Treaty between the Federative Republic of Brazil and the Republic of India (signed 25 January 2020) ('Brazil-India BIT').

[17] See Luke Nottage, "Investor-State Arbitration Policy and Practice after Philip Morris Asia v Australia" in Leon Trakman & Nicola Ranieri, eds, Regionalism in International Investment Law (New York: Oxford University Press, 2013) 452;; Kate Lindeman et al., "Investor-State Dispute Resolution in Australia: A Changing Landscape for Investors", online: (2015) 1 Transnational Dispute Management <www.transnational-dispute-management.com/article.asp?key=2176>; Tania Voon, Tobacco, Health and Investor-State Dispute Settlement: Australia's Recent Treaty Practice (2020) 37(1) Australian Year Book of International Law, 89–98.

[18] Agreement Between Australia and the Oriental Republic of Uruguay on the Promotion and Protection of Investments (signed on 5 April 2019) (Australia-Uruguay BIT).

[19] Investment Agreement Between the Government of Australia and the Government of the Hong Kong Special Administrative Region of the People's Republic of China (signed on 26 March 2019) (Australia-Hong Kong Investment Agreement).

[20] Australia-Indonesia Comprehensive Economic Partnership Agreement, Investment chapter (signed on 4 March 2019) (Australia-Indonesia FTA investment chapter).

10.2 Definition of Investment and IP

The definition of investment in an investment treaty is important because the host State's obligations toward the foreign investor under the BIT are restricted only to "investments that fall within the treaty's scope of applications or treaty definitions".[21] In other words, if an asset is not a protected investment under the BIT, the host State's regulatory measures with respect to that asset cannot be challenged before an ISDS tribunal. Thus, in context of IP, for any foreign investor to challenge IP-related regulatory measures before an ISDS tribunal, the requirement will be to show that IP is a protected investment under the BIT.

10.2.1 Australian Practice

Australia's investment treaty practice contains an asset-based definition of investment. For example, Article 1 of the Australia-Hong Kong investment agreement provides as follows:

> investment means every asset that an investor owns or controls, directly or indirectly, that has the characteristics of an investment, including such characteristics as the commitment of capital or other resources, the expectation of gain or profit, or the assumption of risk. Forms that an investment may take include:
>
> …

(f) intellectual property rights

In addition to providing an asset-based definition of investment, the Australia-Hong Kong investment agreement specifically includes IP rights under the definition of investment. A similar asset-based definition of investment that includes IP rights exists in Australia-Uruguay BIT[22] and the Australia-Indonesia FTA investment chapter.[23] The definition of investment in the Australian treaties talks about three economic characteristics: investment should include a commitment of capital, there should be an expectation or gain or profit and investment should include risk. For IP rights to qualify as a protected investment, they need to satisfy the economic characteristics of investment. To understand this, let us assume that a foreign pharmaceutical company in Australia has been granted a product patent right on a medicine. This product patent will qualify as a protected investment because it will include within its ambit a commitment of capital because without such a commitment, the company will not be able to work the patent. Likewise, the pharmaceutical enterprise will work the product patent toward making a profit, which, in turn, entails a risk.

---

[21] Jeswald Salacuse, *The Law of Investment Treaties* (Oxford: Oxford University Press, 2015), p. 174.

[22] Australia-Uruguay BIT, art 1(a)(iv).

[23] Australia-Indonesia FTA Investment chapter, art 14.1.

10.2.2 Indian Practice

To understand the Indian treaty practice on this issue, our starting point is Article 1.4 (f) of the 2016 Model BIT, which provides:

> "investment" means an enterprise constituted, organised and operated in good faith by an investor in accordance with the law of the Party in whose territory the investment is made, taken together with the assets of the enterprise, has the characteristics of an investment such as the commitment of capital or other resources, certain duration, the expectation of gain or profit, the assumption of risk and a significance for the development of the Party in whose territory the investment is made. An enterprise may possess the following assets:
>
> ...

(f) Copyrights, know-how, and intellectual property rights such as patents, trademarks, industrial designs, and trade names, to the extent they are recognized under the law of a Party.

As against the asset-based definition of investment, which is generally found in most BITs (that India has now unilaterally terminated), the 2016 Indian Model BIT contains an enterprise-based definition of "investment". The enterprise has to satisfy the following economic characteristics of investment: there should be a commitment of capital or other resources by the enterprise, the enterprise should assume risk, there should be an expectation of profit, the enterprise should be in existence for a certain duration and it should be significant for the development of the country where the investment has been made. Out of these five characteristics, the requirement of significant development for the host State may not be easy to satisfy due to its subjective character.

Moreover, it is not sufficiently clear whether these characteristics must be satisfied by the assets of the enterprise or by the enterprise,[24] or both. This confusion arises because there is a comma after the words "taken together with the assets of the enterprise" in Article 1.4. After the comma, the following words appear: "has the characteristics of an investment such as…". If the assets owned by the enterprise have to satisfy the "characteristics test", then in place of the comma, the word "that" should have been inserted. Thus, the text would have read: "taken together with the assets of the enterprise that has the characteristics of an investment…".[25] In the absence of the word "that", it seems that an enterprise alone has to satisfy the "characteristics test".[26]

This might have implications at the practical level. For example, assume that a foreign pharmaceutical company operating in India for say five years gets a product patent on a drug. The question will be whether the company or the patent right or

---

[24] Enterprise is defined in Article 1.3 as '(i) any legal entity constituted, organised and operated in compliance with the law of a Party, including any company, corporation, limited liability partnership or a joint venture; and (ii) a branch of any such entity established in the territory of a Party in accordance with its law and carrying out business activities there'.

[25] 2012 US Model BIT, Art. 1.4(f).

[26] See also Prabhash Ranjan, India and Bilateral Investment Treaties: Refusal, Acceptance, Backlash (2019) (OUP: New Delhi), 312–313.

both need to satisfy the economic characteristics of investment? Further assume that the Indian government, for some public policy reason, revokes the product patent granted in six months. The relevant question here will be whether the pharmaceutical company and the relevant IP right, both, need to show that they satisfy the economic characteristics of investment? Or will it be sufficient for the enterprise to show that it falls within the definition of investment?

Among the BITs that India signed post the 2016 Model, all of them contain the same enterprise-based definition with the requirement to satisfy the five characteristics barring the India-Brazil BIT, which does not require the enterprise to satisfy the requirement of economic development to the host State.

As regards IP rights are concerned, the 2016 Model BITs and the subsequent BITs signed by India include IP rights under the definition of investment. There is a slight variation in the treaty language between the 2016 Model BIT and the remaining BITs. As already mentioned, the 2016 Model BIT includes IP rights such as patents, trademarks, industrial designs, and trade names, to the extent they are recognized under the host State's domestic law. In other words, if something is not recognized under the domestic laws of the host State as an IP right, it will not become a protected investment under the BIT. Thus, the existence of an IP right is linked to this being recognized under the domestic law. On the other hand, in India's BITs with Kyrgyzstan,[27] Taiwan,[28] and Brazil, the existence of IP rights is linked to the Trade-Related Aspects of Intellectual Property Rights (TRIPS) agreement of the World Trade Organization (WTO). For example, Article 2.4(e) of the India-Brazil BIT states that IP rights listed in the TRIPS agreement fall under the definition of investment. This implies that the determination of whether a right constitutes an IP right will be made by referring to the TRIPS agreement and not the domestic law of the host State. In practical terms, this will not have much impact in the case of India because Indian domestic IP laws are consistent with the TRIPS agreement.

10.2.3 Comparison

The following points can be made when one compares the Indian and the Australian treaty practice on this issue. First, both countries specifically include IP rights within the ambit of definition of investment. The slight difference in the treaty formulation is that in the Indian BITs, IP rights are benchmarked either to the domestic law of the host State or to the TRIPS agreement. Whereas, under the Australian BITs, we do not see IP rights being either linked to domestic laws or the TRIPS agreement. However, this variation is of no practical consequence because both India and Australia are WTO members and their domestic IP rights are compatible with the TRIPS agreement.

---

[27] India-Kyrgyzstan BIT, art 1.4(f).

[28] India-Taiwan BIT, art 1.3(f).

Second, while both countries include the economic characteristics of investment within the definition, the Indian treaty practice on this issue is broader. It also includes within its ambit the subjective aspect of investment making a significant contribution to the host State to qualify for treaty protection. Australian BITs do not include this subjective requirement in their definition of investment. Satisfying this subjective requirement is not easy, because it will depend on the assessment made by the host State.[29] Investments that may satisfy the other requirements of commitment of capital, risk, and profit might be devoid of treaty protection because of a subjective assessment that does not contribute to the host State's development. As the ISDS tribunal in *Patrick Mitchell v Russia*[30] held, the requirement of contributing to the economic development of the host State is extremely broad.

Third, another important difference between the two sides on this aspect of treaty practice is that while the Indian BITs focus on an enterprise-based definition of investment, the Australian BITs provide for an asset-based definition of investment, where assets must meet the economic characteristics. In the case of the Indian BITs, as discussed, it is not clear whether the enterprise or the asset, or both has to satisfy the economic characteristics requirement.

10.3 Exclusion of IP-Related Measures from the Ambit of Expropriation

Countries may adopt different kinds of IP-related regulatory measures. For example, countries may revoke the patent on the ground of public interest, as permitted under Section 66 of the Indian Patent Act.[31] Another important IP-related regulatory measure is the issuance of CL. Countries could issue a CL on a patented drug for multiple reasons such as making the drug more accessible to people or increasingly the supply of a drug in response to a health emergency such as a pandemic like Covid-19. An important issue in the interface between IP and investment is whether such IP-related regulatory measures such as the issuance of CL by a host State could be challenged by a foreign pharmaceutical company before an ISDS tribunal as an indirect expropriation of its investment. Several international investment lawyers argue that this is possible.[32] It can be argued that the issuance of CL amounts to indirect

[29] Rudolph Dolzer and C Schreuer, Principles of International Investment Law (2012) (OUP: Oxford/New York), 75.

[30] *Mr. Patrick Mitchell v. The Democratic Republic of Congo*, ICSID Case No. ARB/99/7, Annulment proceeding (1 November 2006) para 33.

[31] Section 66 of the Patent Act, Revocation of Patent in Public Interest: Where the Central Government is of opinion that a patent or the mode in which it is exercised is mischievous to the State or generally prejudicial to the public, it may, after giving the patentee an opportunity to be heard, make a declaration to that effect in the Official Gazette and thereupon the patent shall be deemed to be revoked.

[32] See Bryan Mercurio, 'Awakening the Sleeping Giant: Intellectual Property Rights in International Investment Agreements' (2012) 15 Journal of International Economic Law 871.

expropriation because it has led to the substantial deprivation of foreign investment. As Mercurio argues the prospect of earning a higher compensation might persuade foreign investors to challenge the issuance of CLs before an ISDS tribunal.[33] Moreover, if the concerned BIT does not require the exhaustion of local remedies before bringing international claims, the foreign investor can side-step domestic courts by initiating an action before an ISDS tribunal.[34]

10.3.1 Australian Practice

The Australian practice shows that it is alert to the fact that foreign investors can challenge IP-related regulatory measures such as the issuance of CL as expropriation. Thus, to safeguard its right to regulate, Australian investment treaties exclude the issuance of CL and other IP-related regulatory measures from the purview of the expropriation provision. For instance, Article 14.11(5) of the Australia-Indonesia FTA investment chapter provides:

> The [expropriation provision] does not apply to the issuance of compulsory licences granted in relation to intellectual property rights in accordance with the TRIPS Agreement or to the revocation, limitation or creation of intellectual property rights, to the extent that the issuance, revocation, limitation or creation is consistent with the TRIPS Agreement.

It also contains a footnote, which provides: "For greater certainty, the Parties recognise that, for the purposes of this Article, the term "revocation" of intellectual property rights includes the cancellation or nullification of those rights and the term "limitation" of intellectual property rights includes exceptions to those rights".

Article 7.5 of the Australia-Uruguay BIT provides a similar provision. Article 10.5 of the Australia-Hong Kong Investment Agreement provides as follows:

> For greater certainty, this Article shall not apply to the issuance of compulsory licences granted in relation to intellectual property rights in accordance with the TRIPS Agreement, or to the revocation, limitation or creation of intellectual property rights, to the extent that the issuance, revocation, limitation or creation is consistent with Chapter 14 (Intellectual Property) of the FTA and the TRIPS Agreement.

The common point in all these three treaties is that they exclude the issuance of CL from the ambit of the expropriation provision. Therefore, they confer greater regulatory autonomy on the host State to issue CLs without worrying about the foreign investor challenging such issuance of CL as the expropriation of her investment. Moreover, these treaties also exclude other kinds of IP-related regulatory measures such as those regulatory measures that revoke or limit the IP rights of foreign investors. These treaties explain that revocation of IP rights will include those regulatory measures that lead to the cancellation or nullification of these rights.

---

[33] See also Prabhash Ranjan, 'Issuance of Compulsory Patent Licenses and Expropriation in Asian BITs and FTA Investment Chapters: A Study of India, China, Malaysia and Thailand' in Kung-Chung Liu and Julien Chaisse (eds), *The Future of Asian Trade Deals and IP* (Hart 2019).

[34] Mercurio (2012), 912–913.

However, an important caveat given in these treaties is that these IP-related regulatory measures (issuance of CL or cancellation of IP rights) will be outside the ambit of the expropriation provision only if such measures are consistent with the WTO's TRIPS agreement. In other words, if the IP-related regulatory measure meets the conditions given in the TRIPS agreement, then the expropriation provision does not apply. If not, the expropriation provision will apply and the ISDS tribunal will determine whether the said IP-related regulatory measure amounts to expropriation or not.

To understand this point better, let us assume that Australia issues a CL on a patented drug. Now, if this CL is in accordance with the TRIPS agreement, i.e., it meets all the requirements given in Article 31 of the TRIPS agreement (the provision that provides conditions that have to be met when a State grants a CL), the expropriation provision in the investment treaty will not apply over such issuance of CL. However, if the CL fails to meet the Article 31 conditions, the expropriation provision shall apply to the CL. The conditions given in Article 31 of the TRIPS agreement include that the country must have made efforts at obtaining a voluntary license first (this requirement may be waived in situations of national emergency); the license should have been issued predominantly for supply in the domestic market; the license should be terminated when the circumstances that led to the issuance of the license cease to exist; an adequate remuneration should be paid to the patent holder, etc.[35]

This leads us to the next related issue. The ISDS tribunal will determine whether a country has issued a CL satisfying the conditions given in Article 31 of the TRIPS agreement. Moreover, it is not just the issuance of CL, other IP-related regulatory measures like revocation of patents should also be consistent with the TRIPS agreement for them to fall outside the purview of the expropriation provision. This issue, i.e., whether patent revocation is TRIPS-compliant will also be determined by an ISDS tribunal. Critics may argue that an ISDS tribunal is not an appropriate forum to make such determinations.

Finally, the foreign investor can still challenge the IP-related regulatory measures as breaches of the FET and national treatment provision of the BIT. Thus, even if an IP-related regulatory measure such as the issuance of CL or revocation of patents is consistent with the TRIPS agreement, they can still violate any other substantive provision of the BIT.[36]

---

[35] See TRIPS agreement, art 31.

[36] Another aspect of the Australian practice is that it also exempts IP-related regulatory measures from the ambit of national treatment and most favored nation provisions. For instance, Article 7.3 of the Australia Hong Kong Investment agreement provides that the most favored nation provision "shall not apply to any measure that falls within Article 5 of the TRIPS Agreement, or an exception to, or derogation from, the obligations imposed by Article 4 of the TRIPS Agreement".

10.3.2 Indian Practice

Now, we turn our attention to examining the Indian practice on this issue.[37] The 2016 Model BIT and the subsequent BITs that India has signed do not exclude IP-related regulatory measures from the purview of expropriation. Instead, they go a step ahead and exclude IP-related regulatory measures from the ambit of the entire treaty. For instance, Article 2.4(iii) of the 2016 Model BIT states:

> this treaty shall not apply to the issuance of compulsory licenses granted in relation to intellectual property rights, or to the revocation, limitation or creation of intellectual property rights, to the extent that such issuance, revocation, limitation or creation is consistent with the international obligations of Parties under the WTO Agreement.

Article 2.4(iii) of the India-Kyrgyzstan BIT and Article 3.6(c) of the India-Brazil BIT contain precisely similar language. The language in the two other BITs is marginally different. Article 2.4(iii) of the India-Belarus BIT state that the treaty "shall not apply to the issuance of compulsory licenses granted in relation to intellectual property rights, or to the revocation, limitation or creation of intellectual property rights, to the extent that such issuance, revocation, limitation or creation is consistent with the national law and international obligations of the Party concerned".

Article 2.4(c) of the India-Taiwan BIT states that the treaty "shall not apply to the issuance of compulsory licenses granted in relation to intellectual property rights, or to the revocation, limitation or creation of intellectual property rights under domestic law, to the extent that such issuance, revocation, limitation or creation is consistent with the obligations under the WTO Agreement".

India's new treaty practice excludes IP-related regulatory measures such as the issuance of CL or revocation, and limitation of IP rights, from the scope of the entire treaty.[38] Thus, all the substantive provisions of the BIT including expropriation will be inapplicable to these IP-related regulatory measures. However, this is subject to the condition that these measures should be consistent with the host State's obligations under the WTO agreement, which will include the TRIPS agreement. In other words, if an IP-related regulatory measure is TRIPS-compliant, it will be deemed to be consistent with the BIT.

Importantly, despite excluding all IP-related regulatory measures from the ambit of the treaty, if a foreign investor challenges such a regulatory measure, the ISDS tribunal shall have jurisdiction. The tribunal will determine whether the IP-related regulatory measures are consistent with the WTO's TRIPS agreement or not. If yes, the tribunal will hold that India's IP-related regulatory measures are consistent with its BIT obligations. If not, the tribunal will go on to examine whether the IP-related regulatory measures breach substantive provisions of the BIT.

---

[37] The author has also discussed these issues in detail in the following article: Prabhash Ranjan, 'Compulsory Licenses and ISDS in Corona Times: Relevance of the New Indian Investment Treaty Practice' (2021), 16(7) Journal of Intellectual Property Law and Practice, 748–759.

[38] For a related and detailed discussion on these issues see also Prabhash Ranjan, 'Pharmaceutical Patents and Expropriation in Indian Bilateral Investment Treaties' in Mahdev Mohan and Chester Brown (Eds) The Asian Turn in Foreign Investment (Cambridge University Press: 2021), 29–47.

10.3.3 Comparison

There are similarities and divergences in the Indian and Australian treaty practices on this issue. The following points are worth mentioning. First, given the debate on BITs encroaching on the State's right to regulate in the public interest, both Australia and India are keen to preserve their sovereign right to regulate when it comes to IP-related regulatory measures. This is evident from both countries carving out their IP-related regulatory measures from the scope of BIT provisions.

Second, however, there is an important difference here in the degree of carve-out. While the Australian treaty practice carves out IP-related regulatory measures from the ambit of the expropriation provision, the Indian practice does so from the entire investment treaty. This variance in the treaty practice will have different implications on the ground. Seen from the perspective of the host State, the Indian treaty practice clearly gives a greater regulatory latitude to the State to adopt IP-related regulatory measures. The Indian treaty practice shields the IP-related regulatory measure from a wide range of possible treaty breaches, unlike the Australian treaty practice that firewalls IP-related regulatory measures only from the claim of expropriation. On the other hand, if we look at this from the perspective of the protection of foreign investment, the Australian treaty practice is superior. It allows the foreign investor to contest the IP-related regulatory measures using other treaty provisions such as FET and national treatment. In fact, the Australian treaty practice on this point is a better reflection of the emerging global investment treaty practice. Most countries carve-out their IP-related regulatory measures only from the purview of the expropriation provision.[39] The Indian treaty practice on this issue is an outlier.

Third, another important similarity between the Australian and Indian practices is that they ensure that host States do not abuse their public power to adopt IP-related regulatory measures. Thus, the requirement that the IP-related regulatory measures will be outside the ambit of the relevant provisions of the BIT or the entire treaty only if they are consistent with the TRIPS agreement is an important check imposed on the State's right to regulate. This condition will ensure that countries can take advantage of the carve-out to achieve their genuine regulatory objectives only if they act in an internationally lawful manner and not otherwise.

Fourth, the similarity of the Australian and Indian treaty practice on this issue also extends to allowing the ISDS tribunal to have jurisdiction over IP-related regulatory measures. Thus, an ISDS tribunal has the jurisdiction to find out if the IP-related regulatory measures are consistent with the TRIPS agreement or not.

[39] For instance, Article 6.5 of the United States Model BIT stathes that the expropriation provision "does not apply to the issuance of compulsory licenses granted in relation to intellectual property rights in accordance with the TRIPS Agreement, or to the revocation, limitation, or creation of intellectual property rights, to the extent that such issuance, revocation, limitation, or creation is consistent with the TRIPS Agreement". Article 8.12(5) of the EU-Canada Comprehensive Economic and Trade Agreement also contains a similar provision.

10.4 Performance Requirements and IP

Performance requirements means those obligations that a State may impose on foreign investors to derive maximal benefits for the host State. For instance, a host State may require a foreign investor to necessarily export a certain part of its produce. Another example of a performance requirement is making it mandatory for the foreign investor to use locally produced goods for some of its economic activities or to necessarily transfer technology to the State.[40] These performance requirements are imposed on the foreign investor to ensure that the host State's economy gains from the foreign investment by either adding to the country's export basket or by bringing in new technology, etc.

The first-generation investment treaties, i.e., the BITs that were signed during the 1980s, 1990s, and early 2000s, rarely contained provisions explicitly prohibiting performance requirements. However, the new generation of investment treaties specifically prohibits performance requirements. For example, Article 8(1) of the US Model BIT provides:

"Neither Party may, in connection with the establishment, acquisition, expansion, management, conduct, operation, or sale or other disposition of an investment of an investor of a Party or of a non-Party in its territory, impose or enforce any requirement or enforce any commitment or undertaking:

(a) to export a given level or percentage of goods or services;
(b) to achieve a given level or percentage of domestic content;
(c) to purchase, use, or accord a preference to goods produced in its territory, or to purchase goods from persons in its territory;
(d) to relate in any way the volume or value of imports to the volume or value of exports or to the amount of foreign exchange inflows associated with such investment;
(e) to restrict sales of goods or services in its territory that such investment produces or supplies by relating such sales in any way to the volume or value of its exports or foreign exchange earnings;
(f) to transfer a particular technology, a production process, or other proprietary knowledge to a person in its territory";

...

Thus, the US Model BIT prohibits performance requirements of various types such as a mandatory export obligation or a local content requirement.

[40] For more on performance requirements in investment treaties see Alexandre Genest, Performance Requirement Prohibitions in International Investment Law (2019) (Brill/Nijhoff: Netherlands).

10.4.1 Australian Practice

Australia's investment treaty practice as reflected in the Australia-Indonesia FTA investment chapter on the issue of performance requirements is the same as the US Model BIT practice. The Australia-Indonesia FTA investment chapter specifically outlaws the imposition of performance requirements on foreign investor. Article 14.6(1) provides:

"Neither Party shall, in connection with the establishment, acquisition, expansion, management, conduct, operation, or sale or other disposition of an investment of an investor of a Party or of a non-Party in its territory, impose or enforce any requirement:

(a) to export a given level or percentage of goods or services;
(b) to achieve a given level or percentage of domestic content;
(c) to purchase, use or accord a preference to goods produced in its territory or to purchase goods from persons in its territory;
(d) to relate in any way the volume or value of imports to the volume or value of exports or to the amount of foreign exchange inflows associated with such investment;
(e) to restrict sales of goods or services in its territory that such investment produces or supplies by relating such sales in any way to the volume or value of its exports or foreign exchange earnings;
(f) to transfer a particular technology, a production process or other proprietary knowledge to a person in its territory; or
(g) to supply exclusively from the territory of the Party the goods that such investment produces or the services that it supplies to a specific region or to the world market".

...

Thus, like the provision in US Model BIT, Article 14.6(1) also outlaws the imposition of performance requirements on foreign investors. In the list of performance requirements that are forbidden, the one given in Article 14.6(1)(f) refers to the transfer of technology, production process or transfer of proprietary knowledge. Thus, countries cannot impose requirements on countries to transfer technology or proprietary knowledge.

However, there is an important exception to Article 14.6(1)(f) in the Australia-Indonesia FTA investment chapter. This exception is given in Article 14.6(4), which states:

"Paragraph 1(f) shall not apply:

(a) if a Party authorises use of an intellectual property right in accordance with the TRIPS Agreement, or to measures requiring the disclosure of proprietary information that fall within the scope of, and are consistent with, Article 39 of the TRIPS Agreement".

This provision brings the imposition of performance requirements and IP rights face to face. This exception implies that while countries are generally prohibited from mandating foreign investors to transfer technology, such measures can be imposed if they are consistent with the TRIPS agreement including Article 39 which provides for the protection of undisclosed information.[41] A provision like Article 14.6(4) can prove to be very handy in the situations of pandemics like Covid-19. Countries are negotiating for a waiver of the TRIPS obligations for Covid-19 medical products including vaccines, therapeutics, and diagnostics.[42] If this waiver is adopted, countries will be free to temporarily suspend their IP obligations. They may impose an obligation on foreign pharmaceutical companies to transfer technology on Covid-19 medical products to fast-track the production and distribution of necessary vaccines, medicines, etc. However, foreign investors can still challenge these measures under BITs claiming that the State is imposing outlawed performance requirements on them.[43] In such situations, provisions like Article 14.6(4) can help the State adopting the IP-related regulations to claim that since their measures are consistent with the TRIPS agreement, they are a valid exception to the imposition of performance requirements and thus do not constitute a breach of the BIT.

However, the other two Australian BITs selected for this paper—Australia-Uruguay BIT and the Australia-Hong Kong investment agreement do not contain a provision like this. Arguably, these treaties by not specifically imposing restrictions on the imposition of performance requirements permit the same. Nonetheless, if the host State imposes requirements such as the transfer of technology that affects the IP rights of the foreign investors, there is a possibility of them challenging it before ISDS tribunals. This implies that the regulatory space available to Australia for the adoption of IP-related regulatory measures under the Australia-Uruguay BIT and the Australia-Hong Kong investment agreement is not as strong as in the Australia-Indonesia FTA, which specifically carves out such IP-related regulatory measures.

---

[41] For a commentary on Article 39 of the TRIPS agreement see G. Lee Skillington Eric M. Solovy, The Protection of Test and Other Data Required by Article 39.3 of the TRIPS Agreement (2003) 24(1) Northwestern Journal of International Law and Business, 1–52.

[42] 'Waiver From Certain Provisions of the TRIPS Agreement For the Prevention, Containment and Treatment of Covid-19', Communication from India and South Africa, IP/C/W/669, 2 October 2020 <https://docs.wto.org/dol2fe/Pages/SS/directdoc.aspx?filename=q:/IP/C/W669.pdf&Open=True> accessed 28 February 2022. See also Siva Thambisetty, Aisling McMahon et al., 'The TRIPS Intellectual Property Waiver Proposal: Creating the Right Incentives in Patent Law and Politics to end the Covid-19 Pandemic' (2021) LSE Legal Studies Working Paper No. 06/2021 <https://papers.ssrn.com/sol3/papers.cfm?abstract_id=3851737#> accessed 28 February 2022; Bryan Mercurio, 'WTO Waiver from Intellectual Property Protection for Covid-19 Vaccines and Treatments: A Critical Review' (2021) 62 Virginia Journal of International Law Online 9–32; Prabhash Ranjan and Praharsh Gour, 'The TRIPS Waiver Decision at the World Trade Organization: Too Little Too Late!' (2023), 13(1) Asian Journal of International Law, 10–21.

[43] For more on how foreign investors can challenge TRIPS waiver measures under BITs, see Prabhash Ranjan, Trade-Related Aspects of Intellectual Property Rights Waiver at the World Trade Organization: A BIT of a Challenge (2022) 56(3) Journal of World Trade, 523–546.

10.4.2 Indian Practice

The 2016 Indian Model BIT and the other BITs signed by India do not contain any provision on prohibiting performance requirements. Consequently, one is unsure what will be the outcome if India were to impose an IP-related regulatory measure that takes the form of a performance requirement (mandating the transfer of technology). Arguably, if the foreign investor challenges such a measure before an ISDS tribunal, India can defend its measure relying on the treaty exception for IP-related regulatory measures, as discussed in the previous section.

India can argue that its IP-related regulatory measure limits the IP rights of the foreign investor and thus the treaty provisions are inapplicable. Of course, India will have to show that the IP-related regulatory measure that limits the IP rights of the foreign investor is consistent with the TRIPS agreement.

10.4.3 Comparison

A part of the Australian treaty practice draws a direct link between imposition of performance requirements and IP-related regulatory measures. The other two BITs do not contain a provision like this. This is true for India as well, which is silent on the issue of performance requirement. However, the fact that India excludes IP-related regulatory measures from the ambit of the BIT puts India in a better place in comparison to the Australian treaty practice that neither contains any provision on performance requirement, nor carves out the IP-related regulatory measures from the purview of the BIT.

The provisions that carve-out IP-related regulatory measures such as revocation and limitation of IP rights from the ambit of expropriation cannot be used if an IP-related regulatory measure, say on transfer of technology, is challenged as breach of the FET provision. In such cases, even if the IP-related regulatory measure that mandates transfer of technology is consistent with the TRIPS agreement, the ISDS tribunal will have the jurisdiction to decide whether the measure breaches the provisions of the BIT or not.

10.5 Conclusion

The rise of ISDS claims brought by foreign investors involving IP-related regulatory measures of States has triggered a change in investment treaty practices of several countries including India and Australia. Both States are alert to the fact that such ISDS claims can lead to curtailing their regulatory space on adopting IP-related regulatory measures in the pursuit of public interest. This public interest could vary from ensuring the accessibility of a drug through issuing a CL or achieving other objectives such as ensuring the transfer of technology at the time of a global pandemic like Covid-19.

At the same time, both countries recognize IP rights as part of investments. This shows that India and Australia are willing to provide treaty-based protection to foreign investors for their IP rights. But this right of the foreign investors needs to be balanced with the State's right to adopt IP-related regulatory measures in the public interest such as to address the imperatives of public health.

Notwithstanding this broader similarity, there are important differences between the two sides on the actual treaty practice of how to achieve the goal of maximizing policy space for IP-related regulatory measures. The Australian practice seems to balance investment protection with the host State's right better by ensuring that IP-related regulatory measures are not pushed completely outside the ambit of the BIT. Thus, they exclude IP-related regulatory measures only from the purview of the expropriation provision and provide a few other exceptions. Importantly, at least one Australian investment treaty carves out IP-related regulatory measures from the overall obligation of not imposing performance requirements.

The Indian treaty practice, on the other hand, provides greater regulatory space to the State to shield its IP-related regulatory measures from ISDS claims. However, by making the entire BIT inapplicable to IP-related regulatory measures, the Indian treaty practice tilts the scale in favour of the host State's regulatory power at the cost of the rights of the foreign investor. These differences will be critical as and when the two sides decide to legalize their international investment relations. It will be interesting to see how the two sides bridge their differences in future.

Part IV
Administrative Law

Chapter 11
R2P: A Comparative Study: Between Universalism and Asian Exceptionalism

Rashmi Raman, Lalantika Arvind, Pratyush Gupta, and prithviraj Khanna

Abstract The international community is divided on R2P in the form of intervention for the protection and restoration of human rights. This paper critically examines and compares the application of the Responsibility to Protect ("R2P") doctrine as an established universalist norm as opposed to an Asian *exceptionalism* in its application, using the Rohingya crises in Myanmar as a case in point. The R2P doctrine and its guiding principles are examined to attest that these principles have not been utilized in conflicts in Asia, although the need arose multiple times. In light of the same, the authors argue that the resolution of humanitarian crises as grave as in Myanmar requires a recognition of Asian *exceptionalism.* The same is done through studying the interventions and responses from the international community in Asian conflicts that required humanitarian intervention, mainly, Nagorno-Karabakh (1994), Cambodia (1991), Sri Lanka (2009), and Timor-Leste (1999). We note that in most cases of Asian conflict, the international community does not intervene and instead, dominant regional powers are relied upon for the resolution of the conflict. Such is the nature of the exceptionalism of the application of the R2P doctrine in Asia, because of which the authors theorize that the Myanmar crisis too is likely to respond to regional rather than global intervention.

11.1 Introduction

In the wake of the humanitarian crisis in Myanmar, the stage is set for the international community to take responsibility for the protection and the restoration of human rights of the displaced Rohingya community. Could such a responsibility take the form of interventionist measures? This paper examines whether a future humanitarian intervention may take the form of humanitarian intervention following the accepted *universal* norms of Responsibility to Protect ("R2P") or whether there

R. Raman (✉) · L. Arvind · P. Gupta · Khanna
Centre for International Legal Studies, Jindals Global Law School, O.P. Jindal Global University, Sonipat, Haryana, India
e-mail: rraman@jgu.edu.in

M. John et al. (eds.), *The Indian Yearbook of Comparative Law 2020*, The Indian Yearbook of Comparative Law, https://doi.org/10.1007/978-981-99-5467-4_11

is an *Asian exceptionalism* in understanding normative *universalism* in humanitarian intervention.

This paper is divided into three parts. In the *first* part, we offer an account of the historical evolution of the normative rules that have come to be known as R2P. Through this, we construct the normative *universalism* in R2P – the rules of international humanitarian law that are deemed to be accepted by all states. In the *second* part, we analyze the *universalism* of R2P as a normative rule of international humanitarian law. We critically examine a representative list of cases from non-Asian and Asia geographies to understand how various actors in humanitarian crises have responded to humanitarian intervention. *Finally*, we suggest that there is a regional specificity in Asia that may be called *Asian exceptionalism* in international law. This exceptionalism, developed by the regional equivocation about *universalist* international law is an important factor in how Asian states view the R2P framework.

11.2 Part One: History of the Development of R2P

For a 16-year-old principle, R2P[1] is an exception to the general rule that establishing universalism in international law takes an age.[2] Since 2005, R2P has been invoked in more than eighty-four United Nations Security Council resolutions and presidential statements,[3] fifty United Nations Human Rights Council ("UNHRC") resolutions,[4] and seventeen United Nations General Assembly resolutions ("UNGA").[5] As former UN Secretary General Ban Ki Moon put it:

The primary purpose of the responsibility to protect is to close the gap between State obligations under legal instruments, such as the Convention on the Prevention and Punishment of the Crime of Genocide and the Geneva Conventions of 1949, and the continuing subjection of populations to the violence and terror of atrocity crimes.[6]

[1] In this paper, for congruence, we shall refer to all forms of the evolution of the humanitarian intervention doctrine of responsibility to protect as R2P (including RtoP as sometimes referred to within the argot of the UN), without prejudice to the more technical sense in which the stylised acronym R2P only coming into existence through the Secretary General's Report on Implementation of R2P, 2009 (See note 50).

[2] Pablo de Greiff, 'A Normative Conception of Transnational Justice' (2010) 50 Politorbis 17 <https://www.ihrb.org/pdf/Politorbis_50_Dealing_with_the_Past.pdf> accessed on 29 August 2020.

[3] Global Centre for Responsibility to Protect, 'UN Security Council Resolutions and Presidential Statements Referencing R2P' (*Global Centre for Responsibility to Protect*, 17 June 2020) <https://www.globalr2p.org/resources/un-security-council-resolutions-and-presidential-statements-referencing-r2p/> accessed 24 August 2020.

[4] Global Centre for Responsibility to Protect, 'UN Human Rights Council Resolutions Referencing' (*Global Centre for Responsibility to Protect*, 12 July 2020) <https://www.globalr2p.org/resources/un-human-rights-council-resolutions-referencing-r2p/> accessed 24 August 2020.

[5] Global Centre for Responsibility to Protect, 'UN General Assembly Resolutions Referencing R2P' (*Global Centre for Responsibility to Protect,* 28 October 2019) <https://www.globalr2p.org/resources/un-general-assembly-resolutions-referencing-r2p-2/> accessed 24 August 2020.

[6] UN Secretary General Report 'A Vital and Enduring Commitment: Implementing Responsibility to Protect' (13 July 2015) UN Doc A/69/981, 20 [11].

11.2.1 ICISS Report 2001

The government of Canada, driven by the failures of the United Nations[7] ("UN") and the aspiration to do justice to the Charter of the United Nations Charter[8] ("Charter") set up the International Commission on Intervention and State Sovereignty[9] ("ICISS") in 2000. ICISS' main objective was to reconcile the two contradictory principles of the Charter: sovereignty and use of force.[10] A new international order with new actors, plagued by new security issues, needed a new solution: the ICISS Report of 2001 ("ICISS Report") offered an answer.

> 1.35 ... It is acknowledged that sovereignty implies a dual responsibility: externally – to respect the sovereignty of other states, and internally, to respect the dignity and basic rights of all the people within the state.... Sovereignty as responsibility has become the minimum content of good international citizenship[11];
>
> 2.14 The Charter of the UN is itself an example of an international obligation voluntarily accepted by member states.....There is no transfer or dilution of state sovereignty. But there is a necessary re-characterization involved: from sovereignty as control to sovereignty as responsibility in both internal functions and external duties[12];
>
> 1.38. The kind of intervention with which we are concerned in this report is action taken against a state or its leaders, without its or their consent, for purposes which are claimed to be humanitarian or protective. By far the most controversial form of such intervention is military... But we are also very much concerned with alternatives to military action...[13]

The exercise of sovereignty under the ICISS Report came to include both external accountability toward other states and internal responsibility toward protection of its own peoples.[14] A sovereign state's existing Charter obligations toward its own population expanded to include taking responsibility (and international accountability)

[7] UNSC Res 814 (26 March 1993) UN Doc S/RES/814; UNSC Res 918 (17 May 1994) UN Doc S/RES/918. It was in response to this challenge that the Government of Canada, together with a group of major foundations, announced at the General Assembly in September 2000 the establishment of the International Commission on Intervention and State Sovereignty (ICISS). Our Commission was asked to wrestle with the whole range of questions—legal, moral, operational and political—rolled up in this debate, to consult with the widest possible range of opinion around the world, and to bring back a report that would help the Secretary-General and everyone else find some new common ground.

[8] UNGA 'Secretary-General presents his Annual Report to General Assembly' (30 September 1999) UN Doc SG/SM/7136.

[9] International Commission on Intervention and State Sovereignty 'The Responsibility to Protect' (December 2001) (ICISS Report).

[10] Jonah Eaton, 'An Emerging Norm - Determining the Meaning and Legality of Responsibility to Protect' (2011) 32 Mich J Intl L 765, 770.

[11] ICISS Report (n 9) 8.

[12] Ibid 13.

[13] Ibid 8.

[14] Ibid [1.35].

for failing to do so[15]; the "right to intervene" evolved into a "responsibility" to "intervene."[16]

Historically, the challenge the ICISS Report faced was to give humanitarian intervention legitimacy.[17] While the norms of non-intervention (Article 2.7), prohibition on the use of force (Article 2.4) and self-defence[18] (Article 51) were enshrined in the Charter, state practice throughout the twentieth century showed that the norm of intervention continued in customary international law[19] despite the parallel solidification of principles of sovereignty.[20] During the Cold War especially, states would intervene to aid their allies or to rescue their nationals from foreign territory.[21] The Charter right to self-defence too,[22] occasionally extended to punitive intervention when neighboring states were "unable or unwilling"[23] to protect themselves against their territory being used as launch sites for terror attacks.[24] The ICISS Report resolved this challenge by creating the Three Pillars of the R2P: the Responsibility to Prevent, Responsibility to React, and Responsibility to Rebuild.

---

[15] Ibid [2.14].

[16] James Turner Johnson, 'Humanitarian Intervention, the Responsibility to Protect, and Sovereignty: Historical and Moral Reflections' (2015) 23 Mich St Int'l L Rev 609, 611.

[17] Charter of the United Nations (24 October 1945) 1 UNTS XVI (UN Charter), art 2.7. [2.7 is prohibition to intervene. 2.4 is also in question].

[18] Ibid art 51.

[19] Simon Chesterman, *Just War or Just Peace?: Humanitarian Intervention and International Law* (OUP 2002), 107.

[20] ICISS Report (n 9) [2.9]–[2.10].

[21] Ibid [2.9], '2.9... during the Cold War years state practice reflected the unwillingness of many countries to give up the use of intervention for political or other purposes as an instrument of policy....'.

[22] *Military and Paramilitary Activities in and against Nicaragua (Nicaragua v United States)* (Jurisdiction and Admissibility) [1984] ICJ Rep 441, [91].

[23] Craig Martin, 'Challenging and Refining the "Unwilling or Unable" Doctrine' (2019) 52 Vanderbilt J Transnatl L 1, 5.

The critique offered by Martin to the doctrine offered by Bethlehem was based on the evidence gathered from state positions expressed for endorsing the doctrine as a justification for their own use of force, specifically by Canada, Australia, Netherlands and Germany offering their support for operations against ISIS in Syria and Iraq.

See also page 27–29.

[24] ICISS Report (n 9) 12 [2.10], '2.10 The established and universally acknowledged right to self-defence, embodied in Article 51 of the UN Charter, was sometimes extended to include the right to launch punitive raids into neighbouring countries that had shown themselves unwilling or unable to stop their territory from being used as a launching pad for cross-border armed raids or terrorist attacks. But all that said, the many examples of intervention in actual state practice throughout the twentieth century did not lead to an abandonment of the norm of non-intervention.'

11.2.1.1 Pillar One: The Responsibility to Prevent

Dedicated and decisive prevention under the ICISS Report had 3 conditions: (a) Early Warning Mechanisms (including third-party auditing and observation)[25]; (b) Root Cause Prevention Efforts,[26] as enshrined in Article 55 of the UN Charter[27]; (c) Direct Prevention Efforts (ranging from soft coercion such as threat of sanctions or legal action in the International Court of Justice ("ICJ") to direct use of forceful intervention).[28]

11.2.1.2 Pillar Two: Responsibility to React

R2P entailed the responsibility to react to extreme cases compelling the need for human protection.[29] However, this did not necessarily mean coercive military intervention. Responsibility to react included exhaustion of preventive measures under Pillar One, including diplomatic and non-military avenues.[30] Only when this fails could the decision to militarily intervene must be taken, as a last resort.[31]

Since it is essential to have a clearly defined understanding of extreme cases, the ICISS Report proposed Six Principles[32] defining and limiting military intervention. These included *just cause* (that there is actual or threat of large-scale atrocity crimes)[33]; *right intention* (that intervention is actually for the benefit of those most affected by it and is supported by them - it is not done merely to advance political agenda)[34]; *last resort* (that all other preventive and peaceful means of resolving the conflict have been exhausted)[35]; *proportional means* (the scale, duration, and necessity of the intervention must be the minimum required to achieve resolution of

---

[25] Ibid [3.10]–[3.17].

[26] Ibid [3.18]–[3.24].

[27] UN Charter (n 17) art 55.

[28] ICISS Report (n 9) [3.25]–[3.41].

[29] Ibid [4.13], 'Yet there are exceptional circumstances in which the very interest that all states have in maintaining a stable international order requires them to react when all order within a state has broken down or when civil conflict and repression are so violent that civilians are threatened with massacre, genocide or ethnic cleansing on a large scale.'

[30] Ibid [4.37], '4.37. Every diplomatic and non-military avenue for the prevention or peaceful resolution of the humanitarian crisis must have been explored…military coercion.. justified.'

[31] Ibid [4.13], 'The Commission found in its consultations that even in states where there was the strongest opposition to infringements on sovereignty, there was general acceptance that there must be limited exceptions to the non-intervention rule for certain kinds of emergencies…cases of violence which so genuinely 'shock the conscience of mankind', or which present such a clear and present danger to international security, that they require coercive military intervention.'

[32] Ibid [4.16].

[33] Ibid [4.18]–[4.31].

[34] Ibid [4.33]–[4.36].

[35] Ibid [4.37]–[4.38].

conflict)[36]; *reasonable prospects* (military intervention is not justified if intervention would likely worsen the crises)[37]; and *right authority* (only the UN Security Council is allowed to sanction intervention on humanitarian grounds).[38]

11.2.1.3 Third Pillar: Responsibility to Rebuild

The scope of Pillars One and Two inherently engendered a responsibility to rebuild. Codified as a part of *jus post bellum*,[39] a genuine commitment to helping build durable peace, promoting good governance, and aiding in sustainable development in post-conflict states was the essence of responsibility to rebuild.[40]

Three key areas of focus for rebuilding in the ICISS Report were *security* (including ensuring prevention of retributive violence and reintegration of security forces)[41]; *justice and reconciliation* (like setting up of legal institutions to address rights of IDPs and refugees)[42]; and *development* (economic as well as socio-political).[43]

While it is commendable that detailed principles had been laid down to ensure there is no arbitrary intervention, the text of the ICISS Report left certain loopholes that could subjectively have been used to authorize intervention.[44] For example, while detailing last resort measures, it was acknowledged that there may be situations where there might be no time for the prevention process to be employed, thus tacitly authorizing intervention *before* prevention.[45]

---

[36] Ibid [4.39]–[4.40].

[37] Ibid [4.41]–[4.43].

[38] Ibid [4.17].

[39] Carsten Stahn, Jennifer S. Easterday and Jens Iverson, *Jus Post Bellum: Mapping the Normative Foundations* (OUP 2014) ch 6, 102–22.

[40] The need for prevention of conflict, strengthening of legal institutions, commitment to human rights and provision of development programmes was emphasised in the ICISS Report keeping in mind the commitment to rebuilding as in the 1998 Secretary General's Report. (Report of the Secretary-General, 'The Causes of Conflict and the Promotion of Durable Peace and Sustainable Development in Africa' (24 July 2014) 16 U.N Doc. A/69/162).

[41] ICISS Report (n 9) [5.8]–[5.12].

[42] Ibid [5.13]–[5.18].

[43] Ibid [5.19]–[5.21].

[44] Ibid [4.37], 'This does not necessarily mean that every such option must **literally be tried and have failed….** But it does mean that there must be reasonable grounds for believing that, in all the circumstances, if the measure had been attempted it would not have succeeded.' **(emphasis added)**.

[45] Ibid [4.37].

11.2.2 Recognition of R2P in the United Nations Framework: Path Through the UNSC

In 2004, the UN Secretary-General's High-Level Panel on Threats, Challenges, and Change came out with a report titled "A More Secure World: Our Shared Responsibility" ("2004 Report") redefined R2P as a:

> 203…collective international responsibility to protect, exercisable by the Security Council authorising military intervention as a last resort, in the event of genocide and other largescale killing, ethnic cleansing or serious violations of international humanitarian law which sovereign Governments have proved powerless or unwilling to prevent.[46]

The 2004 Report read R2P as an exception to Article 2.7 of the U.N Charter. Since all States acknowledged atrocity crimes as a violation of international law and a threat to international peace and security, the implementation of existing treaty obligations in this regard legitimized intervention by the UN Security Council ("UNSC").[47]

11.2.3 In Larger Freedom

The 2005 World Summit Outcome[48] ("2005 Outcome") further acknowledged that R2P, i.e., intervention against genocide, war crimes, ethnic cleansing, and crimes against humanity derives from Chapter VI and Chapter VIII of the Charter. Paragraphs 138 and 139 of the document re-iterated the commitment of the UN to take collective action through the UNSC, in a timely and decisive manner when peaceful measures have been rendered inadequate, and states have failed to protect their populations.[49] The 2005 Outcome demonstrated the understanding of the UN Secretary General reflected in the 2005 Report titled "In Larger Freedom", with the latter

---

[46] United Nations Secretary General's High-Level Panel on Threats, Challenges and Change 'A More Secure World, Our Shared Responsibility' (December 2004) 56 [203].

[47] Jonah Eaton (n 14) 771.

[48] UNGA 'Draft Resolution Referred to the High-level Plenary Meeting of the General Assembly' UN Doc A/60/L.1 (2005 Summit Outcome).

[49] Ibid 31, 'Para 138. Each individual State has the responsibility to protect its populations from genocide, war crimes, ethnic cleansing and crimes against humanity. This responsibility entails the prevention of such crimes, including their incitement, through appropriate and necessary means…The international community should, as appropriate, encourage and help States to exercise this responsibility and support the United Nations in establishing an early warning capability.

139. The international community, through the United Nations, also has the responsibility to use appropriate diplomatic, humanitarian and other peaceful means, in accordance with Chapters VI and VIII of the Charter, to help protect populations …we are prepared to take collective action, in a timely and decisive manner, through the Security Council, in accordance with the Charter, including Chapter VII, on a case-by-case basis and in cooperation with relevant regional organizations as appropriate, should peaceful means be inadequate and national authorities manifestly fail to protect their populations…We stress the need for the General Assembly to continue consideration of the responsibility to protect populations…bearing in mind the principles of the Charter and international law. We also intend to commit ourselves… to helping States build capacity to protect

offering an acceptance of the premise of the ICISS Report wherein there was a recognition of the responsibility to protect citizens on the international community if the same could not be undertaken by the national authorities.[50] This premise was further structured by the 2005 Outcome which agreed with the ICISS Report to the extent of the four situations when R2P was to be implemented, and the role of the UNSC in this implementation. In this regard, the 2005 Outcome acted as a bridge between the ICISS Report and the 2009 Report, discussed below, offering the foundation for the institutionalization of the doctrine by the United Nations. While only two paragraphs long, the 2005 Outcome was key to future understanding and adoption of R2P from a doctrinal, policy, and institutional lens. This especially since it drew upon existing international law and was endorsed and agreed upon by both the UNGA and UNSC.

11.2.4 2009 Report

The 2009 Secretary Genera's Report[51] ("2009 Report") is based on the 2005 Outcome's commitment to solidify a framework for the implementation of the R2P. By 2009, The International Criminal Court had arrived, and acceptance for universal jurisdiction and individual criminal responsibility for atrocity crimes had matured in international law.[52] By seeking to end impunity, these factors influenced the 2009 Report which laid down the contemporary Three Pillars of R2P.

11.2.4.1 Pillar One: Protection as Prevention

The Report….

> 13. The first three sentences of paragraph 138 of the Summit Outcome capture unambiguously the underlying principle of the responsibility to protect: … The peoples of the world fully expect each and every Member State to live up to this commitment at all times because this first pillar of the responsibility to protect, which rests on long-standing obligations under international law, is absolutely essential if the responsibility to protect is to move from the realm of rhetoric to the realm of doctrine, policy and action… The State, however, remains the bedrock of the responsibility to protect, the purpose of which is to build responsible sovereignty, not to undermine it.[53]

---

their populations ….and to assisting those which are under stress before crises and conflicts break out.'

[50] UNGA 'In Larger Freedom: Towards development, security and human rights for all: Report of the Secretary-General' (21 March 2005) UN Doc A/59/2005 (2005 Report).

[51] UNGA 'Implementing the responsibility to protect: Report of the Secretary-General' (12 January 2009) UN Doc A/63/77 (2009 Report).

[52] M.M. DeGuzman, 'How Serious are International Crimes? The Gravity Problem in International Criminal Law' (2012) 51 Col J Transnatl L 18, 32.

[53] 2009 Report (n 50) [13].

Prevention, says the 2009 Report, begins at home. It relies on "responsible sovereignty"—that the protection of its people is a defining characteristic of the sovereign state in the twenty-first century, and that an international community can only assist, not replace sovereignty.[54] This also translates to the state building institutions, capacities, and practices for the constructive management of diversity and the tensions it engenders.[55] States must reinforce their commitment to respect for human rights internationally as well as domestically.[56]

> 21. Genocide and other crimes relating to the responsibility to protect do not just happen. They are, more often than not, the result of a deliberate and calculated political choice, and of the decisions and actions of political leaders who are all too ready to take advantage of existing social divisions and institutional failures. Events on the scale of the Holocaust, Cambodia in the 1970s and Rwanda in 1994 require planning, propaganda and the mobilisation of substantial human and material resources. They are neither inevitable nor unavoidable. They require permissive conditions, both domestically and internationally... Candid self-reflection, searching dialogue among groups and institutions, both domestically and internationally, and periodic risk assessment are needed in both fragile and seemingly healthy societies in all regions of the world. We are all at risk if we believe it could not happen to us.[57]

11.2.4.2 Second Pillar: Protection as Assistance (International Assistance and Capacity Building)

> 28. …These provisions suggest that this assistance could take one of four forms: (a) encouraging States to meet their responsibilities under pillar one (para. 138); (b) helping them to exercise this responsibility (para. 138); (c) helping them to build their capacity to protect (para. 139); and (d) assisting States 'under stress before crises and conflicts break out' (para. 139).[58]

The Second Pillar is most effective when the State is weak, divided, unsure, or unable yet willing to protect its people, and is thus responsive to diplomatic interventions.[59] Important manifestations of incubating institutions to tackling the root causes of conflict toward prevention[60] include the presence of the UN, through its specialized agencies, leading strategic tactics like sanctions/disinvestment, the role of the Office of the United Nations High Commissioner for Human Rights ("OCHCR") in strengthening domestic protection capacities for conflict management, states creating a strong, independent national judicial system as a tool for assistance.[61]

While the use of coercive force is a last resort, the deployment of preventive military forces can be used for peaceful, non-coercive purposes.[62] This can only be done

---

[54] Ibid [14] 'The responsibility to protect, first and foremost, is a matter of State responsibility,…'.

[55] Ibid [14] '… Responsible sovereignty is of inclusion, not exclusion based on the politics'.

[56] Ibid [14].

[57] Ibid [21].

[58] Ibid [28].

[59] Ibid [28]–[29].

[60] Ibid [30].

[61] Ibid [32]–[33], [35], [47].

[62] Ibid [40].

with the consent of the host State and ranges from prevention, protection, peace-keeping, disarmament, as well as countering armed non-state actors. Consent-based deployment of an international military presence has achieved success in resolving and preventing conflicts in the past and is thus a valuable assistance tool.[63]

11.2.4.3 Pillar Three: Protection as Action (Timely and Decisive Response)

The threshold for action under Pillar Three is lower than that for Action under Pillar Two, and even under Pillar Three the threshold for action under Chapter VI is lower than that under Chapter VII, which can only be authorized at an inter-governmental level. The advantage of including Chapter VIII in the action is that regional and sub-regional organizations can take non-coercive and non-violent measures without the explicit authorization of the Security Council.[64]

Timely and decisive action by states need not always involve a choice between doing nothing or using force. Intervention against a state that is unable or unwilling to protect its people clears a vast range[65]: such intervention may be pacific or collaborative measures with regional arrangements under Chapters VI and VIII of the Charter, or it can be coercive measures under Chapter VII of the Charter, should peaceful measures be inadequate or national authorities manifestly fail.[66]

For all its insistence on the universality of action and the equality of all three pillars of responsibility to protect, the 2009 Report permits a lot to the subjectivity of the conflict and promotes a case specific customization. This makes it unlike the first R2P instrument in 2001 which set out exact thresholds and standards for coercive action. We suggest that this ambiguity is unsurprising since R2P by then had emerged, with normative universalism, as a rule of customary international law.[67]

11.3 Establishing Universalism

It has been argued that the collective security mechanism[68] of R2P stops it from being recognized as a norm under international law.[69] Evidence of apprehensions regarding the normative value of R2P can be found in state practice in the UN. For

---

[63] Ibid [40].

[64] Ibid [50].

[65] Christophe Paulussen, Tamara Takacs, Vesna Lazić and Ben Van Rompuy (eds), *Fundamental Rights in International and European Law* (TMC Asser Press 2016) 73–97.

[66] 2009 Report (n 50) [49].

[67] 2009 Report (n 50) in paras. 3 and 18, concerning the duty to prevent.

[68] Alexander Orakhelashvili, *Collective Security* (OUP 2011) 6.

[69] *See for instance* J M Welsh, 'Norm Contestation and the Responsibility to Protect' (2013) 5(4) GR2P 365; N Zähringer, 'Norm evolution within and across the African Union and the United Nations: The Responsibility to Protect (R2P) as a contested norm' (2013) 20(2) SAJIA 187; A J

example, India during the 1973 resolution on Libya chose to abstain citing lack of credible sources to information[70]; South Africa, while debating the first draft on Syria, abstained expressing apprehension as to hidden agendas[71]; Russia while vetoing the fifth draft, replying to the UK notes "*How about putting an end to interfering in the affairs of other sovereign States? Just give up these colonial customs and leave the world in peace. The situation would improve in a great many parts of the world.*"[72] These apprehensions are not unique to the modern understanding of R2P.[73] Versions of a democratic deficit in the legitimacy of R2P existed even during the previous iterations of the document; during deliberations over the 2009 Document, Egypt, on behalf of Non-Aligned Movement, expressed concerns over the potential for abuse of authority if applied in situations beyond the scope of the 2005 Outcome, or it being used a tool to interfere in internal affairs of a State[74]; the Philippines called for deliberations on policies and principles on the use of coercive force in extreme situations[75]; Singapore observed that for R2P to become an international norm would require its "*use without political biases and hidden agendas*"[76]; and Benin recommended casting out "*geo-strategic rivalries*" that have paralyzed the UNSC.[77]

However, the progressive development of R2P has closely followed pre-existing obligations under established international law.[78] This alignment meant that R2P did not create new obligations for states but utilized the integration of its principle within the widely accepted framework of international human rights law and humanitarian law to secure its legitimacy.[79] Subsequently, the expansion of the first pillar, strengthening national capacity for preventing atrocity crimes defeated the argument of R2P

Kuperman, 'R2P: Catchy name for a fading norm' (2011) Ethnopolitics *10*(1) 125; N Deitelhoff, 'Is the R2P failing? The controversy about norm justification and norm application of the responsibility to protect' 2019 11(2) GR2P 149; L Glanville, 'Does R2P matter? Interpreting the impact of a norm' (2016) Coop & Conflict 51(2) 184.

[70] UNSC Verbatim Record (17 March 2011) UN Doc S/PV/6498, 5–6. Using the examples of abstention that we have collected in this paragraph follows a deliberate process of arriving at an overview of state practice that occludes the clear existence of a "norm" that may be characterised as R2P but rather points to ambiguity and lack of clear state practice that foregrounds any premature conclusions on the existence of universalism.

[71] UNSC Verbatim Record (04 October 2011) UN Doc S/PV/6627, 11.

[72] UNSC Verbatim Record (08 October 2016) UN Doc S/PV/7785, 16.

[73] *Prosecutor v. Duško Tadic* (Decision on the Defence Motion for Interlocutory Appeal on Jurisdiction) ICTY IT-94-1-AR72 (2 October 1995), [28] 'It is clear from [the] text [of Article 39] that the Security Council plays a pivotal role and exercises a very wide discretion under this Article. But this does not mean that its powers are unlimited…'.

[74] UNGA Verbatim Record (23 July 2009) UN Doc A/63/PV/97, 5–6.

[75] Ibid 10–12.

[76] UNGA Verbatim Record (28 July 2009) UN Doc A/63/PV/98, 6–8.

[77] UNGA Verbatim Record (28 July 2009) UN Doc A/63/PV/100, 24–7.

[78] Ramesh Thakur and Thomas G. Weiss, 'R2P: From Idea to Norm—and Action?' (2009) 1 GR2P 22, 35.

[79] Convention on the Prevention and Punishment of the Crime of Genocide (adopted 9 December 1948, entered into force 12 January 1951) 1021 UNTS 278 (Genocide Convention) art 6.

conflicting with the principle of sovereignty.[80] This was reaffirmed in subsequent reports[81] that focused more on non-coercive methods of assistance under the three pillars to ensure that the need for coercive means was a last resort.[82] The overall challenge of a direct conflict with an established norm of international law was hence overcome by projecting R2P as an ally, not an adversary, of the principle of sovereignty.[83] What therefore emerges is a tempered idea of sovereignty, the international community limiting absolute sovereignty when there is a *just cause* for them to do so.[84]

Structural challenges to the legitimacy of R2P[85] have also been bridged by the systematic integration of the R2P doctrine within UN institutions, as envisaged by the 2005 Outcome[86] and further elaborated upon by the 2009 Report.[87] An example of such integration may be seen in the efforts to utilize the Universal Periodic Review Mechanism of the United Nations Human Rights Council in the early-warning indicators of Pillar One.[88] Another benefit of this integrationist approach is the push toward acceptance of R2P as a rule by the UN; amply demonstrated by the creation of the "UN Office on Genocide Prevention and the Responsibility to Protect"[89] as well as the appointment of the Special Adviser on the Responsibility to Protect, thus creating a channel for responding to concerns of member states expressed in different UN assemblies of states.[90] Moreover, the impact of integration is visible in the strategies undertaken by member states to implement their "obligation to prevent" under R2P,[91] evidenced through National Focal Points.[92]

R2P has arguably overcome these considerable challenges and emerged today as a *jus cogens* norm in international law, situating itself as part of the normative framework of post-conflict justice. The centrum of the debate around peace-making as an object of humanitarian intervention has been traditionally couched in the classical

---

80 Stevie Martin, 'Sovereignty and Responsibility to Protect Mutually Exclusive or Codependent?' (2011) 20 Griffith LR 153, 153.

81 2009 Report (n 50).

82 Ibid [64].

83 Ibid [10].

84 ICISS Report (n 9) 36; Simon Chesterman (n 23) 12.

85 Roland Paris, 'The Responsibility to Protect and the Structural Problems to Preventive Humanitarian Intervention' (2014) 21 International Peacekeeping 569, 593.

86 2005 Outcome (n 48) 31.

87 2009 Report (n 50).

88 2005 Outcome (n 48).

89 United Nations Office on Genocide Prevention and the Responsibility to Protect, 'Mandate' (*United Nations Office on Genocide Prevention and the Responsibility to Protect*) <https://www.un.org/en/genocideprevention/office-mandate.shtml> accessed 30 August 2020.

90 Ibid.

91 UN Secretary General, 'Responsibility to Protect: From Early Warning to Early Action' UN Docs A/72/884 (1 June 2018).

92 Global Centre for Responsibility to Protect, 'Global Network of R2P Focal Points' (*Global Centre for Responsibility to Protect*) <https://www.globalr2p.org/the-global-network-of-r2p-focal-points/ > accessed 30 August 2020.

rules of *jus ad bellum* and *jus in bello*, to the exclusion of a triumvirate conceptualization that extends to the rules and principles governing peace-making in the aftermath of conflict; a move from a negative peace at the end of war, to a positive peace that builds upon what was. While moral philosophy and legal theory have long recognized this third corollary of the whole as a natural limb of the just war theory, it is only now, in the face of heightened concern over human security and the viability of humanitarian intervention, that a legal framework encompassing the normative conception of a *jus post bellum* informs the topic of contemporary debate and straddles the principle of distinction located within.

In deconstruction, the definitional challenge to *jus post bellum* requires an understanding of its parent theme—the R2P doctrine in international law and the sibling branches of international administrative law, namely state building, post-conflict reconstruction, transformative occupation, and transitional justice. In this sense of a vision of what *jus post bellum* "ought" to mean, the answer would be that *jus post bellum* is a teleological or result-oriented indicator of the success or failure of just war. This understanding views *jus post bellum* as a test of the initial justification of the use of force; an understanding corroborated in scholarly writing, which has proposed that a deeper examination of *jus post bellum* might well act as a deterrent to the initial use of armed force in closer consideration of the responsibility of armed interventions, thus seeking to close a systemic gap in the discipline.

11.4 Part Two: Problematising Universalism Through Case Studies

The Annexure table catalogs the implementation of R2P through two sets of case studies. The first studies Libya and Syria as illustrations of a wide range of interventionist mechanisms under R2P in non-Asian geographies. The primary reason for the selection of Libya and Syria is due to the representational capabilities of how R2P functions in practice, specifically in the case of Libya,[93] and have been further documented through various UNSC resolutions. The discussion framework offers two aspects, one of ineffectiveness, as demonstrated in Libya, and inaction, as showcased in the situation of Syria. The second studies four conflicts in (the broadest categorization of) Asian geographies—West Asia (Armenia-Azerbaijan), South Asia (Sri Lanka), South-East Asia (Cambodia), and Asia Pacific (Timor-Leste). These case studies analyze intervention (or non-intervention) and allied actions taken in pursuit of the resolution of humanitarian crises specific to each case.

[93] Simon Chesterman, Responsibility to Protect and Humanitarian Intervention: From Apology to Utopia and Back Again, *The Oxford Handbook on the International Law of Global Security*, (OUP, 2021) 802–820.

11.5 Part Three: Asian Exceptionalism

Asian states have a long history[94] of equivocation with international law.[95] From the politics of history[96] and the region's critical geopolitics in the twenty-first century, a strained relationship with the largely homogenizing western constructions of international law[97] characterize Asian states.[98] Tenuous regional and cultural specificities across the many geographies that may variously be called Asia foster a series of disruptions that are impervious to homogenization and reject the imposition of the structural and grammatical foreignness that international law translates into for the majority of Asian states.[99] They unite instead around shared traditions, values, and economic and social congruencies in the developing world.[100] Today, a plurality of legal systems and histories occludes a singular narrative of Asian approaches to international law; the approaches range from the anti-imperialist rejection of the grammar of international law by post-colonial Asian states,[101] to the fiercely independent preservation of indigenous legal systems in states like Bhutan, Nepal and Thailand, to post-conflict fragile states' mistrust in institutions of international law like East Timor present a chequered model of *exceptionalisms.*[102] The common thread however is that while many Asian states participate in the making of modern international law and are represented in all the critical spaces and decisions[103]; yet they largely maintain a studied aloofness from performing the normative obligations

---

[94] B.S. Chimni, 'Asian civilizations and international law: some reflections' (2011) 1(1) Asian JIL 39.

[95] Anu Bradford and Eric A. Posner, 'Universal exceptionalism in international law' (2011) 52 Harv Int'l LJ 1.

[96] W.A. Callahan, 'Sino-speak: Chinese exceptionalism and the politics of history' (2012) 71(1) J Asian Stud 33; CY Woon, 'China's contingencies: Critical geopolitics, Chinese exceptionalism and the uses of history' (2018) 23(1) Geopolitics 67; J.V. Feinerman, 'Chinese participation in the international legal order: rogue elephant or team player?' (1995) 141 The China Quarterly 186.

[97] D.A. Desierto, 'Postcolonial international law discourses on regional developments in South and Southeast Asia' (2008) 36 Int'l J Legal Info 388.

[98] Bardo Fassbender, Anne Peters, Simon Peter & Daniel Hogger, *The Oxford Handbook of the History of International Law* (OUP 2012) ch 39.

[99] R.P. Anand, 'Attitude of the Asian-African states toward certain problems of international law' (1966) 15(1) ICLQ 55; D.P. Fidler, 'Introduction: Eastphalia Emerging?: Asia, International Law, and Global Governance' (2010) 17(1) Ind J Global Legal Studies 1.

[100] R.P. Anand, International Law and the Developing Countries' Confrontation or Cooperation (Banyan Publications, 1984) 56.

[101] A. Anghie, 'The Evolution of International Law: Colonial and Postcolonial Realities' (2006) 27 (5) TWQ 739.

[102] C. Welzel, 'The Myth of Asian Exceptionalism: Response to Bomhoff and Gu' (2012) 43(7) Journal of Cross-Cultural Psychology 1039.

[103] D.P. Fidler, 'The Asian century: Implications for international law' (2005) 9 SYBIL 19; G.M. Abi-Saab, 'The newly independent states and the rules of international law: an outline' (1962) 8 Howard LJ 95.

that universalist international law demands of them.[104] This is not unique to Asia, in fact it is likely that what we call universalism may be deconstructed into as many exceptionalisms as there are states in international law! It is only possible to observe this aloofness when one isolates the progress of a particular universalist norm and charts its journey in the context of the states in question. This is precisely what our case studies in the previous section have undertaken: the studies follow the path of resistance to internalization of the norm, both internal and external, to the application of a "classic" R2P framework, in the four completely dissimilar Asian states we have studied. We note that unlike interventions in Africa and the Middle East, Asian conflicts are rarely ever intervened into by the international community but tend to respond to regional states and organizations intervening. This is how we understand *Asian exceptionalism* in this paper—a marked departure from the normative universalism of R2P as international humanitarian intervention and the inklings of evidence that a regional framework, lead by Asian actors, may be a more acceptable version of R2P.

As Orend rues,[105] there are not enough restraints on the endings of wars. Codified principles for the justification of the use of force and conduct of hostilities have not, in the twenty-first century, despite several sparks, ignited the process of codification of principles governing the end of hostilities and the responsibility to peaceably settle their aftermath. These sparks were created during periods of transition from war to peace, when each situation was tackled by an ad hoc solution expounded by the international community.

Stories of human displacement, persecution, and atrocity crimes against the Muslim population (the Rohingya community) of Arakan province in Myanmar have been at the center of international litigation in 2019. The forms of concurrent litigation against Myanmar today find articulation in at least three distinct forums—firstly, under the doctrine of universal jurisdiction, Argentina is looking to prosecute individuals in the Myanmar government in its domestic courts, applying Argentinian domestic law, for egregious violations of international human rights law.[106] Secondly, The Gambia, as a party to the Genocide Convention, 1948, brought a request for provisional measures against Myanmar, another party to the Convention, to the International Court of Justice, for alleged breaches by Myanmar of its obligations under that Convention, which are now under documentation and investigation by the UN.[107] Thirdly, the International Criminal Court has found that it has the jurisdiction to adjudicate upon certain portions of the larger story in the Rohingya

---

[104] S.E. Davies, 'The Asian rejection?: International refugee law in Asia' (2006) 52(4) AJPH 562; K. Anderson, 'An Asian Pinochet-Not Likely: The Unfulfilled International Law Promise in Japan's Treatment of Former Peruvian President Alberto Fujimori' (2002) 38 Stan J Int'l L 177.

[105] Brian Orend, *The Morality of War* (Broadview Press 2006) 160.

[106] Md Kamruzzaman, 'Argentinian Court Decision Brings Hope for Rohingya' (*Anadolu Agency*, 2 June 2016) <www.aa.com.tr/en/americas/argentinian-court-decision-brings-hope-for-rohingya/1861967> accessed 30 August 2020.

[107] *Application of the Convention on the Prevention and Punishment of the Crime of Genocide (The Gambia v Myanmar)* (Request for the Indication of Provisional Measures: Order) General List no 178 [2020] ICJ 1, 12.

crisis that are predicated upon crossing an international border into the sovereign territory of Bangladesh, a party to the Rome Statute of the International Criminal Court and therefore subject to the jurisdiction of the Court.[108]

Between the resultant clashing jurisdictional spaces in human rights, state responsibility, universal jurisdiction, and individual criminal responsibility lie the normative claims of the Rohingya people to protection from the state or from a coalition of the willing. The sovereignty challenge resurfaces here when a state refuses to acknowledge that its "internal disturbance" may be "international." This creates two problems; firstly, of representation, in discussions of the situation at the UNSC for authorizing the implementation of R2P.[109] The second problem emerges *post facto*, when the host state to the conflict has to allow third-party adjudication of the crimes committed in its territory. In the Asian context, this problem can easily emerge based on the overall lack of effective utilization of international dispute settlement mechanisms as compared to other geographical regions.[110]

The arguments of representation and effective use of international law stem from four context-driven factors: firstly, shared historical experiences, and secondly the recognition that cultural pluralities in Asia create identity crises in resistance. Sornarajah argues,[111] for example, that an Asian perspective is built into the post-colonial state and the contemporary study of international law in the Asian context must necessarily take into account the role of Asian countries shaping it. Keeping in mind the historic past of subjugation to European powers (that deprived many Asian states of legal personality under international law), the Asian response to humanitarian crises is generally marked by distrust and wariness to external intervention. With emerging economic and humanitarian interventionist norms by hegemonic powers, this past experience and the power that an Asian regional coalition can have must be taken into consideration while theorizing Asian norms for international law. However, with the eventual decline of Asian Solidarity, it is seen that there are stark differences in Asian countries today: their economic growth, scientific advancements, religious ideologies, and foreign affairs.[112] The third and fourth factors are the economic self-interests and the power dynamic in the region, with the rise and decline of certain nations coupled with certain smaller Asian states preferring different forms of arrangement making regional representation difficult.[113]

The lack of representation of the Asian region is evident in the absence of a unified regional organization framework as compared to other regions, such as the

---

[108] ICC Pre-Trial Chambers III, *Situation in the People's Republic of Bangladesh/Republic of The Union of Myanmar* (14 November 2019) ICC-01/19, 51 [114].

[109] Simon Chesterman, 'Asia's Ambivalence about International Law and Institutions: Past, Present and Future', (2016) 27 Eur J Int'l L 945, 960.

[110] Ibid 962.

[111] M. Sornarajah, 'The Asian Perspective to International Law in the Age of Globalization', (2001) 5 Singapore J Int'l & Comp L 284, 310.

[112] Ibid 285.

[113] Ibid 285.

European Union and the African Union.[114] This argument is based on the existing weaknesses of the multiple regional organizations, mainly the Association of South-East Asian Nations ("ASEAN"), to adequately represent a collective Asian identity before the UN or Bretton Woods bodies.[115] Finally, international and multilateral dispute settlement bodies, such as the PCA, WTO, and ICJ, highlight the lack of effective utilization of third-party adjudication for Asian international disputes.

The development of R2P as a principle of international law has placed significant importance on the role of regional organizations in implementing its provisions, starting from the 2011 report.[116] Simultaneously, the growing significance of ASEAN's Political and Security Community has also been highlighted in reducing the number of small armed conflicts and increasing regional cooperation. The institutions of ASEAN have implemented and mainstreamed R2P in member countries when required.[117] This form of strengthened regional cooperation can also be noted in the case of Myanmar, specifically the Rohingya crisis and the Rakhine State issue, where ASEAN has made significant contributions in repatriating and rehabilitating through financial aid and preparation of preliminary needs assessment.[118]

Scarcely before in the history of international law in our times has one set of political events precipitated so rapidly into revealing the fault-lines of the system—to study the contestation of normative claims in the "Rohingya cases" maps an increasingly fictionalized narrative of what amounts to the international legal order or the international legal system in a world of multiplicities. Myanmar therefore presents an interesting setting to apply our understanding of Asian exceptionalism. Thinking beyond litigation into the humanitarian effort in this context could overcome the classic sovereignty challenge of certain states approaching the situation as an "internal conflict."

---

[114] Simon Chesterman (n 109) 957.

[115] Ibid 957.

[116] UNGA 'The Role of Regional and Subregional Arrangements in Implementing Responsibility to Protect' (28 June 2011) UN Doc A/65/877.

[117] High-Level Advisory Panel on the Responsibility to Protect in Southeast Asia, 'Mainstreaming the Responsibility to Protect in Southeast Asia: Pathway Towards a Caring ASEAN Community' <https://www.un.org/en/genocideprevention/documents/responsibility-to-protect/HLAP%20Report_FINAL.pdf> accessed 30 August 2020.

[118] ASEAN 'Indonesia funds US$500,000 to support ASEAN efforts in the repatriation of displaced persons in Myanmar' (20 December 2019) <https://asean.org/indonesia-funds-us500000-support-asean-efforts-repatriation-displaced-persons-myanmar/> accessed 30 August 2020.

Annexure

Geography	Characteristics		Resolutions	Excerpts
Libya 	**Phase (2011-current)** (*Pre-Intervention Laws/ Humanitarian Intervention Laws/R2P*)	R2P	Res. 1970 (2011), Res. 1973 (2011), Res. 2009 (2011), Res. 2016 (2011), Res. 2017 (2011), Res. 2022 (2011), Res. 2040 (2012), Res. 2095 (2013), Res. 2144 (2014), Res. 2146 (2014), Res. 2174 (2014), Res. 2208 (2015), Res. 2213 (2015), Res. 2214 (2015), Res. 2238 (2015), Res. 2240 (2015), Res. 2259 (2015), Res. 2273 (2016), Res. 2278 (2016), Res. 2298 (2016), Res. 2323 (2016), Res. 2357 (2017), Res. 2362 (2017) and Res. 2441 (2018)	Resolution 1970 (2011)- "***Mindful of its primary responsibility for the maintenance of international peace and security*** under the Charter of the United Nations," "4. Decides to refer the situation in the Libyan Arab Jamahiriya since 15 February 2011 ***to the Prosecutor of the International Criminal Court;***" Resolution 1973 (2011)- "2. Stresses the need to intensify efforts … ***decisions of the Secretary-General to send his Special Envoy to Libya and of the Peace and Security Council of the African Union to send its* ad hoc *High Level Committee to Libya*** with the aim of facilitating dialogue…" "4. ***Authorizes Member States*** …acting nationally or through regional organizations or arrangements… ***to take all necessary measures, notwithstanding paragraph 9 of resolution 1970 (2011)***, to protect civilians.. ***excluding a foreign occupation force*** of any form on any part of Libyan territory," Resolution 2009 (2011) "12. ***Decides to establish a United Nations Support Mission in Libya (UNSMIL), under the leadership of a Special Representative of the Secretary-General***…"
	Classification of crisis (*Internal/International*)	Internal		
	Cause for discussion (*Reasons by Secretary General for Reference*)	Report of use of force against civilians		
	Response of UNSC	Imposed various restriction and bans, referred Libyan situation to the ICC, authorised the member states to take all necessary measures, and established the United Nations support mission in Libya		
	Reactions of relevant stakeholders (*Action Taken by neighbouring member states/regional organisations/ other member states*)	Condemnation by the league of Arab States, the African Union, and the secretary general of the organisation of the Islamic conference The Peace and security council of the African Union established an ad hoc high-level committee on Libya		

(continued)

(continued)

Geography	Characteristics		Resolutions	Excerpts
Syria 	**Phase (2011-current)** (*Pre-Intervention Laws/ Humanitarian Intervention Laws/ R2P*)	R2P	Res. 2042 (2012), Res. 2043 (2012), Res. 2059 (2012), Res. 2118 (2013), Res. 2139 (2014), Res. 2165 (2014), Res. 2191 (2014), Res. 2209 (2015), Res. 2235 (2015), Res. 2254 (2015), Res. 2258 (2015), Res. 2286 (2016), Res. 2314 (2016), Res. 2319 (2016), Res. 2328 (2016), Res. 2332 (2016), Res. 2336 (2016), Res. 2393 (2017) and Res. 2401 (2018)	Resolution 2042 (2012) "Reaffirming ***its support to the Joint Special Envoy for the United Nations and the League of Arab States…***following General Assembly resolution A/ RES/66/253 of 16 February 2012 and relevant resolutions of the League of Arab States," "2. Calls upon the Syrian government to implement visibly its commitments in their entirety, as it agreed to do in its communication to the Envoy" "7. Decides to ***authorize an advance team of up to 30 unarmed military observers to liaise with the parties and to begin to report on the implementation of a full cessation of armed violence in all its forms by all parties, pending the deployment of the mission*** referred to in paragraph 5…" Resolution 2043 (2012)- "Decides to establish for an initial period of 90 days ***a United Nations Supervision Mission in Syria (UNSMIS) under the command of a Chief Military Observer, comprising an initial deployment of up to 300 unarmed military observers as well as an appropriate civilian component as required by the Mission to fulfil its mandate***,…" Resolution 2118 (2013)- "***Stressing that the only solution to the current crisis in the Syrian Arab Republic is through an inclusive and Syrian-led political process based*** on the Geneva Communiqué of 30 June 2012…" "7. ***Decides that the Syrian Arab Republic shall cooperate fully with the OPCW and the United Nations***, including by complying with their relevant recommendations…" Resolution 2165 (2014)- "***Reaffirming the primary responsibility of the Syrian authorities to protect the population in Syria*** …"
	Classification of crisis (*Internal/ International*)	Internal		
	Cause for discussion (*Reasons by Secretary General for Reference*)	Violent repression of civilians		
	Response of UNSC	Deployed United Nations Supervision Mission in Syria (UNSMIS) to ensure implementation of the "Preliminary understanding"		
	Reactions of relevant stakeholders (*Action Taken by neighbouring member states/regional organisations/ other member states*)	League of Arab states suspended Syria's membership and imposed sanctions on its failure to abide by Arab league's Peace Plan. Also, Arab league along with UN sent out a joint special envoy to Syria		

(continued)

(continued)

Geography	Characteristics		Resolutions	Excerpts
Cambodia 	**Phase** (1978–1989) (*Pre-Intervention Laws/ Humanitarian Intervention Laws/R2P*)	Pre-IL	Res. 668 (1990), Res. 717 (1991), Res. 718 (1991), Res. 728 1992), Res. 745 (1992), Res. 766 (1992), Res. 783 (1992), Res. 792 (1992), Res. 810 (1993), Res. 826 (1993), Res. 835 (1993), Res. 840 (1993), Res. 860 (1993) and Res. 880 (1993)	Resolution 668 (1990)- *"Also taking note with appreciation* of the efforts of the countries of the ***Association of South-East Asian Nations and other countries involved in promoting the search for a comprehensive political settlement"*** Resolution 717 (1991)- "2. Decides to establish…United Nations Advance Mission in Cambodia immediately…with members of the Mission to be sent to Cambodia immediately after the signing" Resolution 810 (1993)- ***"Recognizes that the Cambodians themselves bear the primary responsibility for the implementation of the Paris Agreement and for the future stability and well-being of Cambodia"***
	Classification of crisis (*Internal/International*)	International		
	Cause for discussion (*Reasons by Secretary General for Reference*)	Implementation of the comprehensive Cambodian peace agreements (Paris Peace Agreements)		
	Response of UNSC	Deployed multiple UN bodies to ensure cease-fire and conduct democratic election as per the Paris peace agreement		
	Reactions of relevant stakeholders (*Action Taken by neighbouring member states/regional organisations/ other member states*)	Attempt to broker peace by association of South-East Asian nations		

(continued)

(continued)

Geography	Characteristics		Resolutions	Excerpts
Azerbaijan-Armenia  	**Phase (1988-current)** *(Pre-Intervention Laws/ Humanitarian Intervention Laws/R2P)*	Pre-IL + R2P	Res. 822 (1993), Res. 853 (1993), Res. 874 (1993) and Res. 884 (1993)	Resolution 853 (1993)- "6. Endorses the continuing efforts by the ***Minsk Group of the CSCE*** to achieve a peaceful solution to the conflict, including efforts to implement resolution 822 (1993)…" Resolution 874 (1993)- "Taking note of the high-level meetings which took place in Moscow on 8 October 1993 and expressing the hope that they will contribute to the improvement of the situation and the peaceful settlement of the conflict," "1. Calls upon the parties concerned to ***make effective and permanent the cease-fire established as a result of the direct contacts undertaken with the assistance of the Government of the Russian Federation in support of the CSCE Minsk Group;*** 2. Reiterates again its ***full support for the peace process being pursued within the framework of the CSCE…"*** Resolution 884 (1993)- 4. ***Demands from the parties concerned the immediate cessation of armed hostilities and hostile acts, the unilateral withdrawal of occupying forces*** …in accordance with the "Adjusted timetable of urgent steps to implement Security Council resolutions 822 (1993) and 853 (1993)"
	Classification of crisis *(Internal/ International)*	International		
	Cause for discussion *(Reasons by Secretary General for Reference)*	Territorial dispute over region of Nagorno-Karabakh		
	Response of UNSC	Condemning the violence and support for intervention attempt by the CSCE		
	Reactions of relevant stakeholders *(Action Taken by neighbouring member states/regional organisations/ other member states)*	Brokering of cease-fire by Russia		

(continued)

(continued)

Geography	Characteristics		Resolutions	Excerpts
Sri Lanka 	**Phase (1983–2009)** (*Pre-Humanitarian Intervention Laws/ Humanitarian Intervention Laws/R2P*)	HIL + R2P	UNHRC- A/HRC/Res/ S-11/1, Report of the secretary general's panel of experts on Sri Lanka, Reports of Secretary General on Armed Conflict in Sri Lanka 2007–2011, UNSC Press Statement- SC/9659 2009	SC/9659 "The members of the Security Council strongly condemn the Liberation Tigers of Tamil Eelam (LTTE) for its acts of terrorism over many years, and for its continued use of civilians as human shields, and acknowledge the legitimate right of the Government of Sri Lanka to combat terrorism The members of the Security Council express deep concern at the reports of continued use of heavy calibre weapons in areas with high concentrations of civilians, and **expect the Government of Sri Lanka to fulfil its commitment in this regard** SECRETARY GENERAL'S PANEL OF EXPERTS ON ACCOUNTABILITY IN SRI LANKA "The Panel's determination of credible allegations reveals a very different version of the final stages of the war than that maintained to this day by the Government of Sri Lanka The Government says it pursued a "humanitarian rescue operation" with a policy of "zero civilian casualties." In stark contrast, the Panel found credible allegations, which if proven, indicate that a wide range of serious violations of international humanitarian law and international human rights law was committed both by the Government of Sri Lanka and the LTTE, some of which would amount to war crimes and crimes against humanity. Indeed, the conduct of the war represented a grave assault on the entire regime of international law designed to protect individual dignity during both war and peace."
	Classification of crisis (*Internal/ International*)	Internal		
	Cause for discussion (*Reasons by Secretary General for Reference*)	Civil War by insurgents (LTTE and breakaway factions), use of civilians as human shields, use of child soldiers		
	Response of UNSC	Authorized the establishment of monitoring and report mechanism at the field level Also created the security council working group on children in armed conflict for Sri Lanka		
	Reactions of relevant stakeholders (*Action Taken by neighbouring member states/regional organisations/other member states*)	In 1987 the Indo-Sri Lankan Accord was signed which implied military intervention in a foreign country and interference in internal affairs		

(continued)

(continued)

Geography	Characteristics		Resolutions	Excerpts
Timor-Leste 	**Phase (1975–1999)** *(Pre-Humanitarian Intervention Laws/ Humanitarian Intervention Laws/ R2P)*	HIL	S/RES/384 (1975), S/RES/1264 (1999), S/RES/1410 (2002)	1. S/RES/384 (1975) "Regretting that the Government of Portugal did not discharge fully its responsibilities as administering Power in the Territory under Chapter XI of the Charter, 1. ***Calls upon all States to respect*** the territorial integrity of East Timor as well as the inalienable right of its people to self-determination … 2. Calls upon the Government of Indonesia to withdraw without delay all its forces from the Territory; 3. Calls upon the Government of Portugal as administering Power to co-operate fully with the United Nations so as to enable the people of East Timor to exercise freely their right to self-determination; 4. Urges all States and other parties concerned to co-operate fully with the efforts of the United Nations to achieve a peaceful solution to the existing situation and to facilitate the decolonization of the Territory;" 2. S/RES/1264 (1999) 15 September 1999 "3. Authorizes ***the establishment of a multinational force under a unified command structure, pursuant to the request of the Government of Indonesia conveyed to the Secretary-General on 12 September 1999***, with the following tasks: to restore peace and security in East Timor, to protect and support UNAMET in carrying out its tasks and, within force capabilities, to facilitate humanitarian assistance operations, and authorizes the States participating in the multinational force to take all necessary measures to fulfil this mandate; ***7. Stresses that it is the responsibility of the Indonesian authorities*** to take immediate and effective measures to ensure the safe return of refugees to East Timor;" 3. S/RES/1410 (2002) "***Noting that the emerging institutions in East Timor remain fragile and that in the period immediately after independence assistance will be required*** …"
	Classification of crisis *(Internal/ International)*	International		
	Cause for discussion *(Reasons by Secretary General for Reference)*	Indonesian invasion of East Timor as it was decolonizing from Portugal in 1975 Anti-independence violence that erupted in 1999, rehabilitation and investigation into the deaths during the 1999 Civil unrest Protecting the independence of East Timor		
	Response of UNSC	In 1975, upon a referral from the UNGA, the UNSC in its resolution S/RES/384 (1975); In 1999 authorised deployment of multinational force pursuant to the request by the Government of Indonesia, through resolution S/RES/1264 (1999)		

(continued)

(continued)

Geography	Characteristics		Resolutions	Excerpts
	Reactions of relevant stakeholders (*Action Taken by neighbouring member states/regional organisations/other member states*)	Indonesia approached the UNSC		

Libya

The first instance of proper application of R2P can be traced back to the situation in Libya where the UNSC authorized intervention under an umbrella of protecting measures, resulting in the intervention being led by the North Atlantic Treaty Organization ("NATO").[119] The implementation of R2P, however, has been criticized heavily after this intervention due to the complexity of foreign involvement created in Libya, which was worsened by the infringement of the NATO mandate by their operations.[120] What emerged was outright warfare against rebel forces and the NATO-backed government that further caused a stalemate in the UNSC.[121] R2P in Libya encountered several criticisms, specifically in Pillar 3, accelerating the redefining of non-coercive measures and respecting human rights in cases of protective intervention.[122]

Syria

The ongoing crisis in Syria[123] straddles a wide range of human rights violations that the international community has been aware of[124] and condemned[125] on multiple occasions since 2011.[126] The implementation of R2P through the UNSC was unsuccessful, initially due to the objections by Russia and China, who anticipated a similar excess of force like the UNSC had approved in the case of Libya.[127] Non-coercive measures such as regional cooperation through the League of Arab States, sanctions, and diplomatic measures have not yielded any success due to an uncooperative Syrian government.[128] Exhausting all the measures apart from direct military intervention leads to the conclusion of inaction in Syria.

---

[119] UNSC 'Security Council Approves 'No-Fly Zone' over Libya, Authorizing 'All Necessary Measures' to Protect Civilians, by Vote of 10 in Favour with 5 Abstentions' (17 March 2011) Press Release SC/10200.

[120] Christopher Zambakari (2016) 'The Misguided and Mismanaged Intervention in Libya: Consequences for Peace' (2016) 25(1) Afr Sec Rev 44, 47.

[121] Marcos Tourinho, Oliver Stuenkel & Sarah Brockmeier, 'Responsibility while Protecting: Reforming R2P Implementation' (2016) 30(1) Global Society 134, 136.

[122] Heidarali Teimouri and Surya P Subedi, 'Responsibility to Protect and the International Military Intervention in Libya in International Law: What Went Wrong and What Lessons Could Be Learnt from It?' (2018) 23(1) J.C. & S.L 3, 29.

[123] M. Nasser-Eddine, 'How R2P Failed Syria' (2012) 28 FJHP 16, 18.

[124] UNGA 'General Assembly Adopts More Than 60 Resolutions Recommended by Third Committee, Including Text Condemning Grave, Systematic Human Rights Violations in Syria' (19 December 2011) Press Release GA/11198.

[125] Security Council Report, 'Chronology of Events: Syria' (*Security Council Report*) <http://www.securitycouncilreport.org/chronology/syria.php?page=all&print=true> accessed 28 August 2020.

[126] Muditha Halliyadde, 'Syria – Another Drawback for R2P?: An Analysis of R2P's Failure to Change International Law on Humanitarian Intervention' (2016) 4 Ind J L & Soc Equality 215.

[127] Ibid 221.

[128] Ibid 227–229.

Nagorno-Karabakh Conflict

An immediate response to the conflict came from the Russia Federation and the Organization for Security and Cooperation in Europe ("OCSE"), who held multiple talks and high-level meetings toward a resolution.[129] The Minsk Group of OCSE was formed primarily to resolve the Nagorno-Karabakh question[130] resulting in the (arguably inconclusive[131]) Bishkek Protocol of 1994 establishing a cease-fire.[132] The role of the UNSC remained limited to observing the Minsk Group's and the Russian Federation's efforts.[133]

Cambodia

The conflict came to an end in 1991 with the Comprehensive Cambodian Peace Agreements ("the Paris Peace Agreement").[134] The document highlights the role of international communities in coming together to broker peace. It not only laid out the process of ending the conflict and building a democratic institution of the people of Cambodia, but also laid out plans for rehabilitation and reconstruction of Cambodia.[135] The Agreement was followed by a UNSC brokered Accord for its implementation, under which the UN established the United Nations Transitional Authority in Cambodia to assist with elections for a new government.[136]

Sri Lanka

UNSC did not make any official statements barring a Press Release in 2009.[137] A report of the UN Panel of Experts in 2011[138] found credibility in several serious allegations that the Sri Lankan Government had committed serious war crimes and

---

[129] Patricia Carley, 'Nagorno-Karabakh: Searching for a Solution' (*United States Institute for Peace* 1 December 1998) <www.usip.org/publications/1998/12/nagorno-karabakh-searching-solution-0> accessed 30 August 2020.

[130] Volker Jacoby, 'The role of the OSCE: An assessment of international mediation efforts' (2005) 17 Accord <https://www.c-r.org/accord/nagorny-karabakh/role-osce-assessment-international-mediation-efforts> accessed 30 August 2020.

[131] Sabine Freizer, 'Twenty years after the Nagorny Karabakh ceasefire: an opportunity to move towards more inclusive conflict resolution' (2014) 1:2 Caucasus Survey 109, 109.

[132] Bishkek Protocol (adopted 5 May 1994) <https://peacemaker.un.org/sites/peacemaker.un.org/files/Bishkek%20Protocol.pdf> accessed on 30 August 2020.

[133] UNSC Res 853 (29 July 1993) UN Doc S/RES/853; UNSC Res 874 (14 October 1993) UN Doc S/RES/874.

[134] Laura McGrew and Scott Worden, 'Lessons from Cambodia's Paris Peace Accords for Political Unrest Today' (*United States Institute for Peace* 16 May 2017) <https://www.usip.org/publications/2017/05/lessons-cambodias-paris-peace-accords-political-unrest-today> accessed 30 August 2020.

[135] Office of the High Commissioner of Human Rights, 'Cambodia - 20 years on from the Paris Peace Agreements' (*Office of the High Commissioner of Human Rights*, 21 October 2011) <https://www.ohchr.org/EN/NewsEvents/Pages/Cambodia-20yearsonfromtheParisPeace.aspx> accessed on 24 August 2020.

[136] UNSC Res 717 (16 October 1991) UN Doc S/RES/717.

[137] UNSC 'Security Council Press Statement on Sri Lanka' (13 May 2009) Press Release SC/9659.

[138] UN Secretary General 'Secretary General's Panel of Experts on Sri Lanka' (31 March 2011).

crimes against humanity. Yet there was no international action invoking R2P through the course of the civil war in Sri Lanka.

Timor-Leste

The UNSC authorized deployment of international force under Chapter VII of the Charter to curb the violence upon the request of the representatives of Timor-Leste under express agreement from Indonesia.[139]

Analysis

Unlike interventions in Africa and the Middle East, our study shows that Asian conflicts are rarely ever intervened upon by the international community and the UNSC and are often resolved through regional cooperation. The four case studies present a broad range of resolutions to potential R2P mandating situations, indicating one important common factor in their diversity, the role of a strong regional power in the main solution. In each of the conflicts, one particular regional organization/ nation played a key role in either involving the international community or resolving the conflict themselves. This is particularly visible in the case study of Sri Lanka and Nagorno-Karabakh, which particularly relied on dominant neighboring countries for resolution. In the case of Timor-Leste as well, the role of Indonesia being the initial intervener in the conflict, coupled with them approaching the UNSC for discussion due to the international nature of the conflict given the involvement of Portugal does further highlight the importance of neighboring nations in such conflicts. The study of Cambodia although the only case of collective international involvement, still shows the importance of regional organizations in implementing the peace agreement.

[139] UNSC Res 1264 (15 September 1999) UN Doc S/RES/1264.

Chapter 12
Intersection of Law, Religion, Customs, and the Problem of Child Marriage in Global South: *A Comparative Study of India, Nigeria and Uganda*

Neha Mishra, Tonny R. Kirabira, and Judith N. Onwubiko

Abstract Despite the existing legal prohibitions, the practice of child marriage remains not just prevalent but has also become a grave concern in the aftermath of pandemic across Sub-Saharan Africa and South Asia. The article takes a comparative approach to describe the key drivers of child marriage in the three country contexts—India, Uganda, and Nigeria. The legal sanctions on child marriage often conflict with the accepted customary and/or religious norms which proliferate when confronted against socio-economic difficulties and cultural realities. The article would reveal a consequent disconnect between the laws and its interphase with the socio-cultural beliefs and hence the need to take into account such elements, when implementing the laws in relevant legal framework. Among the Global South countries, the three countries have substantial similarity in terms of not only the legal framework but also socio-cultural and economic positionality regarding child marriage. While poverty and cultural linkages in Uganda reveals daughters being traded for livestock, each year 1.5 million Indian girls are sold/married off under eighteen and at an estimated 22 million child brides, Nigeria stands at highest rate of child marriages in Africa. Ironically, these countries have comprehensive legal frameworks for child's rights protection, still they remain futile. The paper will deliberate on whether there is a need to look beyond legislative interventions? Further, this paper advances a socio-legal approach within the implementation aspect of rule of law in the three countries studied.

The original version of this chapter has been revised. The author "Tonny R. Kirabira" name and author's "Judith N. Onwubiko" affiliation has been updated and the footnotes are re-arranged. The correction to this chapter is available at
https://doi.org/10.1007/978-981-99-5467-4_14

N. Mishra (✉)
Jindal Global Law School, O.P. Jindal Global University, Sonipat, Haryana, India
e-mail: nehamishra@jgu.edu.in

T. R. Kirabira
Faculty of Humanities and Social Sciences, University of Portsmouth, Portsmouth, UK

J. N. Onwubiko
School of Law and Social Sciences, London South Bank University, London, UK

M. John et al. (eds.), *The Indian Yearbook of Comparative Law 2020*, The Indian Yearbook of Comparative Law, https://doi.org/10.1007/978-981-99-5467-4_12

Keywords Child marriage · Socio-cultural contexts · India · Nigeria · Uganda · Legal pluralism

12.1 Introduction

The marriage of children below the age of 18 is internationally recognized as a breach of fundamental human rights. Although child marriage affects both girls and boys, there is a disproportionate high rate of girl-child marriages across the world. This form of violence against children negatively affects the overall well-being and development of millions of girls in various countries of the global south. According to UNICEF, globally, between 2021 and 2030, up to 10 million girls will be at a greater danger of child marriage. The United Nations Population Fund (UNFPA) believes that the current pandemic will result in an extra 13 million child marriages globally between 2020 and 2030. According to the latest assessment, South Asia would bear the brunt of these child marriages: 191,200 in a single year and 956,000 in five years. It is against this backdrop that this paper examines the problem of child marriage in India, Nigeria, and Uganda.[1,2,3,4]

---

[1] Megan Arthur et al., ibid, 51; UNICEF Data, ibid.

[2] See for instance, UNICEF, *Child Marriage in West and Central Africa: At a Glance* (September 2018) <https://www.unicef.org/wca/media/2596/file> accessed 29 July 2021; Eugene Budu, Bright Opoku Ahinkorah, Abdul-Aziz Seidu, John Elvis Hagan, Wonder Agbemavi, James Boadu Frimpong, Collins Adu, Kwamena Sekyi Dickson, and Sanni Yaya, 'Child Marriage and Sexual Autonomy among Women in Sub-Saharan Africa: Evidence from 31 Demographic and Health Surveys' (2021) 18 Int. J. Environ. Res. Public Health 3754; Sanni Yaya, Emmanuel Kolawole Odusina, 'Prevalence of Child Marriage and its Impact on Fertility Outcomes in 34 Sub-Saharan African Countries' (2019) 19(33) BMC International Health and Human Rights 1; Stella Ojuade, 'Child Molestation in Nigeria: The Way Forward for the Victim' (2019) 10 Nnamdi Azikiwe U J Int'l L & Juris 151, 151; Loretta M Kopelman, 'The Forced Marriage of Minors: A Neglected Form of Child Abuse' (2016) 44 JL Med & Ethics 173; Sheetal Sekhri, and Sisir Debnath, 'Intergenerational Consequences of Early Age Marriages of Girls: Effect on Children's Human Capital' (2014) 50(12) The Journal of Development Studies 1670; Judith-Ann Walker, 'Early Marriage in Africa: Trends, Harmful Effects and Interventions' (2012) 16(2) African Journal of Reproductive Health 231; Anita Raj, 'When the Mother Is a Child: The Impact of Child Marriage on the Health and Human Rights of Girls' (2010) 95(11) Archives of Disease in Childhood 931; Kidangamparampil G. Santhya, Usha Ram, Rajib Acharya, Shireen J. Jejeebhoy, Faujdar Ram and Abhishek Singh, 'Associations between Early Marriage and Young Women's Marital and Reproductive Health Outcomes: Evidence from India' (2010) 36(3) International Perspectives on Sexual and Reproductive Health 132;

[3] UNICEF, "10 Million Additional Girls at Risk of Child Marriage due to COVID-19" (www.unicef.org) <https://www.unicef.org/press-releases/10-million-additional-girls-risk-child-marriage-due-covid-19> accessed September 4, 2021.

[4] United Nations Population Fund, "Millions More Cases of Violence, Child Marriage, Female Genital Mutilation, Unintended Pregnancy Expected due to the COVID-19 Pandemic" (www.unfpa.org April 28, 2020) <https://www.unfpa.org/news/millions-more-cases-violence-child-marriage-female-genital-mutilation-unintended-pregnancies> accessed September 4, 2021.

There is substantial similarity in legal frameworks in India, Nigeria, and Uganda due to the application of mixed systems of civil, customary, and religious law.[5,6,7,8,9,10,11,12,13] Similarly, all the three countries are State members of the Commonwealth, which offers an avenue for harnessing efforts toward the eradication of child marriage. To this end, the national human rights institutions of the three countries agreed to strengthen efforts to prevent and eliminate child, early marriage, under the Kigali Declaration of 2015.[14]

Against this background, the aim of this paper is to critically examine the Indian, Nigerian, and Ugandan legal frameworks on child marriage in order to establish the relevance of a socio-legal approach that addresses the socio-cultural and religious factors enabling the persistence of child marriage in the three countries studied. In

---

[5] Gabrielle Szabo and Jess Edwards, "THE GLOBAL GIRLHOOD REPORT 2020" (Save the Children 2020) <https://www.savethechildren.org/content/dam/usa/reports/ed-cp/global-girlhood-report-2020.pdf> accessed September 4, 2021.

[6] Michael Addaney and Onuora-Oguno Azubike, 'Education as a Contrivance to Ending Child Marriage in Africa: Perspectives from Nigeria and Uganda' (2017) 9(2) Amsterdam Law Forum 110.

[7] UNICEF, Child Protection, Child Marriage, URL Available at: https://www.unicef.org/rosa/what-we-do/child-protection/child-marriage.

[8] Stella Neema et al., "Trading daughters for livestock": An ethnographic study of facilitators of child marriage in Lira district, Northern Uganda' (2021) 25(3) African Journal of Reproductive Health 83.

[9] Supra n. 2.

[10] UNICEF, *Child Marriage in West and Central Africa: At a Glance* (September 2018) 5 available at <https://www.unicef.org/wca/media/2596/file> accessed 29 July 2021; Jacob Wale Mobolaji, Adesegun O. Fatusi and Sunday A. Adedini, 'Ethnicity, Religious Affiliation and Girl-Child Marriage: A Cross-Sectional Study of Nationally Representative Sample of Female Adolescents in Nigeria' (2020) 20(583) BMC Public Health 1, 2.

[11] Tim S. Braimah, 'Child Marriage in Northern Nigeria: Section 61 of Part 1 of the 1999 Constitution and the Protection of Children Against Child Marriage' (2014) 24 AHRLJ 474, 474.; Child Protection Laws in India, http://satyarthi.org.in/wp-content/uploads/BondedLabor/English/Summary%20of%20the%20Child%20Protection%20Laws%20in%20India.pdf.

[12] Megan Arthur, Alison Earle, Amy Raub, Ilona Vincent, Efe Atabay, Isabel Latz, Gabriella Kranz, Arijit Nandi and Jody Heymann 'Child Marriage Laws around the World: Minimum Marriage Age, Legal Exceptions, and Gender Disparities' (2018) 39(1) Journal of Women, Politics & Policy 51, 51; Quentin Wodon, 'Child Marriage, Family Law, and Religion: An Introduction to the Fall 2015 Issue' (2015) 13(3) The Review of Faith & International Affairs 1, 1; Rita Mutyaba, 'Early Marriage: A Violation of Girls' Fundamental Human Rights in Africa' (2011) 19 Int'l J Child Rts 339; Anita Raj, 'When the Mother Is a Child: The Impact of Child Marriage on the Health and Human Rights of Girls' (2010) 95(11) Archives of Disease in Childhood 931; UNICEF Data, 'Child Marriage: Child Marriage is a Violation of Human Rights, but is all too Common' (August 2021) <https://data.unicef.org/topic/child-protection/child-marriage/> accessed 1 September 2021.

[13] For a more elaborate analysis, see UNICEF, 'Child Marriage and the Law: Technical Note from the UNFPA-UNICEF Global Programme to End Child Marriage' (United Nations Children's Fund 2020) https://www.unicef.org/media/86311/file/Child-marriage-the-law-2020.pdf accessed 30 August 2021.

[14] See Kigali Declaration https://thecommonwealth.org/sites/default/files/press-release/documents/Early%20and%20Forced%20Marriage%20-%20Kigali%20Declaration.pdf accessed 16 August 2021.

this sense, the paper is both comparative and socio-legal. Not only does it compare the legal issues and approaches across the three named countries, it also compares the state and non-state legal approaches within each country. Hence, the paper adopts a sociological conception of law within which the concept of legal pluralism is used to draw attention to the state and non-state forms of law regulating child marriages in India, Nigeria, and Uganda.

Sociological conceptions of law view law as 'a practical craft of systematic control of social relations and institutions'.[15] That is, law is seen as a social practice rather than as just the practice of state legal institutions. Such sociological understanding of law acknowledges the existence of state and non-state forms of law and, thus, forms the basis for concepts such as legal pluralism.[16] According to Sally Engle Merry, legal pluralism generally refers to 'a situation in which two or more legal systems coexist in the same social field'.[17] Legal pluralism posits that not all law takes place through the state, but state law exists and operates alongside other non-state forms of law.[18] Legal pluralism is an inherent feature of every society,[19] and remains applicable in modern contexts.[20] Hence, as Merry points out, legal pluralism 'can be seen as the key concept in a postmodern view of law'.[21] It is the 'new common sense' as far as law is concerned.[22]

The concept of legal pluralism is particularly important for understanding law in formerly colonized societies where the colonial imposition of European state law

---

[15] Roger Cotterrell, *The Sociology of Law: An Introduction* (2nd edn., Butterworks, 1992) 4. See also, Robert Cryer, Tamara Harvey and Bal Sokhi-Bulley with Alexandra Bohm, *Research Methodologies in EU and International Law* (Hart Publishing, 2011) 36.

[16] Roger Cotterrell, ibid, 38–39.

[17] Sally Engle Merry, 'Legal Pluralism', (1988) 22(5) Law & Soc'y Rev. 869, 870. See also John Griffiths, 'What is Legal Pluralism?' (1986) 24 Journal of Legal Pluralism 1, 2 and 4.

[18] See Laura Nader and Harry F. Tood (eds.), *The Disputing Process-Law in Ten Societies* (Columbia University Press, 1978); H. W. Athurs, *Without the Law: Administrative Justice and the Legal Pluralism in Mid-19th-Century England* (University of Toronto Press, 1985).

[19] See Stewart Macaulay, 'Private Government' in Leon Lipson and Stanton Wheeler (eds.), *Law and the Social Sciences* (Russell Sage Foundation, 1986); Stuart Henry, *Private Justice* (Routledge and Kegan Paul, 1983); Sally Engle Merry, (n 8), 872; David M. Engle, 'Law, Time, and Community', (1987) 21 Law & Society Review 605; John Griffiths, (n 8), 5; Stuart Henry, 'Community Justice, Capital Society, and Human Agency: The Dialectics of Collective Law in the Cooperative', (1985) 19 Law & Society Review 303; David M. Engle, 'The Oven Bird's Song: Insiders, Outsiders, and Personal Injuries in an American Community', (1984) 18 Law & Society Review 549; David M. Engel, 'Legal Pluralism in an American Community: Perspectives on a Civil Trial Court', (1980) 3 American Bar Foundation Research Journal 425; Sally Engle Merry, 'Going to Court: Strategies of Dispute Management in an American Urban Neighbourhood' (1979) 13 Law & Society Review 891; Sally Falk Moore, 'Law and Social Change: The Semi-Autonomous Social Field as an Appropriate Subject of Study', (1973) 7 Law & Society Review 719.

[20] Jody Sarich, Michele Olivier and Kevin Bales, 'Forced Marriage, Slavery, and Plural Legal Systems: An African Example' (2016) 38 Hum Rts Q 450, 471.

[21] Sally Engle Merry, 'Anthropology, Law, and Transitional Processes', (1992) 21 Ann. Rev. Anthropology 357, 358.

[22] Boaventura de Sousa Santos, 'Law: A Map of Misreading: Toward a Postmodern Conception of Law' (1987) 14 (3) Journal of Law and Society 279, 299.

results in various kinds of interactions and conflicts between state, customary, and religious laws.[23] These interactions and conflicts have become a significant feature of law in countries such as India, Nigeria, and Uganda. Hence, for the purpose of this paper, legal pluralism is useful for understanding the various forms of legal regulation of child marriage in these three countries. Moreover, in countries of the global south, situations of legal pluralism often create 'ambiguity regarding human rights in general and child rights in particular'.[24] The various forms of law involved in the regulation of child marriage often conflict with each other. For instance, while the state law may adopt a minimum marital age of 18 years, some customary and religious laws set lower or no minimum age for marriage.[25] Due to these customary and religious laws, 'there is generally an indifferent attitude to the provisions of the law'.[26] Hence, legal pluralism can be useful for acknowledging the role of customary and religious laws in the continued existence and eradication of the problem of child marriage.

In the literature on child marriage, two of the most common approaches identified for addressing child marriage are education and legal reform of the minimum age for marriage.[27] This paper builds on these studies by pointing out the value of legal approaches that account for the religious and socio-cultural aspects of child marriage.

---

[23] M. B. Hooker, *Legal Pluralism: An Introduction to Colonial and Neo-Colonial Laws* (OUP, 1975) 2–3; Sally Engle Merry, (n 8), 872; John Griffiths, (n 8), 8.

[24] Alexis Foua and Wilson Diriwari, 'Cultural and Legal Perspectives on Child Protection in the Context of Child Trafficking in Nigeria' (2020) 11 Beijing L Rev 11, 11. See also Megan Arthur et al., (n 7), 57; Nkoyo Toyo, 'Revisiting Equality as a Right: the Minimum Age of Marriage Clause in the Nigerian Child Rights Act, 2003' (2006) 27(7) Third World Quarterly 1299, 1299; https://www.unicef.org/media/86311/file/Child-marriage-the-law-2020.pdf; Moore, Gender, Power and Legal Pluralism: Rajasthan, India, American Ethnologist, Wiley, Vol. 20, No. 3 (1993), pp. 522–542; Hoko Horii, Hoko Horii (2019) Pluralistic legal system, pluralistic human rights?: teenage pregnancy, child marriage and legal institutions in Bali, The Journal of Legal Pluralism and Unofficial Law, Routledge, 51:3, (2019) pp. 292–319; Child Mariage in Bangladesh, avaialable at https://www.ohchr.org/Documents/Issues/Women/WRGS/ForcedMarriage/NGO/WomenAndJusticeFellow5.pdf.

[25] Megan Arthur et al., (n 1), 57.

[26] Michael Attah, 'The Age of Marriage Question in Nigeria: How Far Resolved?' (2019) 2 GLR 111, 111.

[27] See for instance, Edilberto Loaiza and Sylvia Wong, *Marrying Too Young: End Child Marriage* (United Nations Population Fund, 2012) <http://www.unfpa.org/sites/default/files/pub-pdf/MarryingTooYoung.pdf> accessed 26 August 2021; Human Rights Watch, *'How Come You Allow Little Girls to Get Married?' Child Marriage in Yemen* (Human Rights Watch, 2011) <http://www.hrw.org/sites/default/files/reports/yemen1211ForUpload_0.pdf> accessed 26 August 2021; Rangita De Silva-De-Alwis, *Child Marriage and the Law: Legislative Reform Initiative* (UNICEF Division of Policy and Planning, 2008) <http://www.unicef.org/policyanalysis/files/Child_Marriage_and_the_Law%281%29.pdf> accessed 26 August 2021; Jain Saranga, and Kathleen Kurz, *New Insights on Preventing Child Marriage: A Global Analysis of Factors and Programs* (International Centre for Research on Women, 2007) <https://www.icrw.org/files/publications/New-Insights-on-Preventing-ChildMarriage.pdf> accessed 26 August 2021; John Mukum Mbaku, 'International Law and Child Marriage in Africa' (2020) 7 Indon J Int'l & Comp L 103; Maria Polyakova, 'Child Marriage and Female Educational Attainment: A Complex Relationship' (2018) 46 Atl Econ J 475; Michael Addaney and Onuora-Oguno Azubike, 'Education as a Contrivance to Ending Child Marriage in Africa: Perspective from Nigeria and Uganda' (2017) 9 Amsterdam LF 110; Belinda Maswikwa,

In response to the problem of child marriage across the word, numerous international agreements were adopted which required state parties to prohibit child marriage by setting a minimum age for marriage in their national laws.[28] The recommended minimum age for marriage is 18 years. However, in special circumstances and with the authorization of a court of law, marriage can be allowed between the ages of 16 and 18 years.[29] Studies have found that the minimum marital age laws have helped to reduce the rates of child marriage in various countries.[30] However, there remain high rates of child marriage across the globe. Hence, the law needs to respond to social realities, and not have a universal imperialistic understanding of abolishing child marriage laws altogether. There is a need for more robust legal approaches against child marriage. What this paper argues is that beyond the minimum marital age laws, there is a need for the law to address the socio-cultural and religious factors that continue to foster child marriage in countries of the global south.

The paper is divided into five sections. After this introduction, sections two, three, and four explore the key drivers of child marriage in the three country contexts—Nigeria, Uganda, and India. The discussions make a comparative approach, highlighting the legal-socio-cultural contexts to help situate our understanding and critique of different legal and policy responses. Finally, section five concludes with recommendations, opening up more sightlines for legal pluralism for countries with similar contexts within the Global South.

Linda Richter, Jay Kaufman and Arijit Nandi, 'Minimum Marriage Age Laws and the Prevalence of Child Marriage and Adolescent Birth: Evidence from Sub-Saharan Africa' (2015) 41(2) International Perspectives on Sexual and Reproductive Health 58; Jennifer McCleary-Sills, Lucia Hanmer, Jennifer Parsons and Jeni Klugman 'Child Marriage: A Critical Barrier to Girls' Schooling and Gender Equality in Education' (2015) 13(3) The Review of Faith & International Affairs 69; Kayode Olatunbosun Fayokun, 'Legality of Child Marriage in Nigeria and Inhibitions against Realisation of Education Rights' (2015) 12 US-China L Rev 812; Ryan Rambudhan, 'For Those without a Voice: An International Plan to Reduce Child Marriage' (2013) 3 Impunity Watch Ann Rev 49; Judith-Ann Walker, (n 3).

[28] These include the 1995 Beijing Platform and Declaration for Action, the 1979 Convention on the Elimination of All Forms of Discrimination against Women, the 1962 Convention on Consent to Marriage, Minimum Age for Marriage, and Registration of Marriages, the 1989 Convention on the Rights of the Child and the 1948 Universal Declaration of Human Rights.

[29] Committee on the Elimination of Discrimination against Women and Committee on the Rights of the Child, 'Joint General Recommendation/General Comment No. 31 of the Committee on the Elimination of Discrimination against Women; General comment no. 18 of the Committee on the Rights of the Child on Harmful Practices' <http://tbinternet.ohchr.org/_layouts/treatybodyexternal/TBSearch.aspx?Lang=en&SymbolNo=CEDAW/C/GC/31/CRC/C/GC/18> accessed 26 August 2021.

[30] Belinda Maswikwa et al., (n 27); Kim Minzee, Wesley Longhofer, Elizabeth Heger Boyle, and Hollie Nyseth Brehm, 'When Do Laws Matter? National Minimum-Age-of-Marriage Laws, Child Rights, and Adolescent Fertility, 1989–2007' (2013) 47(3) Law & Society Review 589.

12.2 Indian Perspective

India has the largest number of child brides in the world, approximately one-third of the global count.[31] Children being married off at young age can be subjected to violations of their fundamental human rights, including their right to self-determination. In India a lot of communities practice marrying their children, although girls remain more vulnerable to being married off before they attain majority. Many such girls are married/ or sold off by their parents or guardians even before they can truly attain physical or mental maturity to undertake such responsibility or handle health and otherwise consequences as a result of such alliances. It is recorded that the degree of child marriage among boys is one-sixth of that of girls.[32] While the number of child marriages across world decreased slightly[33] over last few decades, the grave impact of pandemic may roll this development back extremely fast keeping many more girls in the position of 'at-risk'. Child brides girls are sold (often in the guise of marriage, or trafficked[34]) by their own protectors, guardians, and parents for pittance[35] owing to reasons of poverty as well as the perception of seeing Girl Child as a '*burden*', financial, or otherwise. The parents in Indian society are often riddled with burdens like saving enough for the *Dowry* for the marriage of girl children as soon as they are born.[36] Further, girl is seen as an additional emotional burden because she is prone to be (so-easily and commonly) sexually exploited or may even be raped—hence marrying off the Daughter's early, when they are '*still-pure and virgins*' save the parents and larger families the social outcast by the community. In rural areas which remain afar from development seen via urbanization, child marriage remains a norm, in spite of the clear prohibition via the laws.[37]

Once again the patriarchal norms and consequent attaching inferior status to girl child also results in female foeticide in India on large scale,[38] even though sex determination of foeticide remains illegal in India. Prolonged practice of foeticide has also resulted in a sex-ratio divide,[39] more evident in few states of India. This further

---

[31] UNICEF, "Ending Child Marriage and Adolescent Empowerment" (www.unicef.org) <https://www.unicef.org/india/what-we-do/end-child-marriage> accessed March 4, 2023.

[32] UNICEF, "Child Marriage" (*Unicef.org* 2016) <https://www.unicef.org/protection/child-marriage> accessed 4 March 2023.

[33] From one in four girls at risk to now one in five. For details, Infra n. 10.

[34] Indian girls sold in package deals to Gulf for as low as 150 dollars each. Refer, https://www.reuters.com/article/us-india-trafficking-marriage-idUSKBN1CF1F7.

[35] Many cases of selling girls by poor parents themselves are recorded in India. Refer https://www.indiatoday.in/india/story/andhra-pradesh-parents-sell-12-year-old-girl-rs-10-000-fund-treatment-other-daughter-1773639-2021-02-27.

[36] S. Anukriti, Sungoh Kwon, Nishith Prakash, Saving for dowry: Evidence from rural India, Journal of Development Economics, Elsevier (2021), available at: https://www.sciencedirect.com/science/article/abs/pii/S0304387821001176?dgcid=rss_sd_all.

[37] Prohibition of Marriage Act; Hindu Marriage Act; POCSO.

[38] Refer, https://pha.berkeley.edu/2021/04/10/un-natural-selection-female-feticide-in-india/

[39] With only 900 females against 1000 males as per 2013–2015 data by government through Niti Aayog. Refer https://www.niti.gov.in/content/sex-ratio-females-1000-males.

has aggravated a need among the (discarded/left-out) males to buy the brides,[40] often much younger from them from the other states in India. Girls, still adolescent, with no education (primary or otherwise) and ignorant of their fundamental human rights are often bargained, sold, purchased being the lowest in social hierarchy bear the brunt and long-term impact of such social status which can be avoided through combating child marriage.

The pandemic has been merciless for developing and under-developed nation states and India is no different. It has worsened the situation economically for the marginalized population, migrant workers, rural population. UNICEF states, in addition to 100 million girls who were expected to be married before their eighteenth birthday globally, due to pandemic, it is estimated that a 10 million more girls are at risk[41] and India is home to more than one-third of the child brides globally.

a. **The Confluence of Child Marriage Laws and Customary Practice: Issues and Challenges in India**

Child marriage remains an acceptable and age-old tradition in India. In spite of prohibitions in law, it has been given customary, religious, and cultural assent of population at large. Child marriage victims suffer devastatingly long-term negative effects impacting their right to health and well-being, viz., emotional-physical-mental but also violates their long-term economic, educational, and livelihood independence. Most affected victims remain girl children, whose *Kanyadan*[42] at a young age results in their deprivation of their basic human rights. Furthermore, the prohibitions on legal age of marriage are side-lined by scanty implementation of laws and contrasting acceptance within each religious and cultural groups. Child marriage propositions often also overlap with other crimes against young girls, like, marriage proposals to sell-purchase such young girls in the guise of marriage can be a cover for an eventual technique of trafficking young girls into the sex trade and labor both within and outside the country. In regions like Delhi, Haryana, Uttar Pradesh, and Kolkata, children are married, kidnapped, and forced to labor.[43] In some states, an imbalance in the sex ratio[44] is emerging as a justification for the trafficking of young girls for marriage purposes.

---

40 Refer https://theprint.in/india/mol-ki-bahuein-the-women-haryanas-men-buy-as-brides/549641/.

41 UNICEF, "10 Million Additional Girls at Risk of Child Marriage due to COVID-19" (www.unicef.orgMarch 7, 2021) <https://www.unicef.org/press-releases/10-million-additional-girls-risk-child-marriage-due-covid-19> accessed December 4, 2022.

42 Ritual practiced in Hindu marriages, symbolically representing 'Giving away of girl child in marriage by parents'—although Daan is means to donate. So (controversial) verbatim meaning, 'girl donation' and hence traditionally accepting a view of keeping a girl child akin to property that can be given away.

43 "Child Marriage in India: A Study of Situation, Causes & Enforcement of Prohibition of Child Marriage Act" (*Niti.gov.in*).

44 Female foeticide in India is rampant resulting in alarming sex-ratio imbalance in few States. UNFPA, "Characteristics of Sex-Ratio Imbalance in India, and Future Scenarios" (UNFPA 2007) <https://www.unfpa.org/sites/default/files/resource-pdf/india_0.pdf> accessed December 4, 2022.

Societal, customary, and social acceptance of child marriage has always conflicted with the prohibitive measures in India to combat the same. History of such prohibitive action can be seen as far as the Sarda Act way in 1929[45] which prohibited child marriage of girls below 15 years of age and boys below 18 years of age. This Act was amended later on in 1978 to increase the subsequent ages of girls to 18 years old and boys to 21 years old. The Child Marriage Restraint Act of 1929[46] was the name given to the altered statute. The old law was repealed in 2006, and a new one was enacted called the Prohibition of Child Marriage Act, 2006,[47] which included harsh penalties for those who engaged in such practises, as well as the creation of a cadre of officers known as Child Marriage Prohibition Officers to monitor and work toward its prevention.

Given that India is home to every third child marriage, these figures have serious consequences for the country. While evidence is limited on exact number of child marriages, indirect evidences reinforce similar concerns. A special initiative in India via creating a dedicated phone line for children in distress called 'Childline' was able to record such aggravated number of phone calls during the time of pandemic. For example, 5,584 distress calls were made about child marriage between May and July 2020, reflecting a 33% rise in reports of child marriage to ChildLine between January and June 2019.[48] Jejeebhoy cites analyses of pandemic-related child marriages data from different states in India (Table 12.1).[49]

In India, due to cultural and traditional pressures besides poverty, several castes and tribes marry off their girls while they are quite young. Having a puberty-aged girl still living at home is considered a source of shame for the family, as it implies that the parents failed to find a suitable boy and fulfill their parental role and obligation. Furthermore, in many societies, a female's education is unlikely to be valued as highly as marriage and motherhood, and many cultures place a strong priority on female chastity.[50] Finally, in societies where dowry is highly ingrained, parents may believe

---

[45] "Child Marriage in India: A Study of Situation, Causes & Enforcement of Prohibition of Child Marriage Act" (*Niti.gov.in*) <https://niti.gov.in/planningcommission.gov.in/docs/reports/genrep/Report_Child_Marriage_in_India.pdf> accessed September 4, 2021.

[46] The Child Marriage Restraint Act, 1929 (No. 19 of 1929 dated 1st April, 1930).

[47] The Prohibition of Child Marriage Act, 2006 (No. 6 of 2007 dated 10th January, 2007).

[48] Deepika Bahl, Shalini Bassi and Monika Arora, "The Impact of COVID-19 on Children and Adolescents: Early Evidence in India" (www.orfonline.org March 4, 2021) <https://www.orfonline.org/research/the-impact-of-covid-19-on-children-and-adolescents-early-evidence-in-india/> accessed September 4, 2021.

[49] Shireen Jejeebhoy, "Child Marriages during the Pandemic" (*theindiaforum.in* July 2, 2021) <https://www.theindiaforum.in/article/child-marriages-during-pandemic> accessed December 4, 2022.

[50] Many news reports have reported on the customary practice of Bride Test/Virginity Test/Chastity test. Refer https://www.indiatoday.in/latest-headlines/story/brides-undergo-chastity-test-in-rajasthan-76133-2010-06-08; Also refer, https://asiatimes.com/2019/03/virginity-test-still-haunts-some-indian-brides/; Refer, https://www.indiatoday.in/lifestyle/what-s-hot/story/virginity-test-bride-groom-wedding-night-kanjarbhat-community-first-night-blood-hymen-1152349-2018-01-23; refer, https://www.business-standard.com/article/current-affairs/this-400-year-old-custom-still-forces-virginity-tests-on-brides-in-india-118022100133_1.html;

Table 12.1 Child marriage during the pandemic print and electronic media reports

Date, Author	Title	Location	Change over time
30.4.21 TOI	Covid school closures leads to rise in child marriages in Tamil Nadu's Nilgiris district	Nilgiris, Tamil Nadu	5 marriages stopped
10.4.21 Gupta, The New IE	Covid pandemic led to 27% rise in child marriage	Telangana	27% increase in child marriages averted: from 977 in Feb 2019–March 2020 to 1355 in April 2020–March 2021
24.3.21 Nair, TOI	More child marriage, rise in perversity in pandemic	Maharashtra	51 cases in parts of Baramati and Pune, March 3030-March 2021, even 13–14-year-olds, done surreptitiously; also forced marriage of older girls
25.12.20 Yadav, The Print	How 2 UP girls got their weddings called off as child marriage bids see rise during pandemic	UP	(Quoting ChildLine). Increase in child marriage complaints over 2020, role of teachers crucial. Bulandshahr got 24 distress calls in Aug–Dec 2020 compared to 2 in the same period of 2019, 7 in 2018, 4 in 2017
12.20, Dutta, The Hindu	Pandemic, poverty spur child marriage in MP	MP	46 to 117 (11.2019–3.2020 to 4.2020–6.2020)
17.11.20 Sahu, Scroll	Child marriages were declining in Odisha. Then Covid-19 pandemic struck	Odisha	Economic hardship and social vulnerability. While factors pushing children into marriage strengthened, the system to detect and prevent child marriage has weakened as frontline workers occupied in Covid related work
10.20, Banerjee, National Herald 10.20	Child marriage surge during and after the lockdown, official figures top of the iceberg	MP, Chhattisgarh	Childline reports, 11.2019–3.2020 to 4.2020–6.2020: MP 46 to 117 Chhattisgarh: 18 to 58

Source Jejeebhoy, "Child Marriages during the Pandemic", theIndiaforum

that marrying off their daughter at a young age will reduce the costs of marriage. To protect the community's culture and religious beliefs, most 'pundits, or God Men, or community leaders' promote the practice of child marriage. Due to the community's high regard for such religious or village heads, most families yield to the pressure and engage in child marriage.

Indian central legislation prohibits any solemnization of child marriages under '*Prohibition of Child Marriage Act*', (Hereinafter mentioned as PCMA) and defines solemnization with girl under the age of 18, or the boy under the age of 21 as child marriage.[51] However, confusion and duality is often created because this 'prohibitions' can be overridden and accepted as '*voidable marriage*'[52] by the statute as well as via judicial pronouncements in the light of the personal laws. The child marriage to be void, the grounds are very limited and specific in the statute (PCMA), which provides for where such child might be kidnapped/trafficked or compelled to marry under force or deceit, coercion, etc.[53] PCMA also penalizes the guardians/adults/parents who failed in preventing such marriages.[54] Still in India the law fails against the menace of child marriage as the '*law is by itself rather segmented*' and '*rankled with contradictions*'.[55]

While in India, consensual sex below minimum age is seen as statutory rape, it remains unsanctioned if the girl was married.[56] It further creates confusion even in the cases of some positive legislations, not helping the case of child marriage and allied issues. Protection of Children from Sexual Offence Act, 2012 (POCSO) criminalizes any consensual sex with/between minors.[57] But most of the times, the complaints and allegations under POCSO are made by the parents themselves against their eloped children, especially if these marriages are outside the strict compatibility of religion and caste.[58] As India is a party to CEDAW, the Criminal (Amendment) Act 2013 increased the 'age of consent' from 16 to 18,[59] which was seen as a positive move to protect the children, although, duality with law and implementation was seen in this effect also. Hon'ble Supreme Court in Independent Thought v. Union of India read down the exception to Section 375 which allowed the men to consummate marriage with their brides between 15 and 18 years, such brides still don't have freedom to exercise the option of consent in such cases. The law prohibits sex below 18 years (even if she is married) and after 18 years, the law presumes matrimonial consent, hence the girl doesn't have a freedom to say no.[60] Both age of consent and marital

---

[51] Section 12.2(a), The Prohibition of Child Marriage Act, 2006 (No. 6 of 2007 dated 10th January 2007).

[52] Section 12.3, The Prohibition of Child Marriage Act, 2006. The only exception is recent amendment in Karnataka and Haryana States to define under-age marriage Void.

[53] Section 12, The Prohibition of Child Marriage Act, 2006.

[54] Section 9, 10, 11 The Prohibition of Child Marriage Act, 2006.

[55] Final Report of Red Elephant Foundation, Submission to OHCHR, Child Marriages in India, Abbhi et. al., December 2013.

[56] Ibid; Refer also, UNICEF Background Paper on State of World Children, 2007.

[57] Chapter II, POCSO, 2012.

[58] Pitre, Lingam, *Infra* n. 39. Indian society rigidly follows endogamy within Caste & religion boundaries. There are grave instances of exogamous marriages resulting in Honour Killings in India.

[59] From 1940 to 2012, the age of consent was 16 years for girls and any sexual activity constituted Rape with the exception of when such a girl is married and is 15 years or older. Refer Indian Penal Code 1860.

[60] Deswal V., Need to revisit the concept of age of consent, Nov 2019. https://timesofindia.indiatimes.com/blogs/legally-speaking/need-to-revisit-the-concept-of-age-of-consent/.

rape exception (in India and Uganda) have their roots in colonial legacy.[61] The laws and its enforcement and implementation remains fixated in male patriarchal norm setting. Poor economic status of Indian population, Caste-Religion-based endogamous matrimonial alliances, and culturally-approved arranged marriage makes it even harder to break the vicious cycle of child marriage. While a poor family may agree to 'marry-off' their daughter due to possible economic debts or bad harvest to ease off financial burden on the family as a whole, it creates a chain of weaker families, compromised health care, non-accessibility to basic education, poor economic and bargaining status of such child brides in their matrimonial home. Such child brides often bear children of their own while they are themselves minors and such children again are more prone to being married off, trafficked, or sold, especially if they are girls, resulting in a cycle of intergenerational inequality.[62]

The legislations particularizing child marriage further creates discrepancies with the collated reading of Indian personal laws. Among Hindu's majority population in India, the personal law of Hindu Marriage Act, 1955 (HMA), affirms valid age of marriage for bride and groom to be 18 and 21 respectively but is silent on defining marriages under these ages as Void. Judiciary has on occasions provided 'sanctions' for child marriage but remains silent again on calling such marriages under HMA void.[63]

Similarly, under Muslim personal laws child marriage is not clearly prohibited. A guardian also has the legal authority to marry off minor. The pair does, however, have the 'option of puberty,' also known as khayar-ul-bulugh, where they can refuse to accept the marriage once they reach puberty.[64] They must, however, do so before reaching the age of 18 and only if the marriage has not yet been completed. Under Muslim law, marriage begins at the age of puberty, which is 15 years old. Marriage under the age of seven, even if convened by a legal guardian, is void from the start.

Indian Christian Marriage Act (ICMA) also allows for child marriage. The requirement being that a preliminary notification be published 14 days prior to the wedding. After the time limit has passed, the parties are free to marry without the agreement of their guardians.[65] This very lack of consent and mutual agreement further aggravates the conundrum as more children are forced into engaging in the nuptials.

---

[61] Amita Pitre & Lakshmi Lingam Age of consent: challenges and contradictions of sexual violence laws in India, Sexual and Reproductive Health Matters, 29:2, (2022). available at https://www.tandfonline.com/doi/full/10.1080/26410397.2021.1878656.

[62] Supra n. 54.

[63] Delhi High Court in Jitender Kumar Sharma v. State & Anr. (2010), held, "*It is clear that where, earlier, a child marriage may not have been voidable under personal law, as in the case of the Hindu Marriage Act, by virtue of the Section 12.3 of the Prohibition of Child marriage Act, it has explicitly been made voidable at the option of the child spouse. But nobody other than a party to the marriage can petition for its annulment.*"; Also refer- https://www.thehindu.com/news/cities/Madurai/child-marriages-do-not-become-void-sans-court-order/article8316750.ece.

[64] Mustafa v. Smt Khursida, AIR 2006 Raj 31.

[65] Policy brief, Ending Impunity for Child Marriage in India, Centre for Law and Policy Research & Centre for Reproductive Rights NY, 2018.

Judicial trends repeatedly stress regarding the overriding effect of central legislations in India like PCMA and POCSO over personal laws. However, the decisions often are laced with discrepancies from one High Court to another which further augments the inconsistencies. The PCMA overrides personal laws, according to the Delhi High Court in *Lajja v State.*[66] In *Seema Beghum v State*[67] in 2013, the Karnataka High Court reaffirmed this view. In the case of *Yusuf Ibrahim Mohammad Lokhat v State of Gujarat*,[68] however, it was held in 2014 that according to Muslim personal law, a girl is competent to marry without the approval of her parents no sooner than she reaches puberty or completes 15 years, whichever is earlier. This obviously demonstrates that, in the opinion of the learned judges, personal laws should be used as the principal basis for deciding cases of child marriage. The Madras High Court ruled in 2015 that the PCMA applies to all communities and is not in conflict with Islamic law. There have been no Supreme Court decisions that have resolved this issue. As a result, there is still a state of ambiguity and irregularity. The courts need to protect the interest of children and ensure that any ambiguity is removed which may hinder implementation of laws against child marriage. However, child marriage remains a culturally imbedded practice, where mere State laws can't help in bringing attitudinal transformation. Therefore, legal pluralism must be acknowledged to balance the interaction of the State, religious as well as customary laws for protection of best interest of the children. It is established how child marriage can have lasting consequence on health, economic strength, education, and human rights of children. To bring in a zero-tolerance to child marriage, enforcement agencies must look at grass root advocacy, which will ensure that heterogeneous societal strata will also embrace zero-tolerance to child marriage. At the same time, the laws and the Courts interpreting the intent of law must also clarify the position of underage voidable marriages. There must be all endeavors to ensure that any new solemnized child marriages are stated to be void. In a social-cultural setting of India, authors understand that declaring all child marriages to be void may pose greater difficulty to such woman who married as a child because of the societal-structural issues. Any marriage which if declared void after years of staying in marriage may be detrimental to her, and may even result in stripping of any marital, social, and financial securities that a woman may otherwise get. At the same time, in a stark contrast vulnerable girls who are married off underage will rarely have the power to declare their marriages to be void and succumb to their fate. Balancing the interest of both classes remains vital. It is argued that child marriages are not given validity in the initial phase of getting married itself which may be coupled with a strict enforcement of prohibitory child marriage laws, can yield long term positive result in the larger interest of children. This can be made possible with small steps like sensitization, compulsory registration of marriages, etc., and strict implementation of registering marriages in India. Registration and community sensitization may be addressed through effective

[66] *Lajja Devi* v. *State,* W.P. (Crl.) No.338/2008, H.C. Del., 27 July 2012.

[67] *Seema Begum v. State of Karnataka,* W.P. 75889 of 2013, H.C. Kar., 26 Feb. 2013.

[68] *Yusuf Ibrahim Mohammad Lokhat v State of Gujarat,* R/CR.MA/13658/2014, H.C. Guj., 14 Oct. 2014.

enforcement, which must start at the grassroots instead of a trickle down approach.

Compulsory Registration of Marriages in India: A Step in Right Direction?

In 2017, the Indian Law Commission published a study titled 'Compulsory Registration of Marriages,'[69] which indicated marriages must be registered in each state and acknowledged how child marriage is still common in many sections of the country. Compulsory registration and its implementation can help in tracking child marriage and can prove to be a step in the right direction. Such registrations can also help poor uneducated population against the trafficking traps. It is not surprising to note that there is also an inherent relation between child marriage and trafficking as more often than not, the girl child is sold to brothels and trafficking rings in the garb of child marriage.[70] The border district of North 24 Parganas in West Bengal[71] has long been a major trafficking crossroads in India. Because of the district's porous border with Bangladesh, it has become a hotbed for trafficking girls and women. Within a month of 'unlocking,' as many as 12 child weddings took place in Hingalgunj block[72] alone. Marriage proposals are made to particularly vulnerable families, and it is believed that these are only a ploy for human trafficking. Poor families are forced to choose between two dreadful evils (child marriage or selling young offspring, resulting in trafficking) when and all sources of their money dry up. Despite the penal sanctions of such actions, such families have acknowledged to marrying off their offspring as described earlier in this section.

Each marriage being have to officially registered will leave a trail and help in avoiding illegal buying/purchasing of children and especially brides and hence can considerably contribute toward reducing the exploitation of children at large. Further, the various laws (Central or Personal legislations) also need a relook with the lens of socio-cultural realities of Indian population at large ensuring no exploitation of children be allowed, including getting children married off early by their own guardians.

The next section will explore similarly placed case study of Nigeria from the Global South where the problem of child marriage is severe. It will also highlight the commonalities with the Indian case study, in line with the comparative approach of this article.

---

[69] Law Commission of India, "Compulsory Registration of Marriages" (2007) <https://lawcommissionofindia.nic.in/reports/Report270.pdf> accessed December 5, 2022.

[70] Trafficking includes trafficking for the purpose of marriage. Trafficking in Persons (Prevention, Care and Rehabilitation) Bill, 2021.

[71] Shantanu Ray, "Bengal New Epicentre of Human Trafficking" (*The Sunday Guardian Live* January 14, 2018) <https://www.sundayguardianlive.com/news/12400-bengal-new-epicentre-human-trafficking> accessed September 5, 2021.

[72] Soumashree Sen, "Child Marriage or Trafficking: Choice Covid-19 and Cyclone Amphan Have Left for Bengal's Vulnerable" (*news18.com* August 12, 2020) <https://www.news18.com/news/buzz/child-marriage-or-trafficking-choice-covid-19-and-cyclone-amphan-have-left-for-bengals-vulnerable-2780323.html> accessed December 5, 2022.

12.3 The Influence of Religion on Child Marriage in Nigeria

The case study of child marriage in Nigeria is important because by 2050, Nigeria is forecast to have the highest absolute number of child brides in Africa, while Sub-Saharan Africa will likely have the highest overall number of child brides worldwide.[73] With an estimate of about 22 million child brides, Nigeria currently has one of the highest rates of child marriage in the entire globe.[74] To give a better perspective, about 43% of Nigerian girls are married off before they turn 18, of which 17% are married off before the age of 15.[75] However, child marriage is most common in the North West and North East of Nigeria with prevalence rates of up to 76%.[76]

The high rates of child marriage in Nigeria are attributed to factors such as poverty, illiteracy, political instability, armed conflicts and forced displacements, and harmful traditional and religious practices.[77] One of the contentions of this paper is that these high prevalence rates are also attributable to weak legal frameworks which do not effectively address the socio-cultural and religious factors that foster child marriage in Nigeria. Hence, the Nigerian legal framework needs to incorporate socio-legal approaches that can address the conflicting customary and religious child marriage laws in Nigeria.

Nigeria has one of the most comprehensive legal frameworks for child's rights protection in Africa.[78] In 2003, Nigeria enacted the Child Rights Act (CRA) which domesticates the UN Convention on the Rights of the Child (CRC) and the African Charter on the Rights and Welfare of the Child (African Children's Charter). However, the high rate of child marriages in Nigeria has spanned for decades and given rise to debates on the effectiveness of Nigeria's legal framework for addressing child marriage. These debates often stem from some inconsistencies in the child

[73] UNICEF, *Ending Child Marriage: Progress and Prospects* (2017) 7 <https://data.unicef.org/resources/ending-child-marriage-progress-and-prospects/> accessed 26 August 2021.

[74] UNICEF, (n 3) 5; UNICEF, *The State of the World's Children: Children in a Digital World* (December 2017) <https://www.unicef.org/reports/state-worlds-children-2017> accessed 28 August 2021; Jacob Wale Mobolaji, et al. (n 5) 2.

[75] Girls Not Brides, 'Country Profile-Nigeria' <https://atlas.girlsnotbrides.org/map/nigeria/> accessed 26 November 2022.

[76] Association for Reproductive and Family Health, 'Child Marriage: An Unending Abomination in Nigeria' (2018) <https://arfh-ng.org/news-stories/child-marriage-an-unending-abomination-in-nigeria/> accessed 26 April 2023; Girls Not Brides, ibid.

[77] Dyan Mazurana, Anastasia Marshak and Kinsey Spears, 'Child Marriage in Armed Conflict' (2019) 101 Int'l Rev Red Cross 575; Jennifer Parsons et al., (n 18); Tim S. Braimah, (n 6), 482–485; E. A. Agege, E. U. Nwosu, S. Odjimogbo and E. O. Igumbor, 'Legalities of Child Marriage in Nigeria: Implications on Health and Strategies of Prevention' (2017) Oat <https://www.oatext.com/legalities-of-child-marriage-in-nigeria-implications-on-health-and-strategies-of-prevention.php> accessed 26 April 2023; Girls Not Brides, (n 74).

[78] Tim S. Braimah, ibid, 474.

marriage laws in Nigeria which enable the persistence of child marriage under customary and religious laws.[79]

The prohibition against child marriage is entrenched in Section 23 of the CRA which provides that 'a person under the age of 18 is incapable of contracting a valid marriage. If such a marriage does take place, it should be declared null and void and of no effect'. However, Nigeria does not have a clear legal definition of a child. While the CRA adopts the international legal definition of a child as a person under the age of 18,[80] other legislations adopt definitions which are sometimes contradictory. For instance, Section 29(1) of the 1999 Constitution[81] defines a person of 'full age' as follows:

(a) 'full age' means the age of eighteen years and above;
(b) any woman who is married shall be deemed to be of full age.

Based on Section 29(1)(a), a child is anyone who is below 18 years. However, the implication of Section 29(1)(b) is that married women who are below the age of 18 cannot be deemed as children in law. This provision of the Nigerian Constitution has been heavily criticized for contributing to the problem of child marriage in Nigeria.[82] This is, in part, because such inconsistencies in the law undermine the law's effectiveness against customary and religious child marriage practices.[83]

Childhood is generally understood as a social and political construct.[84] Studies have shown that since the precolonial era, childhood in Nigeria has generally been defined based on the social and cultural values of the various ethnic groups in Nigeria.[85] Hence, attempts by the British colonial administration to impose a unitary definition of a child in Nigeria proved futile due to the existence of conflicting customary and religious laws.[86] In the post-colonial era, attempts to adopt a unitary definition of a child have been significantly undermined by the inconsistencies in the state law. Such inconsistencies weaken the state law against contradictory customary and religious definitions of a child. For want of space, this paper will focus on the issues with the application of Islamic conceptions of a child in Northern Nigeria.

---

79 See for instance, Enyinna S Nwauche, 'Child Marriage in Nigeria: (Il)Legal and (Un)Constitutional' (2015) 15 Afr Hum Rts LJ 421; Tim S. Braimah, ibid.

80 Section 20 of the Child Rights Act 2003.

81 The Constitution of the Federal Republic of Nigeria 1999 (as amended) Cap 23 Laws of the Federation 2004.

82 See for instance, Ibe Okegbe Ifeakandu, 'Child Trafficking and Rights Violations: Examination of Child Protection under International and Nigeria Legal Provisions' (2019) 10 Beijing L Rev 1078, 1080; Kayode Olatunbosun Fayokun, (n 18); E. A. Agege et al., (n 26); Association for Reproductive and Family Health, (n 25).

83 Alexis Foua and Wilson Diriwari, (n 24), 14.

84 Dyan Mazurana et al., (n 78), 578.

85 Alexis Foua and Wilson Diriwari, (n 24), 13; Saheed Aderinto, 'Researching Colonial Childhoods: Images and Representation of Children in Nigerian Newspapers Press, 1925–1950' (2012) 39 History in Africa 241, 242.

86 Alexis Foua and Wilson Diriwari, ibid, 14.

The focus on Northern Nigeria is mainly due to the high rates of child marriage in the region.

In Islamic law, the period of childhood ends when a person begins to show signs of puberty such as menstruation.[87] Hence, the age of childhood varies for boys and girls, and may be dependent on the circumstances of each child.[88] The Islamic definition of a child conflicts with the provisions of the CRA. As a result, several northern states of Nigeria, where Islamic law is widely applied, have been reluctant to adopt the CRA into their state laws.[89] The contention of these northern states is that the provisions of the CRA are contrary to their Islamic beliefs and, thus, in breach of their right to freedom of religion.[90] As Toyo observes, these arguments raise the question of 'whose interpretation, knowledge, and values matter in situations where practices embedded in cultural traditions define social realities'.[91]

Since, under the Nigerian Constitution, the federal government is not given exclusive or concurrent jurisdiction over matters relating to child protection, each federating-state in Nigeria is allowed to adopt the CRA with amendments reflecting the cultural and religious values of the state.[92] To reflect their Islamic values, northern states such as Jigawa State adopted child rights laws which defined a child based on Islamic law. While Section 15(1) of the Jigawa State Child Rights Law 2006 prohibits child marriage, Section12.2(1) of the law narrows the prohibition by defining a child as a person below the age of puberty. That is, the prohibition against child marriage in Jigawa State only applies to children who have not begun to show signs of puberty. The implication being that a child who has begun puberty (which can be as early as 8 years)[93] can be married under the law in Jigawa State. As a result of such laws, the problem of child marriage has remained unabated in various states of northern Nigeria. In fact, such laws have been used to justify, rather than prohibit, child marriage. The case of a Nigerian legislator's marriages to child brides is a good example.

---

[87] Tim S. Braimah, (n 6), 481.

[88] Dyan Mazurana et al., (n 78), 578; Enyinna S Nwauche, (n 29), 428.

[89] Kingsley O. Mrabure and Mudiaga K. Ovakporae, 'Unabated Menace of Child Marriage in Nigeria. The Need for an Enabling Constitutional Provision' (2020) 98 JL Pol'y & Globalization 179, 189; Nkoyo Toyo, (n 24), 1299.

[90] Armstrong Ukwuoma, *Child marriage in Nigeria: The Health Hazards and Socio-Legal Implications (X-Raying The Human Rights & Development Issues in Girl-Child Early Marriage)* (No To Violence Initiative (NOTVI) and International Centre for Development & Budget Advocacy, 2014) 53–54; Kingsley O, Mrabure and Mudiaga K, Ovakporae, (n 40), 189; Enyinna S Nwauche, (n 29), 429; Tim S. Braimah, (n 6), 482.

[91] Nkoyo Toyo, (n 24), 1299.

[92] See the Second Schedule of the 1999 Constitution (n 82).

[93] Belinda Pinyerd and William B. Zipf, 'Puberty – Timing is Everything!' (2005) 20(2) Journal of Pediatric Nursing 75, 75; NHS 'Stages of Puberty: What Happens to Boys and Girls' (16 November 2018) <https://www.nhs.uk/live-well/sexual-health/stages-of-puberty-what-happens-to-boys-and-girls/> accessed 16 October 2021.

In 2006, Senator Ahmad Yerima was reported to have divorced his 17-year-old fourth wife in order to marry another child bride.[94] The girl who was 15 at the time of her marriage to Yerima was nursing his child when he decided to divorce her. By 2010, the Senator got married to a 13-year-old Egyptian girl, after allegedly paying a dowry of $100,000.[95] This marriage raised an uproar across the country. However, the Senator justified his actions on the basis of his religious belief and claimed that he had done nothing wrong.[96]

The Supreme Council for Shari'a in Nigeria (the Council), which initiated legal action against the federal government of Nigeria and the National Assembly to invalidate some provisions of the CRA, including Section 21 which sets the minimum age for marriage at 18 years, backed up the senator's claims. The Council argued that the Holy Quran and the traditions of the Holy Prophet Muhammad were in support of Yerima's marriage to the girl, and the CRA contravened his right to freedom of religion and right to private and family life among others.[97] The actions of the Council show the role that religious institutions play in fostering child marriage practices.

Despite the high rates of child marriage in Nigeria, customary and religious child marriage laws are significantly responsible for the low prosecution and conviction rates for child marriage.[98] As Braimah points out, 'although Ahmad Yerima's conduct seemed reprehensible there was nothing anyone could do about his marriage to the child'.[99] This is because the marriage was supported by Islamic law. Despite numerous calls to prosecute Yerima, the then Attorney-General of the Federation, Mohammed Bello Adoke, maintained that Yerima could not be prosecuted because his marriage was contracted under Islamic law.[100] Even the then deputy leader of the Senate, Ike Ekweremadu, noted that the issues involved in Yerima's controversial marriage went beyond the question of early marriage; it hinged on religion.[101] Due to the religious aspects of Yerima's marriage, not only was the Senate unable to reprimand Yerima but, Yerima also pressured the Senate to reverse a vote that seemed to outlaw child marriage.[102] The inability of Nigerian lawmakers to effectively address

[94] Ogunniran Iyabode, 'Child Bride and Child Sex: Combating Child Marriages in Nigeria' (2011) 2 Nnamdi Azikiwe U J Int'l L & Juris 85, 85.

[95] Tim S. Braimah, (n 6), 486; Al-Jazeera, 'Nigerian Senator Marries Girl of 13' (*Al-Jazeera,* 18 May 2010) <https://www.aljazeera.com/news/2010/5/18/nigerian-senator-marries-girl-of-13> accessed 1 September 2021.

[96] Tim S. Braimah, ibid, 486; Ogunniran Iyabode, (n 44), 85.

[97] Armstrong Ukwuoma, (n 41), 53–54; Enyinna S Nwauche, (n 29), 429.

[98] Kingsley O. Mrabure and Mudiaga K. Ovakporae, (n 40), 190.

[99] Tim S. Braimah, (n 26), 486.

[100] Tim S. Braimah, ibid, 486.

[101] Afua Hirsch, 'Nigerian Senator who 'Married Girl of 13' Accused of Breaking Child Rights Act' (The Guardian, 25 July 2013) <https://www.theguardian.com/world/2013/jul/25/nigeria-senator-accused-child-bride> accessed 1 September 2021.

[102] Ini Ekott, 'Yerima Makes Senate Back Underage Marriage, as Lawmakers Oppose Local Government Autonomy' (*Premium Times,* 17 July 2013) <https://www.premiumtimesng.com/news/141117-yerima-makes-senate-back-underage-marriage-as-lawmakers-oppose-local-government-autonomy.html> accessed 1 September 2021.

Yerima's child marriage reflects the law's failure to deal with the customary and religious practices that foster child marriage in Nigeria.

Despite the laudable provisions of the CRA, it has been unable to tackle the problem of child marriage in Nigeria mainly due to the non-acceptance of the law by northern States.[103] For these northern states to accept the CRA, state legal institutions would need to engage with Islamic institutions and religious leaders in order to adopt a definition of a child in Islamic law that would align with the provisions of the CRA. Such engagement needs to be hinged on the protection of the best interests of the child, rather than the mere imposition of the state law on Islamic law.[104] As scholars such as Mahmood have pointed out, the state often tries to reorganize religious life by stipulating what religion should be.[105] What is suggested in this paper is not the imposition of state conceptions of child marriage on Islam, but the renegotiation of the definitions of a child both in state law and in Islamic law. This would require an engagement with state institutions, Islamic institutions, traditional institutions, civil society organizations, family heads and, where possible, young people.

Since families are often involved in child marriage arrangements, some civil society organizations have pointed out the importance of increasing engagement with families.[106] It is also important to engage with young people. Such an engagement would bring to light the lived experiences of victims of child marriage and help to tailor interventions to the needs of the children. As the Chairman of the National Population Commission, Eze Duruiheoma, noted in relation to the protection of teenage girls, 'The society believes it knows the problem of the teenagers better and this approach runs against the conventional wisdom that he who wears the shoes knows where they pinch. No meaningful and sustainable programs for the improvement of the lives of the teenage girls can be achieved without their inputs and active participation'.[107] Measures need to be put in place for the involvement of children in the negotiation of interventions and policies against child marriage in Nigeria. However, steps need to be taken to ensure that such involvement of children is done ethically without putting the children at risk.

Considering the influence that religious and traditional institutions have on the members of their community, in order to address the issues of child marriage in Nigeria, it is also important for state institutions to work closely with religious and traditional leaders in arriving at a negotiated age for marriage. This is particularly important because traditional and religious leaders can play a significant role in sensitizing members of their community about who a child is and how the child should

---

[103] Kingsley O. Mrabure and Mudiaga K. Ovakporae, (n 40), 179; Tim S. Braimah, (n 6), 485.

[104] Alexis Foua and Wilson Diriwari, (n 15), 11.

[105] Saba Mahmood, *Religious Difference in a Secular Age: A Minority Report* (Princeton University Press, 2016) 210.

[106] See for instance, Coalition of Civil Society to End Child Marriage in Nigeria (8 December 2020) <https://www.facebook.com/ECMNigeria/photos/pb.109394843772213.-2207520000../420043012707393/?type=3&theater> accessed 16 October 2021.

[107] Nigeria Health Watch, 'NGOs Advocate for a Policy to Ban Child Marriage to Enhance Girl Child Education' (19 July 2016) <https://nigeriahealthwatch.com/ngos-advocate-for-a-policy-to-ban-child-marriage-to-enhance-girl-child-education/> accessed 16 October 2021.

be treated.[108] As the National *Coalition of Civil Society to End Child Marriage in Nigeria* has noted, 'individuals and families are usually guided by their religious beliefs and value the preaching of religious leaders. Hence religious leaders are in a strategic position to advocate for social and cultural change through their preachings and sermons by advocating for girls rights, sensitizing on the dangers of child marriage and collaborating with community leaders'.[109] Religious leaders can be critical actors in the fight against child marriage in Nigeria. Hence, they should be brought into conversations and into actions to end child marriage. This is particularly important in rural areas where rates of child marriage are high and yet children have less access to legal and educational institutions or other social amenities that could help them escape from child marriage.[110]

Some religious and traditional leaders have already begun to speak out against child marriage.[111] Hence, involving them in the negotiation of the 18 years minimum age for child marriage would accelerate the effect of the state laws. As Jody Sarich, Michele Olivier, and Kevin Bales point out, 'The question of local acceptance or legitimacy of legal rules is crucial to address the problem of forced and child marriages'.[112] This is because legal rules have little chance of being complied with in societies where they do not enjoy grassroot legitimacy.[113] In essence, when state laws do not reflect the values, beliefs, identities, perceived self-interests, and expectations of those they seek to bind, such laws are unlikely to be effective. Thus, for the state child marriage laws to be effective, they need to be relatable to the people. Engagement with traditional and religious leaders is one crucial way by which state child marriage laws can gain the legitimacy it needs at the grassroot.

However, it is important to bear in mind that the negotiation of issues of child marriage with traditional and religious institutions would not always be an easy task, especially due to the resulting cultural adjustments and religious implications. For instance, in light of the contribution of faith leaders in addressing women's rights issues related to HIV/AIDs and reproductive health, Judith-Ann Walker conducted a study which engaged Islamic scholars as opinion leaders on child marriage in Northern Nigeria.[114] The study found that despite attempts to clarify the need to

---

[108] Ibe Okegbe Ifeakandu, (n 32), 1081.

[109] Coalition of Civil Society to End Child Marriage in Nigeria (7 December 2020) <https://www.facebook.com/ECMNigeria/photos/pb.109394843772213.-2207520000../420043012707393/?type=3&theater> accessed 16 October 2021.

[110] Jody Sarich, Michele Olivier and Kevin Bales, (n 11), 465.

[111] Kingsley O. Mrabure and Mudiaga K. Ovakporae, (n 40), 190. See also, UN Women, 'Engaging Traditional Leaders to End Violence Against Women and Girls and Harmful Practices in Africa' (31 August 2020) <https://africa.unwomen.org/en/news-and-events/stories/2020/08/engaging-traditional-leaders-to-end-violence-against-women-and-girls-and-harmful-practices-in-africa> accessed 16 October 2021.

[112] Jody Sarich, Michele Olivier and Kevin Bales, (n 11), 472.

[113] Ibid.

[114] Judith-Ann Walker, 'Engaging Islamic Opinion Leaders on Child Marriage: Preliminary Results From Pilot Projects in Nigeria' (2015) 13(3) The Review of Faith and International Affairs 48.

address child marriage, there were still scepticisms based on the Islamic view on the age of marriage.

Muslim scholars were reluctant to recommend 18 as the minimum age of marriage upheld in Islam despite participation in leadership development and capacity building training on child marriage conducted by two local NGOs—Girl Child Concerns and Isa Wali Empowerment Initiative.[115] However, the training helped the scholars to understand the importance of delaying marriage in order to prioritize the education and health of young girls.[116] Although the engagement with the Muslim scholars did not lead to an immediate acceptance of the 18 years minimum age for child marriage, it moved them slightly away from their previous position on delayed marriage. With more of such engagements, it is likely that such religious leaders would find the 18 years minimum age requirement more and more acceptable.

In sum, legal attempts to eradicate child marriages in Nigeria have proved futile due to deeply rooted socio-cultural and religious practices that foster child marriages.[117] As a result, the problem requires more than legislative solutions. Hence, a socio-legal approach that addresses the legal and socio-cultural issues of child marriage would be more effective for addressing child marriage. The next section will extend this debate beyond Nigeria, by exploring another Global South case study of Uganda. It will also highlight the common social practices that cut across Uganda, Nigeria, and India, in relation to religious and cultural perceptions on marriage.

12.4 Child Marriage in Uganda: Moving Beyond the Legal Norms

Like Nigeria, Uganda operates a tripartite legal framework of civil, religious, and customary laws on marriage.[118] Crucially, it is important to explore the normative foundation that addresses child marriage in Uganda.

The Constitution of Uganda establishes the minimum age for marriage at 18 years.[119] This provision is similar to Indian law, since a child below the age of 18 cannot legally consent to a marriage.[120] It is important to note that under the Marriage Act of 1904, the age of consent is 21 years, the parents or guardians can

---

[115] Ibid 53.

[116] Ibid, 57.

[117] Jacob Wale Mobolaji et al., (n 5), 2; Stephen Ayo Adebowale, 'Dynamics of Child Marriage and Marital Timing in Nigeria: A Retrogression or Progression?', (2018) 39(9) Healthcare for Women International 975, 976.

[118] Miriam Chinyere Anozie, Millicent Ele and Elizabeth Ijeamaka Anika, 'The Legal, Medical and Social Implications of Child Marriage in Nigeria' (2018) 32 International Journal of Law, Policy and the Family 119.

[119] 68 Article 31(3) of the Constitution of Uganda, 1995.

[120] See *Singh v. Singh*, 67 Misc. 2d 878, 325 N.Y.S.2d 590 (N.Y. Sup. Ct. 1971).

make written consent allowing for marriages below that age.[121] Besides the Marriage Act, there are three other legal avenues for marriage in Uganda: The Marriage and Divorce of Mohammedans Act of 1906; the Hindu Marriage and Divorce Act of 1961; and the Customary Marriages (Registration) Act 1973.

Despite the various philosophical traditions underlying these laws, the general position is that the country's constitution is the Supreme law of the land. Ultimately, child marriage is outlawed in this pluralistic legal regime. 'Child marriage means any union whether formal or informal involving any person below the age of 18 years for the purpose of living as husband and wife'.[122]

Similarly, the Children (Amendment) Act 2016 provides that 'A person shall not expose a child to any customary or cultural practice that is harmful to his or her health, well-being, education or social-economic development'.[123]Besides the harmful socio-cultural practices, the framework includes an explicit protection against child marriage.[124] More notably, influential community members like teachers and medical practitioners are mandated to report any form of child abuse, including marriage, to local authorities.[125] The Local Government System also allows for local authorities to make by-laws to further enforce the national laws against child marriages.[126]

Just like Nigeria, Uganda is a state party to the regional normative framework—the African Children's Charter.[127] This convention provides protection against harmful social-cultural practices that affect the development of children.[128] Against the background of both domestic and national legal frameworks, it is important to draw linkages between cultural norms and the prevalence of child marriage in Uganda.

a. **Child Marriage in Uganda and Socio-Cultural Nexus**

There is a high prevalence of child marriage in Uganda, with 12% of girls marrying before the age of 15, while 40% marry before the age of 18 years.[129] During the two-decade Lord's Resistance Army (LRA) insurgency in Northern Uganda, young girls were taken as 'bush wives' by the LRA rebels under the command of Joseph Kony. Many of the girls were also victims of Sexual and Gender Based Violence

[121] Uganda: Marriage Act 1904, Section 15.

[122] Uganda: The Children (Amendment) Act 2016, Section 12.2

[123] Ibid., Section 7(1).

[124] Ibid., Section 42A.

[125] Ibid., Section 42A(3).

[126] See for example, Joseph Omollo and Fred Wambede, 'Tororo passes law to end child marriage', *Daily Monitor,* 7 July 2021, https://www.monitor.co.ug/uganda/news/national/tororo-passes-law-to-end-child-marriage--3464262 Accessed 29 August 2021.

[127] See Organization of African Unity (OAU), African Charter on the Rights and Welfare of the Child, 11 July 1990, CAB/LEG/24.9/49 (1990), available at: https://www.refworld.org/docid/3ae6b38c18.html (accessed 27 May 2023) {African Charter].

[128] Ibid., Art 21 (1)(a).

[129] Stella Neema and others, '"Trading Daughters for Livestock": An Ethnographic Study of Facilitators of Child Marriage in Lira District, Northern Uganda' (2021) 25 African Journal of Reproductive Health 1.

(SGBV), as highlighted from the recent conviction of LRA commander Dominic Ongwen at the International Criminal Court.[130]

Recent ethnographic research reveals three key underlying drivers of child marriages in rural areas of Uganda: poverty and survival strategies; school dropouts; and cultural beliefs and norms.[131] Ultimately, social and cultural norms of marriage have the potential to limit the legal protection against child marriage. As further observed by civil society and policy analysts, child marriages are deeply entrenched in certain cultures, hence the need for nuanced approaches in order to eliminate the practice.[132]

One area of concern relates to the deeply rooted gender norms within rural societies. Empirical studies in Radical Feminist Theory reveal a connection between cultural practices that undermine women, and the prevalence of child marriage in Northern Uganda.[133] Cultural perceptions of girls as subservient to family and communal demands preclude them from attaining formal education like the boys. A 13-year-old victim of child marriage interviewed by the Daily Monitor newspaper notes that, 'It is part of our culture and when you refuse to go with the man, you are isolated and called all sorts of names'.[134] Such forced child marriages are viewed by some people as an embodiment of their tradition, as highlighted by a local resident; 'It's not a forced marriage as people allege; it is instead a traditional norm which we treasure. We, therefore, have no way we can allow our norm to fade away'.[135]

In the North Eastern region of Uganda, the pastoral communities of Karamoja and Pokot marry off young girls in exchange for heads of cattle.[136] Similarly, the same cultures perceive girls to be ready for marriage when they reach the stage of puberty, as highlighted in qualitative research:

Parents encourage girls to get married early like the case of yesterday. The parents wanted to negotiate for marriage but it is because the case is already brought before the local council that the parents feared to be jailed (Member of local council, key informant interview).[137]

---

[130] *The Prosecutor v Dominic Ongwen*, ICC-02/04–01/15, Trial Chamber IX, Sentence, 6 May 2021; See also, T. R Kirabira, 'Ongwen at the International Criminal Court', 25 ASIL Insights (2021).

[131] Stella Neema and others (n 130).

[132] Esther Nasikye, 'It takes society to end child marriages', *Daily Monitor*, 10 April 2019, https://www.monitor.co.ug/uganda/oped/letters/it-takes-society-to-end-child-marriages-1819038 accessed 30 August 2021.

[133] Chidiebere C. Ogbonna, Margaret Lokawua and Roseann Mwaniki, 'Child Marriage Practices: A "Cultural Siege" Against Girls in the Indigenous Communities in Northern Uganda' (2021) 3 Advances in Social Science and Culture 1, 3.

[134] Ambrose Murangira, 'Over 20 girls rescued from forced marriages in Rakai', *Daily Monitor*, 6 April 2021, https://www.monitor.co.ug/uganda/news/national/over-20-girls-rescued-from-forced-marriages-in-rakai-3351442 accessed 30 August 2021.

[135] Ibid.

[136] Samuel Okiror, 'The Ugandan girl who trekked barefoot to escape marriage at 13', *The Guardian*,26 January 2018, https://www.theguardian.com/global-development/2018/jun/26/uganda-girl-trekked-barefoot-escape-marriage-13 accessed 15 August 2021.

[137] Neema et al. (n 130).

The discourse above points to one other important element; the disconnect between the laws against child marriage on one hand, and social-cultural beliefs on the other. As this disconnect is a common point in all three countries (India, Nigeria, and Uganda), purely legal approaches, divorced from the social realities, cannot eliminate the practices of child marriage. Like is the case in most social-cultural contexts, marriages are usually hierarchical and premised on parental authority over the couple, rooted in the local customs.[138] As suggested by Ugandan judge Elizabeth Nahamya, it is imperative to understand the social dynamics and cultural customs surrounding child marriages, in order to comprehend the drivers of the practice.[139]

b. **Legal Pluralism as a Solution in Uganda?**

The bulk of scholarship on child marriage emphasizes the aspect of education as a key factor in the elimination of child marriages.[140] Of course, access to education is imperative for the realization of childrens' rights, including the protection against harmful practices. However, within the context of marriage, we are mindful about the possible limitations of the law, within socially diverse contexts. Tahir's exploration of 'arranged marriage' invites a closer analysis regarding the perspective of custom and religion, in respect to child marriage.[141] Ultimately, there is a necessity to explore the correlation between laws on child marriage and socio-cultural factors.

It is important to note that the ages of consent under the Customary Marriages (Registration) Act are 16 years for girls and 18 years for boys.[142] As such, the provision is contrary to both Uganda's Constitution and international human rights obligations, since the standard age for marriage is 18 years. According to Judge Nahamya, such provisions that are contrary to the country's Constitution may limit the effective implementation of the laws against child marriage.[143] Her concern reinvigorates earlier recommendations to fast-track the legal reform processes in relation to the Customary Marriages (Registration) Act.[144]

Just like in India, legal pluralism presents certain complexities regarding the enforcement of laws against child marriage in Uganda.[145] Even though Uganda's Constitution affirms the age of consent,[146] there are gaps in enforcing the same

---

[138] Naema N Tahir, 'Understanding Arranged Marriage: An Unbiased Analysis of a Traditional Marital Institution' (2021) 35 International Journal of Law, Policy and the Family 1.

[139] Elizabeth Nahamya, 'Child, Early, and Forced Marriages (CEFM) in the Commonwealth: The Role of the Judiciary' (2017) 43 Commonwealth Law Bulletin 111, 115.

[140] See for instance, Miriam Chinyere Anozie, Millicent Ele and Elizabeth Ijeamaka Anika (n 119); Pintu Paul, 'Child Marriage Among Girls in India: Prevalence, Trends and Socio-Economic Correlates' (2020) 14 Indian Journal of Human Development 304; Addaney and Onuora-Oguno Azubike (n 1).

[141] Naema N. Tahir (supra n.139).

[142] Uganda: Customary Marriages (Registration) Act 1973, Section 11.

[143] Nahamya (n 140) 130.

[144] Jamil D. Mujuzi, 'The Ugandan Customary Marriage (Registration) Act: A Comment' (2013) 30 Journal of Third World Studies 171.

[145] See *Indian case-Court On Its Own Motion (Lajja Devi) vs State* on 27 July, 2012.

[146] Nahamya (n 140).

because of the stalled Marriage Bill of 2017. Among other issues, the proposed Bill seeks to align the laws on marriage and issues like parental consent with the Constitution.

In 2015, Uganda's Supreme Court upheld the customary practice of payment of bride price as a precondition to contracting a valid customary marriage.[147] Even though the case did not concern child marriage, the Court recognized the need to keep the cultural practices within the legal boundaries, noting:

> The issue of parents in some communities in Uganda removing their underage daughters from school and forcing them to marry in order for the parents to get bride price (forced marriages) has been reported by Non-Governmental Organizations (NGOs) concerned with children's welfare, and given wide coverage by the media. Clearly, this is an abuse of the custom of bride price and a reflection on the poor enforcement of the law by the law enforcement agencies...[148]

The Supreme Court decision is regarded as an important judicial intervention that sends out messages against the practice of child marriage.[149]

In Uganda, when cases of child marriage are reported to the local authorities, the cases are usually prosecuted as defilement, like any other criminal proceedings. However, there are only a handful of successful prosecutions, since the parents of the victims are usually bound by the communal pressures that encourage women subservience.[150] Ultimately, many parents are inclined to negotiate 'formal marriages' to validate the practices of defilement and child marriage.[151] Against the backdrop of these challenges, it is important to think of ways in which the laws can be enforced under customary settings. As observed by Judge Nahamya, the lack of connection between formal and customary marriage laws makes it challenging to sanction people that perpetrate child marriage under customary laws.[152]

Over the past years, there have been efforts to revise the marriage laws in Uganda, in the form of the Marriage and Divorce Bill of 2009; the Marriage Bill, 2017; and recent consultations on the Marriage Bill, 2022. Among other provisions, the consent would be limited to the parties to the intended marriage.[153] The Bill has suffered a backlash from many people, that seek to maintain the socio norms and expectations

---

147 *Mifumi (U) Ltd & Anor Vs Attorney General & Anor* (Constitutional Appeal No. 02 of 2014) [2015].
UGSC 13.

148 Ibid page 33.

149 Téa Braun, 'The Role of the Law in Eliminating Child Marriage in the Commonwealth', Commonwealth Lawyers Association, 2018, page 37, http://www.commonwealthlawyers.com/wp-content/uploads/2019/05/CLA-Role-of-the-Law-in-Eliminating-Child-Marriage-T-Braun-2018-FINAL.pdf accessed 31 August 2021.

150 Nahamya (n 140) 119.

151 Ibid.

152 Ibid.

153 See Uganda: The Marriage and Divorce Bill, 2009. Sections 36, 59, 97.

regarding marriage.[154] For example, provisions on the payment of bride wealth or dowry and polygamy elicit strong criticism from feminists that advocate for equality between men and women. While the issues in contention do not directly relate to child marriage, such criticism also illustrates a disjuncture between the normative and socio-cultural perceptions of marriage in general. As such, it is imperative to consider the socio-cultural norms in the implementation of laws against child marriage.

The Uganda Government's Strategy to End Child Marriage and Teenage Pregnancy 2014/2015–2019/2020 entails multiple interventions at the community levels; 'improving access to education for the girl child; improving the quality of sexual and reproductive health services; empowering communities to protect children and influencing social norms'.[155] While such a strategy seems efficient, one would wonder how exactly the said social norms would be influenced.

Uganda's most recent report to the Committee on the Elimination of Discrimination against Women illustrates some critical engagement with socio-cultural elements of child marriage:

> The MGLSD [Ministry of Gender, Labour and Social Development] engaged cultural institutions in the drafting of Declarations and Council Resolutions on child marriages, FGM and HIV/AIDs. The Justice Law and Order Sector (JLOS) developed tools for informal justice systems to assist cultural institutions in their response to VAW [Violence against Women]. These tools include the Karamojong Cultural Principles and the Case Management Handbook for the KerKwaro Acholi.[156]

The strategies outlined above illustrate the limitation of using purely legal approaches to curb child marriage within pluralist communities. While the contentious provisions under the Customary Marriage (Registration) Act that potentially allowed for child marriage are contrary to the Constitution, there is a lack of effective implementation of the existing legal framework.[157] It is therefore a plausible strategy to engage with the cultural leaders when implementing the laws.

Zerald Amalo Opio, a state prosecutor based in the Karamoja region of Uganda, makes a good suggestion to reduce cases of defilement, a prevalent practice within the region:

> Animals are the livelihoods of many people in Karamoja and if these are given out as incentives to keep the girl child in school, it may bring about good results. Once an animal is lost in that region, it will attract all leaders from all levels to look for it until it is brought back. By giving out some animals to these girls, it will enable them complete their education as the parents will have no reason to sell girls off for animals. Without animals, there are no meals due to this area being dry with also few valley dams...[158]

---

[154] See The National Strategy on Ending Child Marriage and Teenage Pregnancy, 2014/2015 – 2019/2020, p.11, <https://www.unicef.org/uganda/media/13666/file/National%20Strategy%20to%20end%20Child%20marriage%20and%20Teenage%20Pregnancy%202022-2027.pdf> accessed 27 May 2023.

[155] See Uganda's Combined eighth and ninth periodic reports to the Committee on the Elimination of Discrimination against Women, CEDAW/C/UGA/8–9, 11 December 2020, para 183.

[156] Ibid., para 41. See also para 183.

[157] Mujuzi (n 145); Nahamya (n 140).

[158] See full remarks in the story, 'Married off at 11: Child marriages still rife', *New Vision*, 14 May 2018, https://www.newvision.co.ug/news/1477620/married-child-marriages-rife accessed 27 May

This idea illustrates the intricate connection between socio-cultural factors and child marriage in Uganda. It also aligns with the suggestions for more community outreach and engagement with parents, customary and religious leaders in order to implement the legal guarantees against child marriage.[159] More importantly, the communities need to be sensitized about the harmful aspects of child marriage, in similar contexts like Nigeria and India.

12.5 Synthesizing the Three Case Studies

The discussions in the previous sections reveal comparative sequences (laws, processes, and patterns) in relation to domestic efforts to combat child marriages. One common aspect across the three case studies relates to the centrality of issues of religious rights and freedom, which have been shown to have intricate links to the formal legal systems, including marriage. As a result, legal pluralism necessitates a high level of concern about the implications of international law protections against child marriage, for both religious freedom and family in the Global South.

In Uganda, the practice of child marriage is mostly observed within the customary traditions. On the other hand, the cases of Nigeria and India mostly hinge on the dichotomy between law, bad implementation of law, and religious practices. Nonetheless, these social-cultural contexts have been shown to present significant barriers toward the equality between men and women, encouraging early marriages of girls. Similarly, the challenges in relation to the implementation of formal laws against child marriage in the three cases are to a large extent, attributed to socio-cultural factors mentioned in the discussions.

International law plays a key role in all the three case studies, providing the basic guarantees under UDHR, CRC, CEDAW, ICCPR, etc., as observed in the normative discussions. However, the implementation gaps illustrate possibilities, but also limits of international law in protecting the rights of children in pluralistic domestic legal orders. As we have seen, international law also contradicts the indigenous legal plural frameworks. As such, we argue that the enforcement of international law standards on childrens' rights is not a linear process. The analysis in the three cases demonstrates the application of multiple legal orders, akin to what is termed 'global legal pluralism'.[160] This practice is similar to the arguments presented by legal pluralists, for a cosmopolitan pluralist approach where different actors interact with each other at global and local levels, in hybrid legal spaces.[161] Conversely, it is

---

2023.

[159] *See* UNICEF (n 5).

[160] *See* Balakrishnan Rajagopal, (2005). The Role of Law in Counter-hegemonic Globalization and Global Legal Pluralism: Lessons from the Narmada Valley Struggle in India, (2005) 18 Leiden Journal of International Law 345, 387.

[161] Paul Schiff Berman, *Global Legal Pluralism: A Jurisprudence of Law Beyond Borders* (Cambridge University Press, 2012).

not merely an interaction among multiple legal systems within the three countries, but also an attempt to use domestic legal systems to implement global standards on childrens' rights. This dichotomy calls for a compromise, as pluralistic discussions in the article.

How best can we support and protect children's rights in the context of the plural legal environment? A similarity gleaned from the cases of India, Nigeria, and Uganda is the role of non-state institutions like NGOs in advocacy and empowerment of vulnerable societies, where child marriages are prevalent. Such initiatives could equally be helpful especially in managing the relations between the state and religious institutions.

12.6 Conclusion

Despite the legal commitments, the enforcement of legislation in the three countries remains problematic. There remains a disconnect between the laws against child marriage and socio-cultural beliefs of population in general. As such, a crucial question remains—what can be done to ensure the successful implementation of the legal framework? As stated before, purely legal approaches, divorced from the social realities, cannot eliminate the practices of child marriage. This paper has presented a case for the consideration of the socio-cultural factors during the implementation of the legal measures to curb child marriage. Effective enforcement of the appropriate legal measures will then be linked with the underlying socio-cultural elements, e.g., custom and religion.

The issue of child marriage remains multi-layered and cannot be viewed in exclusion to its overlapping causes and societal challenges. Combatting child marriage requires more than just bringing in prohibitory legislation. It requires a sensitization of the community, ensuring dowry prohibitory laws are implemented in the harshest manner possible so that girls are not seen as a financial burden by families. It may require a zero-tolerance to child marriage approach and calling such marriages as simply illegal considering the dangers it may expose to young boys and girls who are vulnerable. Child marriage has also been notoriously known for promulgating illiteracy of the girl child. A child bride is forced to leave school and educational institutions for catering to the needs of her husband and her in-laws. Childbearing is an additional responsibility they face, often at risk of their own sexual, mental, and physical health.

In a culturally diverse world, we add our voices to the existing research in comparative legal studies, recommending laws that deal with the dichotomy between universalism and cultural relativism.[162] Meaningful engagement with the relevant contexts and leaders would thus reflect the necessary cultural sensitivity when enforcing both domestic and universal standards of human rights in this case, curbing of child marriage.

---

[162] Markus Kotzur, 'Legal Cultures in Comparative Perspective' in Mahendra Pal Singh (ed), *The Indian Yearbook of Comparative Law* 2016 (Oxford University Press, Oxford 2018) 22–23.

Chapter 13
Developmentalism, Forest Protection, and the Idea of Greater Justice in India

Rajnish Saryal

Abstract In the wake of climate change, the classical debate between environment and development is required to be revisited. The paper analyzes the policies of the Indian Government that primarily treat economic development as freedom. This excessive focus on economic development benefitted India in terms of raising the living standards of its people overall, but at the same time this process also created new victims of development and led to risks or actual deterioration of the environment. By using the case of national forest policy, this paper tries to understand how the Indian Government navigates between the issues of environment and development, given the constitutional mandate of "complete" justice, environmental protection, and aspirations of the people.

13.1 Developmentalism as Freedom

The developmental agenda of the Indian state in the post-independence period was much in line with the elitist vision of the western-trained ruling class. They adopted the hybrid "mixed economy" model of development that basically imbibes the values of two ideological schools of thoughts on development—capitalism and socialism.[1] The underlying common feature of these two systems was their emphasis on intensive industrialization for economic growth. Since poverty eradication and economic development was the central agenda of the Nehruvian State in India after independence, the first two five-year plans emphasized development of mega projects in the area of agriculture, irrigation, power, and industry.[2] During this period Bhakra,

[1] Baldev Raj Nayar, *India's Mixed Economy: The Role of Ideology and Interest in its Development* (Popular Parkashan 1989).

[2] N.A. Sarma, 'Economic Development in India: The First and Second Five Year Plans' (*International Monetary Fund Staff Papers*, 6(2) 1958). <www.elibrary.imf.org/view/journals/024/1958/001/article-A002-en.xml?ArticleTabs=fulltext> accessed on 10 August 2021.

R. Saryal (✉)
Political Science, University Institute of Law, Panjab University Regional Centre, Ludhiana, India
e-mail: rajnish@pu.ac.in

M. John et al. (eds.), *The Indian Yearbook of Comparative Law 2020*, The Indian Yearbook of Comparative Law, https://doi.org/10.1007/978-981-99-5467-4_13

Hirakund, Mettur, and Damodar Valley dams were initiated and five steel plants were established at Bhilai, Durgapur, and Rourkela. Nehru on the eve of inaugurating the construction work of Bhakra Nangal dam famously termed these mega developmental projects as temples of modern India since they were being built "for the good of mankind".[3]

The emphasis on economic growth through energy-intensive industrialization was based on the Indian idea of freedom that was strongly rooted in the Indian national movement. The political freedom without any substantial economic freedom and autonomy was considered distorted and insufficient to the overall health of the Indian State and all-round development of the people. Nehru in his speech in the Constituent Assembly on April 7, 1948 argued:

> [O]ne of our urgent needs was to develop and encourage, to put into operation, these various big schemes and projects in India which would give us greater power, electrical power, more land under irrigation and more power generally for industry etc... these schemes are investments and we must find money for them. If necessary we must borrow money in India or abroad and we must get them through... That I would give first place; and for the rest, at the present moment I believe that the increase of production in every field of activity is most important.[4]

Nehru was very clear about the kind of economic development he wanted for India. While he was clearly inclined toward state-led socialist control mechanisms in certain key industries, he was not averse to allowing private capital a crucial role in the nation-building process. The positive aspect in both these 'isms' that found merit in Nehru's view was the reliance on science and technology for economic development.

An avowed believer in the power of new ideas and scientific discoveries, he deeply believed that a high growth rate could not be ensured without access to such modern means of development. As he observed, "Even looking at it from purely economic point of view … it seems to me that conditions in India today, as in many other parts of the world, are conditions of such rapid change that old ideas and methods cannot possibly be applied without them being changed…".[5] He was a crusader of new India which was ready to embrace the new innovations and ideologies of growth and development. The eradication of poverty and economic growth was ingrained in his idea of freedom. His conception of freedom, however, was slightly different from that of Gandhi. The Gandhian idea of freedom was based on four elements: national independence, political freedom, economic freedom, and self-rule. For Gandhi pursuing one aspect of freedom without acknowledging the importance of another was to distort the very meaning of freedom.[6] Self-rule did not merely

---

[3] Ministry of Information and Broadcasting, GOI, *Jawaharlal Nehru's Speeches: March 1953–August 1957*, (vol 3, Publication Division 1957) 3.

[4] S. Gopal and Uma Iyengar (eds), *The Essential Writings of Jawaharlal Nehru* (vol. 2, OUP 2003) 49.

[5] Ibid.

[6] Anthony J. Parel, 'Introduction' in Anthony J. Parel (ed), *Gandhi, Freedom, and Self-Rule.* (Lexington Books 2000) 18.

underscore political independence but a highly decentralized form of governance. This idea of freedom, however, could not be realized on the Indian political landscape until the 1990s when the 73rd and 74th amendments to the Constitution of India were passed to give constitutional status to the local self-governance system.

13.2 Period of Environmental Ignorance

Given the overwhelming emphasis on economic development in the initial years of India's independence, environmental issues were not a subject matter of serious discussion for the Indian government. This state of political apathy toward environmental issues became firmly grounded in the near total absence of any critical voice which could question or challenge the rationale behind such developmental endeavors. As a consequence, the developmental agenda was carried out fiercely and relentlessly, without any consideration for its impact on the environment. While tracing the historical roots of environmentalism, Ramachandra Guha dubs this period as representing "The Age of Ecological Innocence", as it was marked by complete absence of any protest or resistance. It also came to be characterized as the period of recovery and necessary growth after World War II. According to Guha, the consequences of the end of World War II were much the same for both the North and South at least in one crucial respect: In both contexts, the supreme task of Governments was to fulfill, and if possible to exceed, the economic expectations of their citizens.[7] Thus, under such circumstances, there was no direct deliberation on environmental problems both at the national and international levels. The newly independent colonies of Asia and Africa had soon thereafter got themselves engaged into a mad race for attaining western-style development and modernization in order to wipe away the bitter memories of the colonial period. India also did not encounter any international environmental challenge during the initial phase of her development after independence. At the domestic level, too, there was no forum to pressurize the policymakers on that front. India faced only two challenges at that time. The first was to muster support from both the super powers for her developmental activities and the second was to generate public support at home for her big development projects. India responded to the first challenge, as mentioned above, with the adoption of a foreign policy of non-alignment. The Indian policymakers successfully met the second challenge through the construction of rhetoric like *temple of modern India* for mega projects and dubbed these projects as essential for removing poverty and underdevelopment. The Indian policymakers did not take into consideration the ecological concerns while they framed policies relating to industry, nuclear energy, hydroelectric energy, forest, agriculture, irrigation, etc. In the foreign policy arena, the effort was to establish links with the foreign aid agencies and other countries, which could help India financially in the execution of such policies. Therefore, the first two decades

[7] Ramachandra Guha, *Environmentalism: A Global History* (Longman 1999) 63–68.

since India's independence did witness neither a substantial environmental policy framework nor comprehensive environmental legislation.

The reasons for indifference toward environmental issues during this period were virtually the total absence of debate on environmental issues both at the national and international levels. And moreover, the dominant concern in the whole world during this period was to ensure rapid development. In fact, in the Indian official discourse, expressions such as "India's Policy on Environment" did not exist at all until the post-1970 period. It was only with the emergence of Ministry of Environment and Forests in 1985 and its close association with other Ministries like Ministry of External Affairs, Ministry of Tribal Affairs, Ministry of Agriculture, Ministry of Finance, etc., that a systematic response to environmental issues through a policy framework and legislative structures started taking shape.

The prioritization of development over environmental issues explains two different world views of the Indian political system. One view mostly held by the Indian environmental NGOs "invokes the class-based analyses of India's ruling elite".[8] Guha, who has been one of the prominent supporters of this viewpoint, argues that the prioritization of development over environment owes to "the coalescence of class interests with powerful ideology of modernisation that has been internalized by our elites".[9] The second view is projected by the mainstream political parties and development planners. This view supported the idea of "development first" in order to generate sufficient resources which are essential not only for eradicating poverty but also for protecting the environment.[10] One of the staunch supporters of this viewpoint, Indira Gandhi, asserted in the Stockholm conference that "poverty is the greatest polluter".[11] The overwhelming emphasis on development explains her pragmatic stance putting development before the environment.

Such pragmatism has, however, wittingly or unwittingly resulted in reaffirming and entrenching the State monopoly over the use or abuse of nature. Under such a framework, the State has been viewed as a custodian of natural resources, which could be used by its Government to accomplish the developmental goals. This firmly established the sovereign right of the Government over natural resources which could not be impaired by any internal or external agency under any circumstances. Studies have shown that this approach to forest conservation has not yielded the desired results.[12] The adoption of such a stance by the Indian Government has, however, further alienated especially the tribal people or what Guha calls "eco-system people" from their legitimate claims and natural rights over resources like land and forest use. This was purely a mechanical approach to environmental conservation. Sumi Krishna calls this approach a "Managerial approach". According to this approach, the

---

[8] Mukund Gobind Rajan, *Global Environmental Politics: India and the North-South Politics of Global Environmental Issues* (OUP1997).

[9] Ramachandra Guha, 'Ecological Roots of Development Crisis' (1986) 21(15) EPW, 623–625.

[10] Rajan (8) 35.

[11] Jairam Ramesh, *Indira Gandhi: A Life in Nature* (Simon and Schuster 2017).

[12] M.M. Cernea and K. Schmidt-Soltau, 'Poverty Risks and National Park: Policy Issues and Conservation and Resettlement' (2006) 34(10) World Development, 1808–1830.

State can determine priorities given to the environment over other issues. However, the priority given to one issue over the other will depend upon the nature of urgency attached to it. Thus, the environment for this approach is one of the issues, which can be managed by the State by defining the priorities given to various social issues. As Sumi Krishna puts it:

> The managerial approach ... emphasizes appropriate government policies and interventions to mitigate the adverse consequences of development. It seeks to bring about change in a gradual and incremental manner, through legislation and institutions, rather than through a sharp revoking of processes that have become well entrenched.[13]

Indira Gandhi was the most vocal exponent of this approach. It was in her address to the 1972 UN Conference on Human Environment (UNCHE) in Stockholm that she had emphatically articulated India's priorities for development over environmental issues. She had thus observed:

> ... we do not wish to impoverish the environment any further and yet we cannot for a moment forget the grim poverty of large numbers of people. Are not poverty and need the greatest polluters? For instance, unless we are in a position to provide employment and purchasing power for the daily necessities of the tribal people and those who live in or around our jungles, we cannot prevent them from combing the forest for food and livelihood; from poaching and from despoiling the vegetation. The environment cannot be improved in conditions of poverty. Nor can poverty be eradicated without the use of science and technology.[14]

She further held, "development is not the cause of most of these problems but the cure, and that planned development was an instrument to improve the quality of life".[15] According to her, environmental problems could easily be solved with the right use of science and technology. For her, the industrialization of the developing countries was not the cause of concern because it did not necessarily lead to environmental destruction rather it helped in alleviating the poverty which was responsible for the environmental problems in the developing countries. In other words, environmental problems of the developing countries have basically been the result of "inadequacy of development". Such environmental pragmatism on the part of India was in sync with the general position adopted by the global South. In sharp contrast to the Northern perspective on environment, the roots of environmental problems in the South were identified in the existence of poverty, underdevelopment, and unequal global economic relations. Moreover, the environmental agenda of the North was widely held responsible for perpetuating the plight of the South. According to Wu and Clemente, environmental problems:

---

[13] Sumi Krishna, *Environmental Politics: People's Lives and Developmental Choices* (Sage 1996) 37.

[14] DET Staff, 'Looking back at Stockholm 1972: What Indira Gandhi said half a century ago on man & environment' (31 May 2022) *Down to Earth* <https://www.downtoearth.org.in/news/environment/looking-back-at-stockholm-1972-what-indira-gandhi-said-half-a-century-ago-on-man-environment-83060> accessed 22 May 2023; Gandhi as quoted in Shyam Divan and Armin Rosencranz, *Environmental Laws and Policy in India: Cases, Materials and Statutes* (Oxford University Press 2001) 31–32.

[15] Krishna (no. 13) 38.

> ...are not the by-products of affluence but of poverty: not the symptoms of over-consumption, but the sufferings of under consumption. They cannot cry over the dying lake, but weep for the dying homo sapiens; they cannot be concerned with the doses of DDT, but with eradication of diseases. Their worry is not the smoking chimney, but concern with the vast numbers of jobless people; not a question of clear water, but of obtaining higher productivity from the water. Their advocacy is not of consumerism, but of the struggle against imperialism. The problem is more of survival than of aesthetics.[16]

The same theme echoed in Mrs. Gandhi's address to the UNCHE. Expressing solidarity with the developing countries, she put forward the shared worldview of the developing countries on developmental priorities, with specific focus on environmental equity. She observed that developed countries overexploited the natural resources and subjugated "other races and countries" to attain the current level of their development. She further remarked that any attempt to address ecological crisis through market regulations should not become another opportunity for the developed countries to make profits.[17]

The rationale behind the firm stand of Mrs. Gandhi on environmental issues lies in her domestic as well as international compulsions. She won the 1971 General Elections on the slogan of *Garibi Hatao* (eradicate poverty). She took a number of measures to implement her program of poverty alleviation in India. This set the priorities of the government for development over other issues.

For instance, she nationalized banks and insurance companies, abolished the privy purses of the ex-princes of India, and instituted special employment-generation and poverty-alleviation schemes. Industrialization, and the modernization of the agricultural sector through the "Green Revolution" continued to be Governmental priorities. In short, India's policy on environment during Mrs. Gandhi's reign subscribed to the four fundamental principles, rooted in the fairly long tradition of Indian foreign policy discourse. However, Mrs. Gandhi very eloquently used these principles to justify the apprehensions of developing countries on environmental issues. These principles were concern for sovereignty, concern for equity, solidarity with the Third World, and a high degree of self-esteem and concern for India's international image.

Although India witnessed a huge spur of environmental legislation in the last quarter of the twentieth century particularly after the creation of the Ministry of Environment and Forest, the post-1990s period that opened up the Indian economy to the world through the policies of liberalization and globalization placed additional pressure on the Indian Government to keep pace with the world economies. This led the Government to give clearance to major development projects on a fast track even in the ecologically sensitive sectors under the pressures of foreign creditors. Though during this period the Government rhetoric of environmental protection through development accommodated environmental concerns, the scale tipped substantially toward a high priority for economic growth over environment. This tendency of the Government aptly became clear from the statement of the then Indian Finance

---

[16] Wu and Clemente as quoted in R.P. Anand, 'Development and Environment: The Case of the Developing Countries' [1980] 20(1) Indian Journal of International Law: A Quarterly, 1–19.

[17] DET Staff, 14.

Minister Manmohan Singh, in the early 1990s in which he pitched for necessary environmental auditing and environmental impact analysis of all major developmental projects but at the same time vowed to expand the resource base of Indian economy to absorb the pressure of environmental cost.[18]

India opened its economy to the world in a search for more and more foreign direct investment in all the major sectors. The economic development strategies, however, hardly took a serious note of its environmental impacts despite the caution of the then finance minister Manmohan Singh. The economic success that resulted from the adoption of free market economy during the late 1990s and early 2000, however, could not be extended to the eco-system people. Since their survival depended on the availability of minor forest produce, their condition became worse, because they were denied their legitimate share in these resources by the collective force of State and market in the ensuing age of globalization, liberalization, and privatization.

13.3 The Period of Environmental Consciousness

The National Environmental Policy 2006 (NEP) was the first systematic attempt to articulate an ecologically informed state agenda for fulfilling people's aspirations with recognition of finiteness of the biosphere. The emphasis, however, was laid in NEP on a search for complete justice that should neither be restrained by finiteness of the biosphere nor by the aspirations of the people. In the NEP 2006, Government of India tried to navigate through the often considered conflictual aspirations—state agenda for ensuring decent quality of life, respect for the limits of biosphere, and the idea of complete justice. The Preamble to the NEP 2006, indicated that it was the search for greater justice for the world that struck a balance between the state agenda for economic growth to ensure quality of life and limits of the biosphere (National Environment Policy 2006).[19] Thus, to achieve the above objectives, the NEP 2006 acknowledged and reiterated the urgent need to establish harmony between economic, social, and environmental requirements of the country. This is even more pressing in the wake of climate crisis since the equation between development and environment has become more complex with the rising global mean temperature. In the case of India's long-term economic development plan, the classical debate between environment and development that revolves around the issue of whether to prioritize development over environment or vice versa is no longer applicable. Climate Change poses a unique challenge to India. The sustainable economic growth of India in the long run will largely depend on the stability of climatic conditions. Because of India's unique geography and topographic conditions, the climate

---

[18] Manmohan Singh, 'Environment and the New Economic Policies' (15 September 1992) 36(16) Yojana 4–10 and 28.

[19] Ministry of Environment, Forest and Climate Change, *National Environment Policy 2006* (GOI 2006). <https://www.indiawaterportal.org/sites/default/files/iwp2/National_Environment_Policy__MoEF_2006.pdf> accessed 1 August 2021.

sensitive sectors like agriculture may underperform in the long run and this may also lead to unemployment and social unrest. The objective laid down in the NEP 2006 for establishing harmony between economic and environmental needs of the country by acknowledging the aspirations of the people provides an answer to get through the classical debate of environment and development. The Government of India through its various measures like creation of Prime Minister's Council on Climate Change, a highest nodal agency mandated with power to decide about strategies to deal with climate change, has tried to assign the highest level of priority to Climate Change in the Government setup. The Council in 2008 launched the National Action Plan on Climate Change which included eight national missions to address the challenge posed by Climate Change. Out of the eight national missions, three missions underscore the theme of clean energy and energy conservation and forest conservation. These missions are National Solar Mission; National Mission for Enhanced Energy Efficiency; and National Mission for a Green India. This reflects that policies which address the issues of energy and forests with a focus on equity and social justice would have direct impact on Climate Change and livelihood of people. Therefore, the following section tries to analyze how the Indian Government pursues the Constitutional agenda set for the State under part IV of the Indian Constitution that expects the State to ensure socio-economic development with equity in the wake of ever-growing demand for access to energy resources, climate stability, and forest protection. The issue of forest protection, energy security, and climate stability are interlinked and have direct bearing on the livelihood of people. These issues require a comprehensive policy response which should acknowledge the interlinkages among them and ensure greater justice to the people.

I have taken up the case of India's forest policy to argue that in the post-1988 National Forest Policy period India tried to integrate the objective of forest protection and ecological balance with the objective of greater access to justice by recognizing the role and rights of tribal people and forest dwelling communities in the forest produce and its management. The policy though drew criticism from different quarters for its contradictory and misplaced objectives was a remarkable advancement from its earlier antecedents. In 2018, the Government of India after considering the value of forests for climate stability and energy security developed a Draft National Forest Policy. This draft policy tries to integrate the objectives of forest conservation with greenhouse gases mitigation as well as energy security and carbon neutral commercial supply of timber that would substitute the carbon footprint rich non-timber material. The underlying objective of this draft policy, some critics argue, is the fulfillment of international commitments under the Paris Agreement 2005 on Climate Change, but it may fail on account of ensuring greater justice to the people.

13.4 Forest Protection in India and the Search for Greater Justice

In India, the management and regulation of forests have been governed by both pre- and post-colonial Acts and policy statements. During the colonial period, the first attempt to regulate and manage forest resources was the Indian Forest Act of 1864 which was replaced by another comprehensive legislation on forests in 1878. The legal instrument of 1878 virtually established the State monopoly on forests to the exclusion of customary forest rights of local communities by describing them mere privileges which were extended to them by the local rulers.[20] Subsequently, the National Forest Policy 1894 and especially the Indian Forest Act 1927 provided the legal framework and policy guidelines to manage and regulate the Indian forests. The objective of the National Forest Policy 1894 and Indian Forest Act 1927 was to further bring the forest resources under State control and to facilitate the extraction of resources for building and strengthening the British Empire. Although the colonial forest guidelines and Act did contain some components of forest conservation, the emphasis was on bureaucratization of Indian forests. The intent of introducing forest conservators was to place the Indian forests under a bureaucratic regime. The bureaucratization of forests undermined the claims of the tribal people and local communities for forest produce, essential for their livelihood and survival needs. The State-custodian approach to forest management, in fact, made it easy for the imperial Government to extract the forest resources relentlessly, with a major objective of exporting quality timber.[21] The agenda of the imperial State and the aspirations of the local peoples were, however, at odds with respect to forest resources. The imperial government perceived forests as a major source of revenue generation and the legal framework helped it to institutionalize the extraction of forest resources without any sincere attention to regeneration. While the claims of the tribal peoples and local communities for forests produce were based on a sense of mutual obligation rather than a western notion of private property and intricately interwoven with the customary and cultural practices of forest management, the Indian Forest Act 1927 as an instrument of objective rules of law treated forest dwelling communities in a very impersonal style and thus undermined the idea of mutual obligation of forest dwelling communities toward forests.

In post-independence India, the need was felt to have better forest management to check the overexploitation of forest. With this objective, the Government of India came out with the Forest Policy for independent India in 1952. The forest policy of 1952, although focused on better management of forest resources, continued to ignore the role of local communities and tribal peoples in the management of forest resources. The excessive bureaucratization of forest management reflected the legacy of British policies of forest management in India. During the initial years of the post-independence era, the national economic interests governed every aspect of policy

[20] Ramachandra Guha, 'Forestry in British and Post-British India: A Historical Analysis' [1983] 18(44) EPW 1884.

[21] E.A. Smythies, *India's Forest Wealth: India of Today* (vol. 6, Humphery Milford 1925).

and planning on forest. Therefore, though the forest policy of 1952 emphasized to increase the forest cover, the focus remained on revenue generation from forests. The important aspect of national policy of 1952 was that it classified the Indian forests into national forests, protected forests, tree lands, and village forests. This helped in identifying the forests for commercial use and local needs. But due to State-controlled forests management policy, the objectives of this scheme could not be materialized. Moreover, there were some apparent contradictions in the objectives of National Forest Policy of 1952 which reflected the colonial legacy. For example, it emphasized both on checking denudation and generating revenue from the supply of timber and other forest produce.[22]

With the growing awareness of environmental problems at the international level and the overexploitation of Indian forests due to misplaced priorities in the earlier National forest policies, the Government of India in 1980 enacted a Forest Conservation Act to check the conversion of forest land into non-forest uses. In 1988, the Government of India came out with a new National Forest Policy that prioritized environmental stability and maintenance of ecological balance over economic value of the forests.[23] This policy paved the way for participatory forest management by recognizing the symbiotic relationship of tribal people with forests. Given this relationship, the policy called for a need to associate tribal people with all the programs of forest management for its protection, regeneration, and development and to create "a massive people's movement with the involvement of women" to achieve the objectives of National Forest Policy.[24]

The National Forest Policy 1988, however, has largely failed to achieve its set goals in the wake of some contradictory objectives. Economic development remained a central objective of the Government of India which got a further fillip in the post-1990s period with the introduction of economic liberalization. The development projects that involve even forest land were cleared without any consideration of their adverse impact on the eco-system as well as the life of tribal people and forest dwellers. Information sought under the Right to Information Act 2005 by environmental lawyers Ritwik Dutta and Rahul Choudhary in 2013 revealed that the average loss of natural forest in India due to various development schemes is 135 hectare per day.[25] Moreover, in a single year in 2017 the Government cleared 10,000 cases of forest diversions.[26] These facts clearly indicate the priority of the Government of India assigned to economic development over forest preservation. Nevertheless, during this period one can sense the rhetorical shift at least in the usage of slogans and choices of words by the political class at different platforms that indicate the growing

---

[22] Guha (no 21) 1888.

[23] Department of Environment, Forest and Wildlife, *National Forest Policy* (GOI 1988).

[24] Ibid.

[25] Ananda Banerjee, 'Why India's draft national forest policy needs and urgent course correction' *Mint* (New Delhi 9 April 2018). <https://www.livemint.com/Politics/vWEeMB1KZvvE2VzvJ0zv9I/Why-Indias-draft-national-forest-policy-needs-an-urgent-cou.html> accessed 14 August 2022.

[26] Ibid.

sensitivity of the Government of India towards protection of forest and maintenance of ecological balance.

13.5 The Forest Protection in the Age of Climate Change

The Draft National Forest Policy 2018 was prepared to keep pace with the changing environmental situation in the country. The National Forest Policies of 1894 and 1954 had their focus on revenue generation from the forests, while the National Policy of 1988 emphasized on achieving environmental stability and maintaining ecological balance including atmospheric equilibrium. Considering the changed priorities with respect to the forests in the twenty-first century, the Draft National Forest Policy 2018 is more ambitious in its objectives. The central goal of the Draft Policy is to "safeguard the ecological and livelihood security of people, of the present and future generations, based on sustainable management of the forests for the flow of ecosystem services".[27] The Draft National Forest Policy 2018 entails a number of objectives like ecological stability, conservation of biodiversity, reverse degradation of forests, improving the life of people through sustainable use of eco-system services, checking denudation and soil erosion, mitigating climate change through enhancing green cover and fulfill India's commitments under Nationally Determined Contribution, etc.[28] These broad ranges of objectives make the Draft National Forest Policy 2018 quite appealing. Despite these broad ranges of objectives, however, the draft policy has been criticized on account of being too focused on water conservation followed by climate change through carbon sequestration. It sets securing livelihood as the last objective by ignoring the fact that problems like Climate Change first impacts the livelihood of people.[29] The overemphasis in the draft policy on increasing the forest productivity for mitigation of climate change by encouraging the usage of carbon neutral timber and thus reducing the dependency on high carbon footprint wood substitute material has actually drawn much criticism for its misplaced priorities. It places emphasis on afforestation with commercially suitable timber species and the development of public–private partnership for achieving such goals.[30] This plan, however, ignores the role of tribal people and forest dwelling communities in forest conservation. The draft policy in the area of participatory forest management is rather one step backward from that of the National Forest Policy 1988.

---

[27] Ministry of Environment, Forest and Climate Change, *Draft National Forest Policy 2018* (GOI 2018).

[28] Ibid.

[29] Ishan Kukerti, 'Draft National Forest Policy Cleared: Cabinet to take decision' (2019) Down to Earth <https://www.downtoearth.org.in/news/forests/draft-national-forest-policy-cleared-cabinet-to-take-decision-67945> accessed on 18 August 2021.

[30] Gopikrishna S. Warrier, 'India's new forest policy draft draws criticism for emphasis on industrial timber' *Mongabay* (New Delhi 9 April 2018). <https://news.mongabay.com/2018/04/indias-new-forest-policy-draft-draws-criticism-for-emphasis-on-industrial-timber/amp/?print> accessed on 19 August 2021.

There are three central issues that the government wants to address through the Draft National Forest Policy 2018. The first is to increase the forest cover to enhance their carbon sequestration capacity, second is to encourage industrial forestry to ensure sustainable supply of timber for commercial use and the third is to ensure rights of the forest dwelling communities in forest produce and its management for their sustainable livelihood. The first two goals consider forests as mean to an end and rely on its extrinsic value. The third goal, although it treats forests as a means to sustain the livelihood of tribal people and forest dwelling communities, the relationship between these communities and forests is not just based on a means and end binary, rather it is more intricate. In the cosmological vision of tribal people and forest dwelling communities, the forests exist in the first place and they establish their relation with the forest to fulfill their spiritual, cultural, and economic needs. This relationship between the forest and tribal people and forest dwelling communities does not underscore only the extrinsic value of forests but also their intrinsic value.

13.6 Looking for a Solution

The judiciary has played an important role in the evolution of forest policy through judicial activism in India.[31] Judicial activism in the area of forest conservation and environmental protection is linked to another important development—the growth of non-governmental environmental advocacy and people's movements in India. Therefore, it is essential to analyze the respective role of judiciary, environmental NGOs and Government in the field of regulation, management and activism for forest protection to decipher whether their respective roles underscore the idea of greater justice for the people, or in what ways the Government and Judiciary has maintained a balance between the claims of the tribal peoples and forest dwelling communities for forest access and protection of forests.

As pointed out above, the Government of India's interests in forests during the initial phase of the post-independence period were strongly shaped by the colonial policies of forest management. The forests were perceived by the Government as an important source for the economic growth. In the first three decades of post-independent India, the management of the forests was done keeping in view its economic value, with scant regard to its importance in the life and livelihood of tribal people and forest dwelling communities. The period that followed the initial phase of complete ecological ignorance or innocence on the part of the Central Government was a period where attempts were made to adopt a holistic approach to forest conservation. This approach did not only acknowledge the need to maintain some kind of equilibrium among the different components of the environment, but also the place

[31] Armin Rosencranz and Sharachchandra Lele, 'Supreme Court and India's Forests' (2008) 43(5) EPW 11–14; Naveen Thayyil, 'Judicial Fiats and Contemporary Enclosures', Conservation and Society (2009) 7(4) 268–282; See also Ayesha Dias, 'Judicial Activism in the Development and Enforcement of Environmental Law: Some Comparative Insights from the Indian Experience', (1994) 6(2) Journal of Environmental Law, 243–262.

of tribal people and forest dwelling communities in the protection and conservation of forests. The National Forest Policy (NEP) 1988 advocated this approach to forest management. The NEP 1988 considered forest as a composite whole and not a single unit with just economic value. The tribal people and forest dwelling communities are also a part of this whole which got its first acknowledgement in the NEP 1988. The legal recognition of forest rights of these people could only be secured with the enactment of the Forest Rights Act in the year 2006 known as Scheduled Tribes and Other Traditional Forest Dwellers (Recognition of Forest Rights) Act (FRA), 2006.

The Act was passed to give legitimacy to individual as well as community claims of tribal people and other forest dwelling communities over the forest resources. The legal entitlement of forest rights to the tribal people and forest dwelling communities was essential to undo the historic injustice that these communities had been subjected to for centuries. The Act, however, soon became embroiled in a controversy when the claims of the tribal people and forest dwelling communities under the Act were challenged by some non-governmental environmental organizations in the Supreme Court of India. In 2008 Wildlife First, the Wildlife of India, Nature Conservation Society, and other conservationists challenged the FRA 2006 in the Supreme Court (Wildlife first Vs Ministry of Forest and Environment & Others) on two grounds. First, it challenged the constitutional validity of the Act since forests being a State subject, the Center has no power to frame such an Act. Second, the recognition of forest rights of these communities would have an adverse impact on the wildlife and flora and fauna.[32] The first objection to FRA 2006, however, did not find much appeal from the Court, but the Supreme Court paid serious attention to the second argument. In 2014 the petitioner filed an interlocutory application in the court requesting it pass an order to evict illegal forest dwellers. The Supreme Court on 13 February 2019 passed an order directing 21 states to forcefully evict more than 100,000 forest dwellers and other forest dwelling households whose claims under the FRA 2006 had been rejected by the state governments on or before 24 July 2019, the next date of hearing. The Supreme Court, however, on 28 February 2019 acting on an application filed by the Central Government, placed a stay on its earlier order and directed all the states to submit an affidavit before it whether due process of law has been followed in the processes of granting recognition of forest rights under FRA 2006.[33]

The approach of the Indian Government on this issue has not been consistent. The Government, though publicly supported the cause of tribal people and forest dwelling communities, did not defend the case in the court seriously. The failure on the part of a counsel of the Central Government to appear in the Supreme Court on 13 February 2019 gave an opportunity to the petitioner's counsel to portray tribal people and

---

[32] Raghav Srivastava, 'What's worrying about the SC order on FRA?' (2019) Down to Earth <https://www.downtoearth.org.in/news/forests/what-s-worrying-about-the-sc-order-on-fra--63330> accessed 15 July 2021; Geetanjoy Sahu,. 'Forest Rights Act: A litmus test for govt to protect forest dwellers' (2019) Down to Earth <https://www.downtoearth.org.in/blog/forests/forest-rights-act-a-litmus-test-for-govt-to-protect-forest-dwellers-65816> accessed 8 August 2021.

[33] Krishnadas Rajagopal, 'SC stays Feb 13 order for eviction of tribals, forest dwellers' *The Hindu* (28 February 2019). <https://www.thehindu.com/news/national/sc-stays-feb-13-order-for-eviction-of-tribals-forest-dwellers/article26396154.ece >accessed 16 August 2021.

forest dwellers as encroachers and a threat to the sustainability of the forest. During the proceedings of the Court, the Central Government did not bring attention of the Court to the facts and material that may establish that in most cases the claims of the tribal peoples and forest dweller communities were rejected without following the due process of law as was laid in the FRA 2006.[34] Under Section 13.4(5) of the Act, it is clearly mentioned that no person should be evicted from the forest land under his/her possession till the proper recognition and verification of claim is completed by following the due process of law.[35]

After drawing severe criticism from different quarters for its indifferent approach to the issue of rights of tribal people and other forest dwelling communities, the Solicitor General Tushar Mehta representing the Central Government made the stand of Government clear in the Supreme Court of India, while filing an application to request the Court to place a stay on its 13 February 2019 order. He said that the FRA 2006 is a "beneficial legislation which should be construed in favour of the Poor".[36] Taking into consideration the impact of such an order of the Court on the life of millions of tribal people and forest dwellers and its political fallout, the Central Government argued in the Court that this issue required a more humane approach since it was more a human problem rather than just a legal one. On the inconsistent approach of the Central Government to the issue of rights of tribal people and forest dwelling communities for forest produce and its management some critics argued that the collusion of powerful interests of both public and private ventures prevented the Government to take a consistent stand on this issue.[37]

In fact, the electoral concerns of the Government were also at stake because barely two months after the Supreme Court 13 February 2019 order, the 2019 general election was scheduled to be held. An electoral study, published on 18 March 2019, conducted by an NGO network—Community Forest Resource-Learning and Advocacy by using the data of 2014 general election pointed out that in 133 parliamentary constituencies "the number of voters eligible for land rights under the FRA is more than the margin of victory in more than 95% of the seats".[38] This meant that the issue of implementation of FRA and the position of Government on this issue could influence the electoral outcome in these parliamentary seats. Therefore, the Government took an assertive position in the Supreme Court to secure stay on its 13 February 2019 order. The environmental NGOs have also taken a narrow view of forest conservation. The FRA 2006 was a progressive legislation and clearly recognized the role of tribal

---

[34] Nishant Sirohi, 'Forest Rights Act case: Supreme Court directing eviction of over a million tribals is gross injustice' *The Leaflet: Constitution First* (24 February2019). <https://www.theleaflet.in/validity-of-the-forest-rights-act-supreme-court-directing-eviction-of-almost-two-million-tribal-peoples-is-a-gross-travesty-of-justice/> accessed 17 August 2021.

[35] The Scheduled Tribes and Other Traditional Forest Dwellers (Recognition of Forest Rights) Act 2006 (aip 6).

[36] Rajagopal (34).

[37] Sirohi (35).

[38] Bhasker Tripathi, 'Forest Rights could Decide Election Results in 133 (25%) Seats' *India Spend* (20 March 2019). <https://www.indiaspend.com/forest-rights-could-decide-election-results-in-133-25-seats/> accessed 20 September 2021.

people and other forest dwelling communities in forest conservation. The implementation of FRA 2006, however, mired into some controversy because of the polarized view of environmental NGOs, Government and the Judiciary and obstructions of forest department officials, as many researchers have reported. The tribal people and other forest dwelling communities have developed methods of coexistence with nature over the centuries and maintained ecological balance with the forests.[39] Forest resources constitute the life line of these communities. The environmental NGOs which approached the courts to establish that presence of these communities in and around the forest is harmful to the forest conservation lacked sufficient information and material on the relationship between forest and tribal communities. These communities, in fact, possess a high level of environmental consciousness and value the forest not only for its economic benefits but for the sacredness attached to it. It is integral to their cultural heritage.

13.7 Conclusions

The forest management in India is a classical case of marginalization of tribal people and other forest dwelling communities and presents a tension between the State agenda, constitutional directives, and aspiration of the people. The State agenda, which claims to be in conformity with constitutional directives, revolves around economic development and considers forests as one of the means for such development. The above discussion, nevertheless, indicates that the constitutional directives that were meant for securing greater justice most of the time came into conflict with the State agenda. The aspirations of the tribal people and other forest dwelling communities in respect of forest rights and management are clearly at odds with the State agenda and therefore contradict with constitutional directives.

Of late, however, with the enactment of the FRA 2006, the Government tried to resolve the contradiction between the State agenda and people's aspiration by legally recognizing the rights of tribal people and other forest dwelling communities in the forest produce and its management. The FRA 2006 is a classic case that touches upon the issue of environment protection, complete justice, and development. The implementation of the FRA 2006, however, has been a controversial issue because of the divergent approaches of different agencies involved and the different perspectives of stakeholders.

People want development and economic resources for their growth. The process of development in India and for that matter in any part of the world has established that economic development of some, however, comes at the cost of others. These people may be termed as what Menski calls "victims of development".[40] Indian

---

[39] Aniruddha Jena, 'Communities of Judges, Protection of Tribal Cultures, and the Principle of 'Complete Justice'" 2021 41(3) *South Asia Research.*

[40] Werner Menski, 'Final Rallying Call on the Brutal Realities of the Anthropocene and the Necessity of Cosmoprudence to Minimise Human Suffering' in Domenico Amirante and Silvia Bagni (eds),

development narrative evinced the suffering of millions of victims of development who were either displaced because of loss of land and habitat due to the construction of dams and other development projects or were declared illegal inhabitants in their own ancestral habitat as is the case of forceful eviction of tribal people and other forest dwelling communities from the forests following the Supreme Court order of 13 February 2019.

To resolve the moral tension of prioritization between development and the environmental protection with the objective to achieve greater justice, we need to answer the following questions: Does the Government recognize the need to pay proper compensation to the victims of development? Does it really need to change the trajectories of development to accommodate environmental issues as well as ideas of greater justice? These are vital questions, and the Indian State should answer them affirmatively.

Moreover, considering the deteriorating condition of the environment and its impact on development, it is essential not only to talk about necessary compensation to the victims of development but also create awareness among the people to develop eco-friendly consumption patterns to minimize the stress on natural resources. Recognizing the role of resource efficiency in the economic development as well as environment protection, the Government in 2019 came out with a Draft National Resource Efficiency Policy to invite suggestion from different stakeholders and the public in general to develop an overarching national policy for encouraging resource efficiency as well as promote the usage of secondary raw material across different sectors.[41] In the area of energy efficiency and climate trajectories, the performance of India has been remarkable over the past decade.[42] India has considerably reduced its emission intensity over the period of time and is well in line with achieving the targets under the Paris Agreement and probably the first in the club of G20 to achieve that feat (Ibid).[43] Certain programs of the Government like creation of a Bureau of Energy Efficiency and star rating of electrical appliances and launching of Pradhan Mantri Ujjwala Yojana (PMUY) have performed fairly well in terms of achieving energy efficiency and reducing energy intensity per unit of GDP. PMUY is a flagship scheme of the Central Government to provide clean cooking fuel like liquid petroleum gas to rural and deprived households with the objective to replace the traditional cooking fuel such as firewood, coal, cow-dung, which had an adverse impact on the health of rural women and environment.[44] Despite all this, India still has to do a lot to resolve the moral tension between development and environment by taking up affirmative action in the area of awarding due compensation to the victims

Environmental Constitutionalism in the Anthropocene: Values, Principles and Actions (Routledge 2022).

[41] Ministry of Environment, Forest and Climate Change, *Draft National Resource Efficiency Policy 2019* (GOI 2019).

[42] Annapurna Mitra, (ed), *Reconciling India's Climate and Industrial Targets: A Policy Roadmap* (ORF 2021).

[43] Ibid.

[44] Ministry of Petroleum and Natural Gas, 'Pradhan Mantri Ujjwala Yojana' (GOI 2016) <https://www.pmuy.gov.in/about.html> accessed 20 September 2021.

of development and creating balance in the constitutional objectives of development, environment protection, aspiration of people and greater justice. Only then will the august promises of the Constitution about complete justice be fulfilled.

Correction to: Intersection of Law, Religion, Customs, and the Problem of Child Marriage in Global South: A Comparative Study of India, Nigeria and Uganda

Neha Mishra, Tonny R. Kirabira, and Judith N. Onwubiko

Correction to:
Chapter 12 in: M. John et al. (eds.), *The Indian Yearbook of Comparative Law 2020*, The Indian Yearbook of Comparative Law, https://doi.org/10.1007/978-981-99-5467-4_12

The original version of the chapter 12 was inadvertently published before incorporation of the final corrections. The chapter has been updated with the following: The author "Tonny R. Kirabira" name and author's "Judith N. Onwubiko" affiliation has been updated and footnotes are re arranged.

The correction chapter and the book have been updated with the changes.

The updated version of this chapter can be found at
https://doi.org/10.1007/978-981-99-5467-4_12

M. John et al. (eds.), *The Indian Yearbook of Comparative Law 2020*, The Indian Yearbook of Comparative Law, https://doi.org/10.1007/978-981-99-5467-4_14

SPRINGER NATURE

GPSR Compliance

The European Union's (EU) General Product Safety Regulation (GPSR) is a set of rules that requires consumer products to be safe and our obligations to ensure this.

If you have any concerns about our products, you can contact us on ProductSafety@springernature.com

In case Publisher is established outside the EU, the EU authorized representative is:

Springer Nature Customer Service Center GmbH
Europaplatz 3
69115 Heidelberg, Germany

The manufacturer's authorised representative in the EU is Springer Nature Customer Service Centre GmbH, Europaplatz 3, 69115 Heidelberg, Germany. If you have any concerns regarding our products, please contact ProductSafety@springernature.com

Printed and bound by CPI Group (UK) Ltd, Croydon, CR0 4YY
30/09/2026
02225322-0009